teach yourself...

VISUAL BASIC 4.0 FOR WINDOWS 95

JOHN SOCHA &

DEVRA HALL

a subsidiary of Henry Holt and Company, Inc.
115 West 18th Street
New York, NY 10011

Printed in the United States of America.

Library of Congress Cataloging-in-Publication Data

Socha, John
Teach yourself-- Visual Basic 4.0 / John Socha and Devra Hall
p. cm.
Includes index.
ISBN 1-55851-399-4
1. BASIC (Computer program language) 2. Microsoft Visual BASIC.
I. Hall, Devra. II. Title.
QA76.73.B3S635 1995
005.265--dc20 94-43532
CIP

10 9 8 7 6 5 4 3 2 1

MIS:Press books are available at special discounts for bulk purchases for sales promotions, premiums, fund-raising, or educational use. Special editions or book excerpts can also be created to specification.

For details contact: Special Sales Director
MIS:Press
a subsidiary of Henry Holt and Company, Inc.
115 West 18th Street
New York, New York 10011

Associate Publisher: Paul Farrell
Development Editor: Mike Sprague
Copy Edit Manager: Shari Chapell
Managing Editor: Cary Sullivan
Production Editor: Maya Riddick
Copy Editor: Melissa Burns

Dedication

JS: *To Michele, for being Michele.*

DH: *To John, in celebration of 15 years.*

TABLE OF CONTENTS

STARTING WITH BASIC

* Introducing Visual Basic
* Using the Debug window
* Learning simple Basic commands: Beep, End, and Print
* The basics of command syntax
* Computer arithmetic and precedence

In this chapter, we're going to get off to a quick start. After we cover some introductory material to make sure we're all starting in the same place, we'll get straight to the business of learning about programming.

Our first journey into programming will be relatively easy, and you won't need to learn a lot before you actually write some very short Basic programs. Each program will be one line long, and you'll be able to run these programs directly from within Visual Basic, so you'll see what they do. You'll be surprised at how much fun learning Basic can be.

First, though, we need to cover a few preliminaries.

Starting Visual Basic

The first thing you'll want to do is make sure that you've installed Visual Basic. If you haven't already done so and you want a little more help than you'll find in Microsoft's manual, you can find further details in Appendix A. Return here when you're finished with it.

At this point you should have a program group called Microsoft Visual Basic, which is created by the Setup program. This program group should look something like the one in Figure 1.1 when you open it.

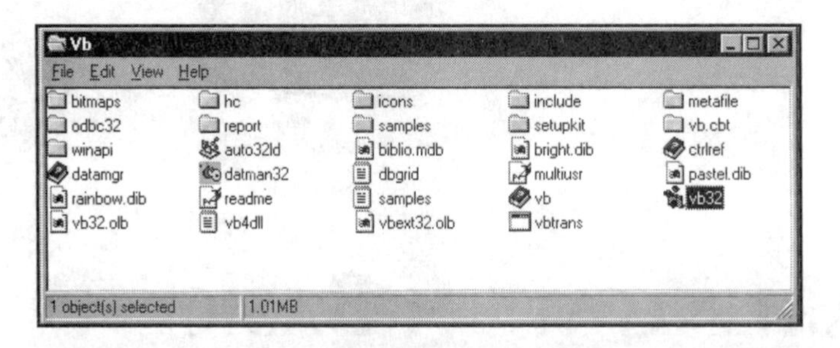

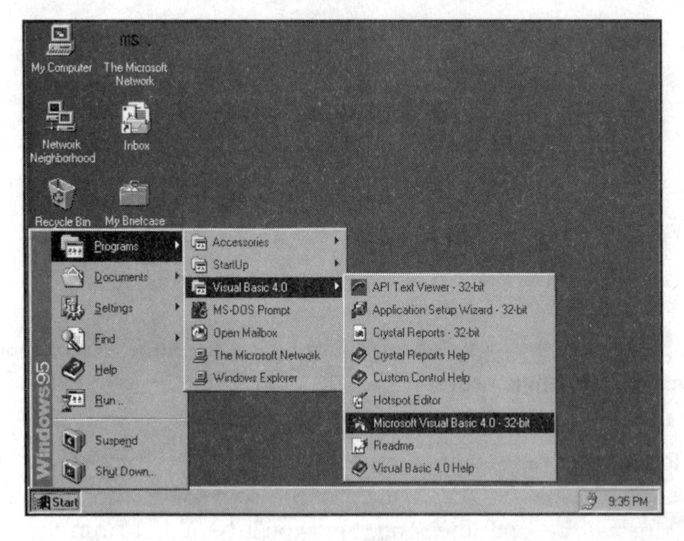

FIGURE 1.1a + b *After installing Visual Basic, you should have a program group that has the Visual Basic icon in it.*

(Notice the small clock icon at the lower right? This is a small program that displays the current time. It's like the Clock.exe program that's part of Windows 3.1, but it looks a lot nice. Not only that, but you'll write your own completely in Visual Basic, and you'll find the entire program later in this book! You'll also find an enhanced version on the disk included with this book.)

Double-click on the Microsoft Visual Basic icon to start Visual Basic. Within a few chapters, you'll become quite familiar with the Visual Basic screen as shown in Figure 1.2.

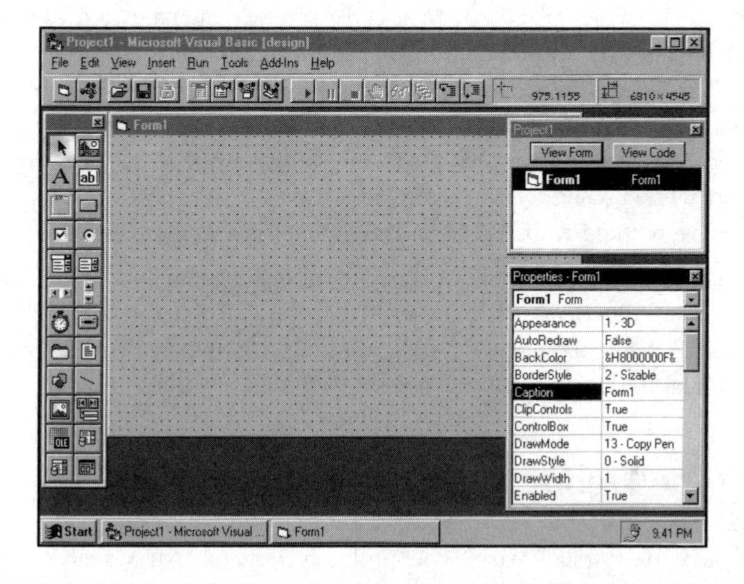

FIGURE 1.2 *You should see a screen like this one when you first start Visual Basic. If the Properties window is not visible on your screen, press **F4** to bring it into view. (The Program Manager's Minimize on Use option in the Options menu was used to get its windows out of the way after starting Visual Basic.)*

Exiting Visual Basic

If you've used other Windows programs, you probably already know how to exit from Visual Basic. But in case you're new to Windows, here's how: Pull down the File menu (Press **Alt+F**) and select the **Exit** item (**X**).

What is Programming?

In the next few chapters, you'll learn that programming in Visual Basic consists of writing instructions that tell Visual Basic what steps you want it to perform. Programmers tend to use several names to refer to such instructions—*statements*, *instructions*, *commands*, and *code* being the most common. In Chapter 1, we'll usually refer to them as *commands*.

You'll also see the term *programming language*. There are a number of programming languages, including Basic, C, Pascal, and Assembly Language, that you can use to write programs. In a sense, these languages are like different spoken languages because each one has its own grammar and set of words, and different languages have their strengths and weaknesses. Many professional programmers (including the ones at Microsoft) write their programs using the C language because of its power and flexibility. C, however, tends to be difficult to learn, and writing Windows programs in C takes a lot of work. Of all the languages we've worked with, Visual Basic is the easiest to learn and use.

In this chapter you're going to learn about three commands in the Basic language by using the *Debug window* in Visual Basic. This window lets you enter commands and run them right away. Running a command simply means that you tell Visual Basic to actually do the steps you've asked it to follow.

Using the Debug Window

When you started Visual Basic, you probably noticed that Visual Basic uses a number of windows—five, to be exact. We're going to ignore all of these windows for now, because you'll be working entirely within a sixth window for the rest of this chapter. (You'll start to use the other windows in Chapter 3, where you'll learn how to draw lines in the large window called Form1.)

The sixth window is called the Debug window, which you'll use to write one-line programs. It's called the Debug window because it allows you to type in commands (parts of a program) that Visual Basic will run immediately. If this doesn't make sense, don't worry; it will become quite clear after a couple of examples.

Showing the Debug Window

Before you can work with the examples, though, you have to find out how to open the Debug window. This is quite simple. The steps are as follows:

- ✱ Press **F5**, or pull down the Run menu and select **Start**. This tells Visual Basic to switch from *design mode,* which you'll use later to design programs, to **run mode,** which you use to run programs.
- ✱ Press **Ctrl+Break**, or pull down the Run menu and select **Break**. This tells Visual Basic to switch to *break mode,* brings the Debug window to the front, and makes it the active window.

You should now see a Debug window like the one shown in Figure 1.3.

FIGURE 1.3 *The Debug window. The blinking insertion point in the upper-left corner shows where text will appear as you type.*

You can also select the Debug window option from the View menu, or press **Control+G**. The difference between this method and pressing F5 or selecting Start from the Run menu is that this way you remain in design mode. You are not going to use this method here, because we want you to be able to enter commands in the Debug window, and you can't do that when in design mode. When you want to set breakpoints to test code in the Debug window, or view output that you directed to the Debug window after your program finishes executing, you'll find the View menu option approach useful.

Key Concept: The Debug Window

The Debug window is a great way to test new commands because you can type a command and immediately see the result. Because you'll be using it often, the steps for showing the Debug window are as follows:

- ✱ Press **F5**, or select the **Start** item from the Run menu.
- ✱ Press **Ctrl+Break**, or select the **Break** item from the Run menu.

Typing in the Debug Window

The Debug window is like a text editor because characters appear as you type, and you can use the mouse to select and edit what you've typed. But the Debug window differs from a text editor in one very important way: When you press Enter, the Debug window does more than just move the insertion point to the next line—it also tries to run what you've typed.

To understand this more clearly, you'll enter a very simple Basic command, called *Beep,* that emits a sound from your computer. Try entering this command now. Simply type **beep** and press **Enter** (see Figure 1.4). The insertion point moves to the next line and your computer makes a sound.

It was a number of years ago, but we both recall being very excited the first time we were able to enter a command like this. There's something very exciting about typing a word on your computer and having it respond with an action. Programming, after you get the hang of it, can be very addictive.

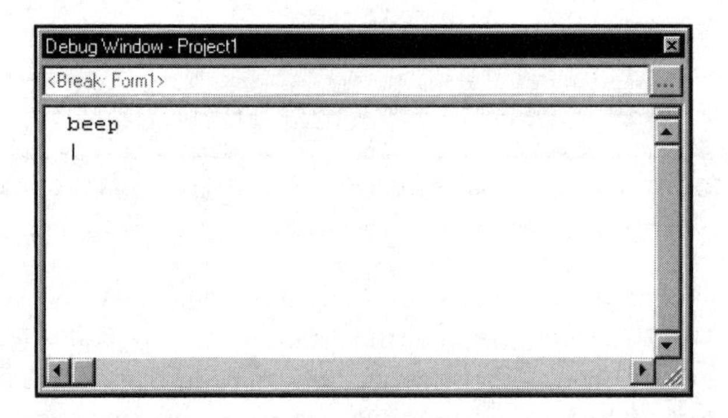

FIGURE 1.4 *The Debug window after entering the Beep command, which tells Visual Basic to generate a beep sound.*

Reference: Beep Command

The Beep command tells Visual Basic to emit a sound from its speaker.

Since you'll be using the Debug window rather heavily to test out new commands, let's spend a few minutes exploring some other aspects of this window. First, press Backspace. This causes the insertion point to move back to the previous line. If you press Backspace again, you'll delete the letter *p* at the end of *Beep.* Type *p* again, and then press **Enter**. Visual Basic beeps again.

Now let's explore even further. Click the left mouse button between the two *e*'s so the insertion point looks like the following:

```
be|ep
```

Press **Enter**. Notice that instead of moving *ep* to the next line as you might expect, Visual Basic again emits a beep sound. In other words, pressing Enter in the Debug window tells Visual Basic to run the command on the line that contains the insertion point.

Let's explore one final aspect of the Debug window before we move on. You can also edit previous commands. Let's say you made a mistake when typing in the Beep command and that you typed *Beeo* instead of *Beep*. When you press Enter, Visual Basic displays an alert box to let you know that you made a mistake, as shown in Figure 1.5. At this point, the message probably seems mysterious. As it turns out, it actually isn't all that mysterious. In essence, it means that Visual Basic couldn't find a command with the name you typed.

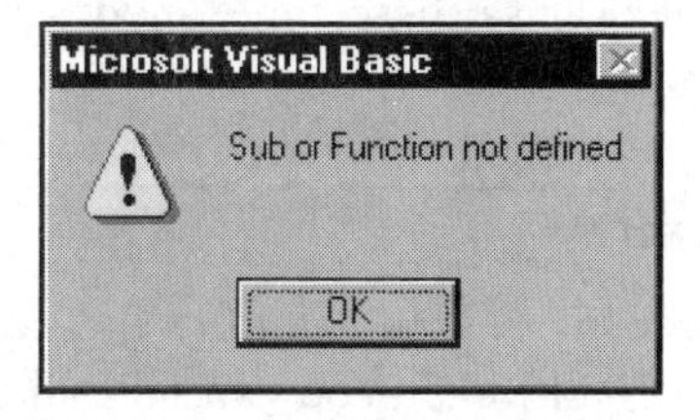

FIGURE 1.5 *You'll see this alert box if you mistype a command, such as typing Beeo instead of Beep. Basically, it means "huh?"*

You can press Enter to dismiss this alert box. Then you can edit what you typed, with either the mouse or the cursor keys. When you're done making corrections, press Enter to run the corrected command.

Leaving Run Mode

The next command you'll learn about is called the *End* command, which tells Visual Basic to stop running a program. In other words, End tells Visual Basic to switch back from run mode (which you're in whenever you can see the Debug window) to design mode.

REFERENCE: END COMMAND

The End command tells Visual Basic that you're finished running your program. Visual Basic returns to design mode when it executes this command.

Try entering this command now. Type **End** in the Debug window, and press **Enter**. You'll notice that the window disappeared from the screen and Visual Basic is now back in design mode. By the way, you can tell which mode you're currently in by looking at the top of the screen. When you're in design mode, the top line on the screen should read the following:

```
Microsoft Visual Basic - Project 1 [design]
```

The word in square brackets, [design] in this case, indicates which mode is currently active. If you enter run mode again (press F5), you'll notice that the mode changes to [run]; and when you press Ctrl+Break to show the Debug window, it switches to [break]. We'll discuss these three modes when you graduate from using just the Debug window.

VISUAL BASIC'S MODES

Visual Basic has three modes and, during the course of reading this book, you'll work with all three. You can tell which mode is active by looking at the word in square brackets at the top of the screen: Microsoft Visual Basic [design].

[design]	Appears while you're designing programs
[run]	Appears while Visual Basic runs the current program
[break]	Appears while the program is stopped, which allows you to use the Debug window.

You can also use the pull-down menus, rather than the End command to exit from programs: Pull down the Run menu and select **End**.

You've now learned two simple Basic commands, Beep and End. You've learned just about everything there is to know about them. In the next section, we'll discuss a more interesting command that can do a number of things. You'll use it quite a bit in your explorations of the Basic language, as well as in programs that you write.

The Print Command

In this section you'll learn about the *Print* command, which you'll use to explore how Basic handles arithmetic.

How Print Got Its Name

The name Print is a little misleading. Most people tend to think of printing as the act of sending output from a computer to a printer. The Print command, on the other hand, sends it to the screen. Why is it called Print and not Display? The reasons are entirely historical.

The Basic language was originally created by two professors, John G. Kemeny and Thomas E. Kurtz, at Dartmouth College between 1963 and 1964. At that time people worked with large mainframe computers rather than personal computers. These computers filled large air-conditioned rooms with very expensive equipment. To communicate with such computers you used a teletype rather than a CRT screen. So whenever a program sent output to the user, it was actually printed on a piece of paper, rather than displayed on a screen. This is the reason why Kemeny and Kurtz chose the name Print, rather than Display for this command.

The name Basic is an acronym that stands for Beginner's All-purpose Symbolic Instruction Code, and most of the time is written in all uppercase letters: BASIC. In Visual Basic, however, Microsoft chose to change the spelling to mixed case.

Make sure the Debug window is visible, because you're going to use this window to learn about the Print command. The first thing you'll do is have Print display a number. If you type **Print 10**, and then press **Enter**, you'll see the following:

```
print 10
 10
|
```

Notice that 10 appears after you press Enter, and then the insertion point moves down another line.

Now try something a little more involved: adding two numbers together. Type **Print 11+23**, and press **Enter**. Notice that Print did the arithmetic for you, and just "printed" the answer:

```
print 11+23
  34
|
```

The Making of a Basic Command

So far, you've been working with very simple Basic commands. Beep and End are the simplest commands you can type: they're only one word long. In a sense, these commands are like one-word sentences in the English language—for example,"Run!"

But one-word sentences don't convey much meaning. To communicate effectively with your computer, you need to build longer sentences. For longer sentences, however, you need rules telling you how to combine words. For spoken languages, these rules make up what is called grammar. For programming languages, on the other hand, rules make up what is called *syntax* (computer scientists rather than linguists chose the word), and they describe how to combine various elements to form a command.

Any command you write must have at least one word, which is called the *keyword.* Keywords are the names given to commands, such as Beep, End, and Print (you'll learn other keywords as well).

Commands can also include additional information, such as the equations you asked Print to calculate and display. These equations are known as *arguments.* The syntax rules and then spells out how to combine keywords and arguments. For Print, there is a syntax rule that says the keyword must appear first, followed by arguments. The following is correct:

```
print 10+2
```

The following is incorrect:

```
10+2 print
```

Another syntax rule says you can display the results of several equations using one Print command. You do this by typing a space between each of the arguments (equations) as follows:

```
print 10+2 3
  12 3
|
```

ARGUMENTS AND DELIMITERS

Whenever you have more than one argument, you need to separate the arguments somehow so that Visual Basic will know where one argument ends and the next begins.

Visual Basic has very definite rules on what characters you can use to separate arguments. In the Print example, a space was used, but you can also use a comma or a semicolon in a Print command. These characters, which you use to separate arguments, have a special name: *delimiters.* They are called delimiters because they delimit, or set the boundaries, between two arguments next to each other.

The following is a list of the delimiters that you can use in the Print command (other commands use other delimiters):

Delimiter	What it does in Print
;	Displays one value after the other, with no gap between them. Print always puts a space in front of positive numbers and a minus sign (without a space) in front of negative numbers.
space	Same as a semicolon. Actually, Visual Basic converts a space internally to a semicolon.
,	Move to the next tab stop before displaying the next value.

You can also place a comma between the 10+2 and the 3 to tell Print to move over to the next tab stop after it displays the first result as follows:

```
print 10+2, 3
 12      3
|
```

There is one major difference between English grammar and Basic syntax: Unlike English, the Basic programming language is very precise. A given Basic command has one, and only one, meaning. (A single English sentence can have many meanings, which allows us to write poetry, but would make it difficult for a computer to figure out what we want.) Another difference is that each Basic command has its own syntax rules, whereas English tends to have general rules for the entire language rather than for specific words.

WHY WE DON'T PROGRAM IN ENGLISH

Have you ever wondered why you have to learn a programming language like Basic rather than write your programs in English? It's because computers are very dumb, and they can't understand the subtleties of English. Computers are like idiot savants: They can perform amazing feats of computation, but they have no idea what they're doing or what it means.

The English language is ambiguous, at best, and some sentences can have a number of meanings. Even we, as humans, don't always understand a sentence correctly. So computer scientists created programming languages, like Basic, in which each "sentence" you write has one, and only one, meaning. Of course, you might not understand Basic's rules and you may write the wrong sentence, but that is another issue.

Let's use the Print command again to make this clear. The syntax for the Print command looks like the following:

```
print expression [{;|,| } expression] ...
```

What this means (we'll show you how to read it in a minute) is that you can display the results of one or more equations, which we call *expressions* in computer science jargon. You separate expressions, when you have more than one, with a semicolon, a comma, or a space. You saw how this worked in the previous two examples.

Now let's take a look at how to read this syntax. First, you'll notice that the Print command appears in bold letters. Anything you see in bold letters, such as print, is known as a *keyword*, which is a command in the Basic language. You type it in as you see it.

Words that appear in italics, such as *expression*, are place holders for other pieces of information. In this case, you supply an expression, which can be a number, an equation, or (we haven't covered this yet) a string of characters that you want Print to display.

You'll notice that syntax descriptions often include some special characters. The square brackets, [and], for example, indicate parts that are optional. So the second expression here is optional. The braces, { and }, and vertical bar, |, are used to show choices. When you see something like {;|,| }, it means you must choose one of the options separated by the vertical bars. So in the {;|,| } notation, your options are a semicolon, a comma, or a space. In other words, you must use one of these three characters between expressions in the Print command. Finally, the ellipsis, ..., indicates that you can repeat this process; in other words, you can have one, two, three, or more expressions in one Print command.

LANGUAGE SYNTAX

print *expression* [{;|,| } *expression]* ...

The following is a chart that shows you what the different parts of a syntax description mean:

command	Words in bold are words that you type as you see them. These are the keywords that exist in the language, such as Print.
expression	Italic type indicates additional information you need to supply to the command. For example, you might substitute 3+4 for expression in the Print command.
[*something*]	Anything you see in square brackets is optional. You don't type the brackets—they indicate only that what appears inside the brackets is optional.
{*a* | *b*}	The braces indicate that you must choose from one of the options separated by the vertical bar, |. You must choose only one of these options. In this example, you must choose either *a* or *b*. In the Print command, the braces indicate you must choose a semicolon, a comma, or a space.
...	An ellipsis indicates that you can repeat an element. In the Print command, this means that you can combine any number of expressions in one Print command.

What's the difference between an argument and an expression? The answer is subtle. An expression is a value or equation by itself. In other words, 10+2 and 3 are both expressions. An argument, on the other hand, is a value used in a command to supply information to that command (see Figure 1.6). This means that an expression used in a Print command is also an argument to the Print command. It's a little confusing now, but you'll get the hang of it after a few more chapters.

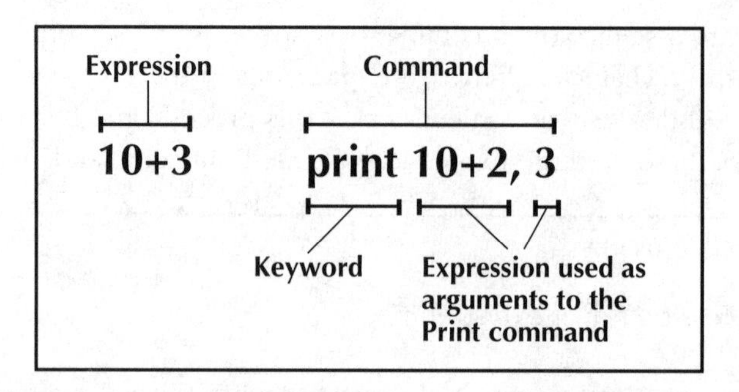

FIGURE 1.6 *An example of an expression, showing the parts of a Basic command.*

Reference: Print Command

The Print command displays numbers and strings of characters (more on this later) on the screen. In Chapter 1, you're using Print only within the Debug window, but you'll use it in other windows later in the book.

Print can display multiple expressions. If you have more than one expression, separate them with spaces, semicolons, or commas (commas tell Print to move to the next column before printing the next expression; spaces or semicolons tell Print not to move before printing the next expression).

print

Without any parameters, Print displays a blank line.

print *expression*

Displays the expression on the screen.

print *expression* [{;|,| }***expression***] ...

You can display more than one expression with a single Print command by separating each expression from the previous one with a semicolon, a space, or comma.

Doing Arithmetic

You've probably already guessed that in addition to adding numbers, you can subtract, multiply, and divide them. Table 1.1 shows a list of arithmetic *operators,* which are symbols like + that you use between numbers.

TABLE 1.1 *Visual Basic's Arithmetic Operators*

Symbol	Meaning	Example	Result
+	Addition	10+3	13
–	Subtraction	10–3	7
*	Multiplication	10*3	30
/	Division	10/3	3.333333
\	Integer Division	10\3	3
^	Exponentiation	10^3	1000
Mod	Remainder (modulo)	10 mod 3	1

You can also put a minus sign in front of a number to type a negative number, for example, –23.

There are probably a few operators in Table 1.1 that are either new to you or a little different from what you're used to. As you learn to write software applications, you'll find that arithmetic is a very important aspect of programming. Let's spend a few minutes going through each of these operators so you understand what they do and how to use them.

The Calculator Functions

Most simple electronic calculators provide only four functions: addition, subtraction, multiplication, and division, so you're certainly used to the +, –, *, and / symbols. The only difference from what you might be used to is the multiplication symbol. Some people (usually scientific types) use one of the following forms to indicate multiplication:

2 x 3
2 · 3
2 3

None of these forms work in Basic—you must use the form 2*3. And the same thing applies for division. You can't use 2 ÷ 3—you must type 2 / 3.

Quotient and Remainder

Two of the operators, \ and Mod, provide functions that you may not have thought about since grade school, so we'll review them very quickly. When you first learned division, you learned that 7 / 3 = 2 with a remainder of 1. In other words, you can divide 3 into 7 evenly only two times, with one left over. Of course, now that you've gotten past grade school you know that 7 / 3 = 2.33333, which is exactly the result Print displays, as follows:

```
print 7/3
  2.333333
|
```

But what if you want to get only the whole part of this division? Or what if you want only the remainder? Both these operations are things you'll want to do from time to time when you're writing a program, and Basic has two operators designed to return exactly these two parts.

The first operator, \, is called the *integer division* operator. What this means is that the result returned will always be a whole number (like 1, 2, 3, ...) rather than a fractional or mixed number (like 2.3). In computer jargon, such whole numbers are called *integers*. In other words, \ produces an integer that is the whole part of the division as follows:

```
print 7 \ 3
  2
|
```

(By the way, you can put spaces between the numbers and operators, as we've done in this example. Sometimes such spaces make it easier to read a complex equation.)

There is another operator, called *Mod*, which calculates only the remainder of a division. For example, if you want to display the remainder of 7 / 3, you type the following:

```
print 7 mod 3
  1
|
```

That's all there is to it. The Mod operator gets its name from the mathematical operation called *modulo*, which calculates the remainder of a division.

Now, just for the fun of it, we're going to show you something a little ahead of time: Print can display more than one result at a time, and it can show strings of characters enclosed by double-quote characters as follows:

```
print 7 \ 3 "remainder" 7 mod 3
  2 remainder 1
|
```

We've now discussed all of the operators in Table 1.1 except for the exponential operator. Let's look at it next.

Exponentiation

Exponentiation is an operator you may not use very often, if ever. Nevertheless, because programmers sometimes use it, a brief explanation is in order—at least you'll recognize it when you're reading someone else's program. You probably learned about the exponentiation operator in algebra when you were learning about powers, and you probably saw something like the following:

$$10^{2}$$

This means 10 to the second power, or 10 * 10. The way to write this in Basic is 10^2, as you can see in the following example:

```
print 10^2
  100
|
```

Now that you've learned all of the arithmetic operators, there are actually two more issues we should cover: operator precedence and parentheses. These aren't the most scintillating topics, but a little information can go a long way toward saving time when your program crashes and you can't figure out why.

Complex Equations

The next concept that we're going to look at will probably take a little time to get used to. It's a very important subject because almost all programs deal with equations of one form or another. Your equations could be as simple as adding numbers. You can use several operators in a simple expression to create a complex equation.

If you use more than one operator in a single equation, it's not always obvious how Basic will handle the calculation. For example, if you have an equation with both addition and multiplication, such as 3+4*5, you know from algebra class that you have to multiply (4*5=20) before you can add (3+20=23) as follows:

```
print 3 + 4 * 5
  23
|
```

But what happens when you mix the integer division operator, \ , with multiplication?

Most programming languages use a concept known as *precedence* to determine which operators are more important. Operators with higher precedence, such as multiplication in the previous example, are calculated before operators with lower precedence, like addition. Table 1.2 shows all of the arithmetic operators from Table 1.1, grouped by precedence. The most important (highest precedence) operators are at the top of the table.

TABLE 1.2 *Operator Precedence*

Operator	Meaning
^	Exponentiation (to the power of)
–	Minus (negative) sign
*, /	Multiplication, division
\	Integer division
Mod	Remainder
+, –	Addition, subtraction

Rules:

1. **Highest precedence first.** Basic first calculates operators that appear higher in this table (such as 4*5 in 3+4*5).
2. **Left to right, same precedence.** If two operators are at the same level (such as * and /), Basic starts with the left-most operator, then moves to the right (such as calculate 2+3 first in 2+3+4).
3. **Parentheses.** You can override these rules using parentheses, such as (3+4)*5 to force Basic to calculate 3+4 and then multiply by 5.

These rules take a little time to get used to, and you can often make a mistake. For example, you might expect the integer division operator \ to be on equal footing with normal division, and expect the result of 3\2*2 to be 2. But as you can see from Table 1.2, this isn't the case. In fact, multiplication has the same precedence as regular division, but a higher precedence than integer division. So Basic calculates 2*2 before doing the integer division.

We've both made this mistake before, and if you don't think to look for it, it can take a long time to find the error. If you're at all in doubt about what order Basic will use in such a calculation, use parentheses to tell Basic how to calculate the result. So instead of writing 3\2*2, you would write (3\2)*2.

If you have a really complex equation, you might wish to use more than one set of parentheses, like this: 1/((3+4)*(2+5)), which is the same as the following:

$$\frac{1}{(3+4)\mathrm{x}(2+5)}$$

As you can see, too many parentheses can become a bit complicated, and you'll need to make sure you put them in the right place.

Matching Parentheses

As you've seen here, some equations can have a lot of parentheses in them. How can you make sure you have the correct number of both left and right parentheses?

The pros use a method called *counting parentheses.* You go through the equation counting parentheses. But you count in a very special way. Each time you see a left parenthesis, **(**, you count up. And each time you see a right parenthesis, **)**, you count down. If you start with 1 for the first left parenthesis, you should have a count of zero at the end of the equation. If you don't, you're missing a parenthesis. If your final number is 1, you need another right parenthesis. And if your final number is –1, you need another left parenthesis.

Let's look at an example that is incorrect. If you count parentheses on the following equation, you won't end with a count of zero:

```
1/((3+4)*(2+5)
```

This is what you'll end up with when you count this equation: 1, 2, 1, 2, 1. The final 1 means you're missing a right parenthesis.

One final note before we close this chapter. You might have noticed in Table 1.2 that there are two – signs: one for subtraction and one for a negative sign. The negative sign is a little different because all of the other operators work with two expressions, such as 3+4. The negative sign, on the other hand, modifies just one expression: –(2+3) returns the result –5. You can also write something like 3+–2, which means 3+(–2) and equals 1.

Related Tools

Because Visual Basic is such a rich language, we won't be covering every aspect of Visual Basic in this book. But to help you explore Visual Basic on your own, you'll find a section called Related Tools at the end of each chapter. In this section, you'll find a list of commands and features related to the ones you learned about in the chapter. You might find some of these commands of interest, and you can explore them on your own.

We should warn you, however, that sometimes (and often near the beginning) these related tools will use knowledge you don't yet have. So if you don't understand this section now, you will later, after you've read more of the book.

* **Tab Stops.** In Chapter 1, you briefly used the comma to display two numbers in different columns. You can also use the Tab function for more control over which column Visual Basic moves to between items you want to display on a line. For example, "print 1 tab(15) 2 tab(30) 3" displays the 2 in column 15 and a 3 in column 30, which produces a display very much like "print 1,2,3."
* **Format$ Command.** You'll need to use this command if you want more control over how your numbers appear than you get with the Print command. For example, if you're displaying money information, you might want to display the number 2.3 as $2.30 (with a dollar sign and two decimal places). Format$ will do that for you, and much more. Right now Format$ is an advanced command. But by Chapter 7, where you'll use Format$ to display time information, you'll know enough to use it yourself.
* **Exp—e to the x Power.** This is a rather advanced function related to exponentiation. Many people working in the sciences often need to calculate powers of the constant *e* (which is related to natural logarithms). You can calculate e^2 by writing Exp(2). There are many other such functions you might also find useful, such as Log and Sqr (square root).

Summary

We've covered a lot of introductory material in this chapter, and we've actually learned three Basic commands. The following list is a summary of what you've learned so far:

✷ **Starting Visual Basic.** You learned how to start and exit Visual Basic.

✷ **Debug Window.** The Debug window is a window you'll use quite heavily in the next few chapters to learn about new Basic commands. Press **F5** to enter run mode, and then press **Ctrl+Break** to show the Debug window and make it active.

✷ **The Beep and End commands.** These two commands are very simple. Beep emits a sound from your computer; End tells Visual Basic to exit run mode and return to design mode.

✷ **Arithmetic and the Print command.** You used the Print command to learn about Basic's arithmetic operators and took a quick look at how you can send text strings to your screen.

✷ **Precedence.** You learned about the precedence of operators, which determines in what order Basic will calculate expressions when you have a complex equation.

In the next chapter you'll learn about *variables*, which let you give names to numbers and other pieces of information.

LEARNING ABOUT VARIABLES AND VALUES

- What are variables
- Values and Types
- Introduction to strings and string operators

In this chapter we're going to talk about two things that are at the very heart of all but the simplest of programs: *variables* and *values*. Variables, as you'll see shortly, are places that store numbers and strings of characters. These numbers and strings are values.

You may wonder why you have to learn about variables and values. Why can't you just graduate to building windows and dialog boxes? Well, nearly every program you write, no matter how small, will have to use variables and values. Programs aren't very useful if they don't do anything, and programs you build in Visual Basic won't be able to do anything unless you use variables and values. That's why you have to learn about them before you can move on to the fun stuff.

You'll also learn much more about strings of characters and the operators that you can use to work with strings.

What are Variables?

Variables are places where you can store numbers and strings, which you'll do often in programs to keep track of intermediate results. The easiest way to demonstrate this idea is with an example.

Make sure you have Visual Basic running and the Debug window is visible and active (press **F5** to enter run mode, followed by **Ctrl+Break**). Then, type the following line in the Debug window and press **Enter**:

```
n=2
|
```

What does this mean, and what did it do?

The equal sign is a new command called the *assignment operator*. It's not an equation—see the sidebar called "Equal is not Equal—It's Assignment." The assignment operator saves a value in part of your computer's memory, and we'll show you where it saves this value in a moment. But first, let's make sure this number is actually in memory.

You can use the Print command to display the value stored in a variable simply by supplying the variable's name. Try it.

```
print n
  2
|
```

As you can see, the value of 2 is still in *n*.

We chose to use the letter *n* here because it's short for the word number. Programmers sometimes use a single letter, like *n*, for a name rather than spelling it out. In most of this book, we'll use more descriptive names, but for now, using a single letter makes the examples a little easier.

Notice that the *n=2* line is still in the Debug window. You might be wondering what would happen if you edited this line to something like *n=3*. Would this change the value of *n*? The answer is yes and no. If you change this line and press Enter while the insertion point is still in the line, Visual Basic *will* change the value of *n*. But if you move the cursor to another line *without pressing Enter*, Visual Basic won't change the value of *n*. Here's why.

The text you see inside the Debug window is merely a string of characters, as far as Visual Basic is concerned. It only treats this text as a command when you press **Enter**, at which point Visual Basic runs the command. So the moral of the story is this: Previous commands inside the Debug window are merely text until you press **Enter**. Pressing **Enter** only runs one command—the command on the line that contains the insertion point when you press **Enter**.

REFERENCE = COMMAND

The = command is an assignment operator. It assigns a value to a variable:

name = expression

Assign the value of *expression* to the variable called *name*.

The next thing you'll do is really interesting. Let's say you want to add 3 to the value already in *n*; in other words, you want to add 3 to 2 and put this result back into *n*. How do you do this? By writing n=n+3, as follows:

```
n = n + 3
print n
  5
|
```

It worked. (We added some spaces around the = sign to make this statement more readable. Basic doesn't care whether or not you use spaces.)

EQUAL IS NOT EQUAL—IT'S ASSIGNMENT

The equal sign in programming languages is very different from the equal sign in algebra. In algebra, *num* = *num* + *3* is an equation with one unknown: *num*. (This particular equation doesn't have a solution.) Basic, on the other hand, treats the equal sign as a command.

Here's what happens in the Basic language. When Basic sees an equal sign, it looks on the right side of the equal sign and calculates the value of the expression it finds there (*num* + *3*, which results in 5 because *num* is currently 2). Then Basic assigns this value to the variable *num*, which appears on the left side of the equal sign.

Because this can be a little confusing, some programming languages actually use a left-pointing arrow for assignment, like this: *num* ←2+3. The Pascal language uses := rather than =, as in *num*:=2+3.

Where are Variables?

The simple answer to this is that variables are stored in memory. Each program in Windows has its own areas of memory that it uses and works with. Visual Basic, for example, has a number of pieces of memory that it uses for itself and the programs you write. Some of this memory is available for storing variables.

What happened when you typed *n = 2*? First Visual Basic looked through its memory for a variable named *n*. One didn't exist, so Visual Basic *created* a new variable with the name *n*. Because Visual Basic "forgets" all variables whenever you leave run mode, this variable only exists when you're running a program. So if you type **End** to exit run mode, and then press **F5** and **Ctrl+Break** again (to return to run mode), you'll discover that *n* no longer has the value 2. Try it for yourself. Enter the following:

```
n=2
end
```

Then press **F5** and **Ctrl+Break**, and enter the following:

```
print n

|
```

Why did Print display a blank line rather than telling you that *n* doesn't exist anymore?

It turns out that Visual Basic defines a new variable for you automatically whenever it sees a name it hasn't seen before. So when you entered Print *n*, Visual Basic automatically defined a variable called *n*. And because you didn't assign a value to *n this time*, it had no value. All new variables are empty until you assign a value to them. We'll talk more about empty variables shortly.

All new variables are empty until you assign a value to them.

Naming Variables

The only variable name we've used so far is *n*. But you can actually use much longer and more descriptive variable names. The sidebar "Naming Variables" gives the rules you must follow when naming variables. The following are some examples of names that are allowed, by using these rules:

lastName	Mixed case, starting with a lowercase letter
first_Name	Underscore in the name
NumNames	Mixed case, starting with an uppercase letter
Name3	Includes a number that isn't the first character
München	Uses an international character: ü
last_Name_3	Combines several of the elements above

The following are some examples of names that are not allowed:

1Name	Variables cannot have names that start with a number
beep	Variables cannot have the same name as a Basic keyword. Basic ignores the case of a word, so beep, Beep, and BEEP are all considered to be the same keyword.

As you can see, you have quite a bit of freedom in choosing variable names. We'll have more to say about variable names and how to choose them later when we start writing programs. For now, though, let's work with short simple names because the names really aren't important yet. We're more interested in the concepts of variables and values.

Naming Variables

Variable names can be almost anything you want, as long as you follow these rules:

- **Length.** Names can be up to 255 characters long.
- **Characters.** You can use any upper- or lowercase letters, numbers, and the underscore (_) character. But the first character *must* be a letter. Letters can include international letters like ü, but not symbols such as @.
- **No Keywords.** You can't use names like Print or Beep, or even beep, because these are keywords in the Basic language, nor can you use any other Basic keywords as variable names. Visual Basic has many keywords, so it's best to check names that you want to use against the words listed in the *Language Reference Manual* included with Visual Basic.

Values and Types

Most of the examples until now have dealt with numbers, but you did work briefly with what is known as a *string* in Chapter 1. There you wrote the following command:

```
print 7 / 3 "remainder" 7 mod 3
```

This command generated the following output:

```
 2 remainder 1
|
```

The text "remainder" is called a string because it's a *string of characters.* You must enclose strings with a pair of double-quote marks to tell Basic that the characters are a string rather than a variable name.

Reference: Strings

Strings are strings of characters that you work with in Basic. Whenever you write a string in a Basic command, you must surround all the characters with double-quote marks (one on each end) as follows:

```
"any string of characters"
```

You can use any character inside a string. However, if you want to use a double-quote character (") itself as part of a string, you must write it twice for each time you want it to appear in the string. For example, the following:

```
print "A double-quote "" character"
A double-quote " character
|
```

What happens if you try to assign such a string to a variable called *s*?

```
s = "remainder"
|
```

It seems to have worked, and you can verify that it did using the Print command as follows:

```
print s
remainder
|
```

You can assign a string to a variable just as easily as you can assign a number to a variable. Now try to assign a number to the variable *s*. Can you change the type of value stored in this variable? Give the following a try:

```
print s
remainder
s = 10
print s
 10
|
```

Every value has a specific type—for example, a string or a number. And Visual Basic's variables are storage containers that can store any type of value.

Now you might be wondering if a *single* variable can contain both a string and a number. The answer is no. Variables in Basic can only contain one value at a time. (Some languages, like LISP, actually do allow you to assign multiple values to a single variable. Basic does not.)

While we're on the subject of strings, there is one operator you can use on strings. The + operator *concatenates* two strings, which means it creates a new string by combining the two strings. The following is an example that shows exactly how the process works (notice the use of the different variables):

```
s1 = "Text in"
s2 = " two parts."
s = s1 + s2
print s
Text in two parts.
|
```

This example creates two variables, *s1* and *s2*, and assigns part of a sentence to each variable. The third string, *s*, is a combination of *s1* and *s2* using the + operator. String concatenation is really quite easy and very useful. (Note that we put a space before "two" when assigning the value of *s2* to prevent "in" and "two" from being combined as "intwo.")

REFERENCE: STRING CONCATENATION WITH +

When placed between two strings, the + sign creates a third string that contains both the other strings as follows:

```
sCombined = s1 + s2
```

This command creates a string *sCombined* that contains *s1* followed by *s2.*

Variables and Types

You've seen that values have a specific type, such as a number or a string, and you'll see more types of values in later chapters. You've also seen that the variables you created can contain either a number or a string. You may think that because variables can contain any value, they have no type. But that isn't actually true.

The variables you've been using so far do have a type. They are called *variant* variables and can contain any number or string. You can also create other types of variables that are more restrictive. You just have to tell Basic what kind of value the variable can contain. If you create a string variable, then that variable can only contain a string type of value. Does this sound unduly restrictive? There are several reasons you would want to use such variables.

First, there are times when you'll need to use a specific type of variable, such as when you're writing programs that read and write data to the disk (which you'll see in a later chapter). But more important, perhaps, is that before the introduction of Visual Basic 2.0 (in late 1992), programmers had to use explicit types because the variant variable type did not exist yet. So if you want to read other people's programs—which is a good way to learn programming—you'll need to be able to understand the different variable types.

You can tell Basic that a variable has a specific type by adding a special character at the end of the variable name. Adding a dollar sign ($) to the end of a variable name signals Basic that the variable is a string. So if you type *s$ = "remainder"* rather than *s = "remainder"*, you're telling Basic that it's working with a string variable called *s$*, rather than a variant variable called *s*. Or you can add a percent sign (**%**) to the end of a variable name to signal Basic that the variable is an integer. Using a variable named *T*, define it as an integer and assign it the value of 10, as follows:

```
T% = 10
Print T%
  10
|
```

Now we want you to try assigning the number 10 to this same integer, only place the value in quotation marks indicating that it is a string, like so:

```
T% = "10"
Print T%
  10
|
```

It worked. Did you think it wouldn't? How could Basic assign a string value to an integer variable? Earlier versions of Visual Basic wouldn't have been able to do it, but version 4.0 has added some new automatic conversion features. Basic evaluated the contents of the string and determined that it could be converted into an integer.

Okay, so what happens when you try to assign a string that cannot be converted? Try it using the following code, and you'll see the Alert Box shown in Figure 2.1:

```
T% = "string"
```

In this case, the error message, Type mismatch, means that you tried to assign a string to an integer variable. The string did not contain a numeric value that could be converted, so Basic decided that the assignment didn't make sense.

FIGURE 2.1 *You'll see this warning message box when you try to assign one type of value to a variable of a different type and Basic cannot automatically convert the value.*

NOTE

The Alert Box also identified this error as run-time error number 13. Whenever a run-time error occurs, Visual Basic assigns the error number to the *Err* variable, and advanced programmers use those values in their program code to write error-handling routines.

More about Types and Numbers

You've now seen two different types of values: numbers and strings. In fact, there are actually five different types of numbers. How's that? Calculators get by with just one type of number, so why do computers need five?

This question is hard to answer because it has to do with the microprocessor inside of your computer. For the most part, computers have very limited native abilities to perform mathematical calculations. The 80386 microprocessor, for example, can multiply integers, which are whole numbers such as 1 or 200. But to multiply two floating-point numbers, such as 1.3 and 6.87, someone had to write a small program telling your computer how to do this calculation. In the case of Visual Basic, these programs were written by Microsoft. But if Microsoft did the work for us, why do we need other types of numbers?

Floating-Point Numbers

You'll often read and hear about *floating-point* numbers in connection with computers. Let's take a couple of minutes to learn exactly what they are and why they're called floating-point numbers.

Any number with something after the decimal point is called a floating-point number. Thus, both 1.1 and 3.14159 are floating-point numbers.

The reason they are called floating-point numbers is more subtle. All floating-point numbers are represented inside of your computer as whole numbers. Another piece of information tells your computer where the decimal point should be in a number. Because the decimal point can move left or right, depending on the actual number (for example, 123.4, 12.34, and 1.234), it can float around in the number.

The digits in the number make up what is known as the *mantissa* (you don't need to remember this). The information on the location of the decimal point is known as the *exponent.* For example, the number 12.34 has a mantissa of 1234 and an exponent of –2, which means the decimal point floats two places to the left.

The answer has to do with speed. The native arithmetic provided by your computer for working with integers is much faster than the floating-point arithmetic provided by Visual Basic. When you're writing programs, the difference in speed can be very important. Almost all programs written by professional programmers make very heavy use of the native arithmetic to make their programs run more quickly. You'll see examples of this speed difference later in the book.

For now, just be aware that Visual Basic uses several different types of numbers. Table 2.1 provides a list of all the types of values that are built into Basic. In this book you'll be working mostly with three types: Variant, Integer, and String.

TABLE 2.1 *Types of Variables and Values in Basic*

Type	Suffix	Range of Values
Integer	%	–32,768 to 32,767
Long	&	–2,147,483,648 to 2,147,483,647
Single	!	Largest number: ±3.402823 ¥ 10^{38}; smallest number: ±1.401298 ¥ 10^{-45}
Double	#	Largest number: ±1.797693134862315 ¥ 10308; smallest number: ±4.94066 ¥ 10^{-324}

continued

Type	Suffix	Range of Values
Currency	@	–922,337,203,685,477.5808 to 922,337,203,685,477.5807
String	$	From 0 to about 65,535 characters.
Variant	(none)	Null, Error, any number up to the range of a double, or any character text, object, or array.
Byte	(none)	From 0 to 255
Boolean	(none)	True or False.
Date	(none)	January 1, 100 to December 31, 9999.
Object	(none)	Any object reference.

Note: In the old days, the Basic programming language needed to use type-declaration characters, or suffixes, in order to identify the data types. As the language evolved, the suffixes were no longer needed, so the newer data types were never assigned any. The original type-declaration characters are still supported for the sake of compatibility with older code.

Notice how the ranges for numbers use rather strange values? Like –32,768 to 32,767 for integers? Why these particular limits?

Again, these limits are a result of the way your computer works. If you're interested, you'll find more information about this in the sidebar "Bytes and Numbers." The main thing we'll be concerned about in this book is the set of limits on the size of numbers. You need to make sure that you don't work with numbers that are too large. Let's explore these size issues a little bit.

Bytes and Numbers

Your computer's memory is divided into many small storage locations called bytes (most computers running Windows, for example, have at least 4 megabytes of memory). Each byte can hold a single character of information. A string of characters requires one byte for each character, plus a few extra bytes that keep track of how many characters are in the string. For example, the string "word" is six bytes long: four bytes for the characters, and two bytes to keep track of the *length* in characters of the string.

You might guess that numbers would require one byte for each digit in the number, but there's actually a much more efficient way to store numbers. As it turns out, a single byte can represent any number between 0 and 255. Two bytes together can represent any positive number between 0 and 65,535. In actual practice, half the numbers are defined as negative, producing a range of -32,768 and 32,767—exactly the range allowed by an Integer type. In other words, an integer is exactly two bytes long.

Microsoft has introduced a Byte data type that is new to Visual Basic 4.0. Like all bytes, it can represent any number between 0 and 255. This data type is most useful for passing values to external program components such as DLLs and OLE Objects (a subject beyond the scope of this book).

Exploring the Limits on Numbers

We're almost finished with our discussion of numbers, and soon we'll move on to more entertaining topics. Let's spend a little time exploring different types of numbers and their limits. This will give you a better feel for the range of numbers that you can work with and help you understand what happens when you pass the limits.

Let's do some more work in the Debug window. You already know how to define a variable as an integer. Let's use another letter to represent the variable. Type the following:

```
z% = 5
|
```

You can verify that this worked correctly by typing the following:

```
print z%
  5
|
```

That's all there is to defining *z%* as an integer.

WARNING

Be careful of using a command like Print *z%* = 5. Don't expect this command to assign *z%* = 5. It won't. Instead, this command tests *z%* to see if it's equal to 5. It prints False when *z%* is not 5, and True when *z%* is equal to 5. You'll learn about this kind of command in Chapter 4, when we talk about *Boolean expressions*.

Now let's do some arithmetic so you can see how differently Integers behave from the floating-point numbers in variant variables. The value of *z%* is currently 5. If you divide 5 by 3, you would normally expect the answer to be 1.666667. But here, because *z%* is an Integer (whole number) type of variable, the answer is 2 (again, a whole number). Try the following:

```
z% = z% / 3
print z%
  2
|
```

Why did this result in 2 rather than 1? Because Basic rounds the real answer, 1.666..., to the nearest whole number, which is 2.

HOW VISUAL BASIC ROUNDS NUMBERS

When you want to turn a fractional number into a whole number, the most accurate method is to round the number to the closest whole number. In other words, if the fractional part is above 0.5, you round up to the next highest number. If the fractional part is below 0.5, you round down. But what happens when the fractional part is exactly 0.5?

You may think that you should always round 0.5 up to the next highest number, but this isn't mathematically correct. Instead, you round up half the time, and down the other half of the time. The rule is that you round up when the whole part of the number is odd, and down when it's even. For example, 1.50 is rounded up to 2 (because 1 is odd) and 2.50 is rounded down to 2 (because 2 is even).

Let's see what happens if you always round up 0.5, rather than only when the whole part is odd. Let's say you're adding together a group of numbers that all end with 0.5: 1.5 + 2.5 + 3.5 + 4.5 = 12.0. If you round all of these numbers up before adding them together, you get: 2 + 3 + 4 + 5 = 14, which isn't correct. On the other hand, if you use the rule Basic uses, you get: 2 + 2 + 4 + 4 = 12. The bottom line is that rounding up half the time gives more accurate answers than rounding up all the time.

Now let's see what happens when you multiply two large numbers together. First, set z% to 30,000; and then multiply this by 30,000 (note that Basic doesn't allow you to type commas between the thousands) as follows:

```
z% = 30000
z% = z% * 30000
|
```

You'll see the warning message box shown in Figure 2.2. *Overflow* means that the result is too large to fit into an Integer. In other words, the number (900,000,000 in our example) *overflows* the size limits of an Integer (32,767).

FIGURE 2.2 *Whenever a result is too large for a type of variable, you'll see this warning message box.*

Another message you'll sometimes see is Division by zero, which means you tried to divide a number by 0 as follows:

```
z% = 1/0
|
```

You might want to experiment a little with the limits on Integers before you move on.

Scientific Notation

Next let's look at what happens when you work with really large numbers using the variable *r!*, which is of type Single because it has an exclamation at the end of the name. Numbers of type Single are floating-point numbers, which means that you can work with very small numbers, like 0.000001 as well as large numbers, like 10000.2. Notice that the decimal point "moved" between numbers.

First, set *r!* to 1,000,000 as follows:

```
r!=1000000
print r!
  1000000
|
```

Multiply this by 1,200,000, which should result in 1 trillion 200 billion (11 zeros in all). The following is what you'll actually see:

```
r! = r! * 1200000
print r!
  1.2E+12
|
```

The answer, 1.2E+12, is what's known as *scientific notation.* If you remember back to grade school, you learned that you could write large numbers like 1.2 X 10^{12}. But this is impossible to write on a computer that can't use superscripts, so you must write it as 1.2E+12. The E+12 means that the number (1.2 here) is multiplied by 10 to the 12th power.

Now that we're done with our discussion of numbers, we can start having some real fun. In the next chapter you'll learn some new commands that will let you draw on your screen.

Related Tools

* **Converting Between Types.** Visual Basic has a number of functions (you'll learn about functions later in the book) that allow you to convert between the different types of numbers and to convert between strings and numbers as follows:

CCur	Valid numeric or string expression to Currency
CDbl	Valid numeric or string expression to Double
CLng	Valid numeric or string expression to Long
CSgn	Valid numeric or string expression to Single
CInt	Valid numeric or string expression to Integer, rounds to the nearest whole number

Fix Numeric expression to Integer, truncates the fractional part

Int Numeric expression to Integer, largest whole number less than or equal to Number. (3.2 Æ 3 and -3.2 Æ -4)

Str Numeric expression to String

Cbool Valid numeric or string expression to Boolean

Cbyte Valid numeric or string expression to Byte

Cdate Valid numeric or string expression to Date

Cstr Valid numeric or string expression to String

Cvar Valid numeric or string expression to Variant

Val String expression to Number

A valid numeric or string expression is one where the value falls within the allowable value range of the data type to which the expression is being converted. If the expression does exceed the range, an error occurs.

- **String Functions.** Visual Basic has a very nice set of tools that you can use to work with strings. These tools are a combination of functions and commands that allow you to, for example, search strings, break strings up into pieces, or convert to upper- or lowercase. The following is a brief overview of these functions:

InStr Searches to see if one string is contained inside another.

Left$ Builds a new string that contains the first (left-most) *n* characters from another string.

**Mid$** Builds a new string that contains characters from the middle from another string. You can also use this function to replace part of a string with another string. Using InStr and Mid$, you can do search and replace operations.

Right$ Builds a new string that contains the last (right-most) n characters from another string.

LTrim$ Builds a new string with any spaces at the start of the string removed.

RTrim$ Builds a new string with any spaces at the end of the string removed.

LCase$ Returns a copy of a string with all letters converted to lowercase.

UCase$ Returns a copy of a string with all letters converted to uppercase.

Len Returns the length, in characters, of a string.

✱ **Variant Functions.** There are several functions you can use with variant variables to determine what's in the variable.

VarType Tells you what data type is currently stored inside the variant variable.

IsEmpty Reports if a variant variable is empty. All new variant variables are empty when they're first created.

IsNull Reports if a variant variable contains the special Null value, which is used to indicate that the variable contains no data. Null is like empty, except that empty applies only when a variable hasn't had *any* value assigned to it.

IsNumeric Returns True if the value in a variant variable is a number.

IsDate Returns True if the value in a variant variable is a date/time value.

IsArray Returns True if the variable is an array.

IsError Returns True if an error is identified.

IsMissing Optional arguments or parameters can be passed from procedure to procedure. IsMissing returns True if a specified optional argument or parameter was not passed to the procedure.

IsObject Returns True if the expression represents an valid Object.

Summary

This chapter was filled with new material. We'll slow down a little in the next chapter, where you'll learn how to draw on your screen. Here's a quick review of the material in this chapter.

✱ **Variables** are named locations in memory where you can store values. Each variable has a type that determines what you can store in it.

✱ **Values** are pieces of information and can be numbers or strings. We spent quite a bit of time exploring the range of values that you can use with variables. For Integers, numbers can range from –32,768 to 32,767 (but you can't use the commas when you type the numbers in Basic).

✱ **Types.** All of Basic's variables have specific types, and there are a total of six different types: one string type and five numeric types. In this book you'll work almost entirely with the Integer, Variant, and String data types, but if you're writing scientific programs, you may need to use the Double type because it provides more precise results. (Note, however, that calculations with Double values are slower than calculations with Integer values.) If you're writing financial programs, you might want to use the Currency type.

DRAWING ON THE SCREEN

- Drawing in a window using the Line command.
- Windows' coordinate system and twips.
- Forms, which are windows created by Visual Basic programs.
- Objects, which are things like forms and the printer.
- Properties, special variables attached to forms and objects.

In this chapter, you'll learn about a new window in Visual Basic: the Form1 window. You'll start drawing pictures inside of this window by using a couple of new commands in the Basic language. Through these commands you'll also learn about the coordinate system used by windows in Visual Basic.

Drawing in a Window

If you look at your screen when you start Visual Basic, you'll notice a window called Form1; it's probably the largest window. You're going to draw some lines in this window.

You'll want to make sure you have Visual Basic started, and the Debug window should be active and visible (press **F5** then **Ctrl+Break**). You'll also want to make sure that your Debug window is about the same size and location as the one shown in Figure 3.1 so it won't cover up much of the Form1 window. This is important because we'll be drawing in the Form1 window and don't want the Debug window hiding Form1 (except for a small amount at the bottom, which is okay).

Visual Basic has a command called *Line* that lets you draw lines in windows. Line accepts several pieces of information (*arguments*) that tell it where the line should start and where it should end. Type the following Line command into the Debug window and press **Enter**:

```
Form1.line (100,100)-(1000,1000)
|
```

At this point you should see a line appear inside the window Form1, as shown in Figure 3.1.

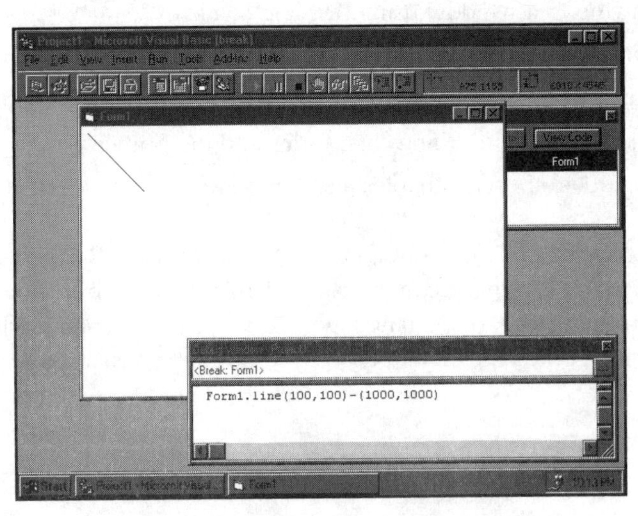

FIGURE 3.1 *The sample Line command draws a line about one inch long in the window Form1.*

There are a couple of things to notice here. First, this Line command has a starting point and an ending point for the line. Each of these points is described by two numbers in parentheses. Now think about what the line looks like for a minute. Notice how the line goes from the upper left to the lower right? Is this what you expect? Probably not.

The starting point is at (100,100) and the ending point is at (1000,1000). If this were the normal Cartesian coordinate system you learned in school, you would expect to see the line start near the bottom-left corner of the window. And you would expect the end of the line to be above and to the right of the starting point. So what's going on here?

It turns out that Microsoft Windows (and some other computers like the Macintosh) uses an upside-down coordinate system, so the origin (0, 0) appears in the upper-left corner of a window (see Figure 3.2).

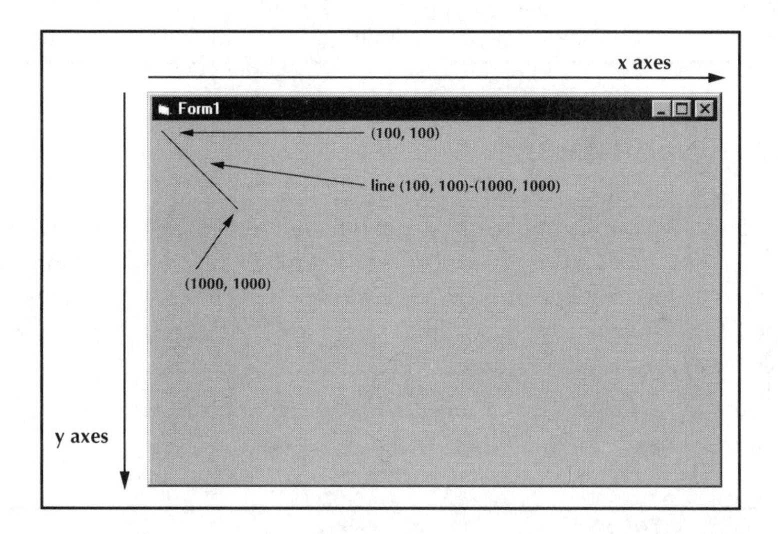

FIGURE 3.2 *Windows programs have an inverted coordinate system, with the point (0,0) in the upper-left corner. Increasing numbers move to the right and down (rather than up).*

WHY WINDOWS ARE UPSIDE DOWN

You're probably wondering, and rightly so, why the coordinate system is turned upside down in Windows. It is a result of how your monitor and the display adapter inside your computer work. Your computer's screen is very much like a television screen, only of higher quality and price. Televisions and computer monitors both create an image by scanning electron beams across a phosphor screen. This beam moves from left to right and from top to bottom—the same as the way we read.

The image you see on your screen is also formed from a number of small dots, called *pixels* (short for *picture elements*). Your display adapter has a memory location for each pixel you can see on the screen. These memory locations appear in the same order as they're drawn on the screen. In other words, the top left pixel is first in memory because it's drawn first on the screen, followed by the next pixel to its right. The lower right pixel is the last pixel in memory.

The programmers at Microsoft who wrote Windows used this knowledge of how pixels are stored in memory to make Windows programs run faster. By inverting the coordinate system, you don't have to change the sign for locations on the y-axis, and that makes calculating the memory address of a pixel just a little easier and therefore faster.

Drawing and Twips

You may also be wondering just how long the line is. You asked Visual Basic to draw a line that goes from (100,100) to (1000,1000). But what distance is this? The screen in Figure 3.1 is from a VGA display, which is 640 pixels wide and 480 pixels high. Obviously, then, the distance isn't measured in pixels because the line doesn't go 900 pixels down and across.

It turns out that the unit of measure is something called a *twip*. A twip is equal to 1/1440 inch.

What's a Twip?

A twip is a unit of measure that Microsoft created, and it means "a twentieth of a point." A *point* is a unit of measure used in the typesetting world, which is equal to approximately 1/72 inch. So a twip is equal to 1/1440 inch and is measured in terms of points, not pixels.

The number of twips per pixel varies under Windows and depends on the type of display your computer has. On a normal VGA display, for example, a pixel is 15 twips wide and high. You'll find more information about twips and pixels later in this book.

Let's try an example that enables you to actually measure the size of a twip on the screen and on the printer. You'll use a slightly different form of the Line command that draws a box instead of a line, but first, you'll need to erase the line you just drew by using a new command. *Cls* stands for clear screen. Enter Cls into the Debug window and you'll notice the line disappear from Form1. Now try the new Line command, and don't forget to type in two commas before the *b*, like the following: :

```
cls
Form1.line (100,100)-(1540,1540),,b
|
```

Now you should see a small square on your screen. You've told Basic to make this box 1440 twips wide and high, which should be one inch. On John's screen (which is a 14-inch VGA screen) this box comes out to be about 1.5 by 1.5 inches. The letter *b*, by the way, is short for the word box.

NOTE

Because the screen on your computer could be any size from 12 inches (or even 9 inches for lap-top computers) to 21 inches, the actual size of a pixel can vary considerably. Windows doesn't have any way of knowing how large your monitor is, so an "inch" (as in 1440 twips) may not be one inch long when you measure it on your screen. But as long as you work with twips in your programs as if they're real inches, anything you print out on paper will print at the correct size. (You'll find a much more detailed discussion of this entire issue in Chapter 14.)

Command Reference: Cls

The Cls command "clears the screen," which in this case means it clears the current form, or window. In this chapter, it clears the window called Form1. Cls takes no arguments.

Now let's see what happens when you try to print the sample box on the printer. You'll find that it's just as easy to draw on the printer as it is in the Form1 window. All you have to do is put *Printer.* in front of any Line commands. Then follow this up with a *Printer.EndDoc* command to tell Windows that you have finished printing a document. If you have a printer connected to your computer, make sure it's turned on and ready; then try the following commands (Basic will take longer to run each of these commands):

```
printer.line (100,100)-(1540,1540),,b
printer.enddoc
|
```

After a little delay, your printer should print a page that has a box on it. And this box should be exactly one inch wide and high. There may be some small variation in size because not all printers are built exactly alike.

REFERENCE: LINE COMMAND

```
object.Line [[Step](x1!, y1!)] - [Step](x2!,
y2!)[,[color&],B[F]]
```

draws a line in a window. Notice that you have a number of options you can use.

```
(x1!, y1!)
```

is the starting point of the line, which is optional. If you leave the starting point out, Line continues drawing from the previous endpoint, as you'll see later in this chapter. Visual Basic uses numbers of type Single for the start points and endpoints (hence the ! after the arguments). You don't need to type the ! after each number.

```
(x2!, y2!)
```

is the endpoint for the line.

```
color&
```

allows you to use any color when you draw a line. You'll normally use a command called RGB to create these numbers, as you'll see later.

```
,B[F]
```

These two arguments allow you to draw a rectangle (B is short for box) or a filled rectangle (BF which means box, filled).

```
Step
```

tells Visual Basic that (*x1!,y1!*) or (*x2!,y2!*) are distances from previous positions, rather than positions themselves. In other words, the command *Line (500,500)-Step(100,100),,B* will draw a box exactly 100 twips wide and high, with the top left at (500,500).

A Peek at Objects and Forms

Notice how we used exactly the same Line command on the screen and the printer? As you'll see later, there are a number of *objects* in Visual Basic, and Printer is one of them. Visual Basic allows you to use the same command on different objects by putting the object name, followed by a period, in front of the command. But what happens when you don't supply an object name? It defaults to the current object.

KEY CONCEPT: OBJECTS

Visual Basic has a number of objects that you can work with, such as forms, the printer, and many others you'll see in coming chapters. Commands such as Line can actually work on different objects by putting the object's name in front of them, such as Printer.Line. By default, commands like Line draw to the current form, which is Form1 in the examples.

If you take a look again at the Debug window in Figure 3.1, you'll notice that the caption says the following:

```
Debug Window - Project1
```

The name in the square brackets (Form1.frm) identifies the current object—in this case it's telling you that the current object is a form (.frm) called Form1. This means that all commands, like Line, that draw in a window (also known as a *form* in Visual Basic jargon) will be drawn in the Form1 window unless you supply a different object name (like Printer).

KEY CONCEPT: FORMS

Visual Basic has its own jargon in addition to using much of the jargon from Windows. Because many programs are built out of a number of "forms," Microsoft chose not to call windows "windows" for programs written in Visual Basic. Instead, windows are called *forms*. The reference manual states that a form is "a window or dialog box that you create with Visual Basic."

This brief detour into printing is a little off our track, so let's get back on track and learn a little more about the Form1 window and drawing in it.

More Explorations in Drawing

Our next subject is something you may already have stumbled upon. The question is this: What happens if you cover your window and then show it again? Will the line still be there? You might guess so, but let's find out what really happens.

Enter the following commands in the Debug window:

```
cls
Form1.line (100,100)-(1540,1540)
|
```

This draws a line in the window Form1. Now drag the Debug window so it completely covers the line you just drew and release the mouse button. Then drag the Debug window back to the lower right corner. Is the line still there? No.

Neither Visual Basic nor most Windows programs keep track of what you draw on the screen. Instead, they have to redraw their windows every time something erases part of it. In other words, you will have to tell the programs you write to redraw when part of a window is erased. We'll come back to this later, but for now, it isn't important for the lines to stay on the screen.

Exploring the Step Keyword

The Step keyword isn't actually a command by itself—instead it modifies the Line command. For this reason we call it a keyword rather than a command.

The Step keyword allows you to specify, for example, how wide a box will be without doing any arithmetic. For example, if you want a box one inch wide, you could write the following command:

```
Form1.line (100,100)-step(1440, 1440),,b
```

This command draws a box exactly one inch wide and high (1440 twips = 1 inch). So in the case of the endpoint, Step means that the endpoint is (*width, height*) rather than (*x2, y2*). But what does Step mean for the starting point?

Type in the command above (if you haven't done so already), and then type in the following command:

```
Form1.line step(500,500)-step(1440,1440),,b
```

You know that the second part, Step(1440,1440), means that you want to draw a one-inch box. But what does the first Step mean? The distance 500 twips is about 1/3 inch. And as you can see from Figure 3.3, the top left of this new box is about a third of an inch below and to the right of the previous box. In other words, the starting point of this new box is 500 twips down and to the right of the previous end point. How does Visual Basic keep track of the previous endpoint?

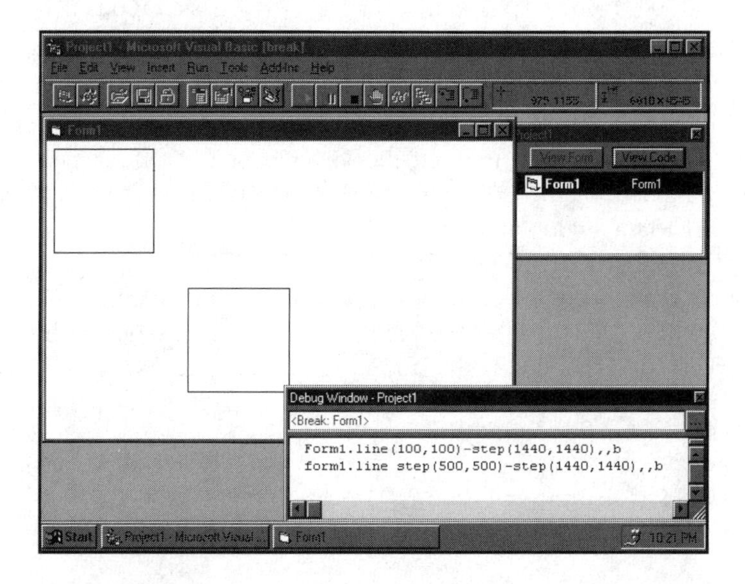

FIGURE 3.3 *This figure shows how the Step keyword works. For the endpoint, Step tells Line to treat (x2,y2) as a width and height instead of as coordinates. And for the starting point, Step tells Line to set the starting point to (x1, y1) twips from the previous endpoint.*

The CurrentX and CurrentY Properties

In the last chapter you learned a lot about variables, the areas in memory where you can store values. All the variables you saw in Chapter 2 were variables you created yourself. But Visual Basic also has another type of variable, called a *property*, that it creates. Two of these properties keep track of the previous location of something called the *pen*, which is a fictitious tool for writing on the screen.

Let's see what the current values are for these two properties, called CurrentX and CurrentY as follows:

```
print currentX, currentY
 3480      3480
|
```

The endpoint for the last box you drew is something you can calculate easily. The first box ends at 100+1440=1540. Therefore, the endpoint of the second box will be 1540+500+1440=3480, and this is what Visual Basic reports here.

Reference: CurrentX and CurrentY

The CurrentX and CurrentY variables are called *properties* and are of type Single. They keep track of the location of the writing pen. Each time you use a Line command, Visual Basic resets CurrentX and CurrentY to the endpoint of the new line.

Try a simple experiment to see what happens when you change these numbers. Use the command Line –Step(1440,1440),,B to draw a box one inch wide with the upper-left corner located at the current location (CurrentX, CurrentY):

```
currentX = 100+1440+500
currentY = 100
Form1.line -step(1440,1440),,b
|
```

You should now see a third box on your screen, to the right of the first box and above the second box. In other words, you can change the value of CurrentX and CurrentY as easily as you change any other variable.

What Property Means

The meaning of *property* in Visual Basic to describe variables like CurrentX and CurrentY is based on a different definition of property than the usual one. Here is the closest definition from Webster's dictionary: "a quality that defines or describes an object or substance."

CurrentX and CurrentY are thus properties (characteristics) attached to the form Form1 that describe the location of the drawing pen. As you'll see later, each form or other object in Visual Basic has a number of properties that you can use to change the way an object looks or behaves.

Knowing about CurrentX and CurrentY and how they work gives you a lot of freedom in how you write your programs. For example, if you want to draw a figure, like a triangle, it's much easier to use the Step keyword. Try the following example:

```
cls
Form1.line (1000,1000)-step(500,500)
Form1.line -step(-500,0)
Form1.line -step(0,-500)
|
```

These commands draw a right triangle (see Figure 3.4), starting with the top at (1000,1000). The first line is drawn from (1000,1000) to a location 500 twips down and to the right of the starting point. The next Line command draws a line continuing from there to a location 500 twips to the left (the base of the triangle). The final Line command draws a line back up (remember the coordinate system is inverted, so –500 moves up, not down) to the starting point.

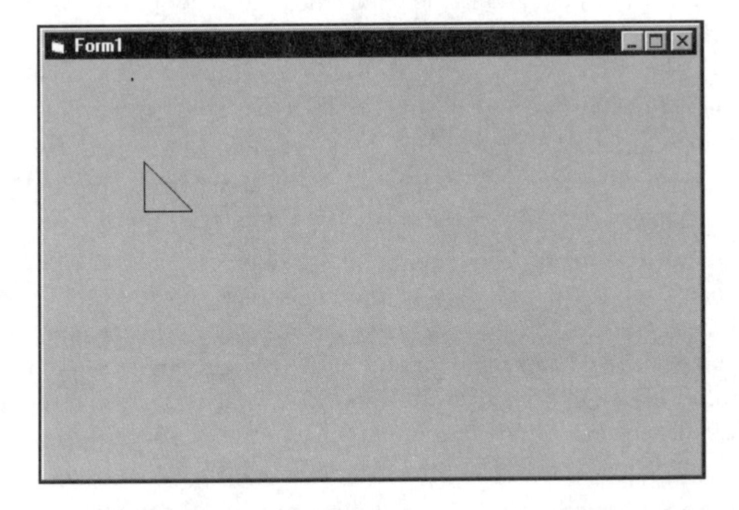

FIGURE 3.4 *This is the right triangle drawn by the three Line commands, using steps of 500 twips.*

Before we leave this subject, let's try another simple experiment. We mentioned before that both CurrentX and CurrentY are defined by Visual Basic and are of type Single. What happens if you try to use these names as Integers by putting a % at the end? If you type the following:

```
currentX% = 1
|
```

Then you'll see a warning message box from Visual Basic that says the following:

```
Type-declaration character does not match declared data type
```

This means you don't have the freedom to change a variable's type when the variable is a property created by Visual Basic.

Related Tools

* **Circle.** In addition to the Line command, Visual Basic also has a Circle command that allows you to draw circles, ellipses, arcs, and pie segments. This command is rather complicated, but it can do a lot.
* **Colors.** The Line and Circle commands can draw objects with different colors, which you'll do in Chapter 7. You use the RGB function to describe the color you want to use. You can also use the FillStyle and FillColor properties to tell Visual Basic how to fill boxes and circles.
* **Line widths.** You can change the width of lines you draw by using the DrawWidth property, which you'll learn about in Chapter 5. You can also change the color of these lines by using the ForeColor property.
* **Size of the form.** There are several properties that you can read (and change) to get information on the current size of the form (in drawing units), and the left and top edges: ScaleWidth, ScaleHeight, ScaleLeft, and ScaleTop. These are very useful if you're trying to write a program that will use the full size of a form for any drawing you're doing. You can also change the ScaleLeft and ScaleTop values so that the origin will be anywhere you want, rather than in the upper-left corner.
* **ScaleMode property.** In this chapter you've been working with screen units measured in twips. But you can use the ScaleMode property to set the units to points (1/72 inch), pixels, inches, millimeters, or centimeters.

✱ **Custom scales.** The Scale command allows you to create a custom scale that's anything you want, so you're not limited to working with just the modes provided by ScaleMode. You'll do this in Chapter 7.

✱ **Printer.** There are several related commands you can use with the printer that we haven't talked about in this chapter: NewPage starts a new page, and Page is the number of the page you're currently drawing. The Page property is useful when you need to keep track of the page number, such as when you want to display "Page *nn*" at the bottom of each page.

Summary

You learned a number of things in this chapter about drawing inside a window. And you learned a little about printing and a new type of variable called a property. The following list is a review of what we've covered here:

✱ **Line command.** The Line command allows you to draw lines inside a window. The coordinate system is inverted from the Cartesian coordinate system, so (0,0) appears in the upper-left corner of a window. The unit of distance is called a twip and equals 1/1440 of an inch.

✱ **Forms.** Windows that you create with Visual Basic are called forms. You can tell which form a Line command will draw on by looking at the title in the Debug window.

✱ **Printer.** You can draw with the printer by using Printer.Line rather than Line by itself. The Printer.EndDoc command sends everything you draw to the printer.

✱ **CurrentX and CurrentY properties.** Visual Basic keeps track of the previous endpoint of a Line command by using the properties CurrentX and CurrentY. These are type Single variables created by Visual Basic for each form.

✱ **Objects.** Visual Basic supplies a number of objects for you to work with, such as Form1 and Printer. Commands, such as Line, can draw on these different objects, and you indicate which object you want to use by putting its name before the command. For example: Printer.Line.

✱ **Property.** Properties are special variables attached to objects, such as forms, that allow you to change the way an object looks or works.

CHAPTER 4

BUILDING PROGRAMS

- Events, subroutines, and functions
- Building the Sketch program
- The If..Then command and Boolean expressions
- Saving and loading projects

At this point, you're ready to roll up your sleeves and start writing some real programs in Visual Basic. By real programs we mean programs that will run by themselves, without your having to type commands in the Debug window. In fact, we're only going to use the Debug window to explore new commands.

The first program you'll build will beep when you click. After you've learned the basics with this simple beep program, you'll move on to build a real program. This program, called Sketch, will let you sketch lines inside a window. We'll spend the next two chapters building Sketch, and most of the work will be learning about new features in Visual Basic and how to write programs.

Building Your First Program

To start building your first program, exit from Visual Basic, and then start it again. This will clear any changes you may have made.

Your first program will be a very simple one-line program: It will show a window, called Form1, and will beep as soon as you click in the Form1 window. Then you'll add a second line to exit after the beep. To build this program, you're going to start working with another new window, called the Code window. This is the window that you'll use to write your programs. To display this window, double-click on the window called Form1. You could also select **Code** from the View menu, or press **F7**. You should then see the Code window called Form1 (see Figure 4.1).

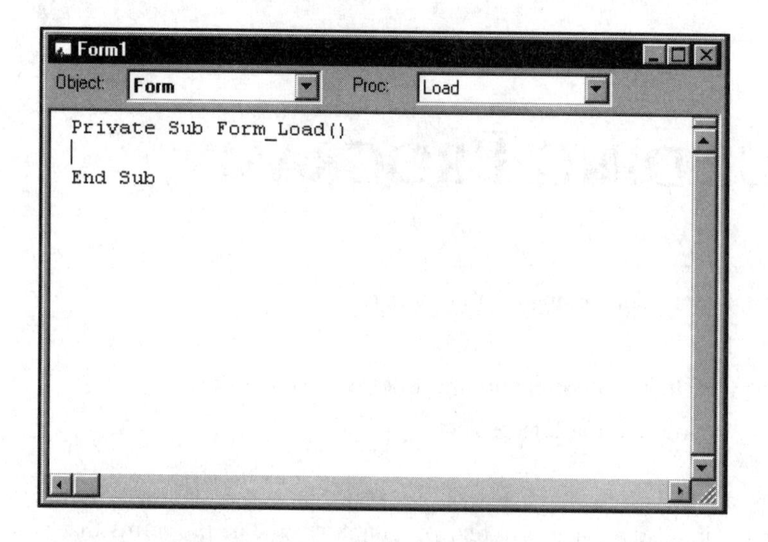

FIGURE 4.1 *To display Form1's code window, called Form1, double-click on the Form1 window (which is now behind Form1).*

We'll explain what this window is all about in a minute. But first, let's try a simple experiment.

Click on the down-pointing arrow for the Proc combo box (which has the word Load inside it) to display a list of names. Type the letter **C**; the combo box should highlight the word Click. Then press **Enter**. You should see the following in the Code window:

```
Private Sub Form_Click ()

End Sub
```

Press the Tab key on your keyboard. This moves the insertion point four spaces to the right. Most programmers like to indent lines because it provides a visual clue as to where groups of instructions start and end. Here it won't make much difference now, but it will in later chapters when you write longer programs.

Next, type the word **beep** and you should see something like the following:

```
Private Sub Form_Click ()
  beep
End Sub
```

Press **F5** to run this simple program (but don't press **Ctrl+Break** because you won't be working with the Debug window here). You'll see the window Form1 come to the front again. Also, notice that the caption at the very top of the screen reads as follows:

```
Project1 - Microsoft Visual Basic - [run]
```

This tells you that you're running this program.

Your program should beep every time you click inside the white part of the Form1 window. When you've had enough fun, quit this program and return to design mode by clicking on the control box (the square icon at the upper-left of the Form1 window) and selecting Close from this menu, or double-clicking on the Control box.

We'll look at what happens in this small program in just a second. But first, you may have noticed something interesting. You probably typed the Beep command into the code window using all lowercase letters, but this is what it now looks like:

```
Private Sub Form_Click ()
  Beep
End Sub
```

Visual Basic automatically capitalized the word Beep. As you'll see, Visual Basic automatically capitalizes all keywords in its language whenever you move to the next line or run the program. In addition, if you're using a color monitor, you'll notice that the keywords appear in blue.

Anatomy of an Event Handler

This small piece of code, which consists of three lines, is called an *event handler* because it handles mouse click events inside the form. There are a number of different types of events in Windows programs. Clicking is an event. Pressing a key is an event. Even redrawing (or repainting) a window is an event. And Visual Basic allows you to write instructions (subroutines) for handling each of these events. In this example, you're handling the click event, which means that you're running the Beep command whenever you click inside the Form1 window.

NOTE

Visual Basic programs are built around *events,* which are various things that can happen in a program. As you'll see in this book, you can write code to handle a number of events —such as clicking, double-clicking, painting (drawing a window), pressing a key, and moving the mouse.

Any event handler consists of three parts: the event definition, lines of code you write, and the End Sub line.

The first line defines the name of the event handler. In this case, Visual Basic has created an event handler called *Form_Click().* (In a minute we'll take a look at the rules Visual Basic uses to define event names. But first, let's finish looking at the structure of this event handler.) The word Sub stands for *subroutine,* which is another piece of computer-science jargon. A subroutine is a small piece of code that stands as a separate package. This will become clearer later when you have more than one subroutine. The first word, Private in this case, indicates that the subroutine can only be accessed by statements that are inside the form or module containing the private subroutine. In other words, commands inside other forms and modules can't access that subroutine. If it were Public instead of Private, then it would be available to all other commands in all other forms or modules. We won't be using Public subroutines in this book, but we will talk more about forms and modules later.

NOTE

Subroutines are small pieces of code that have a name. They begin with the word Private or Public, followed by Sub *Name,* and end with End Sub. Any lines of code you write must appear between the Sub statement and the End Sub statement. For example:

```
Private Sub Name
  [statements]
End Sub
```

These statements define a private subroutine with the name *Name*. You can place as many statements as you want, or none at all, between the Sub and End Sub lines.

Subroutines must end with an End Sub statement. It's not actually a command because it doesn't perform any action—it just marks the end of the subroutine. To make this clearer, let's look at how Visual Basic works with this subroutine. Whenever you click inside of the Form1 window, Visual Basic automatically runs the code inside Form_Click(). By the code inside, we mean any code that appears between the Sub Form_Click() and the End Sub statements. In our example, this means Visual Basic runs the Beep command. After it finishes running that command, it sees the End Sub statement, which tells Visual Basic that it has finished running this subroutine.

The name of this event procedure, Form_Click() has two parts (see Figure 4.2) separated by an underscore character (_). The first part of the name is the object you're working with. When you're working with forms this name is always "Form." For some reason, it never has the name of the form itself. That's why this event handler is called Form_Click() and not Form1_Click(), which would have matched the actual name of the form from our example. But as you'll see later, for other objects this part of the name will be the name of the object.

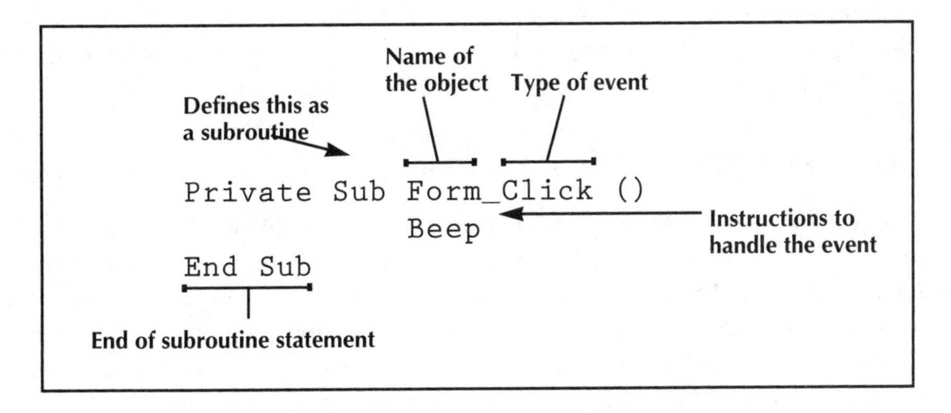

FIGURE 4.2 *The various parts of an event-handling procedure.*

The second part of the name is the name of the event this subroutine will handle. In this example, you're handling the Click event for mouse clicks inside the form, so it's called Form_Click().

All subroutines end with the line End Sub.

A Multiline Program

Let's make this program a little more interesting by adding another line to it. Use either the cursor keys or the mouse to move the insertion point after the *p* in Beep, and then press **Enter**. Finally, type the word **end**. Your Click subroutine should now look like the following:

```
Private Sub Form_Click()
  Beep
  end
End Sub
```

Now run the program and see what it does. Notice how it quits and returns to design mode as soon as you click the mouse? The End command, as you'll recall, tells Visual Basic to stop running the current program, so when Visual Basic ends your program it returns you to design mode. You may have observed that Visual Basic capitalized the End keyword when you ran your program, just as it did before with your Beep command.

You'll also notice something potentially confusing. There are two Ends in this subroutine: The End command, and the End Sub statement. The End in each case has a slightly different meaning. Although the End command ends the current program, the End Sub statement marks the end of the current subroutine, similar to the way a period marks the end of a sentence.

A Look at Event-Driven Programs

Most of the time that your program is "running," it's not actually doing anything. This is because your Visual Basic program has returned control back to Windows. All Windows programs are built around what's known as the *event model* of programming. In this model, Windows watches your computer to see what's going on, and as soon as something interesting (an event) happens, Windows figures out which program the event belongs to, and then sends that event off to the correct program (see Figure 4.3).

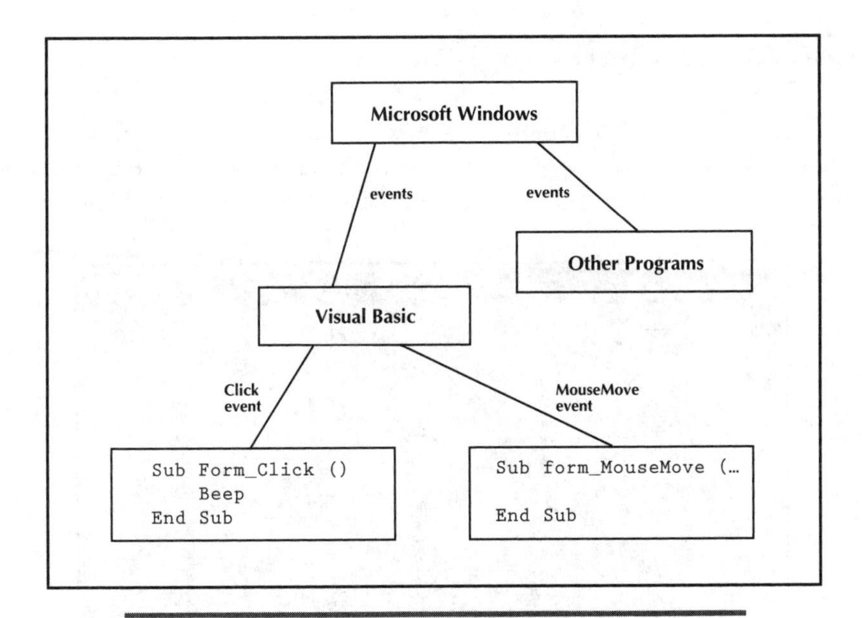

FIGURE 4.3 *This figure outlines the kind of event model used in Windows programs. In this model, your program only receives control of, and runs in response to, events generated by Windows.*

In this model your Visual Basic program won't actually be running, in a sense, until you click on your Form1 window. At this point, Windows notices that the click belongs to a window owned by Visual Basic, so it sends the click event to Visual Basic. Visual Basic, in turn, notices that the click is for your Form1 window, so it sends the event to your code in Form_Click(), which beeps. When Visual Basic encounters the End Sub statement, it returns control back to Windows, to await the next event.

When you added the End command to Form_Click(), you altered the picture a little. This command generates a "quit" message, telling Visual Basic that you want to quit your program. Visual Basic removes your program from the event-handling system and returns to design mode. When you're in design mode, clicking on the Form1 window sends a message to Visual Basic rather than to your program.

All of these concepts will become clearer in the next few chapters, where you'll continue to work with events. The concept of an event is one that most people have a little trouble learning at first. But when you get the hang of it, it's a nice and simple way to write programs. So hang in there.

Building a Sketch Program

Now we're going to change course. You're going to build your first real program, called Sketch, that will allow you to sketch on the screen. Figure 4.4 shows what this program will do when you finish it at the end of Chapter 5.

FIGURE 4.4 *Sketch lets you use the mouse to draw on the screen. It includes a pull-down menu that lets you erase the picture, change the width of the pen, and exit the program.*

Think for a couple of minutes about where you're going to start building this program. So far, you don't know very much about programming, so we'll start you off with the easiest thing you know how to do. In the last chapter, you learned how to draw lines. In this chapter, you learned how to attach some commands to an event. So the first thing you'll do is combine these two pieces so that you can draw lines inside this window as you move the mouse. This is very easy to do, but you'll run into a couple of simple problems that can be solved using some new commands.

After you've polished the part of your program that draws lines as you move the mouse, we'll move on to adding the pull-down menu. This is remarkably easy, especially if you ever see how much work "real" programmers have to do to get menus running in *their* programs.

Drawing Lines to Follow the Mouse

Before we continue, you'll need to remove the two lines of code you added to Form_Click() at the start of this chapter. There are two ways to do this. You can either quit Visual Basic and start over again, or you can delete the two lines of code. If you quit Visual Basic, you'll see a message like the one in Figure 4.5. This message box is informing you that you'll lose the two lines of code you typed into Form_Click() if you don't save Form1.frm. Click on the **No** button—you don't want to save this click program.

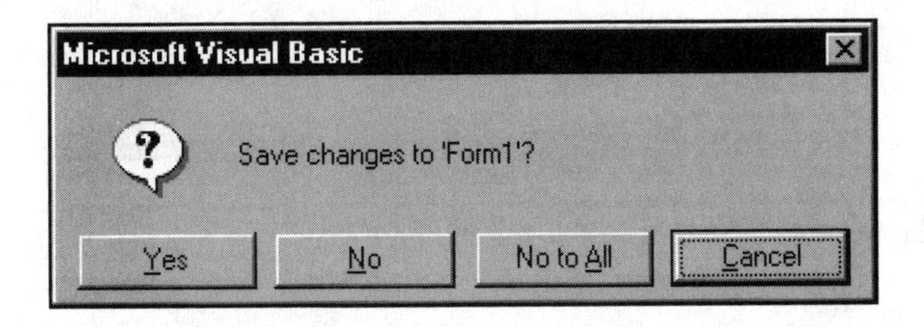

FIGURE 4.5 *You'll see this message box if you try to quit Visual Basic after you've entered some commands for Form_Click(). Press **N** or click on the **No** button to cancel the save.*

To remove the two command lines, delete them by using the usual Windows methods for editing text. For example, you could use the mouse to select these two lines, and then press the **Del** key to remove them.

Choosing the Event

The Form_Click() event isn't the event you actually want to work with. Instead, you want to work with an event called Form_MouseMove. This event occurs whenever you move the mouse. (Big surprise, right?)

You get to this event by clicking on the down-pointing arrow in the combo box called *Proc* in the code window. (Proc is short for *procedure*, which is another name for subroutine.) Figure 4.6 shows this combo box pulled down with the MouseMove event highlighted. Click on this event to show it in the window.

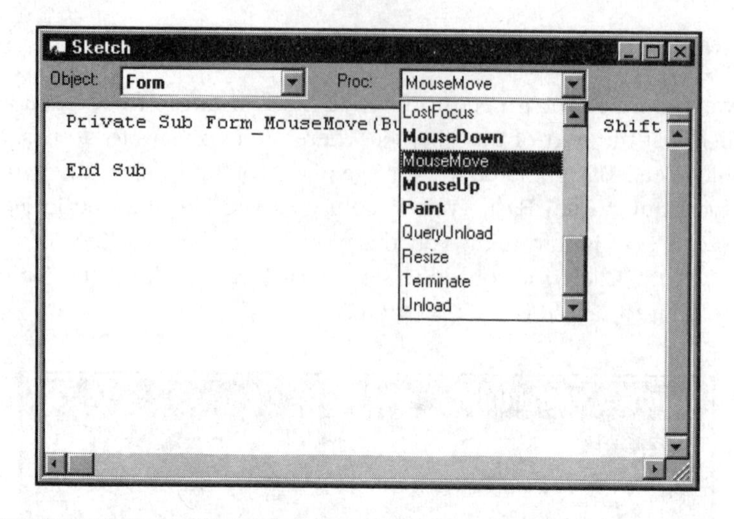

FIGURE 4.6 *Click on the down-pointing arrow for the Proc combo box to show the procedures (event handlers) available, then click on MouseMove to select this event procedure.*

WHY IT'S CALLED THE PROC COMBO BOX

You may have noticed that you used the Proc combo box to change the subroutine (event handler) we were looking at. If you're changing subroutines, why is this called Proc and not Sub? Good question.

The word *procedure,* as it turns out, is a more general name for a set of statements than the word *subroutine* or *function.* (A function is like a subroutine, but it returns a number or a string of characters.) Because Proc is more general, Microsoft chose to call this combo box Proc, rather than something longer like Sub/Function.

If you use the horizontal scroll bar, you can see that the MouseMove event procedure actually has a number of arguments that it receives (these are the names inside the parentheses) as follows:

```
Sub Form_MouseMove (Button As Integer, Shift As Integer, _
X As Single, Y As Single)
```

(Even though this is one code statement, we've written it as two lines so it will fit on this page.)

NOTE

Lines of code in this book are restricted to about 65 characters because the page is not wide enough to fit more. So all the lines you write will not, for the most part, be longer than 65 characters. But Visual Basic itself often creates subroutine definitions that are longer than 65 characters. To make it easier to read code in the code window, Visual Basic 4.0 has added a line-continuation character so that you can write single code statements on more than one line. To continue a statement onto the next line, use a space followed immediately by an underscore character at the end of the first line, then continue your statement on the subsequent line.

This subroutine definition includes four arguments. If you remember back to Chapter 1, you learned that the Print command can work with a number of arguments. Like Print, the MouseMove event handler also has some arguments it can receive:

Button Gives us information on which mouse button is pressed. This will be 1 if just the left button is down, 2 if just the right button is down, and 3 if both buttons are down.

Shift Which shift keys (like the Left Shift, Right Shift, Alt Shift, or Ctrl Shift) are currently down. We won't be using this information here.

X, Y Gives information on where the mouse is inside the window. You'll use these two numbers for the endpoint of your lines.

Writing Event Code

Make sure you have the Form_MouseMove subroutine visible in the Code window, and then type the following line of code, between the Private Sub and End Sub lines:

```
Line -(X, Y)
```

(You can indent this line by pressing the Tab key.) Now press **F5** to run this program. Move your mouse. See how it draws lines to follow the mouse (see Figure 4.7).

When you want to exit from this program, click on the control menu in the upper-left corner of the window and choose **Close** (or press **Alt+F4**).

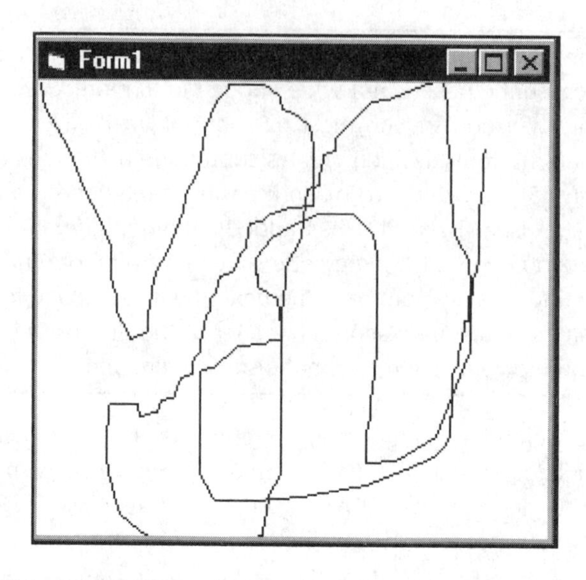

FIGURE 4.7 *As you can see, the line followed the movements of the mouse; however, this program started by drawing a line from (0,0) to our mouse's location.*

There are a couple of problems with this program, which we'll show you how to fix next. First, notice how your Sketch program began by drawing a line from (0, 0) to the mouse location. This happens because the Line –(X, Y) command draws lines from the last location. Because the "last location" is initially (0, 0), the first line starts at (0, 0). Second, you want Sketch to draw lines only when you press the mouse button.

Both of these problems are easy to fix, and we could fix both problems at the same time. But it's actually better to fix one problem at a time and test your solution. If you change too many things at once, you may forget what you're doing and not test a change you made. Let's start by changing Sketch so it won't start drawing until you click.

Let's think about what you need to do. You need some way of knowing when the mouse is down and drawing only then. If you look again at the arguments received in the MouseMove event subroutine, you'll notice one of them is called Button, and it tells you which mouse button is pressed. How can you use this information?

Clicking to Draw

A command called *If..Then* will run a command (or set of commands) *only* if some condition is true. This is the perfect command to use for drawing a line only if the left button is down. Before we look at all the details of If..Then and how it works, let's try it out in the program. Replace the current Line command in Form_MouseMove() with the following:

```
If Button = 1 Then Line -(X, Y)
```

Try running this program. Sketch should only draw lines when you hold down the left mouse button.

Now we need to cover some more theory, so save this project before we continue.

Saving Sketch

Visual Basic actually saves a number of files for each program you work on. Each program is called a *project* in Visual Basic's jargon. And each project minimally consists of a project file (with the extension .mak) containing information on what other files belong to the project, such as forms like Form1.frm.

Forms are saved as separate files with the .frm extension. The current form is called Form1, which isn't a very descriptive name. You'll need to change this to a more descriptive name before you save the project. The name Sketch jumps to mind.

You'll need to return to design mode before changing the form's name. Make sure the Sketch form is active (click once on it), then press **F4** to make the Properties window visible and active. Finally, use the scroll bar on the right side of the Properties window to scroll the list until the line with Name becomes visible (see Figure 4.8).

Click on the Name property. Notice that the combo box at the top of the Properties window now reads Form1. This is the current name of your Form, as you saw in the Debug window. To change this name, simply type **Sketch** and press **Enter** (see Figure 4.9).

The Properties window allows you to change various properties. The Name item that you selected is a property of this form, as are the CurrentX and CurrentY properties we discussed in Chapter 3. As you can see, there are a number of other properties that you can also change by using this window.

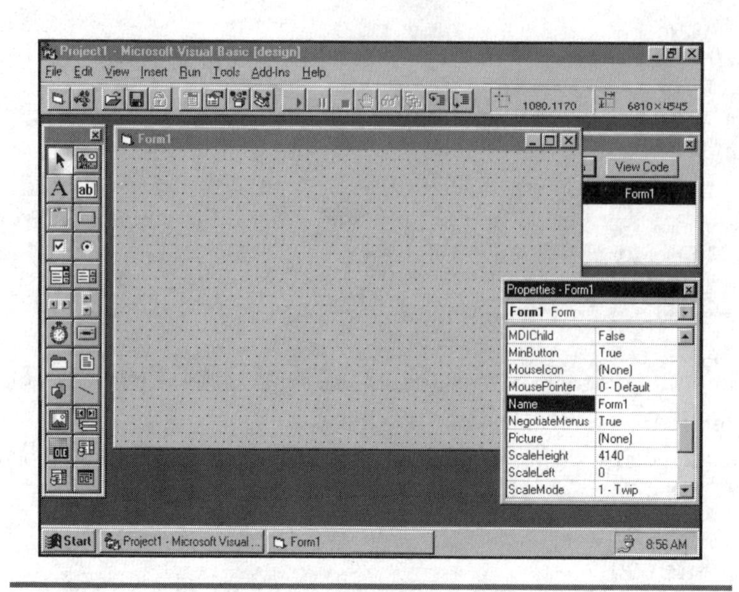

FIGURE 4.8 *Use the Properties window to change the name of this form. Scroll the list until the Name property is visible, click on it, and type in the new name (Sketch in our example).*

FIGURE 4.9 *This figure shows the Property Bar after you've typed in a new form name, Sketch, but before pressing Enter. You can use the mouse or cursor keys to edit what you've typed.*

NOTE

You may have noticed that the CurrentX and CurrentY properties don't appear in this combo box. Why not? These two properties are known as *run-time* properties, which means they only have meaning when you're running a program. On the other hand, the properties you see in this combo box are known as *design-time* properties. Some properties are both run-time and design-time properties, but only the design-time properties are shown in the Properties window.

In addition to changing the form's name, you'll also need to change the caption in the window (which currently reads Form1) so that it, too, reads Sketch. To do this, again use the Scroll bar to display the line with Caption, and click on it to select the Caption property. Then type **Sketch** and press **Enter**. Your Sketch window should now say Sketch, rather than Form1, at the top.

Now you're ready to save your project. Instead of allowing the files to be saved in Visual Basic's directory, we suggest you use the Explorer to create a directory for your projects, and a subdirectory called Sketch for all of your Sketch files. We made PROJ a subdirectory of the C: root directory, and SKETCH a subdirectory to PROJ. Then pull down the Visual Basic's File menu and select Save Project. Visual Basic will first try to save the form Sketch (see Figure 4.10). Because we've already provided the form name, it has supplied us with the file name SKETCH saved as a FRM type file. Click **SAVE** to save the form.

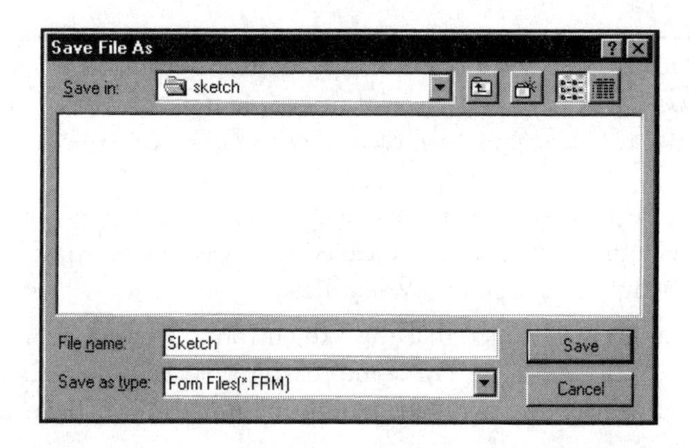

FIGURE 4.10 *When you ask to save the project, Visual Basic will first prompt you for the name and directory of the Sketch form.*

Next, Visual Basic displays a Save Project As dialog box, with a default name of Project1.vbp for the project file. Type **SKETCH.VBP** and press **Enter** (the directory will already be the one where you stored SKETCH.FRM). That's it. You've now saved Sketch, so you can exit Visual Basic and then load your project back into Visual Basic by selecting Open Project... in the File menu.

Opening Your Sketch Project

When you start Visual Basic again, you'll need to know how to load your Sketch Project back in. Quit from Visual Basic and start over. When you have Visual

Basic running again, select **Open Project...** from the File menu. You'll see a dialog box like the one in Figure 4.11.

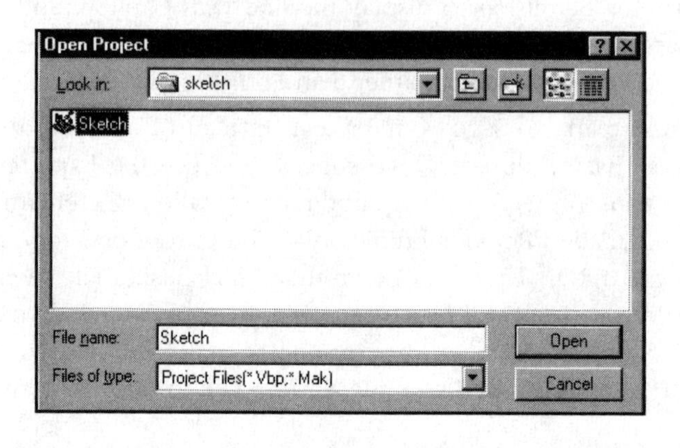

FIGURE 4.11 *When you select Open Project... in the File menu, the Open Project dialog box appears showing Visual Basic's directory. Use the LookIn listbox to change to the directory that contains your project as shown here.*

Change the directory shown in this dialog box to the one you created for Sketch, at which time you'll see a file called SKETCH Double-click on this file to load your Sketch project back into Visual Basic.

At this point, you'll notice that the Sketch form (window) isn't visible (see Figure 4.12). Where did it go? For some reason, Visual Basic doesn't automatically open a form when you load a project. Instead, you have to open the form yourself.

You can open a form by clicking on the name SKETCH.FRM that appears at the top of the project window (you may have to select Project Window from the Window menu to make the project window visible) and then clicking on the View Form button. The project window is the window on the right called SKETCH. You can also open the Sketch form by double-clicking on SKETCH.FRM in the project window.

The If..Then Command

Now that you've saved your project, let's spend a few minutes on the theory behind the If..Then command. You've probably already figured out how the If

Button=1 Then Line command works, but let's try a few simple experiments anyway. Make sure you have the Debug window visible and active and enter the following to test the If..Then command as follows:

```
if 1=1 then print "True"
True
|
```

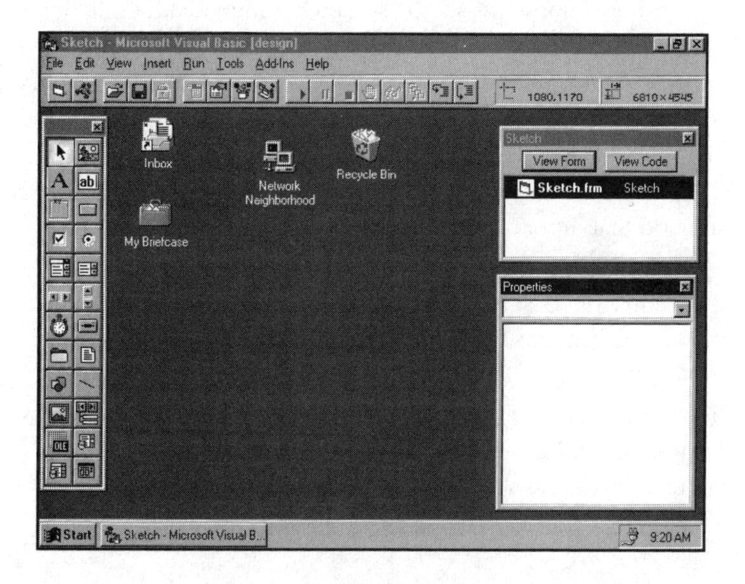

FIGURE 4.12 *You'll see a screen like this one when you load your Sketch project back into Visual Basic. Double-click on the name* ***SKETCH.FRM*** *that appears inside the project window (the window with the caption SKETCH.MAK). (Note that you may have to select Project Window from the Window menu to make the project window visible.)*

As you can see, the If..Then command checked to see if 1=1, and since it does (meaning that 1=1 is true), Visual Basic ran the command after the Then: Print "True".

You can also try using this command with something you know isn't true, like 1=0 as follows:

```
if 1=0 then print "True"
|
```

You'll notice that Visual Basic completely ignored the Print "True" command, which is exactly what you want it to do. In other words, it only executes the Print command if the condition is True. Since 1=0 is not true, it didn't print.

Boolean Expressions (Conditions)

You'll notice that the equal sign here is actually a test, rather than an assignment. Such tests are called *Boolean expressions* in the jargon of computer science. Although this name may sound somewhat intimidating, all Boolean really means is that an expression can be either true or false. In other words, it can only have one of two values.

There is also another piece of computer-science jargon, which should make a little more sense. When you use a Boolean expression like 1=0 in an If..Then statement, it's called a *condition.* In other words, If..Then runs a command only on the condition that an expression is true.

But how does Visual Basic represent true and false? Versions of Visual Basic prior to 4.0 didn't have a Boolean data type with values of True and False. Instead, the earlier versions used numbers to represent True and False, and two predefined variables called True and False to contain these two values.

Let's try some more tests with the Debug window to see how Visual Basic 4.0 handles true and false now. Because there are only two values, you can use two Print commands to display both of them as follows:

```
print 1=1
True
print 1=0
False
|
```

You can see from this reply that Visual Basic 4.0 uses the words True and False as values for the Boolean data type. So if everything works as expected, you should be able to use the words as conditions just as easily as expressions.The following are the same Print commands as previously mentioned by using the Boolean data value rather than expressions:

```
if true then print "True"
Continue
if false then print "True"
|
```

A Boolean expression will *always* return either True or False.

BOOLEAN EXPRESSIONS

The term Boolean is named after an English mathematician named George Boole, who in the mid-1800s developed a type of mathematics called *Boolean algebra*. This type of algebra deals with values that are either true or false. It is invaluable for use with computers because computers work fundamentally with 0 and 1 (false and true) signals inside.

Earlier versions of Visual Basic did not have a Boolean data type, so Boolean expressions had to return a number. With Visual Basic 4.0, the new Boolean data type shows us the words True and False, but internally, Visual Basic is still storing the value numerically. The number 0 represents False, and –1 represents True.

You can see this for yourself by using the CInt command (it stands for "Convert to Integer") in the Debug window, as follows:

```
Print CInt(True)
  -1
Print CInt(False)
  0
```

The reason Microsoft chose these two numbers has to do with an operator called Not because the expression Not True = False.

The Not operator, in turn, works with something called a bit, which is the smallest unit of storage inside your computer and is either 0 or 1. An Integer number, which is how true and false are represented, is built out of 16 of these bits. If we write the numbers for true and false as bits, you get the following:

Boolean	Basic	Binary
False	0	0000 0000 0000 0000
True	–1	1111 1111 1111 1111

The Not keyword inverts all the bits in a number, changing 0s to 1s and 1s to 0s, which means that Not 0 = –1. This, of course, means that Not True = False, which is exactly what we want Not, True, and False to mean.

As to why Not 0 is negative, you learned in Chapter 1 that half of the values in an Integer number are defined as being negative. The microprocessor inside of your computer determines whether or not a number is negative by looking at the first digit in the binary number: All numbers that start with a 1 are negative numbers. So Not 0, which starts with a 1 will be a negative number, which happens to be minus 1.

The Else Part of If..Then

The If..Then command is actually a very powerful command. So far we've only looked at the simplest case, where you run just one command if a condition is true. But you can also have If..Then run a different command if the condition is false, as you'll see in the next example.

The following example executes one command if a condition is true and another command if it's false:

```
if 1=0 then print "True" else print "False"
False
|
```

You can see that all you have to do is add an Else keyword, followed by another command. The If..Then command is a very useful command that you'll use often in this book, so you'll learn more of the details in coming chapters.

COMMAND REFERENCE: IF..THEN..ELSE

You'll learn more about the If..Then..Else command and how to use all its pieces in following chapters.

```
If condition Then command1 [Else command2]
```

There are several pieces to this command. The first piece, *condition*, is a test that the If command performs. If the result of this test is True, Visual Basic runs *command1*; otherwise it will do nothing or, when you have an Else, it will run *command2*.

```
If condition1 Then
  [statements]
[ElseIf condition2 Then
  [statements] ]
[Else
```

```
    [statements] ]
End If
```

When you want to run more than a single statement in any part of the If..Then command, you'll need to use this format, which places the statements on separate lines from the If..Then and Else keywords.

Boolean Operators

In addition to the simple = comparison that you've been working with so far, there are a number of other operators, as you can see in Table 4.1. Some of these operators should be fairly clear, but others, such as Xor, are more advanced, and we won't cover them until later chapters when you need them.

We will, however, take a quick look at the Or operator, which is quite useful when you have more than one condition and only need one condition to be true. For example, if you have the Boolean expressions 1=1 and 1=0, and you write (1=1) or (1=0), the result should be true because the first expression is true. Try it by using the Print command and you'll discover that it is true as follows:

```
print (1=1) or (1=0)
True
|
```

The And operator is quite useful when you have multiple conditions that must all be true. The following two examples should give you a better idea of how And works:

```
print (1=1) and (2=2)
True
print (1=1) and (1=2)
False
|
```

The first example returns True since both expressions are True, but the second example returns False because the second expression (1=2) is not True.

One final word of advice. When you have a number of operators in one expression (there are two equal signs and one Or in the example above), it's a good idea to use parentheses to make sure that Basic correctly interprets what you write. If you're not intimately familiar with operator precedence (which you learned about in Chapter 1), you could easily write a statement that looked correct to you, but which Visual Basic calculated in an order different from what you might expect.

TABLE 4.1 *Boolean Operators*

Operator	Meaning
=	Equal to; returns True if the values on both sides are the same
<>	Not equal; the values on the two sides differ
<	Less than; True if the left side is less than the right side
>	Greater than; True if the left side is greater than the right side
<=	Less than or equal
>=	Greater than or equal
Not	Invert all the bits in the number to its right; Not 0 = –1
Or	Bit-wise Or
Xor	Bit-wise Exclusive Or
Eqv	Equivalent
Imp	Implication

Finishing Sketch

Enough theory! Let's get back to your Sketch program and fix the remaining problem. If you run Sketch again, you'll notice that it draws a line from (0, 0) to your mouse location when you first click. You'll also notice that you can't draw unconnected lines. This turns out to be the same problem.

All of these extra lines appear because the Line –(X, Y) command draws a line continuing from the last point. In the last chapter, you learned that Visual Basic remembers the last point using the CurrentX and CurrentY properties, and that they're set to 0 when you first start your program.

What you need to do is set CurrentX and CurrentY to the location of the mouse when you first click the mouse. How do you do that? By using a new event called Form_MouseDown.

Visual Basic runs the code you write in this event subroutine whenever you click the mouse button, but not during the rest of the time you hold down the mouse button. (On the other hand, the Form_Click() event that you worked with before only runs when you click *and then release* the mouse button.) In other words, if you click and hold and then move the mouse, Visual Basic first runs MouseDown, then it runs MouseMove (and finally Click when you release the button). And this is exactly what you want. You'll set CurrentX and CurrentY to the mouse position (X, Y) inside the MouseDown subroutine.

NOTE

The MouseDown and Click events are quite different. MouseDown is called as soon as you click the mouse button. But Click is not called until you release the mouse button.

Make sure you're in design mode and the Sketch form is visible, then double-click on this form to show the Code window. Next, pull down the Proc combo box and select the MouseDown event. The following code is all you need to add:

```
CurrentX = X
CurrentY = Y
```

After you've entered these two lines in the Form_MouseDown event, run your program and see how it works. You should now be able to draw lines without the initial line from (0, 0). You'll also notice that Sketch now allows you to draw lines that aren't connected to one another.

Well, that was pretty easy. But there is one last problem. If you click and release the mouse button *without* moving the mouse, you'll notice that Sketch doesn't draw anything. It should draw at least a point, so let's add yet another command that will draw a point even if you don't move the mouse.

To draw a point, you'll use another Basic command called PSet, which stands for Point Set, and draws a single point (pixel) on the screen. The command PSet(X, Y) will draw one pixel at (X, Y). Add this command to the Form_MouseDown subroutine, which should now look like the following:

```
Private Sub Form_MouseDown (Button As Integer, Shift As Integer, _
X As Integer, Y As Single)
  CurrentX = X
  CurrentY = Y
  PSet (X, Y)
End Sub
```

(The first line is too long to print as a single line, so we've wrapped it to two lines, using the continuation character—a space immediately followed by an underscore character—indicating that the second line is a continuation of the first line.)

Reference: PSet Command

```
[object.]PSet [Step](x!, y!)[,color&]
```

The PSet command draws a single point (pixel) at (x!, y!). You can also use the same Step keyword and *color&* argument used by the Line command.

You've done as much work on Sketch as you're going to in this chapter, so you might want to save your work. You can use the Save Project command in the File menu to save the project file, as well as any other files (Sketch.frm) that you've changed. In the next chapter, you'll add a menu bar to your Sketch program.

Related Tools

* **Select Case.** This command is similar to the If..Then command. It's most useful when you have a single variable that you're testing against several values. In other words, if you want to run a different statement for any value in a variable, use this command.
* **Functions.** Functions, which you'll learn about later in this book, are very much like subroutines, except that they return a value (either a number or a string of characters).

Summary

You learned a lot about building real programs in this chapter, and you'll learn even more in the coming chapters.

* **Code window.** You'll use the code window throughout the rest of this book to write your programs. You display this window by double-clicking on the form window, which is called Form1 in new projects.
* **Events.** Visual Basic programs are built around event subroutines (also known as event handlers) that handle such events as clicking the mouse

button, moving the mouse, and pressing a key. In this chapter you worked with the Click, Form_MouseMove, and Form_MouseDown event subroutines.

✷ **Sub.** Any subroutine begins with the word Sub and the subroutine's name. Event subroutines are formed from the object name (such as Form) and the event name (such as MouseMove). Subroutines end with the line End Sub. Any lines of code you write must appear between these two lines.

✷ **If..Then.** The If..Then..Else command allows you to choose which code you want to run, based on the result of a condition. Conditions are Boolean expressions that result in a True or False. In the Basic language, True = –1 and False = 0, and Boolean expressions return numbers of type Integer.

✷ **Properties window.** You saw how to use the Properties window to change the form Name and Caption properties of your Sketch program, and how to save the project to the disk.

ADDING A MENU BAR

- Mnemonic access characters
- Control names and menus
- Using the Menu Design window
- Control arrays
- The Index argument

In this chapter you're going to add a menu bar to your Sketch program. As you'll see, this is something that's quite easy to do, which means that you won't have to learn as much new material in Chapter 5 as in previous chapters.

Building a Menu Bar

Because Visual Basic provides a visual tool (which is why it's called *Visual* Basic) for building menu bars, building them is very simple. Anyone who's ever written a program using a language like C or Pascal will tell you it's a lot more work using those languages.

If you don't already have Sketch loaded in Visual Basic, select Open Project... from the File menu to open Sketch.mak. To use the menu tool, you'll need to close the Code window (if you still have it open) so your Sketch form will be visible and active. You might want to click once on it to make sure it's active. Next pull down the Tools menu and click on **Menu Editor**. This will bring up a window like the one shown in Figure 5.1.

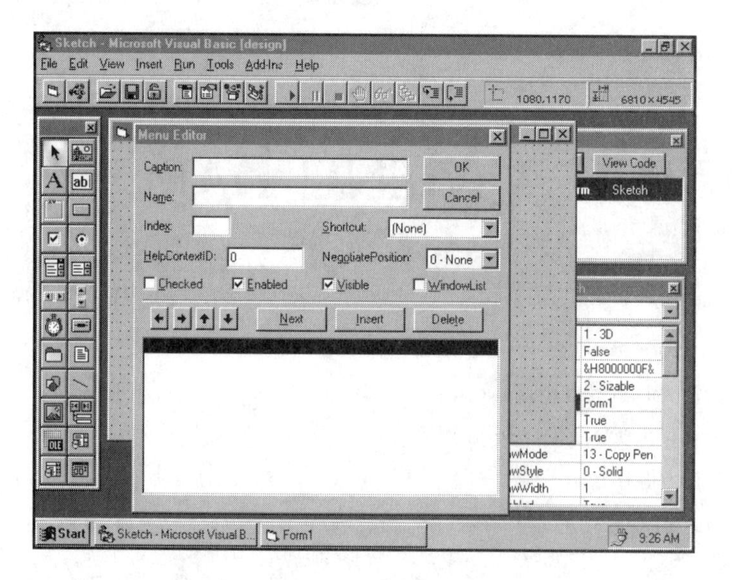

FIGURE 5.1 *The Menu Design window.*

This window lets you create an entire menu bar, with all of the menus and items you want. There are only a couple of new concepts for you to learn here, but first, let's quickly review the menu you'll create (see Figure 5.2). You'll actually start with a simpler version of the Draw menu, using only a single menu item—Exit. This will allow you to get a menu up and running quickly, without learning everything you'll need to know for the full menu.

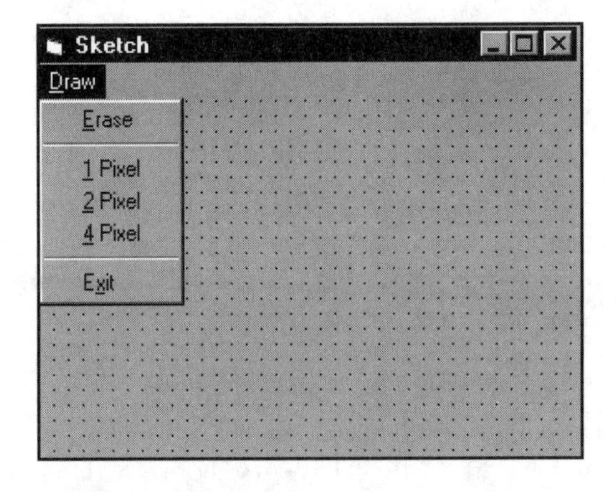

FIGURE 5.2 *The Draw menu you'll create. Notice that there's only one menu on the menu bar.*

Creating the Menu Title

The first part of creating a menu is easy. Type in the name of the menu, which in this case is Draw. Notice in Figure 5.2 that the D in Draw is underlined. This tells Windows that you can use the Alt+D key combination to pull down this menu.

Such underlined letters are called *mnemonic access characters* in Windows jargon. This is quite a mouthful, but what it means is quite simple. Mnemonic characters are characters you can remember more easily than function keys, like F4, as shortcuts for some action. Such letters usually have some obvious connection to a longer name, such as the first letter. For example, when you think of Draw, the first sound you hear is the D sound. In other words, the letter *d* has a mnemonic connection to the word Draw.

Sometimes, however, you have two or more menus or menu items that start with the same letter, like File and Format in Word for Windows. In these cases, you'll have to use other rules to choose which letter to underline. See the sidebar "How to Choose Mnemonic Characters" for the rules that Microsoft suggests.

Windows, and therefore Visual Basic, uses an ampersand character (&) in front of a letter to mark that letter as a mnemonic access character. To make the *D* in Draw the access character, type the following into the Caption text box of the Menu Design window:

```
&Draw
```

Next press the Tab key. This moves the insertion point to the next text box, called Name, which is the name of the control.

How to Choose Mnemonic Characters

Microsoft has a number of suggestions on how to choose what letter to use for a mnemonic access character. These rules apply to all menu names and to the names of all the menu items in any one menu. Here are the rules, in order of preference:

- **First letter.** Use the first letter when you can. If you have more than one menu or item that starts with the same letter (such as File and Format), you'll have to choose a different mnemonic character for all but one name. You may also decide that another letter is more meaningful than the first letter, such as *x* for Exit. When you have a two-word title, you can use the first letter in the second (or third) word. For example, many programs have a Save and a Save As... menu item. Notice that the A in Save As... is underlined.
- **Distinctive.** Consonant If you can't use the first letter, use a consonant that stands out. For example, the *t* in Format stands out more than the *r* or *m* because it's at the end of the word. On the other hand, the *b* in Ribbon is more distinctive than the *n*. There are no hard-and-fast rules here.
- **Vowel.** If all else fails, use a vowel in the title. For example, Word for Windows has the following menus: File, Format, Tools, and Table. You can see how they chose the F for File, the T in Format, and the vowels in Tools and Table by following all three rules.

In all cases, you mark the mnemonic access character with an ampersand (&) in front of the mnemonic character. For example, T&able marks the *a* in Table.

Controls and Control Names

What is a control? It's a special type of object. You learned about objects in Chapter 3, when you looked at forms and the Printer object. There are other types of objects in Visual Basic, and most of these objects appear inside forms.

The menu bar and its items, for example, will appear inside your Sketch program (as soon as you finish building it). All objects that appear *inside* a form are called *controls*. All menus and menu items are controls.

A control name is the name you give to each control (object). In the Name field for your &Draw title, type the following:

```
menDraw
```

Here we're using a naming convention we'll use throughout this book for the names of controls. We've put the letters "men" in front of Draw to indicate (to you, not Visual Basic) that this control is the name of a menu.

When you've finished typing in this control name, press **Enter**. This is the same as clicking on the Next button, which takes you to the next menu or item name.

Why do you have to provide a control name? So Visual Basic can provide an event handler for each menu and item. As you'll recall from Chapter 4, the name of an event handler is the object's name followed by the event name, such as Form_MouseMove. Here the names will look something like menDraw_Click( ). Even though you won't use this event, Visual Basic still requires you to give Draw a control name.

Creating the Exit Item

The next thing you'll create is the menu item Exit. First, type **E&xit** into the Caption text box, and then press the **Tab** key. Next type **miExit** in the Name field (mi is a naming convention that tells you this is a "menu item"), but don't press Enter. First, you need to tell Visual Basic that you want this to be a menu item rather than a menu. To do that, you'll need to click on the right-pointing arrow (see Figure 5.3).

Finally, click **OK** to close the Menu Design window. You'll notice that your Sketch window has a menu bar, with a single menu called Draw.

NOTE

You may be wondering why we had you underline the x in Exit rather than the E. It turns out that Microsoft has a number of standard menu names and items, and Exit is one of these. If you look at most Windows programs, you'll notice they have a File menu with the last menu item being Exit.

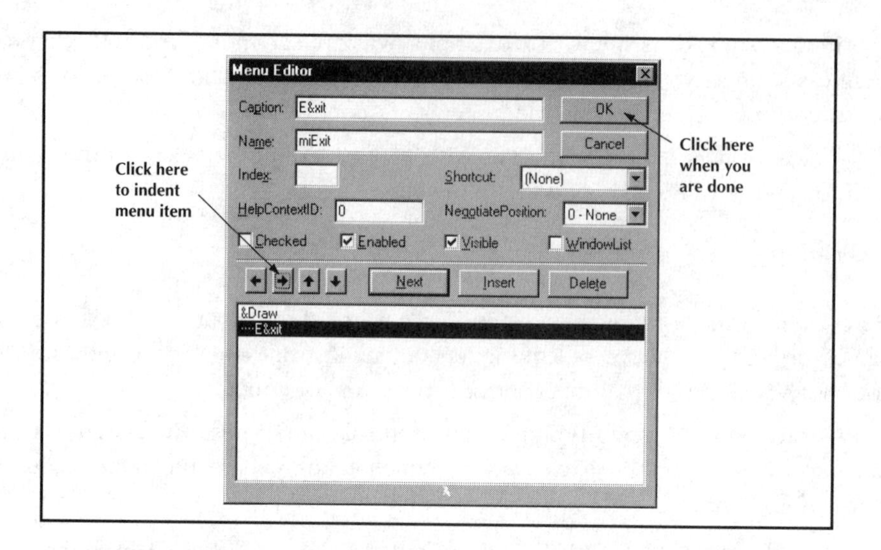

FIGURE 5.3 *Click on the right-pointing arrow to indent the Exit menu item so Visual Basic will know it's a menu item, rather than a menu title. Click on the Done button to finish editing the menu bar.*

Adding Code to a Menu Item

You're now ready to write some code to handle your new menu bar. The only menu item you have is Exit, which should exit your program. This is the same as double-clicking on the control box in the upper-left corner of the window.

Each menu item has an event handler called *Name_Click()* that is called by Visual Basic whenever you click on a menu item. The control name you gave to the Exit menu item is miExit, so the event handler should be called miExit_Click(). How do you get to this event handler? If you click on the Draw menu, then on the Exit item, Visual Basic displays the code for miExit_Click() in its code window, which should look something like the following:

```
Private Sub miExit_Click ()

End Sub
```

Do you know what code we want to put into this subroutine? When you select the Exit menu item, you want the program to exit, which means you want to use the End command. Type the **End** command into this subroutine and run your program.

```
Private Sub miExit_Click ()
  End
End Sub
```

Did selecting the Exit menu work the way you expected?

Adding the Erase Menu Item

Let's go back and add another item to the menu. You'll add the Erase item, which erases whatever you've drawn into the Sketch form. If you remember back to Chapter 3, you learned about the Cls command, which erases a form. You'll use Cls here. But first, you have to add the Erase menu item.

Click on the Sketch form to make sure it's the active window. Then select **Menu Editor** from the Tools menu. At the bottom of this window you'll see a list of the menus and items you've created so far, and it should look something like the following:

```
&Draw
....E&xit
```

Click on the second line, which is the one that reads E&xit. Then click on the **Insert** button just above this list. This will insert a new line (and therefore menu item) into your menu. It should look something like the following:

```
&Draw
....
....E&xit
```

You can then click in the Caption text box and start typing (you'll have to click in the Caption box because, as you can see, the insertion point won't be there until you click). Type **&Erase** for the caption, and then press the Tab key and type **miErase** for Name. Finally, click **OK**. You should now have a menu bar with two items: Erase and Exit.

Finally, pull down the Draw menu and click on Erase. Then type the Cls command into the miErase_Click() event handler as follows:

```
Private Sub miErase_Click ()
  Cls
Sub End
```

That's all there is to it! Now you have a simple menu bar that actually works. Try drawing in your Sketch window, then use the Erase command. Nice, huh?

Now you should save your project (using the Save Project item in the File menu) before you move on. In the next section, you'll add menu items that allow you to change the width of the lines drawn in Sketch.

Completing the Menu Bar

In this section, you'll add a total of five new menu items to your menu: three line-width menu items (1 Pixel, 2 Pixels, and 4 Pixels) and two separating lines. The first thing you'll need to do (can you guess?) is to bring up the Menu Design window. In the last section, you saw how to insert menu items before another menu item. You'll be using this technique to insert all five new menu items, so we won't step you through entering each menu item. But there are a couple of new techniques you'll learn.

Inserting Lines in Menus

First, let's look at how you insert the two separating lines. If you type a hyphen (–) into the Caption text box, this tells Windows to draw a line across the menu. You'll also need to provide a control name for these two separating lines, even though you can't click on them. Consistency in naming is a good habit to get into, so we suggest that you use the names miLine1 and miLine2.

Go ahead and insert the first line between your existing Erase end Exit menu items. Remember to set the Caption to – and Name to miLine1.

Adding Control Arrays

Next add the three line-width menu items. The first one should have a caption of &1 Pixel and a control name of miPixel. But before you add the next menu item, there is another piece of information you'll want to add. If you look at the Menu Design window, you'll notice there is a text box labeled Index. Press the **Tab** key to move the insertion point into the Index box, and then type **1**.

What's this for? It turns out you can create a number of menu items, or other controls for that matter, that are closely related to each other, and the Index field labels each control in a group. This will become clearer after an example, so let's continue creating the menu bar.

At this point your Menu Design window should look something like Figure 5.4. You can now enter the other two menu items and the final line using the information in Table 5.1 (which shows an index of 2 for the 2 Pixels item, and an index of 4 for the 4 Pixels item).

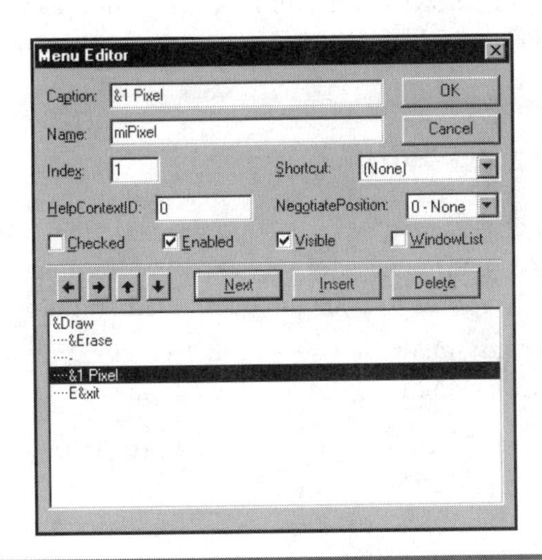

FIGURE 5.4 *Your Menu Design window should look like this after you've entered the first line-width menu item, &1 Pixel. Notice the 1 (one) in the Index field.*

TABLE 5.1 *Menu Names and Control Names*

Caption	Name	Index
&Draw	menDraw	
....&Erase	miErase	
....–	miLine1	
....&1 Pixel	miPixel	1
....&2 Pixel	miPixel	2
....&4 Pixel	miPixel	4
....–	miLine2	
....E&xit	miExit	

Notice that the Index field is blank for everything except for the three n Pixel menu items. Also notice that the Name is the same for all three n Pixel menu items. The four dots (....) mean that a caption is a menu item and show the indent you'll see at the bottom of the Menu Design window.

Finally, close the Menu Design window by clicking **OK**. You should now have a menu bar like the one shown in Figure 5.2. After doing all this work to build your menu, you might want to save your project. It's a good idea to save changes to your project often, in case Windows encounters the dreaded General Protection Fault (also known as a GPF), which most people encounter every now and then. GPFs result in a loss of all your work from the last time you saved your project.

Changing the Line Width

In the final section of this chapter, you'll add the code that allows you to change the width of your drawing pen. After you see how it's done, you might want to add several more line widths to your program by adding more menu items.

Pull down the Draw menu and select the 1 Pixel menu item. The code window should appear showing the following event handler:

```
Private Sub miPixel_Click (Index As Integer)

End Sub
```

There are two things different about this Click event handler. First, if you look at the Object: combo box, you'll notice it says miPixel(). There are now two parentheses after the control name, indicating that we're dealing with a control array (which includes all three *n* Pixel menu items) rather than a single control.

You'll also notice that this event handler has an extra piece of information that you've never seen before: the *Index As Integer*. What does this mean, and what is it used for?

The word *Index* is an argument to our Click event handler. Because you're now dealing with three controls that all have the same control name, you need some way to determine which menu item you clicked on. This is exactly what Index is for. It reports the value of the Index field from the Menu Design window. So Index will be 1, 2, or 4 because these are the three values you entered for the 1 Pixel, 2 Pixel, and 4 Pixel menu items. And you can now see why you used 1, 2, and 4 in the Index field—these are the line widths you'll need to support.

Anatomy of an Argument

Any argument you see in Visual Basic appears in three parts as follows:

```
ArgumentName As Type
```

The first part, *ArgumentName,* is the name of the argument (Index in miPixel_Click). In the last chapter you worked with the Button, Shift, X, and Y arguments in the Form_MouseDown event handler.

The next part, *As,* is one of Visual Basic's keywords that tells you the next word will be the type of value this argument holds.

Finally, the variable's type can be Integer, Long, Single, Double, Currency, String or Variant. See Table 2.1 for a refresher on Types.

The way to change the width of a line you draw is to use the DrawWidth property of a form. If you like, you can use the Debug window to try out different line widths. The following are some examples you can try:

```
Sketch.Line (0,0)-(1000,1000)
DrawWidth=2
Sketch.line (500,0)-(1500,1000)
DrawWidth=4
Sketch.Line (1000,0)-(2000,1000)
|
```

These commands will draw three lines, each with a different line width. The first line will be one pixel wide, since Visual Basic initially sets DrawWidth to 1 when you run a program. The next line will then be 2 pixels wide, with the last line 4 pixels wide. Unlike the measurement used for start points and endpoints, notice how the line widths are measured in pixels rather than twips. One of the things you'll discover about Visual Basic is that's it's not consistent, which makes learning it a little more challenging.

REFERENCE: DRAWWIDTH PROPERTY

The DrawWidth property of a form determines the width of the lines drawn on the form. DrawWidth is measured in pixels, *not* twips. By default, DrawWidth equals 1 when you first start a program.

When in design mode, you can change the default DrawWidth value for any form. To do so, click on the form you want to change, select the DrawWidth property in the Properties window, and type in a new number for the default DrawWidth.

By now you've probably figured out what code you need to put into the Click event handler, and you may even have tried it. The following is the code in its entirety:

```
Private Sub miPixel_Click (Index As Integer)
  DrawWidth = Index
End Sub
```

That's all there is to changing the width of the drawing pen. Try running this program and changing the line width. Everything should work as advertised. But there is one last thing you'll add to this program before we end this chapter. If you look again at the menu in Figure 5.2, you'll notice that the current width has a check mark next to it. We're going to add yet another piece of code to keep this check mark up to date. As you'll see, this takes only two lines of code: one line to remove the current check mark, and one to check the new line width.

Checking Menu Items

Each menu item has a property called Checked, which controls whether or not Visual Basic draws a check mark next to the menu item. By default, all menu items you create will not be checked. But you can easily check the correct menu item with this code as follows:

```
Private Sub miPixel_Click (Index As Integer)
  miPixel(DrawWidth).Checked = False  ' Uncheck current
                                        width
  DrawWidth = Index                   ' Change width of
                                        the pen
  miPixel(Index).Checked = True       ' Check the new
                                        width
End Sub
```

Try this code, and then we'll go back and see how it works (remember to save your project before you run your program). You'll notice that none of the menu items are checked initially; we'll fix this shortly. But now, after you select a width, it will be checked. And you can also change which width is checked.

Menu Property: Checked

Every menu item has a property called *Checked* that determines whether or not a check mark will be drawn next to it. The menu shown in Figure 5.2 has a check mark drawn next to the 1 Pixel menu item.

```
menName.Checked = False|True
```

Setting Checked to False removes the check mark, and setting it to True adds a check mark.

Now let's look at this code to see how it works. There are a couple of new concepts here that you'll learn about in the process. Let's look at the first line as follows:

```
miPixel(DrawWidth).Checked = False   ' Uncheck current width
```

What does all this mean? Well, you know that DrawWidth tells you the current width of the pen. And you know that the current width can be 1, 2, or 4, because these are the possible DrawWidth values you defined for Sketch. You also know that you want to change the Checked state on the menu item for the current width. In other words, if DrawWidth is 2, you want to remove the checkmark from the menu item called 2 Pixels. And that's what this command does. Let's go through each part.

The miPixel control, as we mentioned, is a control array, which means that you have more than one control and that you can refer to each control in the array by a number. The number is the Index value that you typed into the Menu Design window. By writing miPixel(DrawWidth), you're telling Visual Basic that you want to work with the menu item with an Index value equal to DrawWidth.

Control Arrays

The three menu items, 1 Pixel, 2 Pixels, and 4 Pixels, are a control array because you gave them all the same control name. You can refer to any control in a control array using the following syntax:

```
Name(Index)
```

Name is the name of the control, and *Index* is number that must match one of the Index values for a control in the array.

For a control array of menu items, the Index numbers can be any of the numbers you typed into the Index field of the Menu Editor window.

This is also the first time that you've changed a property on anything other than a form. As you'll recall from Chapter 3, properties are like variables, except that they're predefined by Visual Basic. All objects, such as forms, menu items, or the Printer object, have some properties. The Checked property you're using here is only available for menu items. You set a property by writing the menu item's name, followed by a period and the name of the property.

Accessing Properties in Objects

You can read or change any property in an object, such as a menu item, using the following syntax:

```
ObjectName.Property
```

ObjectName is the name of the object (which can be a form, a control, or Printer), and *Property* is the name of the property that you want to set or read. Notice that you put a period between ObjectName and Property.

You can read a property by writing, for example, miPixel(1).Checked, and you can set it using the assignment operator: miPixel(1).Checked=0.

The last part of this command is something called a *comment.* Comments are descriptions you can add to your programming code. This makes your programs easier to read in the future, when you no longer remember what you were thinking when you wrote the original code. Anything on a line that appears after a single vertical quote (') is treated by Visual Basic as a comment and is therefore ignored.

You'll use comments often in programs you write from now on. You can consider the comments to be English-language descriptions of the Basic code you're writing. We can't say enough about using comments (and indeed, we'll say more in later chapters). Without comments, programs are very difficult to read. You'll probably be able to figure out what individual statements do, but you may not be able to figure out the programmer's overall plan. Good comments should give you an idea of why the programmer (you) did something.

Now the only thing you have to do before you're finished is figure out a way to get the 1 Pixel menu item checked when your program first runs. This is really easy. Bring up the Menu Editor window and click on the 1 Pixel menu item in the list at the bottom of the window. Then all you have to do is click on the check box called Checked. This will cause the 1 Pixel menu item to be checked initially.

Save your project now, because this is a version you'll want to keep. Before we move on to the next chapter, we're going to show you a neat trick that was new to the standard edition of Visual Basic 3.0—pop-up menus.

Pop-up Menus

A pop-up menu is the same as any other menu you've created, except that it doesn't have to drop down from the menu bar. Instead, a pop-up menu appears on top of your form. Figure 5.5 shows what your Sketch program Draw menu would look like as a pop-up.

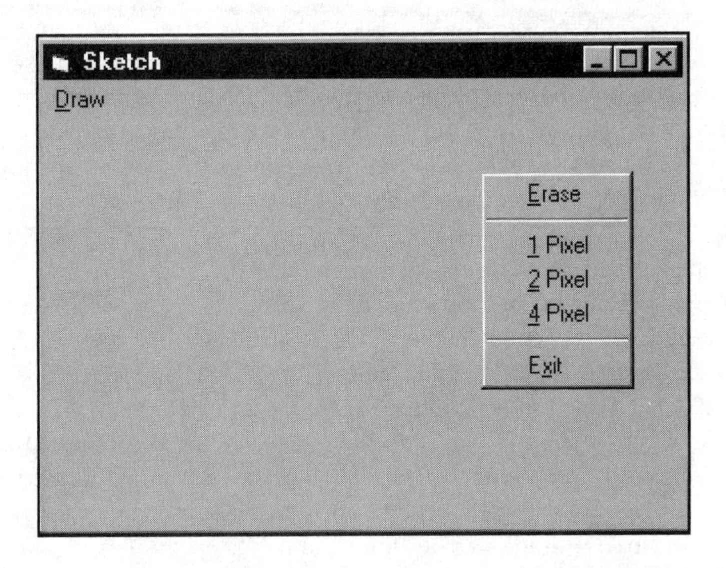

FIGURE 5.5 *Your Sketch program with the Draw menu added and displayed as a pop-up menu.*

The PopupMenu method makes it easy to display menus this way. First you'll need to decide which event you want to trigger the pop-up. A right mouse event, either MouseUp or MouseDown, seems to be a common choice. Try adding the following code to your Sketch program's Form_MouseUp procedure:

```
Private Sub Form_MouseUp (Button As Integer, Shift As Integer, _
X As Single, Y As Single)
  If Button = 2 Then            'Right mouse button clicked?
    PopupMenu menDraw           'Yes. Display menDraw as popup.
  End If
End Sub
```

Now press **F5** to run Sketch, and then click on your right mouse button. Your screen should look similar to the one in Figure 5.5. You can click on the menu items. Continue drawing, even use the regular Draw menu and verify that check marks are still being maintained while you are using the Draw menu both ways (the pop-up and from the menu bar). Okay, now stop the program (select End from the Run menu) and then double-click on the form to bring back the code window.

NOTE

Although for the purposes of this exercise we had you use the Right Mouse-Up event to display the PopupMenu, we suggest that you use the Right Mouse_Down event for any real programs you create. The reason is purely one of user perception: the pop-up menu seems to appear on screen faster, so your program will seem faster.

Did you notice while you were experimenting that every time you clicked the right mouse button you were also leaving marks (i.e., drawing) on the form? That's because of the code in the Form_MouseDown subroutine. Unlike the code in the Form_MouseMove subroutine, the Form_MouseDown event does not check to see which mouse button you're using. If you really like the pop-up menu and want to keep it, you can alter the code in the Form_MouseDown event to make it dependent on which mouse button is clicked. Use the MouseMove event as a model and add an If statement to check for Button = 1, indicating left mouse usage. If you don't want to keep the Draw pop-up menu, delete the code you put in the Form_MouseUp subroutine, and we'll move on.

You can also create a menu for pop-up use that does not appear on the menu bar. If you look at the Menu Editor window (see Figure 5.1), you'll notice a check box marked Visible. If you select your menu name and uncheck this box, your menu will not appear on the menu bar. It will, however, still be available for use with the PopupMenu method. The PopupMenu method also uses optional flag parameters with X and Y variables to control the location and behavior of the pop-up menu. This is detailed in the *Language Reference Manual.*

In the next chapter you'll continue doing work on Sketch, which will allow you to print out your sketches. In the process you'll learn even more about the Basic language. Then in Chapter 7 you'll write another program, called *Icon Clock,* which produces the program you've seen at the lower-left corner of the screen shots throughout this book.

Summary

You're now finished writing your very first "real" Windows program. And you've learned a great deal in the process.

- **Menu Editor Window.** You learned how to use the Menu Design window to add a menu bar to your programs. The only real trick is to make sure you're in design mode (not run mode) and that your window is active (you might have to click on it) before you select the Menu Design item from the Window menu.
- **Mnemonic Access Characters.** You create mnemonic access characters by placing an & in front of the letter to be underlined.
- **Controls.** Menus and menu items are all controls, which are objects that appear inside forms. Controls must have names.
- **DrawWidth.** The DrawWidth property allows you to change the width of the drawing pen. This width is measured in pixels.
- **Control Arrays.** Related controls (menu items) can be grouped into a control array. All menu items in a control array share the same control name, but each item must have a unique Index number. This number allows you to reference individual controls in a control array.
- **Checked.** The Checked property for menu items allows you to check or uncheck items in a pull-down menu.

USING ARRAY VARIABLES TO SAVE LINES

* Defining array variables
* Working with arrays
* The For..Next command
* Creating new subroutines

The goal of this chapter is twofold. First, you're going to make some modifications to Sketch so it will remember all the lines you've drawn. This will allow you to add a Print command to Sketch, and it will make it possible for Sketch to redraw your picture when part of its window is erased (for example, by dragging another window over it). Second, you'll learn more about variables and writing Visual Basic programs. Variables are probably one of the most important aspects of any computer language, and they take a little getting used to. In this chapter, you'll learn about some new forms of variables and how to work with them.

Designing a New Sketch

To redraw or print the figures, you'll need to be able to remember all the lines you drew. For that you'll use something called an *array.*

In Chapter 5, you learned about control arrays. These are controls that are related and therefore all share the same name. You can also have a whole list of variables that all have the same name and are referenced using a number in parentheses (just as you referenced controls in a control array). These variables are called arrays and are very simple to work with, as you'll see shortly.

Here's an outline of what you need to do. First, you'll create two arrays, called *saveX* and *saveY,* in which you'll save all the points in the lines you've drawn. You'll also need a way to keep information on where one line ends and the next line begins and on how thick each line is (remember that you can change the line thickness, so all lines may not have the same thickness).

We'd like to say a few words about writing programs. Whenever we have a program in mind, we think for a while about what we'd like this program to look like and what we'd like it to do. After we've figured that out, we don't sit down and write the entire program; that's a very difficult thing to do. Instead, we start with a simple piece and get it working. Then we add another piece. Adding one piece at a time is much easier than writing the entire program at once, because each piece is small and easy to work with. This process is known as *step-wise refinement,* and it's how most programmers write real programs.

What you're going to do with Sketch is start with a very simple piece. First, you'll write some code to keep a list of points as you draw them. Then you'll try to redraw these points when Sketch's window is erased. But here you'll just connect all the points you've stored without concern for where one line ends and the next begins or for the thickness of each line. We'll help you refine these additions later to add these features.

So with that in mind, let's examine array variables so you can start to modify Sketch.

A Word About Variable Names

You'll notice that we chose to use variable names, saveX and saveY, that start with a lowercase letter. But all the variables you've seen so far, like CurrentX, have started with an uppercase letter. Why did we choose to start these variable names with a lowercase letter?

When you start to read other people's programs, you may find it difficult to tell the difference between properties and variable names. How can you tell if a name is a property or a variable name? If all names start with uppercase letters, you can't. You'll have to look each name up in your *Language Reference Manual* to see if it's there. If, however, you start your variable names with a lowercase letter and all property names with an uppercase letter, you'll be able to tell at a glance whether a name refers to a variable or a property.

If you're thinking that Visual Basic uses blue lettering to display keywords and green lettering to show comments, this may not seem like such a big deal. But there may be times you'll need to read code from a printout or use a monochrome monitor. It's always a good idea to develop habits early on that can make your life easier in the long run.

You'll also notice that we use an uppercase letter at the start of each new word, which makes reading variable names easier. For example, "longVariableName" is much easier to read than "longvariablename." (Of course, in languages like German you can have long names without mixed case, like *Damfschiffskapitänwitwe*, which means the widow of a steamship captain—no kidding.)

Array Variables

As you can see from the preceding discussion, two variables, saveX and saveY, will play an important role in your new version of Sketch. These variables are arrays in which you can store a number of X and Y points.

To create an array variable, you have to define that variable, which also tells Basic how many "slots" the variables will have. For example, the following defines saveX as an array with index values from 0 to 1000, which means it has 1001 slots of type Single (all slots must have the same type):

```
Private saveX(1000) As Single
```

These slots, by the way, are called *elements* of an array in computer-science jargon. So in the example above, there are 1001 elements in the saveX array.

If you have ever used or seen program code from an earlier version of Visual Basic, you may have expected us to use the Dim keyword to define a variable. Although Dim still works in Visual Basic 4.0, the preferred declaration statement uses either the Private or Public keywords. We'll talk more about defining variables in a moment, but first we'd like to spend a moment talking about arrays.

VARIABLE ARRAYS

A variable array is a group of variables that all have the same name and type. You define a variable array by placing a number in parentheses after the variable name. This number is the maximum index value you'll be able to use with this array. Because the first element of an array has the index value of 0, the number of elements in an array will be one greater than the number you provide in the Private statement.

You refer to elements in an array by putting the index value in parentheses after the name. For example, saveX(10) refers to the 11th element in the saveX array because the first element is saveX(0).

By the way, you can change the index of the first element in an array so it will be a number other than 0. There are two ways to do this, in case you're interested: You can use the To keyword (look up Private in the *Language Reference Manual*) or use the Option Base statement.

There are a number of things that are new about this statement (see Figure 6.1). First, you'll notice we used the Private keyword, which tells Visual Basic that you're defining a variable. All the variables you've used so far have been defined *implicitly*; in other words, when you first used a variable, Visual Basic automatically defined it.

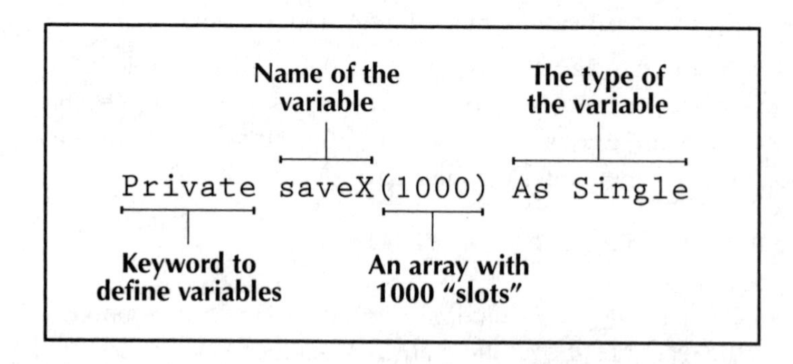

FIGURE 6.1 *The different parts of a Private statement in Visual Basic. If you leave out the type (As Single) Visual Basic will create a variable of type Variant.*

However, you must define array variables *explicitly* so Visual Basic will know how large to make the array (how many elements you want). The Private keyword, therefore, explicitly defines a variable. (You can also use Private to explicitly define any variable, not just arrays.)

You'll also notice the keywords As Single after the variable. The As keyword is a new keyword used to tell Visual Basic the variable type. In previous chapters, you always used special letters, like $ for a string, to define the type of a variable, but you have a choice. You can use either the type character (for example, % or $) or As Single. In other words, both of these statements have the same effect, except you must use the trailing $ in the second case, as follows:

```
Private someString As String
Private someString$
```

Which form you use is really a matter of personal taste. If you look at other people's programs (which is a good way to learn, by the way), you'll notice that some people tend to use As String, and others tend to use $. You'll also find people who use both methods for defining variables. So it's really up to you.

In this book, we'll mostly use the As String form of defining variables because we find it easier to remember words like String rather than characters like $.

THE AS KEYWORD VERSUS TYPE CHARACTERS

Whether you use the As keyword or a type character to define a variable's type is really up to you. The following table lists the corresponding words and characters for all the types defined by Visual Basic:

Type Keyword	Type Character
As Integer	%
As Long	&
As Single	! or none
As Double	#
As Currency	@
As String	$
As Byte	
As Boolean	
As Date	
As Object	
As Variant	

The only thing you have to remember when using the type character is that it becomes part of the name. So if you create a variable called someStr$, you must always write someStr$ with the trailing dollar sign. You will have to use the As keyword when working with the newer data types because they do not have a type character.

Defining Form Variables

Getting back to the modifications to Sketch, you want to define two variables, saveX and saveY, in such a way that you can read and write these variables from several subroutines inside your form. In particular, you'll want to add points to saveX and saveY from inside Form_MouseMove and Form_MouseDown. And you'll want to use these same points inside Form_Paint to redraw the picture whenever part of it is erased.

If you define variables inside a subroutine, you would use the Dim or Private keyword, and they would only be available from inside that subroutine. (You can't use Public inside a subroutine.) There is, however, a special place where you can define such variables so they'll be available to all subroutines in a form. If you have closed the program, restart Visual Basic and open your Sketch program. Make sure your Code window is visible (double-click on the Sketch form). Click on the down-pointing arrow in the combo box called Object (see Figure 6.2). Finally, click on **(general)** at the top of this list.

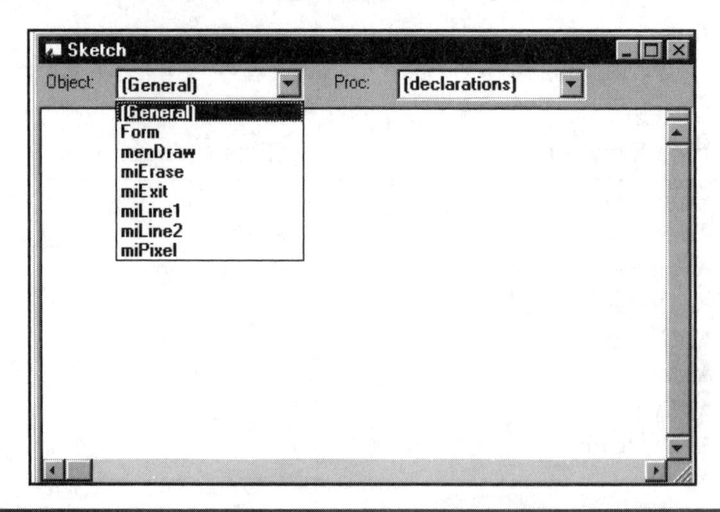

FIGURE 6.2 *The Object combo box allows you to switch between different objects in the form. You'll notice our Form object, as well as miErase and so on.*

You'll notice this combo box lists all the objects (the Form and controls) we created inside this form. It provides an easy way for you to move between the code for different objects inside of a form. You'll probably find yourself using this combo box often to change from one object to another as you're writing programs.

The special entry at the top of this list, called (*general*), is used for things other than objects. This is where you use Private to define variables you want to be available to all the code you write inside a form. (If you define a variable inside a subroutine, it's only available inside that subroutine—see "A Word on Scope and Location of Variables.")

When you click on (**general**), it may seem as though nothing happens. After all, the Object combo box doesn't change. So what happens? So far, the only change is a subtle one. Your cursor was moved to the top of the code window. As soon as you enter the statements shown below, the Object combo box will change to show (**general**), and the Proc combo box will read (**declarations**), which means you're looking at the declarations part of the form.

Enter the following three lines at the top of your Code window:

```
Private numPoints As Integer      ' Number of points saved
Private saveX(1000) As Single     ' Saved X coordinates
Private saveY(1000) As Single     ' Saved Y coordinates
```

Notice that comments are used to say what these variables are for. We'll use comments often, because even if you have a good name for a variable, you can always make it clearer with a comment.

A Word on Scope and Location of Variables

Visual Basic 4.0 has changed the rules for how you define variables. In the past, you always wrote Dim to define form-level variables and Global in modules to define module-level variables. This can actually be quite confusing if you're new to programming, especially when you're trying to figure out which variables are visible outside a form or module. The new rules are that you should use Private or Public to define form-level and module-level variables, and Dim should be reserved for defining local variables inside a subroutine.

Subroutine When you define a variable inside a subroutine, it's only available about that variable. Visual Basic creates the variable again the next time it runs that subroutine. Use the Dim keyword.

Form When you use Private to define a variable in the (general) section of a form under (declarations), the variable is available to any subroutine inside the form. Use Public if you want the variable to be available to other forms and modules.

Module You can define variables in any module (but not in forms), which you'll do later in this book. Use Public to define these variables, and they will be available anywhere in your program, rather than just in a form. This will become important when you begin to have programs with more than one form.

What happens when you define a variable inside a subroutine that has the same name as a form-level variable? In such cases, Visual Basic ignores the form-level variable. In other words, you won't be able to read or write the form-level variable in any subroutine where you've defined a subroutine variable with the same name.

Saving Points in Sketch

The next thing you'll do is modify MouseMove and MouseDown so they save points in these variables. To do this, you need to switch the current object back to the Form object; you should be looking at the (general) object. Pull down the Object combo box and select **Form** from this list. You should see the Form_MouseDown event handler.

The MouseDown subroutine saves the starting point for a line, so let's add some code to save this point in saveX and saveY. The following is the new version of Form_MouseDown that saves these points in the arrays and draws the starting point:

```
Private Sub Form_MouseDown (Button As Integer, Shift As
                          Integer, X As ...
  CurrentX = X                  ' Start point for next Line
  CurrentY = Y
  PSet (X, Y)                   ' Draw first point in line
```

```
    numPoints = numPoints + 1     ' The next free point
    saveX(numPoints) = X          ' Remember this point
    saveY(numPoints) = Y
  End Sub
```

The three lines at the end of this subroutine are new, and you'll notice we added comments to the other lines.

As mentioned in the last chapter, if you chose to include the pop-up menu feature in your Sketch project, you'll need to add an If...Then statement to the code in the MouseDown subroutine shown above. The first statement inside the subroutine (just before `CurrentX = X`) should be:

```
If Button = 1 Then
```

and the last statement just before the `End Sub` should be:

```
End If
```

Next you'll want to modify MouseMove so it will save the endpoints of all the lines you draw. You can scroll to the MouseMove subroutine or move there automatically by selecting it from the Proc combo box. Or you can use a keyboard shortcut: Press **Control-PgUp** and **Control-PgDn** to move back and forth between subroutines in the form.

The new version of Form_MouseMove, which is much like the new form of Form_MouseDown is as follows:

```
Sub Form_MouseMove (Button As Integer, Shift As Integer,
                    X As ...
  If Button = 1 Then               ' Is the left button down?
    Line -(X, Y)                   ' Yes, draw a line

    numPoints = numPoints + 1      ' Next free point in array
    saveX(numPoints) = X           ' Remember this point
    saveY(numPoints) = Y
  End If
End Sub
```

You'll notice that this is a different form of the If..Then command here. In Chapter 5 you used a form of If..Then that fit on a single line. But here you're using the multiline version, which allows you to include a number of commands in the Then part of the If statement. Thus, if Button = 1, Visual Basic will run all four lines between the Then and the End If.

Keyboard Shortcut: Page Up and Page Down: You can easily move between the subroutines in your form by pressing **Control-PgUp** and **Control-PgDn** in the Code window. If you have long subroutines, these keys will scroll one subroutine at a time until you reach the top or bottom of the form or module. Using the **PgUp** or **PgDn** keys alone will scroll one page or screenful at a time.

We've also introduced another level of indenting. Programs are usually much easier to read (and therefore write) if you use indenting to make it visually obvious how a program is built. Whenever you have some code that will be run if a condition is true, it's a good idea to indent it, so it will be visually obvious that this *block* of code is at a different conceptual level than other parts of the code. You'll see many more examples of this in this book, as we're very big on using indenting to show how a program is built.

Now you can run your program to make sure there are no errors in what you've typed. The program won't do anything different from the previous version because you're not using any of the points being saved, but at least you can make sure there isn't anything Visual Basic objects to, such as a typographical error.

Redrawing Forms

Most Windows programs have a way to redraw parts of a window that have been covered and then uncovered. Whenever a part of a window is uncovered and needs to be redrawn, Windows sends a *paint* message to that window telling it to redraw itself. Visual Basic works the same way.

Your form will receive a Paint event whenever your window (or part of it) needs to be redrawn. Pull down the Proc combo box and select **Paint**. This will display the Form_Paint event handler, which is responsible for redrawing your windows.

Let's try a simple experiment to give you an idea of when Form_Paint gets called. Put a Beep command in the Form_Paint subroutine to hear a beep whenever Visual Basic sends a Paint event to your program, as follows:

```
Private Sub Form_Paint ()
  Beep
End Sub
```

Now run this program. You'll hear a beep when Sketch first starts running. This means you're asked to paint the window as soon as Sketch starts. After all, when Sketch starts, the window is blank (except for any controls you put into it, such as the menu bar).

Next, click on the **Minimize** button (the down-pointing arrow in the upper-right corner) to iconize Sketch. This simply makes the form invisible, so Visual Basic doesn't run Form_Paint. Finally, double-click on the iconized Sketch near the bottom of your screen. Sketch will return to a form and you'll hear a beep, telling you that Visual Basic sent a *paint* message.

You might want to try other experiments on your own. Try covering up part of Sketch's window with another window, and then uncovering part of Sketch's window. Sketch should beep whenever part of its window becomes uncovered.

Seeing Which Events Have Code

There is a nice feature of the Proc combo box you might be interested in. If you look at Figure 6.3, you'll notice that some of the lines in the Proc combo box are bold. The bold event handlers are the ones where you've added code, so you can tell at a glance which event handlers have code attached to them—in this case, MouseDown, MouseMove, and Paint.

This feature was especially handy in earlier versions of Visual Basic because each subroutine had a code window of its own and you couldn't see the form's other routines. Even though all of a form's subroutines are now shown in the same code window, we think you'll still find this useful in lieu of scrolling through lots of code.

Redrawing Sketch's Lines

From the preceding example, you can see that you'll need to write code in Form_Paint to redraw the lines saved in the saveX and saveY arrays. For this, you'll need a new command called *For..Next,* which allows you to run a set of commands a number of times.

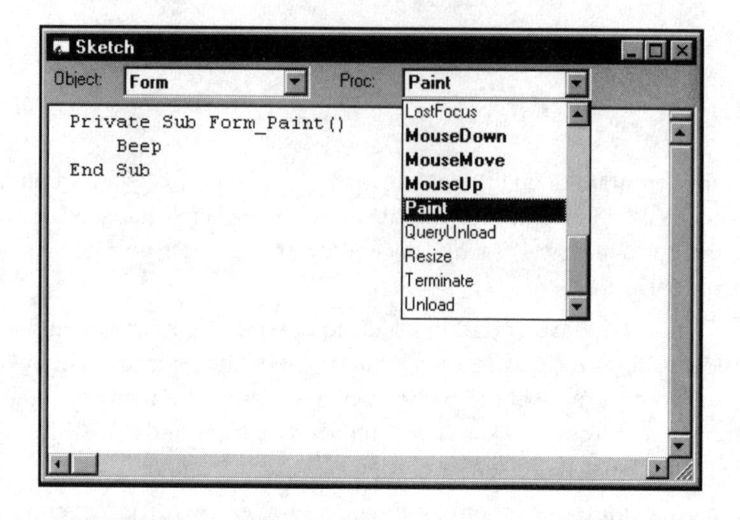

FIGURE 6.3 *The Proc combo box uses bold characters to show which event handlers have code attached to them.*

But before we get to the theory, the new Form_Paint subroutine that uses For..Next is as follows:

```
Private Sub Form_Paint ()
  PSet (saveX(1), saveY(1))       ' Draw first point in line
  For i = 2 To numPoints          ' Repeat numPoints - 1 times
    Line -(saveX(i), saveY(i))    ' Draw the i'th point
  Next i                          ' Got to the next point
End Sub
```

Now try running this program. Draw something, cover a portion with some other window, and then uncover your Sketch window. See how nicely that works? This program will now redraw any lines you've drawn. Of course, there are a few things it doesn't do correctly, but we'll fix those problems next. At least now you have some code that redraws something.

Let's take a close look at what this new subroutine does. The first line should be clear, because you've used PSet before. If you look at the MouseDown event handler, you'll notice that PSet draws the first point in a line. But you'll notice one difference from the MouseDown subroutine. In MouseDown, you set CurrentX and CurrentY to the mouse location and *then* you called PSet.

As it turns out, the `CurrentX = X` and `CurrentY = Y` lines in MouseDown aren't necessary because the PSet command automatically sets CurrentX and CurrentY after it draws a point. Now that you know this, let's go back and change MouseDown so it's a little cleaner (in other words, as simple as it can be).

```
Private Sub Form_MouseDown (Button As Integer, Shift As
                              Integer, X As ...
  PSet (X, Y)                   ' Draw first point in line

  numPoints = numPoints + 1     ' The next free point
  saveX(numPoints) = X          ' Remember this point
  saveY(numPoints) = Y
```

NOTE

We'd like to mention again that if you are using a pop-up menu in your Sketch project, your MouseDown subroutine should include the If..Then statement to identify the left mouse button. Now it's up to you to remember this throughout the rest of the Sketch project, because our code examples will not show the If..Then statement for this subroutine.

Now that you've made Form_MouseDown a little simpler, let's get back to Form_Paint. As you just learned, the PSet command draws the first point in lines saved in the saveX and saveY arrays. But think about that for a second. When you first run Sketch, Visual Basic calls Form_Paint even though Sketch hasn't saved any points yet. So the first line, PSet(saveX(1), saveY(1)) tries to draw a point that hasn't been saved. What happens?

New variables of type Single are initially set to zero, including all of the elements in an array. So the first time Visual Basic runs Form_Paint, both saveX(1) and saveY(1) are set to zero. If you look very closely at your Sketch form when you run Sketch, you'll see a small dot in the upper-left corner of the window because of PSet(0, 0). That's one problem with this program, which you can fix very easily by adding an If..Then command to see if there are any points before trying to draw the first point, as follows:

```
Private Sub Form_Paint ()
  If numPoints > 0 Then          ' Are there any points?
    PSet (saveX(1), saveY(1))    ' Yes, draw the first point
  End If
```

```
    For i = 2 To numPoints          ' Repeat numPoints - 1 times
      Line -(saveX(i), saveY(i))  ' Draw the i'th point
    Next i                          ' Go to the next point
End Sub
```

Now let's look at the rest of this subroutine.

The For..Next Command

The rest of this subroutine relies on the new command For..Next. This command is a type of command called a *loop*, which allows you to run a set of commands more than one time. There are actually several different types of loop commands, but we'll only cover For..Next here.

The For..Next command allows you to specify the number of times you want to run the commands inside the loop. It also uses a variable you supply as a *loop counter*, which starts with some value and counts up, adding one each time through the loop.

When you write the following, you're telling Basic to set *i* to 2 before running any commands:

```
For i = 2 To numPoints
   ...
Next i
```

The variable *i* will then be increased by 1 each time Basic sees the Next *i* statement. And finally, the To part of For tells Basic when to stop repeating the loop. As soon as *i* is greater than numPoints, Basic stops running this command.

Why We Use the Variable *i*

You're probably wondering why we chose to use a variable called *i*, rather than something more descriptive like *count*. Most programmers use the variable *i* whenever they need a counter, and if they need more than one counter, they also use *j*, *k*, *l*, and so on.

The reason for this is entirely historical, having to do with a programming language called FORTRAN, one of the first popular computer languages used by scientists and other programmers. FORTRAN, unlike Basic, uses the first letter of a variable name to determine the type of variable. Therefore any variable name that starts with *i* through *n* is defined to be an integer. Because most counters (like *i* in the For..Next loop) are integers, programmers use the letters *i* through *n* as loop counters.

Even though many programmers these days have never learned or used FORTRAN, this tradition of using *i* through *n* for loop counters persists. And it's not likely you'll see this practice disappear because it's been passed from one generation of programmers to the next.

Let's use the Debug window for a few experiments to see exactly how the For..Next command works. Enter the following commands into the Debug window:

```
for i = 1 to 3: print i: next i1
2
3
print i
4
|
```

Here we've used a new fact: You can place several commands on a single line by separating them with a colon, as in the first line of this example.

You can see that Basic ran `Print i` three times, with i starting at one and ending at three. You can also see that *i* has the value of four after the For..Next command finishes.

Try another experiment. See what happens when the To value is less than the initial value. Will Basic run the Print command once in this case, or not at all? To find out, enter the following command:

```
for i = 1 to 0: print i: next i
|
```

As you can see, For..Next won't run any of the commands inside its loop if the initial value is greater than the final value.

COMMAND REFERENCE: FOR..NEXT

The For..Next command runs a set of commands inside a loop a specific number of times.

```
For varName = initialValue To finalValue [Step increment]
   statements
Next [varName]
```

This command repeats the *statement* between the For and Next lines. The variable *varName* starts at *initialValue* and increases by 1 (or by *increment*) each time through the loop. Basic stops running the loop when *varName* is greater than *finalValue*.

To make this command clearer, the following list is an English-language description of how Basic runs a For..Next command:

1. Set *varName* to *initialValue*.
2. If *varName* > *finalValue*, you're all done.
3. Run *statements*.
4. *varName* = *varName* + 1 (adds *increment* rather than 1 if you use Step)
5. Go to step 2.

If Step is negative, step 2 becomes "If *varName* < *finalValue*...." In other words, the values go down to *finalValue* rather than up to *finalValue*.

Enough theory. You can see from this short description of For..Next that Form_Paint will call Line for each line saved, starting with the second point. You'll also notice that For..Next won't draw *any* lines if numPoints < 2. For..Next will only draw lines if there are lines to be drawn.

Remembering Separate Lines

You've now managed to redraw all of the lines you drew using the mouse. But you're not keeping the data on where one line ends and the next begins. So if you draw several separate lines (by releasing the mouse button between lines), your program will draw a single line, rather than separate lines (see Figure 6.4).

To fix this problem, you'll need to add two more arrays to keep track of the starting and ending points of lines. We'll call these arrays lineStart and lineEnd, and we'll save enough room for 500 lines (which is a truly arbitrary number).

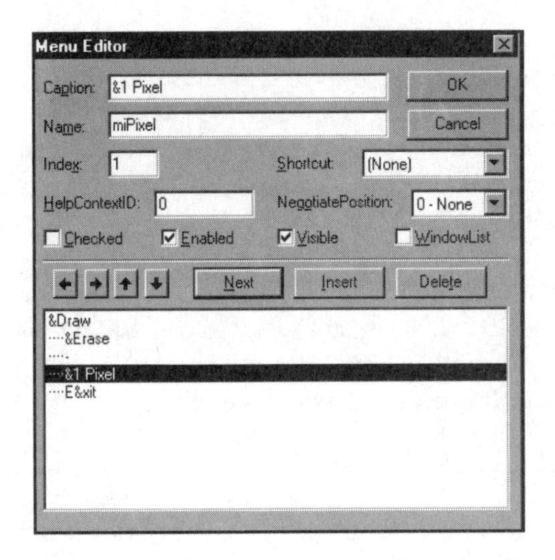

FIGURE 6.4 *This figure shows how our current version of Sketch connects separate lines when they're redrawn with the Form_Paint subroutine. This is because we're not keeping track of where one line ends and the next begins.*

Add the following three lines to the (general) section of your form:

```
Private numLines As Integer           ' Number of separate lines
Private lineStart(500) As Integer     ' Start of each line
Private lineEnd(500) As Integer       ' End of each line
```

Now you'll need to modify Form_MouseDown, Form_MouseMove, and Form_Paint to save and use these starting and ending points.

First modify Form_MouseDown so it will save the starting point (as well as an initial ending point). All the "points" you'll be saving in the lineStart and lineEnd arrays are actually indexes into the saveX and saveY arrays. The following changes are the changes to Form_MouseDown that save the starting index of each new line (add the three new lines at the end):

```
Private Sub Form_MouseDown (Button As Integer, Shift As
                            Integer, X As ...
  PSet (X, Y)                       ' Draw first point in line

  numPoints = numPoints + 1         ' The next free point
  saveX(numPoints) = X              ' Remember this point
```

```
    saveY(numPoints) = Y

    numLines = numLines + 1             ' Next free line
    lineStart(numLines) = numPoints ' Index of the first point
    lineEnd(numLines) = numPoints     ' Initially a single point
End Sub
```

Next you'll modify Form_MouseMove to update the index for the endpoint in a line. Each time Visual Basic calls MouseMove, you add another line segment to the line you're drawing. The following code is the new version of Form_MouseMove with one new line at the end.

```
Private Sub Form_MouseMove (Button As Integer, Shift As
                              Integer, X As ...
  If Button = 1 Then                   ' Is the left button down?
    Line -(X, Y)                       ' Yes, draw a line

    numPoints = numPoints + 1          ' Next free point in array
    saveX(numPoints) = X               ' Remember this point
    saveY(numPoints) = Y

    lineEnd(numLines) = numPoints      ' New ending index for line
  End If
End Sub
```

Finally, you'll need to modify Form_Paint to use this information. As you can see from the new version of Form_Paint below, Form_Paint needed more changes than the other two subroutines. In fact, this version is practically a new subroutine, so you might as well replace everything in Form_Paint with the following code rather than try to modify what you have now:

```
Private Sub Form_Paint ()
  For Lin = 1 to numLines          ' Draw each line
    aStart = lineStart(Lin)        ' Start index of this line
    anEnd = lineEnd(Lin)           ' End index of this line
    PSet (saveX(aStart), saveY(aStart))

    For i = aStart To anEnd         ' Draw parts of this line
      Line -(saveX(i), saveY(i))
    Next i
```

```
    Next Lin
End Sub
```

This new version of Form_Paint has two For..Next loops inside it. The outer loop (`For Lin = 1 to numLines`) runs the variable *Lin* from one to the number of separate lines you've drawn. The inner loop (`For i = aStart to anEnd`) draws all the parts of a single line.

We've added a couple of extra variables in this subroutine to make it a little easier to both write and read. By setting aStart to the starting index of a line, and anEnd to the ending index for the same line, we can use these values in both the PSet command and the For..Next command, which means you don't have to write something like the following:

```
PSet (saveX(lineStart(Lin)), saveY(lineStart(Lin)))
```

This line is hard to read because there are too many parentheses. Rather than write lines like this, we prefer adding a few lines of code to break long lines into several steps. So we find the following much easier to read (and write):

```
aStart = lineStart(Lin)
anEnd = lineEnd(Lin)
PSet (saveX(aStart), saveY(aStart))
```

You've made quite a bit of progress so far. You only have a few things left to do in this chapter, and then you'll be done with Sketch. First, you'll need to modify Sketch so it will remember the thickness of each line. This isn't very hard to do, so you might want to try making this change yourself before you read the next section.

Then you can have some fun. You'll add a Print menu item and some extra code that will allow you to print your drawings. Finally, you'll turn Sketch into an EXE file that you can run directly like any other program.

Remember the Line Widths

If you haven't guessed yet, you don't have to do much to remember the thickness of each line. All you have to do, in fact, is add another array, called lineThickness, and then save the value of DrawWidth on each mouse click. Here are the changes you'll need to make.

Add the following line to the (general) area of your form to declare the lineThickness array:

```
Private lineThickness(500) As Integer   ' DrawWidth for
                                        ' each line
```

Next add the following line to the end of your Form_MouseDown subroutine (on the line before the End Sub statement):

```
lineThickness(numLines) = DrawWidth
```

Finally (yes, you're almost done adding this feature), add the following line to Form_Paint immediately before the PSet command:

```
DrawWidth = lineThickness(Lin)
```

That's all there is to remembering the line thickness for each line. Try this program and see how it works. (Remember to save your project by pressing **Alt-FV**, before you run this program.)

Before we move on, there is one other small problem with your program. Do you know what it is? Have you tried all of the menu items to make sure they work the way you expected?

It turns out that if you select the Erase menu item, Sketch doesn't forget all of the points you've drawn, as it should. You can see this by drawing some lines, erasing them, and then minimizing and restoring your window. This will redraw the lines that should have been erased.

You'll need to modify miErase_Click so it clears all the lines you've drawn. You can do this simply by setting the numLines and numPoints variables to zero, as follows:

```
Private Sub miErase_Click ()
  Cls                         ' Clear the form
  numPoints = 0               ' Set to no points
  numLines = 0                ' Set to no lines
End Sub
```

In the next section you'll modify Sketch so it can print your sketches, and then you'll turn Sketch into a stand-alone EXE program you can run like any other program.

Printing Your Picture

Now that you've modified Sketch so it will redraw your picture, let's make one last change. You'll add another menu item, called Print, that will draw sketches on the printer. As you'll recall, you can draw on your printer by putting *Printer.* in front of each command.

Bring up the Menu Design window and add another line and a Print menu item (see Figure 6.5).

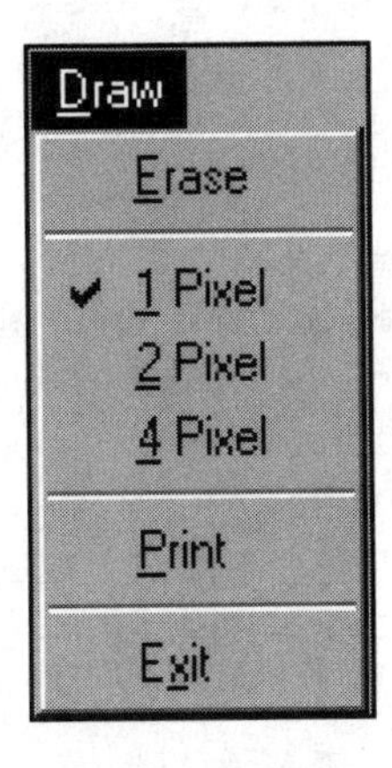

FIGURE 6.5 *The menu item Print and the line that you'll need to add to your Sketch program. The control names should be miLine3 for the line and miPrint for the Print menu item*

When you've added miPrint to the menu bar, add the following code to miPrint_Click:

```
Private Sub miPrint_Click ()
  For Lin = 1 to numLines           ' Draw each line
    aStart = lineStart(Lin)         ' Start index of this line
    anEnd = lineEnd(Lin)            ' End index of this line
    Printer.DrawWidth = lineThickness(Lin)
    Printer.PSet (saveX(aStart), saveY(aStart))

    For i = aStart To anEnd          ' Draw parts of this line
      Printer.Line -(saveX(i), saveY(i))
    Next i
```

```
    Next Lin
    Printer.EndDoc
End Sub
```

You can see that this subroutine is identical to Form_Paint, except for the Printer. in front of each command that draws or changes properties (like DrawWidth). We also added a Printer.EndDoc command at the end of this subroutine. You need to use this command to tell the printer to print the page you've just drawn.

Your Sketch program should now be able to print anything you draw. Give it a try. Did you notice anything interesting? If you try different line widths, you'll notice that the lines are much narrower on your printer. Why?

If you remember back to Chapter 5 where you learned how to change a line's width, you learned that line widths are measured in pixels, and the starting and ending points are measured in twips. What this means is that anything you draw on the printer, using points measured in twips, will keep the same size no matter what printer you use. But line widths, because they're measured in pixels, will be much smaller on high-resolution printers like laser printers.

So what do you do if you want a line to keep its width in twips? The easiest thing to do for now is to modify the DrawWidth line in miPrint_Click like the following:

```
Printer.DrawWidth = lineThickness(Lin) * 3
```

Multiplying by three is correct if you're using a laser printer, but it may not be correct for other printers. Figure 6.6 illustrates these ideas.

Later in this book you'll find a section (Adjusting DrawWidth on Printers in the Toolbox for Drawing chapter) that describes how to calculate the correct multiplier for any printer.

Creating an EXE Program

Now that you have a finished program that's fun to play with, you'll want to turn this program into an EXE file so you can run it without starting Visual Basic. To create an EXE file, pull down the File menu and select **Make EXE File...**. You'll see a dialog box like the one shown in Figure 6.7.

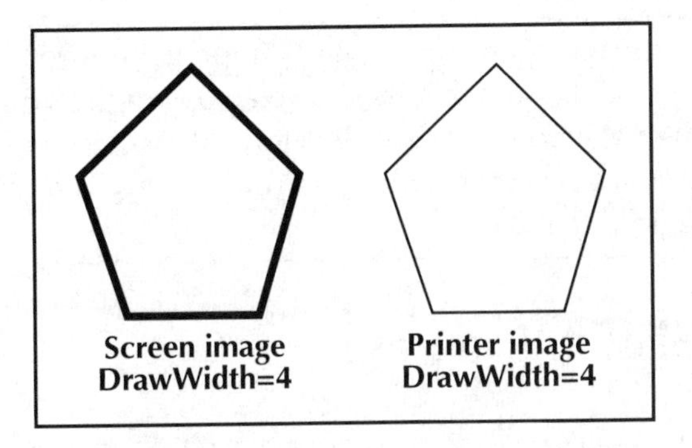

FIGURE 6.6 *DrawWidth set to 4 on both the screen and a laser printer. The lines won't be as thick on the printer because DrawWidth is measured in pixels, and pixels are smaller on a printer.*

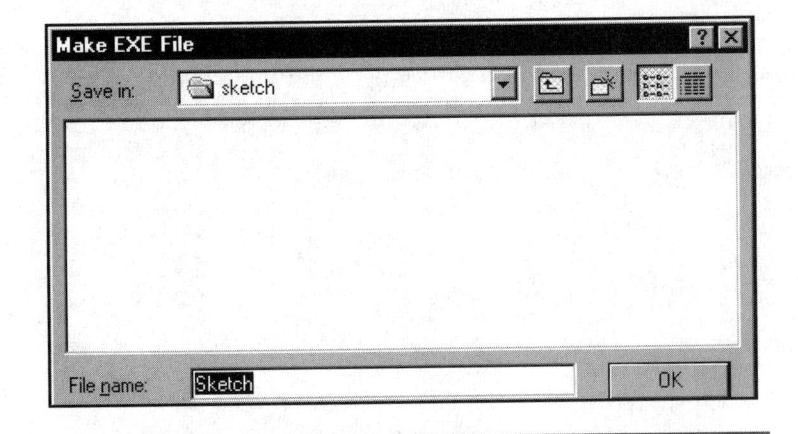

FIGURE 6.7 *You'll see this dialog box when you select **Make EXE File...** from the File menu. Simply click **OK** to create SKETCH.EXE.*

Press **Enter** (or click **OK**) to create an EXE program called SKETCH.EXE. Now you can run Sketch from the File Manager, just as you can run any other Windows program. You can give a copy of this program to anyone you like, and they don't have to have Visual Basic on their computer. They do, however, need a copy of VBRUN300.DLL in their Windows' System directory.

If you want to give your new EXE program to other people, you'll have to make sure that they have a copy of the VBRUN300.DLL file in their Windows' System directory. Microsoft gives you permission to give a copy of this file to anyone, along with any programs you write in Visual Basic.

The Final Sketch Program

You've made a number of changes to your Sketch program, so in this section you'll find a full listing of Sketch, as it stands now. Table 6.1 shows all the captions, control names, and index values for the pull-down menu in your Sketch program.

TABLE 6.1 *Menu Names and Control Names*

Caption	Name	Index
&Draw	menDraw	
....&Erase	miErase	
....–	miLine1	
....&1 Pixel	miPixel	1
....&2 Pixel	miPixel	2
....&4 Pixel	miPixel	4
....–	miLine2	
....&Print	miPrint	
....–	miLine3	
....E&xit	miExit	

The following lines should be in the (general) section of your form:

```
Private numPoints As Integer        ' Number of points saved
PrivatesaveX(1000) As Single        ' Saved X coordinates
PrivatesaveY(1000) As Single        ' Saved Y coordinates

PrivatenumLines As Integer          ' Number of separate lines
```

```
PrivatelineStart(500) As Integer    ' Start of each line
PrivatelineEnd(500) As Integer      ' End of each line
PrivatelineThickness(500) As Integer   ' DrawWidth for each
line
```

The following lists all of the event handlers in Sketch, in alphabetical order:

```
Private Sub Form_MouseDown (Button As Integer, Shift As
                            Integer, X As ...
  PSet (X, Y)                         ' Draw first point in line

  numPoints = numPoints + 1           ' The next free point
  saveX(numPoints) = X                ' Remember this point
  saveY(numPoints) = Y

  numLines = numLines + 1             ' Next free line
  lineStart(numLines) = numPoints     ' Index of the first point
  lineEnd(numLines) = numPoints       ' Initially a single point
  lineThickness(numLines) = DrawWidth
End Sub

Private Sub Form_MouseMove (Button As Integer, Shift As
                            Integer, X As ...
  If Button = 1 Then                  ' Is the left button down?
    Line -(X, Y)                      ' Yes, draw a line

    numPoints = numPoints + 1         ' Next free point in array
    saveX(numPoints) = X              ' Remember this point
    saveY(numPoints) = Y

    lineEnd(numLines) = numPoints     ' New ending index for
line
  End If
End Sub

Private Sub Form_Paint ()
  For Lin = 1 to numLines        ' Draw each line
    aStart = lineStart(Lin)      ' Start index of this line
    anEnd = lineEnd(Lin)         ' End index of this line
    DrawWidth = lineThickness(Lin)
```

```
    PSet (saveX(aStart), saveY(aStart))

    For i = aStart To anEnd       ' Draw parts of this line
      Line -(saveX(i), saveY(i))
    Next i

  Next Lin
End Sub

Private Sub miErase_Click ()
  Cls                   ' Clear the form
  numPoints = 0         ' Set to no points
  numLines = 0          ' Set to no lines
End Sub

Private Sub miExit_Click ()
  End
End Sub

Private Sub miPixel_Click (Index As Integer)
  miPixel(DrawWidth).Checked = False ' Uncheck current width
  DrawWidth = Index                  ' Change width of the pen
  miPixel(Index).Checked = True      ' Check the new width
End Sub

Private Sub miPrint_Click ()
  For Lin = 1 to numLines         ' Draw each line
    aStart = lineStart(Lin)       ' Start index of this line
    anEnd = lineEnd(Lin)          ' End index of this line
    Printer.DrawWidth = lineThickness(Lin) * 3
    Printer.PSet (saveX(aStart), saveY(aStart))

    For i = aStart To anEnd       ' Draw parts of this line
      Printer.Line -(saveX(i), saveY(i))
    Next i

  Next Lin
  Printer.EndDoc
End Sub
```

Related Tools

- **Array Lower Index.** The arrays in this chapter have a starting index of 0 and count up from there. You can also change the first index number for an array in two ways. First, you can use the Option Base statement to change the lower bound from 0 to any other number; this will apply to all arrays. Second, you can use the To keyword when you define an array. For example, Dim A(– 10 to 10) defines an array with index values that range from – 10 to 10.
- **Array Bounds.** The UBound and LBound functions allow you to find out the lowest and highest index value for any array. So if you define an array with Dim A(– 10, 10), then LBound(a, 1) returns – 10. For more details, see your *Language Reference Manual.*
- **Erasing Arrays.** If you ever need to erase all of the variables in an array (set them to 0 or to an empty string for String variables), you can use the Erase command. For example, to erase an array called A, you would type **Erase A**.
- **Dynamic Arrays.** Sometimes you may want to change the size of an array when your program is running. For such cases, Visual Basic has a type of array called a *dynamic array.* Dynamic arrays can change in size as your program runs.

  You define a dynamic array by leaving out the size in the Dim statement. For example, Dim A() defines an array A as a dynamic array. To use this array, you need to set a size for the array using the ReDim command. This command erases any elements that might have been in the array and creates a new array of the size you ask for. You can use ReDim Preserve to resize an array without erasing the values stored in the array.
- **Loops.** In addition to the For..Next statement, Visual Basic supports several other loops. Each type of loop has its own advantages. The following is a summary of the types of loops in Visual Basic:
  - **For..Next.** Repeats a set of statements a specific number of times. The following is the syntax:

    ```
    For counter=start To end [Step increment]
      [statements]
    Next [counter]
    ```

* **Do..Loop.** Allows you to repeat a loop as long as (or until) a condition is True (like you'd use in If..Then). There are five forms, summarized below. Which form you use depends on which is most convenient for solving a specific problem.
* **While..Wend.** Works exactly like the Do While..Loop statement. We suggest that you use Do..Loop instead since this is a more recent addition to Basic language, and is more flexible.

In general, it's best to use For..Next if you want to repeat some commands a specific number of times, and to use the Do..Loop command whenever you need to test a condition to tell when you're finished running the loop. The following is a summary of the five versions of Do..Loop you might want to use and a discussion of how they're different:

Repeat statements as long as condition is True (could be zero times):

```
Do While condition
  statements
Loop
```

Repeat statements until condition is True (could be zero times):

```
Do Until condition
  statements
Loop
```

Repeat statements as long as condition is True (at least one time):

```
Do
  statements
Loop While condition
```

Repeat statements until condition is True (at least one time):

```
Do
  statements
Loop Until condition
```

Repeat statements forever:

```
Do
  statements
Loop
```

Summary

This is the last chapter on the Sketch program. In the next chapter you'll build a new program, which is the clock you see at the bottom-left corner of the screens in this book.

In this chapter you learned more about building Visual Basic programs. In particular, you've learned the following:

- **Step-wise refinement.** You had your first introduction to building programs through step-wise refinement. With this technique you build a program one step at a time, and each step is fairly small. After each step, you test your program and see how it works. Building a program one small step at a time is much easier than trying to build too much at a time.
- **Array variables.** You learned about array variables, which are variables that share the same name and type. Each array consists of a fixed number of elements, and you get to any element using an index in parentheses. For example, saveX(9) returns the tenth element of the saveX array. You use the Dim keyword to define array variables.
- **Form variables.** Any variable defined in the (general) area of a form, which you get to by using the Object combo box, is available to all subroutines inside a form. You defined several variables and arrays so they would be available to all your subroutines.
- **Form_Paint.** Every time your program needs to redraw parts of its window because part of it is being erased by another window, Visual Basic calls your form's Form_Paint event handler. You used this subroutine to redraw the lines in Sketch.

* **For..Next.** You used the For..Next command to repeat a group of commands so we could draw all the lines you saved. For..Next allows you to specify how many times a group of statements (called a *code block*) should be run. It also uses a *counter variable*, which counts up from a starting value to an ending value. You used this counter as the index into your saveX and saveY arrays.
* **Creating EXE Programs.** Finally, you turned your Sketch program into an EXE program that you can run just like any other Windows program (without using Visual Basic).

BUILDING A CLOCK PROGRAM

- Working with minimized icons
- Using timers
- Reading the clock
- Formatting times
- Custom-drawing scales
- Constants
- Drawing in color
- Erasing lines

Building programs is what Visual Basic is all about, and that's exactly what you'll be doing in Part II of this book. In Chapter 7, you'll build another small program, called Icon Clock, that displays the current time inside of an icon.

As you're building this program, which is a little larger than the Sketch program, you'll learn more new concepts. You'll also get a chance to gain more experience with ideas you learned in previous chapters.

In Chapter 8 you'll start on a completely new program, called Address Book. That project will take a number of chapters to build. Through this program, you'll learn more about the Basic language and building programs with Visual Basic. You'll also learn more about how to go about building a program once you have an idea.

Designing Icon Clock

Before starting to build any program, you'll need to take at least a few minutes to think about what you want to build. Building a program without some game plan is difficult because it's hard to know where to start.

The first thing to think about is what you want your program to look like, and what you want it to do. For Icon Clock, it will look like Figure 7.1. And you also have a pretty good idea about how it should work, because it works much like a real clock.

FIGURE 7.1 *What you'll want Icon Clock to look like when you're done.*

But there are a few things to review just to make sure that we're all headed in the same direction. First, you'll notice that our program draws the clock hands inside of the icon. As you'll see in this chapter, it's actually very easy to draw inside an icon when you're using Visual Basic.

The icon you'll use is a blank clock face—everything you see in Figure 7.1 except for the clock hands—so you'll need to draw the clock hands. Both the hour and minute hands are drawn in black, as two-pixel-wide lines. To make the second hand stand out like the clocks in kitchens, you'll draw the second hand in red rather than black.

Writing a program that does all of this can be somewhat daunting unless you start with something simple, and then work your way to a more complicated (and complete) program. As we mentioned in the last chapter, this process in known as step-wise refinement.

In this case we'll start with the very basics. You'll experiment with minimized programs to learn a little about how they work and how to change the caption in the task bar. Then you'll learn how to get the current time from your computer, and how to put it into the caption under the cursor.

Only then will we tackle the problem of drawing the clock hands inside the window and changing them every second. Now that you know the game plan, you can get to work, starting with minimized programs.

Working with Icons

As promised, the first thing you'll do is experiment with changing the caption of a minimized program in the task bar. Fire up visual Basic with a new project (the default when you start Visual Basic), which will ensure that you have an empty window (form) called Form1. Next clock on the Minimize button of the Form1 window to turn it into a button on the task bar (see Figure 7.2).

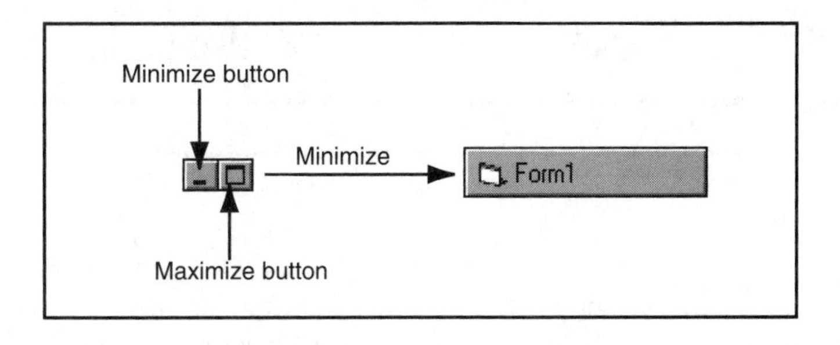

FIGURE 7.2 *If you click on the* ***Minimize*** *button of Form1, it will turn into an icon near the bottom-left corner of your screen. It should look like the icon labeled Form1 in this figure.*

The icon used for Form1 is a generic icon that Visual Basic supplies to any new form you create. In a short while you'll learn how to change this to an icon of your choosing, but for now we're going to work with this icon.

Setting the Caption

The first thing you'll do is experiment with changing the caption in the task bar. Press F5 to switch to run mode, then minimize the Window again (Visual Basic uses a property to determine whether or not a form should be minimized when you run the program). Finally, press Ctrl+Break to show the Debug window.

If you remember back to Chapter 4, you learned that the title of a window is controlled by a property called Caption. You used the Properties window to change the caption of your Sketch window to Sketch. Another way to change a window's caption is to use a command inside your program. All you have to do is assign a new string to the Caption property, like the following:

```
caption = "testing..."
|
```

Try entering this command in the Debug Window, and you'll see something like Figure 7.3. Changing a windows caption couldn't be easier. By the way, a window's caption appears inside the title bar when a window is open and to the right of the icon when a window is minimized, as in Figure 7.3.

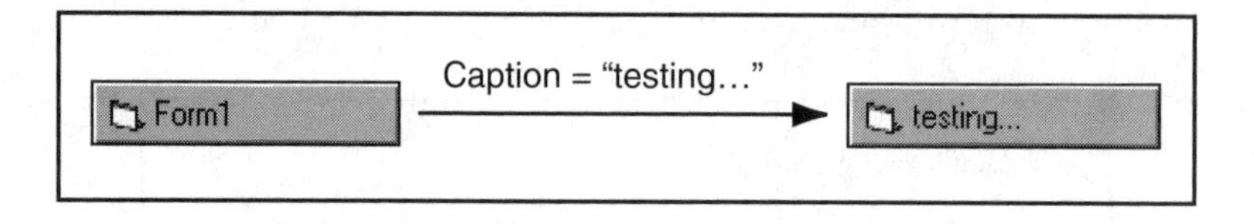

FIGURE 7.3 *Changing the caption on a minimized form.*

Incidentally, we know one professional programmer who spent several days figuring out how to change the caption in a program he was writing using a "real" programming language called C. Isn't it nice that Visual Basic makes this so simple? You've now learned everything there is to know about changing the caption inside a Visual Basic program!

Reading the Clock

You're making good progress doing your initial research. You now know how to set the caption beside an icon. As soon as we show you how to get the current time, you can actually start to write the program.

Visual Basic has a very special string called Time$ that will give you the current time. The easiest way to see how this works is to try an example, by using the Print command to display the value of Time$, as follows:

```
print time$
13:48:43
|
```

If you try the following again after only a short pause:

```
print time$
13:49:22
|
```

You can see from these examples that Time$ isn't like other variables because each time you use it, it has a different value. In many ways, though, it acts like a variable. In fact, you can even assign a value to this "variable," which changes the time of the clock (you probably don't want to run this example because it'll reset your clock to 1:20 AM), as follows:

```
time$ = "1:20"
print time$
01:20:04
|
```

You may have noticed from this example and the one before it that Visual Basic reports the time using a 24-hour format. We don't know about you, but we find it easier to read times with AM/PM, probably because that is what we grew up with. (The standard time display in almost all countries except for the U.S. and Latin America is 24-hour time.)

For now, we'll use this 24-hour time to build our program. Later in this chapter we'll show you how to display the time by using the AM/PM format.

Using Timers

Now you can go back to design mode (type **End** in the Debug window or select **End** from the Run menu) to start building Icon Clock.

There is another window in Visual Basic that we're going to use in this chapter. It's called the *Toolbox* (see Figure 7.4).

FIGURE 7.4 *You'll see this toolbox on the left side of your screen (except when you're in Run mode). It allows you to create various types of controls on your form.*

Restore the Form1 window to its normal size by clicking on its icon in the task bar at the bottom of the screen. You'll use the toolbox to create a new control inside this form, called a *timer control.* Timer controls have an event handler, called *Timer,* which you'll use to display a new time in the caption every second.

Creating a Timer

To create a timer, first click on the icon in the Toolbox that looks like a stop-watch (it's the one shown in Figure 7.5). This highlights the stop watch, but it won't actually create the timer. To do that, you'll need to use the mouse.

Click the mouse anywhere inside of the Form1 window and hold the mouse button down. Drag the mouse down and to the right until you have a gray square about 0.5 inch on each side. When you release the mouse button, you'll see a small clock inside a box, as shown in Figure 7.5.

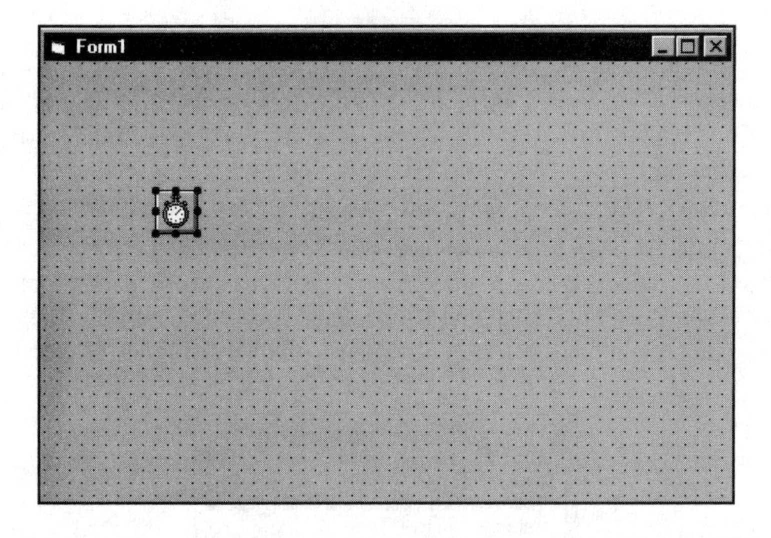

FIGURE 7.5 *Your form should look something like this after you create a timer object by clicking and dragging. The eight black squares along the outside of this timer are called handles and appear whenever you click on the object in design mode.*

Before we move on, let's take a look at what you've done. First of all, you've just created a new object, which is different from all the other objects you've been working with so far. Until now, you've only worked with Forms, Printer, and menu objects. But Visual Basic allows you to create a number of other objects, and you'll use many of them by the end of this book.

USING THE TOOLBOX TO CREATE OBJECTS

With the exception of the pointer (top left), all the icons you see in the Toolbox (Figure 7.4) are objects you can create inside a form. You create any object by following these steps:

1. Click on the icon for the object you want to create (the timer in our example).
2. Click and drag to outline the area you want the object to cover. The timer object will always be the same size, but other objects can be different sizes.
3. Release the mouse button, and you'll see your new object.

You'll notice that this object has a total of eight black squares around it. These squares are known as *handles,* because you can use them to change the size of objects. (As it turns out, the timer object is the only object that you can't change the size of.) If you don't see the handles around the timer, click on the timer inside of the form.

Finally, take a look at the Properties window (see Figure 7.6). If the Properties window is not readily visible, press **F4**. You'll see that the control name for this new object is *Timer1.* Visual Basic automatically assigns a name to new objects, but as you can see, it may not be the most informative one. The control name does tell you it's a timer, but it gives you no idea about what you plan to do with the timer.

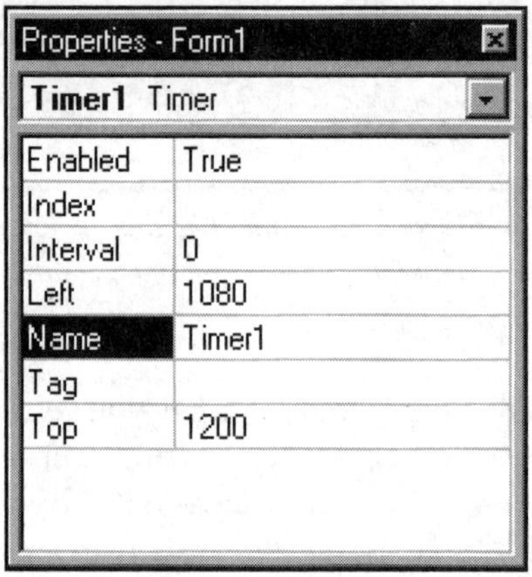

Properties - Form1

Timer1 Timer

Enabled	True
Index	
Interval	0
Left	1080
Name	Timer1
Tag	
Top	1200

FIGURE 7.6 *The control name for the new timer object is Timer1.*

Let's rename this control so it has a name that more closely resembles the function that you intend to use it for. You're going to use this control to update your clock, so a better name might be something like *Tick.* Go ahead and change the Name property to Tick.

Setting the Timer

Your next step will be to run a very simple test program. We've mentioned before that it's best to work in very small steps, and we can't overemphasize the value of working with small pieces at one time. Instead of making all the changes so this timer will update the caption, all in one sitting, let's start with just making the timer beep every second.

There are two things you'll need to do to make your timer will beep. First, you need to tell the timer how often to generate a Timer event. To do this, make sure your timer object has handles around it (by clicking on it), and then click on the Properties window and use the scroll bar to select the *Interval* property (click once on it).

The initial interval will be 0, which means this timer will never generate a Timer event. You'll want to set this value to a number other than zero. But what number? What units are the intervals measured in?

Intervals are measured in milliseconds (0.001 second), so if you want to generate a Timer event every second, you need to set this to 1000 milliseconds. To do this, type **1000** and press **Enter**. You should now see the number 1000 in the Properties window (see Figure 7.7).

Finally, double-click on the timer object inside your form. This will bring up the Code window, showing the Tick_Timer subroutine. Add the Beep command to this subroutine, so it looks like the following:

```
Private Sub Tick_Timer ()
  Beep
End Sub
```

Now run this program. What you'll discover is that the timer object isn't visible in this window (it's only visible at design-time), but your program should beep faithfully (or almost so; see the sidebar "The Timer Interval") every second.

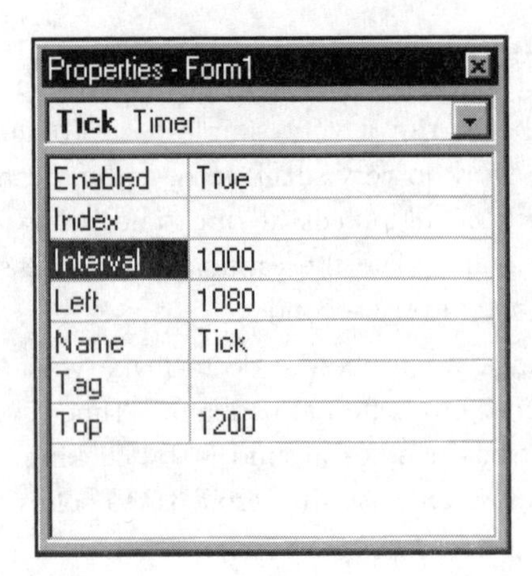

FIGURE 7.7 *The Properties window after changing the timer's interval to 1000.*

THE TIMER INTERVAL

The Interval property, measured in milliseconds (0.001 second), tells a timer object how often to generate a Timer event. But for a couple of reasons, you don't actually have this much control over how often your program receives Timer events.

- Windows uses a timer inside of your PC to determine how much time has elapsed from the last Timer event. But this internal timer only ticks 18.2 times every second, which is about 55 milliseconds. So you can never set the interval more accurately than 55 milliseconds.
- Windows won't always generate a Timer event as soon as the interval has elapsed, because Windows doesn't actually allow more than one program to run at a time. Instead, it lets one program process an event, and then it lets the next program process an event, and so on. If you have a program that takes a long time to process an event, your program won't receive a Timer event until after that program finishes processing its event.

If this sound confusing, just remember that your program will usually get a Timer event at about the right time, but sometimes it may take much longer than interval value.

Try experimenting with different interval values. Also, see what happens when you work with other programs while your Visual Basic program beeps away. For example, if you run another program, you may discover that your program doesn't beep for a short while.

Showing the Time

Now that you've got the Timer event handler working, let's make it a little more interesting. In your next small program, you'll update your window's caption every second to display the current time. But before we show you the code, can you write it yourself?

Think about it for a minute. What you want to do is read the current time each second, and then set the Caption property by using this time. You've already learned all the pieces you need to build this program. All you have to do is put them together in the correct order, so give it a try.

Are you done yet? Now we'll show you our solution to this problem. As you may have already guessed, the new version of Tick_Timer only requires the following single line:

```
Private Sub Tick_Timer ()
  Caption = Time$
End Sub
```

Try out this program. Notice what happens when you minimize it? You'll see the caption flicker every second (unless you have a very fast computer). Flickering like this tends to draw your attention to the source of the flicker, which is great fun when you've just finished writing a program. But after a while, this kind of flickering bothers most people, especially when they're trying to work on something else. It can be downright distracting.

What can you do about this? Well, if you update the caption every minute instead of every second, you probably won't notice the flicker anymore. This is exactly what Icon Clock does, as you can see in Figure 7.1.

The problem, though, is that Time$ always returns a time showing seconds. So you need some way to get a time that doesn't include the seconds.

Using Time Functions

To do this, you'll need to use some new commands in Visual Basic, and one of them is something called a *function*. A function is a command (or some code you write) that returns either a number or a string. Let's look at an example to make this clearer.

Functions in Visual Basic are very similar to the functions that you learned about in math class. *Sine* and *Cosine* functions (which you'll use later in this chapter) are mathematical functions that you can use to describe a circle. If you recall your geometry class, you'll remember that Cos(0) equals 1. In fact, you can write this exact equation in Visual Basic, by using the Debug window as follows:

```
print cos(0)
 1
|
```

You can use functions in very much the same way you use numbers or strings, so you can print the value returned by a function, assign it to a variable, and so on.

Visual Basic has other functions as well, including one called *Now*. The Now function returns the current time and date information as a special date number (which is represented inside Visual Basic as a number of type Double). Microsoft doesn't say what the number actually means, but fortunately they do provide some other functions that take a date number apart. We'll use these other functions shortly, but first an example.

If you print the value of Now, you'll notice it's displayed as a full date and time, which is more information than you need for Icon Clock, as follows:

```
print now
10/27/94 9:23:11 AM
|
```

The return value of the Now function, by the way, has the type Date, which you'll need to keep in mind for later, when you define a variable to remember the value of Now at a single instant.

Reference: Now Function

The Now function returns a special date number of type Date. This single number contains all the information on the current time and date.

```
someVar = Now
```

Returns the current time and date information in a date number of type Date.

There are a number of functions you can use with the information returned by Now. The following functions are the ones that you'll use in this chapter:

```
s% = Second(Now)
```

Returns the seconds, which is a number between 0 and 59.

```
m% = Minute(Now)
```

Returns the minutes, which is a number between 0 and 59.

```
h% = Hour(Now)
```

Returns the hours, which is a number between 0 and 23.

```
s$ = Format$(Now, "h:mm AM/PM")
```

Returns the current time, using the U.S. 12-hour format (such as 9:55 AM).

Visual Basic has four functions you'll use with the value returned by Now: one each to return the hour, minute, and second information, and one to nicely format the time.

Let's start first with the function that will nicely format the time reported by Now. This new function, called *Format$*, returns a string. It's a very useful and powerful function for formatting numbers of all kinds. Here you'll use just the part of this function that formats a date serial number using the AM/PM time display (rather than the 24-hour display) that doesn't show seconds. Try the following command in the Debug window:

```
print format$(now, "h:mm AM/PM")
9:55 AM
|
```

The format$ function takes two arguments. The first argument is the Date returned by the Now function. The second argument is a pattern that tells format$ how you want the time formatted. If, for example, you want to display the time in 24-hour format rather than 12-hour format, you could use this string instead: "h:mm". Give this a try.

Let's rewrite Icon Clock so it will use the Format$ command, as follows:

```
Private Sub Tick_Timer ()
  Caption = Format$(Now, "h:mm AM/PM")
End Sub
```

When you run this program, you may notice the caption still flickers when your program is minimized, but now it displays the time in exactly the same format shown in Figure 7.1. (Note: if you're in a country other than the U.S., you may see the time displayed in your country's standard format instead.)

Now let's look at how you can keep the caption from flickering. There are actually two approaches you can take. First, you could change the interval to 60,000, which is 1 minute. But because you'll need to draw a new second hand every second, this isn't the solution that you'll use.

The second approach takes a little more work. You'll create a form-level variable, called *lastMinute*, that keeps track of the minute currently displayed. As soon as the current minute is different from lastMinute, you'll change the caption. If this sounds a little confusing, it'll become clearer after a little more work.

Getting Information from Dates

Visual Basic has yet another function, called *Minute*, that returns the minute part of a Date. So if you type the following, you'll see just the minutes part of the time:

```
print time$
9:58:04
print minute(now)
 58
|
```

(The minutes might will be different in this example if you wait too long between running these two commands.)

So here's what to do. First, define the variable lastMinute in the (general) section of your form, as follows:

```
Private lastMinute As Integer       ' Last minute shown in
                                    ' caption
```

Next, you'll use this information in Tick_Timer, as follows:

```
Private Sub Tick_Timer ()
  Dim t                         ' The time information

  t = Now                       ' Get the current time
  min = Minute(t)               ' Get the current minute
  If min <> lastMinute Then     ' Update caption if new minute
    Caption = Format$(t, "h:mm AM/PM")
    lastMinute = min            ' Remember new current minute
  End If
End Sub
```

(If you changed the Interval property, make sure you set it back to 1000.) Try out this new program, and then think about what it does before you read on.

There are a few things in this subroutine that may not be obvious. For starters, you'll notice that we defined the variable *t* without a type after it. Any variables you define without an explicit As *type* are created as Variant variables, which is exactly what you want in this case. The Now function returns a Date value, and Variant variables can contain Date, as well as other types of values.

You'll also notice that we used a very short name, *t*, to save the date number. Why didn't we use a longer, more descriptive name like *time*? In this case you can't use the word *time* because Visual Basic already has a function called Time. (The Time function returns a date number without the date information—it just contains the time.) You could use an even longer name, like *dateNumber*, but because you're going to be using this variable a couple of times, we suggest using a very short name. When you use one variable a number of times in a single subroutine, a short, single-letter variable name can actually make the code easier to read and write.

Let's look in detail at how this subroutine works. First, it assigns the value of Now to the variable *t*. You do this, rather than continue to use Now in the rest of the subroutine, to make sure you're working with a single time. If you don't do this, the time might change before Tick_Timer finishes.

Next, it gets the minutes from this time and saves this value in the *variable min*. It then compares the value in min to the value in lastMinute. The symbols <> mean *not equal to*. So if min is not equal to *lastMinute,* Visual Basic runs the next two statements. In other words, it only updates the caption when *min* is different from *lastMinute*.

Finally, Tick_Timer updates the caption and saves the new minute value in the *lastMinute* variable. This ensures that it won't update the caption again until the minute changes.

Displaying the time in the caption was the easy part. Now for the hard part: Drawing the hands on the clock face.

Drawing the Clock Face

Writing the rest of Icon Clock is a little more difficult because you'll be dealing with some trigonometry to draw the hands on the clock. Fortunately, there is something much simpler you can start with: hanging the icon used for your minimized program.

Setting the Icon

The icon we use in this program is a special icon John created by using the Icon Works program that came with Visual Basic 3.0. But you don't have to create this icon yourself because it's included on the disk at the back of this book. We'll show you how to use this icon in your own program.

Make sure you're in design mode. Then click on the icon in the Toolbox that looks like a picture with a cactus and a sun (if you pause the mouse over this button, you'll see a tool tip appear with the name PictureBox). Click and drag the mouse inside the form to create a PictureBox control, just as you previously created a Timer control.

In the Properties window you'll also want to change several properties for the PictureBox control:

Appearance	0 – Flat
AutoSize	True
BackColor	&H00C0C0C0& (light grey)
Border Style	0 – None
Name	Clock

Next select the Picture property in the Properties window.

At this point you'll see a small button with three dots (...) to the right of the (Picture) property value. Click on this button, and you'll see a dialog box like the one shown in Figure 7.8.

If you haven't installed the files from the disk at the back of this book, you'll need to do so now. Then use the Directories part of the Load Icon dialog to switch to the ICONCLCK directory. You'll find a file called *Clckface.ico* in this directory. Double-click on this file to load it into Visual Basic.

Now click on your Form1 window to make it the active window. If the picture box control has handles around it, click anywhere else in the form (except on the timer control). This will ensure that your form, rather than the picture box or timer, is the currently selected object. Now click on the Icon property and repeat the process you used above for the picture box's Picture property to set the form's icon to Iconclck.ico. You will notice that the icon in the upper-left of your form now looks like a clock instead of the standard Visual Basic form icon. Your window should now look just like Icon Clock, except for the lack of hands. Your next project will be to draw the hands on the clock face.

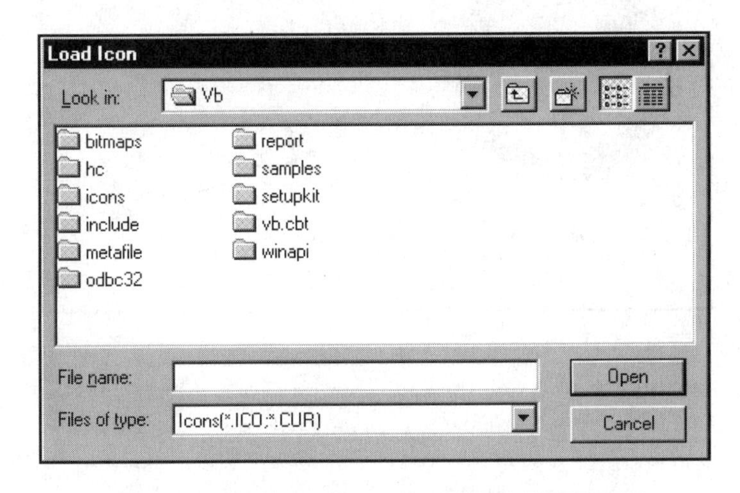

FIGURE 7.8 *The Load Icon dialog box. You can then change drives and/or directories to load the* ***Clckface.ico*** *file.*

Drawing the Clock Hands

Drawing the clock hands really isn't that hard to do, but it will take a much longer subroutine to do this than you've ever written before. And you'll actually use several subroutines to do all the work.

Why does it take so much code? Well, for one thing, you'll be drawing three hands on the clock: the hour hand, the minute hand, and the second hand. This is in addition to updating the caption, which you're already doing.

Let's start by drawing the second hand; since it will move each second, you'll be able to see if it works correctly in all positions (and it will only take a minute). To do this, we'll need to review a little math, which is necessary to calculate where to draw the second hand. You'll be able to use the same code for both the hour and minute hands.

Figure 7.9 shows a blowup of the clock face, along with the hands drawn on the screen and a review of the trigonometry involved in drawing the second hand.

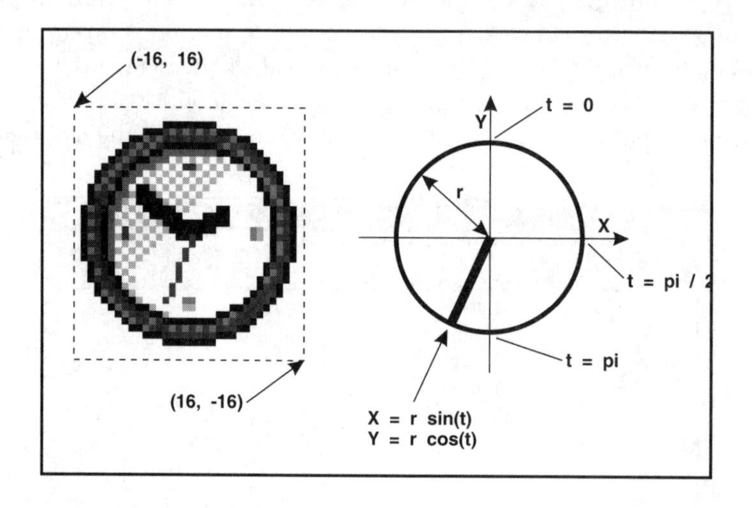

FIGURE 7.9 *This figure provides a brief review of the trigonometry that you'll be using to draw the hands on the clock. You'll define the coordinate system to go from –16 to 16 because the icon is 32 pixels wide and high.*

If you remember the drawing you've done so far, you'll remember that (0, 0) has always been in the upper-left corner, with increasing Y values moving *down* rather than up. But here you'll want to use a Cartesian coordinate system, with (0, 0) at the center of the icon, and increasing Y values moving *up*. How do you do this? You can fake it, by writing the equations to work with the standard coordinates. Or better yet, you can redefine the coordinate system so it's more to your liking.

It's easy to change the coordinate system. You use a command called *Scale*. This command lets you tell Visual Basic what numbers you want to use for the top-left and lower-right corners of your form. In the case of the icon, you'll use a range of numbers from –16 to 16, as you can see in Figure 7.9. Why these numbers?

REFERENCE: SCALE COMMAND

The Scale command allows you to define a custom coordinate system for any form.

```
Scale [(x1, y1) - (x2, y2)]
```

Sets up a custom coordinate system, with the upper-left corner at (*x1, y1*) and the lower-right corner at (*x2, y2*).

If you don't provide any coordinates, Visual Basic resets the coordinates back to the default coordinate system, with each unit equal to a twip, (0, 0) at the upper-left corner, and Y increasing down.

Any icon for a minimized window in Microsoft Windows is 32 pixels (dots) wide and 32 pixels high. So by creating a coordinate system that spans the range from –16 to 16, you're creating a coordinate system where each unit is exactly one pixel wide. It's really not important in this case that each unit be one pixel wide, but you'll do it anyway because it really doesn't matter how large a unit is, as long as (0, 0) is at the center of the icon.

Let's try a simple experiment using Scale. Start your clock program again. Then press **Ctrl+Break** to show the Debug window, and enter the following two commands:

```
Clock.Scale (-16, 16)-(16, -16)
Clock.Line (0, 0)-(10, 10)
|
```

The "Clock." in front of the Scale and Line command tells Visual Basic that you want these commands to apply to the picture box called Clock instead of to the form. This is exactly what you want in order to draw inside the icon.

This Line command draws a line starting at the center of your icon, and ending 10 pixels up and to the right of the center (Figure 7.10).

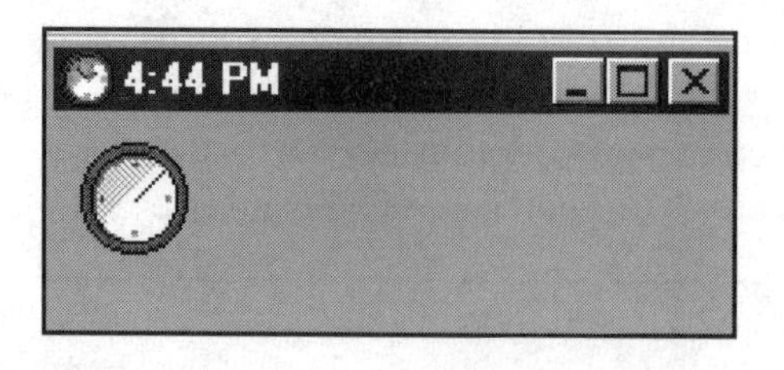

FIGURE 7.10 *The effect of changing the Scale, then drawing a line from (0, 0) to (10, 10).*

Now let's write the code to draw this second hand using the real time. Return to design mode, and make sure you're viewing the code for Tick_Timer(). Enter the following changes (notice we're using the equations in Figure 7.10 to calculate the position of the second hand):

```
Private Sub Tick_Timer ()
  Const pi = 3.141592653          ' Define the value of pi
  Dim t                           ' The time information

  t = Now                         ' Get the current time
  sec = Second(t)                 ' Get seconds, 0..59
  min = Minute(t)                 ' Get the current minute,
                                    0..59

  If min <> lastMinute Then       ' Update caption if new minute
    Caption = Format$(t, "h:mm AM/PM")
    lastMinute = min              ' Remember new current minute
  End If

  Scale (-16, 16)-(16, -16)       ' Set scale for clock icon
  x = 10 * Sin(sec * pi / 30)     ' Calculate end of second hand
  y = 10 * Cos(sec * pi / 30)
  Line (0, 0)-(x, y)              ' Draw the second hand
End Sub
```

Then run this program.

You'll find one problem. Tick_Timer isn't removing the second hand after it draws it, so after a minute, your clock face will be filled with 60 second hands.

Before we move on, there is a new keyword in this program: *Const.* The Const keyword defines a special type of variable, called a *constant,* which has a fixed value. In other words, you can never change the value of a constant. You'll use Const whenever you have a constant value in a program, such as *pi* (which is written as π in mathematics, but as pi in programs because you can't use Greek letters in programs).

REFERENCE: CONST KEYWORD

The Const keyword allows you to define constants in your programs. You can assign a name to a number or a string of characters, as follows:

```
Const name = value
```

Defines *name* to be a constant equal to *value.*

Showing One Second Hand

You now have a program that has the problem with the second hand. Right now you're drawing the hand, but you're never erasing it, so you're filling the icon with black lines.

Think about this problem for a moment. How would you fix it? The first thing you need to do is identify exactly what the problem is; only then can you solve it. In this case, the problem is very simple. You're not erasing the previous second hand before you draw the new one, so you need a solution that erases this old second hand.

Right now you only know one way to erase anything—using the Cls command. You learned that Cls automatically redraws the icon in your minimized program, so it erases everything *except* for the icon. In other words, the Cls command will erase only the second hand, since that's all you've drawn on top of the icon. Try adding Cls to your program, then run it. What happens now? (By the way, if you haven't made the change yet, here's how to do it. Put a Clock.Cls command into your Tick_Timer event handler on a line immediately before the Line command.)

At this point you'll notice that the second hand moves around the clock face. But the clock face flickers now, just as the caption flickered earlier in this chapter when you changed it every second. What you really want is some way to erase the second hand without having to use the Cls command. In other words, you want some way to "undraw" a line. We'll show you how to do it after a brief side trip into colors.

Drawing with Color

At the start of this chapter, we promised that your second hand would be red in color, so let's examine how to change the color of the line. Doing this before learning a better way to erase a line may seem like we're getting off the track, but we're actually not. What you learn here will help make the next step clearer because the technique you'll use has to do with colors.

The Line command has an optional argument that you haven't used yet. This argument allows you to draw lines with other colors. There is also a function, called *RGB*, that allows you to calculate a color number. RGB stands for Red-Green-Blue because it takes three arguments: a red, a green, and a blue component. For a red line, you'll want to use 0 for green and blue, and 255 (the maximum value allowed for each part) for red.

The following line is the new version of the Line command in Tick_Timer that draws a red line (instead of the normal black line):

```
Clock.Line (0, 0)-(x, y), RGB(255, 0, 0)
```

Now your program should draw a nice red second hand.

Reference: RGB Function

```
colorNumber = RGB(redNumber, greenNumber, blueNumber)
```

Returns a color number, which you can use in the Line command to draw a line of any color.

The red, green, and blue color numbers can be any number between 0 and 255. White is (255, 255, 255) and black is (0, 0, 0). The number returned by RGB is of type Long.

The RGB function builds color numbers used by the Line command, and stands for red-green-blue, which are the primary colors used for television screens. If you remember back to your art classes in grade school (or later) you'll probably remember learning that the primary colors are red, yellow, and blue. So why do we use red, green, and blue here?

The primary colors you learned about in grade school are for *subtractive* colors, because if you use paint and combine all the primary colors, you'll end up with a very dark mess. On the other hand, when you're working with light rather than paint, you're working with *additive* colors. In this case the primary colors switch to red, green, and blue. This should be familiar if you've done any work with theater lighting, where you create a white spot by combing red, green, and blue spot lights.

Using Xor to Erase a Line

Now that you've learned about colors, you might guess that you could erase the line you drew before (without having to redraw the icon) by drawing a white line. You can try that using RGB(255, 255, 255), but it will also erase anything on the clock face that wasn't white before. So you need a different technique to undraw lines without erasing what was there before. Sounds like the impossible, but there is a way to do this.

Windows actually has a way to undraw lines, as long as you draw them properly. All the drawing you've done so far has been drawn lines on top of other objects. But you can also draw lines by "inverting" dots on the screen. If you invert the dots twice, they end back at their original color. What this means is that you can erase a line you drew by drawing that line a second time.

To see how this works, let's do some experiments with the Debug window. Run your program and let it start ticking, then press **Ctrl+Break** to show the Debug window. Next see what happens when you draw a line twice, without changing anything else, as follows:

```
Clock.cls
Clock.line (0,0)-(10,10)
Clock.line (0,0)-(10,10)
|
```

The first Line command here will draw a line from the center, going up and to the right 10 pixels. And the second Line command does the same thing, which is what you're probably used to.

Now let's add another command to this test. You're going to use the DrawMode property to change the method used for drawing in a form. By default, DrawMode is set to 13, which tells Visual Basic to draw lines on top of anything on the screen. But here you'll set DrawMode to 10, which tells Visual Basic to use the inverting mode of drawing, as follows:

```
Clock.cls
print drawmode
 13
Clock.drawmode = 10
Clock.line (0,0)-(10,10)
Clock.line (0,0)-(10,10)
|
```

When you run the first Line command, you'll see a black line appear, just as before. But this time, the second Line command will erase the original line! And that's all there is to this trick.

Now let's take a look at how it works. First a comment. If you look in your *Language Reference Manual* under DrawMode, you'll find a list of 16 different drawing modes you can use. What you'll also find is that the descriptions of the different drawing modes don't make much sense. And DrawMode 10, which is what we're using here, is called the *Not Xor Pen* mode. What does all this mean?

It's a little hard to explain, especially because most professional Windows programmers don't fully understand all the different drawing modes. You may not really want to understand *how* it works as long as you know it works. If you're interested, however, the sidebar on the DrawMode Property will give you all of the information that you should need. And it will be here, waiting for you, if you ever need to learn more about DrawMode.

Reference: DrawMode Property

The DrawMode property allows you to control how Visual Basic draws colored lines (and shapes) on your screen. This is a little like the difference between using water colors and oil paints. With oil paints, you can paint one color over another color, and it will completely replace the old color. But water colors don't work the same way: When you paint a water color over an existing color, the two colors blend together where they overlap to give you a third color.

Visual Basic has two drawing options similar to the painting examples, and it also has 14 other drawing modes. One of the nice things about computers is that you have much more freedom than you might have in the physical world. But it also takes a little while to understand all of the nuances and meanings. You won't need to understand most of the material in this sidebar. But later, when you're ready to experiment, you'll find this sidebar to be a very useful reference, because much of this information isn't documented well anywhere else. You're only going to be using two modes in this chapter: 10 and 13.

Understanding all the DrawMode values takes quite a bit of work, and we weren't able to find a good explanation in any of the books we looked at (including Microsoft's Windows programming reference manuals). Below you'll find a very complete description of each of the 16 modes supported by Visual Basic.

There are three groups of modes here (Mask, Inverse, and Merge) that are not at all easy, so we'd like to say a few words about them. But first, we'd like to point out which modes are the most commonly used in real programs, and give you an idea of what they do.

Type of DrawMode	DrawMode numbers
Combining light	15
Draw over (replace old color)	13 (the default)
Erasable draw	10, 7, or 6

Figure 7.11 shows a color wheel for the additive colors (using light rather than paint). The inverse of any color on this wheel is the color on the opposite side of the circle. You can also see that bright colors are turned into dark colors when they're inverted.

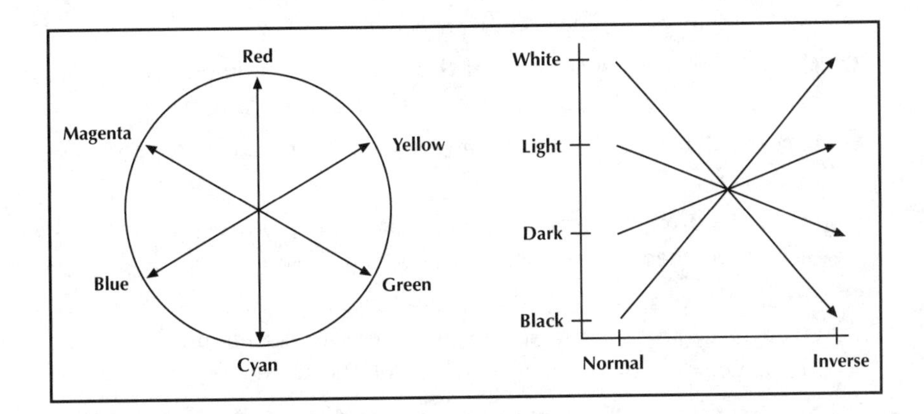

FIGURE 7.11 *The left side shows which colors are the inverse of other colors. The right side shows how the brightness of a color changes when you invert it.*

The Merge and Mask groups use color information from both the pen and each pixel currently on the screen where the shape will be drawn. Color in Windows have three components: red, green, and blue. The merge modes work with one pixel at a time and add together each color component (red, green, and blue) from the pen color and the color of the pixel being drawn over. For example, if you draw a bright red pixel (RGB = 255, 0, 0) over a bright blue pixel (RGB = 0, 0, 255), you get a bright magenta pixel (RGB = 255, 0, 255). And drawing a green pixel on top of a bright magenta pixel gives you a white pixel. The Merge modes act very much like combining the light from two lights with different colors.

The other group is the Mask group, which requires a little explanation. In the mask modes, either the pen or the current pixel color (or it's inverse) is used as a mask. A mask, in this case, limits the amount of red, green, and blue in the final pixel drawn on the screen. For example, if the mask color is (127, 127, 0), the red and green components of the final pixel will be limited to 127 or less, and the blue component will be 0. For example, if we use a mask of (127, 127, 0) to mask bright magenta (255, 0, 255), you'll get a light red pixel (127, 0, 0).

The following values are the DrawMode values:

1. **Black.** Always draw in black. This ignores the pen color, and it draws over anything currently on the screen.
2. **Inverse of Merge.** Windows merges the pen and pixel colors, then draws the inverse of this on the screen.
3. **Mask Screen using Inverse of the Pen.** This mode masks the colors on the screen, using the inverse of the pen color as a mask
4. **Inverse Pen Color.** Draws using a color that's the inverse of the pen color.
5. **Mask the Inverse Screen.** Inverts the colors on the screen, and then masks them by using the pen color.
6. **Invert Screen.** In this mode, anything you "draw" will simply invert the colors on the screen. In other words, this mode ignores the pen color and just changes what's on the screen.
7. **Xor Draw.** Use this mode when you need to draw lines that you can erase by drawing them again. This mode will keep the correct color for lines you draw against a *black* background. Use Mode 10 for a white background.

8. **Inverse of Mask Screen.** This mode displays the inverse of the colors displayed by mode 9. It uses the pen color to mask the screen color, and then it inverts this color.

9. **Mask Screen.** Windows breaks the pen and pixel colors into red, green, and blue components, then "clips" the red, green, and blue components so they're no larger than the RGB components of the pen. For example, if you mask a white pixel (RGB = 255, 255, 255) using a dark blue pen (RGB = 0, 0, 127), you get a dark blue pixel on the screen.

10. **Inverse Xor Draw.** Use this mode when you want to draw lines that you can erase by drawing them again. This mode will keep the correct color for lines you draw against a *white* background. Use Mode 7 for a black background.

11. **Transparent.** Doesn't draw anything. You'll probably never need to use this mode.

12. **Merge Screen and Inverse of Pen.** Merges the inverse of the pen color with the screen colors. To draw any pixel, Windows first inverts the pen color, and then it adds together (individually) the red, green, and blue components of these two colors. Windows does this for each pixel being drawn over.

13. **Pen Color (default).** Draws using the pen color. It draws over anything currently being shown.

14. **Merge Pen and Inverse of Screen.** Merges the pen with the inverse of the screen colors. To draw any pixel, Windows first inverts the pixel being drawn over, and then adds together (individually) the red, green, and blue components of these two colors. Windows does this for each pixel being drawn over.

15. **Merge Pen and Screen.** Merges the color of the pen with what's currently on the screen. For each pixel drawn, Windows adds together each color component (red, green, and blue) of the pen color and the pixel being drawn over. For example, if you draw a bright red pixel (RGB = 255, 0, 0) over a bright blue pixel (RGB = 0, 0, 255), you get a bright magenta pixel (255, 0, 255). Drawing a green pixel on top of a bright magenta pixel gives you a white pixel. (If any component adds up to a number greater than 255, it's set to 255.)

16. **White.** Always draw in white This ignores the pen color, and it draws over anything currently on the screen.

That said, you can now use DrawMode = 10 to display an erasable second hand. So now you need to figure out exactly how you're going to use this drawing mode. First we'll describe what you want to do in simple English. Then we'll try to describe it in a way that makes it easy to write this program. For the second way, we'll be using something called *pseudo-code*, which is a cross between a programming language and English.

But we're getting ahead of ourselves—first the English description. What you need to do here is draw the second hand. Then when you get the next Tick_Timer event, you'll need to erase the last second hand you drew, and then draw a new second hand.

Sounds simple enough. But this is only the first step in solving the problem. In reality, there are a number of special conditions to look at, known as *boundary conditions*. You'll want to try to identify all the places where you might have to do something a little different. In other words, you want to find the boundaries of the problem.

For example, the very first Tick_Timer event you get after your program starts is slightly different from all the others. Why? Well, the English description of what you want to do says you want to erase the last line you drew before drawing the new second hand. But the first time you get a Tick_Timer event you haven't drawn a line yet. So there's nothing to erase, which means you'll want to handle this case a little differently. This is the type of thing you'll need to look for when you're looking for boundary conditions.

There are some other boundary conditions as well that you'll find later. But for now, the initial call to Tick_Timer is only boundary condition you'll need to worry about.

Now let's rewrite our simple description of how to draw an erasable second hand, but this time in more detail, using pseudo-code. The solution will look like the following:

```
Tick_Timer()
     If previous line Then
          Erase the previous second hand
     End If
     Draw the new second hand.
```

As you can see, this is a cross between real Basic code and English. We're using the Basic If..Then command, but for the condition and the statements we're using an English-language description. This technique is a very powerful way to express your ideas in a way that's much easier to turn into a program.

PSEUDO-CODE: THE TOOL OF PROS

Pseudo-code is a very powerful tool for writing complex programs, and it's one you'll find many professional programmers and professors using, to try to express their ideas before they start to write programs. There aren't any hard-and-fast rules about how to express ideas in pseudo-code. The main idea is that you want to use some of the "control structures" like If..Then, but use English descriptions for other statements and even for the conditions that will appear in the If..Then statements.

When writing pseudo-code, you need to avoid defining things in too much detail, because that can easily get you bogged down. Write as simple a description as you can, then fill in the details later. If you're working with a very complex idea, you'll probably find yourself rewriting your pseudo-code several times, with a little more detail each time.

When you have this idea of what you're going to do, it's time to turn it into real code. Before we show you our solution, try writing a solution yourself; we'll give you a couple of hints. You'll need to keep track of where the last second hand was so that you can erase it. The obvious place (and best solution) for saving this information is in some form-level variables. See if you can write this new Tick_Timer event handler yourself.

Now for our solution. First, we've created two variables, called *lastX* and *lastY* to keep track of the end-point for the second hand. Because the second hands always start at (0, 0), this is all the information needed to keep track of the last second hand. Put these two definitions into the (general) area part of your form, as follows:

```
Private lastX As Integer        ' End point of last second hand
Private lastY As Integer
```

Next, you need some way to let Tick_Timer know when there isn't a previous second hand for it to erase. You could do this if there were some way to set lastX to a special value before your program starts running. We've chosen to use 999 because X for the second hand ranges between minus 10 and 10, so it can never reach 999.

How can you set lastX to 999 before your program starts? Well, there's another event handler, called *Form_Load,* that's only called when your form is first loaded. In other words, it's only called once at the start of your program. (Later, when you work with programs using multiple forms, you'll see that it's called whenever a form is loaded again).

Use the Object combo box to select **Form,** then select **Load** from the Proc combo box. then enter **lastX = 999** in the following event handler:

```
Private Sub Form_Load ()
  lastX = 999                  ' No previous second hand
End Sub
```

Finally, you need to modify Tick_Timer so it will erase the old second hand and remember the location of the new second hand. Since Tick_Timer is getting rather long, instead of showing you the entire event handler, we'll just show you the changes for the following lines starting with the Scale command (which you won't change):

```
Clock.Scale (-16, 16)-(16, -16)      ' Set scale for clock icon
Clock.DrawMode = 10                  ' Set for erasable drawing
red = RGB(255, 0, 0)             ' Define red color

x = 10 * Sin(sec * pi / 30)    ' Calculate end of second hand
y = 10 * Cos(sec * pi / 30)
If lastX <> 999 Then             ' Erase any old second hand
  Clock.Line (0, 0)-(lastX, lastY), red
End If
Clock.Line (0, 0)-(x, y), red        ' Draw the new second hand

lastX = x                        ' Save end point of new hand
lastY = y
End Sub
```

Most of this new code should be fairly clear. There is one small trick we've pulled to cut down on any flicker you'll see in the second hand. You'll notice that you're now calculating the new x and y position *before* you erase the previous second hand. This allows the two Line commands to be as close together as possible. The closer together they are, the less time there will be no second hand at all on the screen. Trigonometric functions, such as Sin and Cos, tend to be rather slow.

In fact, you might want to try an experiment with this. If you move the three lines that erase the previous second hand (starting with If lastX <> 999) up two lines so they're before the x and y calculations, you'll notice that the second hand flickers slightly each time it's moved. The way we wrote them above, you won't see a flicker. Small differences like this can make the difference between a good program and an excellent program.

Drawing the Hour and Minute Hands

You're almost finished writing the Icon Clock program. At this point you only have a couple things left to add. First, and most obvious, you need to draw the hour and minute hands.

But there is also a slight "glitch" in the way your program works now. If you cover up part of the clock, and then uncover it, you'll notice that the clock face will be erased, and Icon Clock may become confused about the previous second hand. In other words, it may leave behind a second hand. This happens because Visual Basic clears the entire clock face whenever you uncover part of the icon. This problem is a little tricky to fix, and we won't show you how to fix it here. But the version of Icon Clock on the disk accompanying this book fixes this problem, and includes a few more nice touches as well.

There is also a slight problem in which the old second hand sometimes stays behind. This happens now because the *x* and *y* variables are floating point numbers, whereas lastX and lastY are of type Integer. So it's possible for lastX to be different from the previous *x* as a result of rounding. You can fix this problem by defining *x* and *y* as Integer in Tick_Timer. Or you can redefine lastX and lastY so they're of type Variant. Either solution will work.

As to adding the hour and minute hands, you'll find the new version of Tick_Timer below. You'll also need to add the variable lastHour to the (general) section of your form, and there are a couple of other things we'll comment on. First, you'll notice a line that calculates a variable *h*. This line creates a fraction hour that includes the minute information, which allows the hour hand to move every minute. A real clock changes the position of the hour hand every minute, so it will be between two of the hour marks at 30 minutes past the hour.

You'll also notice we've carefully changed the drawing mode between erasable mode (10) for the second hands, and non-erasable mode (13) for the hour and minute hands. This allows you to have an hour and minute hand such that the hour hand doesn't erase part of the minute hand. If you want to see what we mean, remove the line that sets DrawMode to 13.

Finally, we set lastX to 999 when the hour or minute changes. This is because whenever the hour or minute changes, the clock face is erased, so there won't be a previous second hand in such cases. The rest of this program should be familiar.

The final clock program has a single Timer control added to the form, called Timer1, with the Name Tick. The property for the form is Icon, with the setting Iconclck.ico.

The following definitions are in the (general) part of your Form:

```
Private lastMinute As Integer    ' Last minute shown on clock
Private lastHour As Integer       ' Last hour shown on clock

PrivatelastX As Integer          ' End point of last second hand
PrivatelastY As Integer

Private Sub Form_Load ()
  lastX = 999                    ' No previous second hand
End Sub

Private Sub Tick_Timer ()
  Const pi = 3.141592653         ' Define the value of pi
  Dim t                          ' The time information
  Dim x As Integer               ' Use same type as lastX
  Dim y As Integer

  t = Now                         ' Get the current time
  sec = Second(t)                 ' Get seconds, 0..59
  min = Minute(t)                 ' Get the current minute, 0..59
  hr = Hour(t)                    ' Get hours, 0..23

  Clock.Scale (-16, 16)-(16, -16)       ' Set scale for clock icon
  '
  ' If the hour or minute has changed, update the caption,
  ' then remove all the hands and redraw them
  '
  If min <> lastMinute Or hr <> lastHour Then
```

```
    Caption = Format$(t, "h:mm AM/PM")
    lastMinute = min                 ' Remember new current minute
    lastHour = hr
    Clock.Cls                              ' Clear all clock hands
    lastX = 999                      ' No previous second hand

    Clock.DrawWidth = 2                    ' Draw 2-pixel wide lines
    Clock.DrawMode = 13                    ' Draw non-erasable lines

    h = hr + min / 60                ' Decimal hour, for hour hand
    x = 5 * Sin(h * pi / 6)          ' End point of hour hand
    y = 5 * Cos(h * pi / 6)
    Clock.Line (0, 0)-(x, y)               ' Draw the hour hand

    x = 8 * Sin(min * pi / 30)       ' End point of minute hand
    y = 8 * Cos(min * pi / 30)
    Clock.Line (0, 0)-(x, y)
    Clock.DrawWidth = 1                    ' Set back to 1-pixel lines
  End If

  Clock.DrawMode = 10                      ' Set for erasable drawing
  red = RGB(255, 0, 0)               ' Define red color

  x = 10 * Sin(sec * pi / 30)        ' Calculate end of second hand
  y = 10 * Cos(sec * pi / 30)
  If lastX <> 999 Then               ' Erase any old second hand
    Clock.Line (0, 0)-(lastX, lastY), red
  End If
  Clock.Line (0, 0)-(x, y), red            ' Draw the new second hand

  lastX = x                          ' Save end point of new hand
  lastY = y
End Sub
```

You might want to create an EXE version of this program so you can run it. But we'd suggest using the version that comes on the companion disk, because it fixes a couple of boundary conditions we didn't address in this chapter. For example, the version on the disk will redraw itself properly when it becomes uncovered. It also has a nicer icon.

Related Tools

- **Format$** This command is very powerful, and can format many types of numbers. For example, if you want to display money information, such as displaying 2.3 as $2.30 (with a dollar sign and two decimal places), this is the command for you. You'll find details in your *Language Reference Manual.*
- **Time/date functions** There are a number of time and date functions we haven't used in this chapter that you might find useful, as follows:

TimeSerial	Calculates a Date value given the hour, minute, and second.
TimeValue	Converts a string (such as "12:34PM") into a Date value.
Date$	Returns the current date in a string.
DateSerial	Calculates a Date value given a year, month, and day.
DateValue	Converts a string (such as "3/6/92") to a Date value.
Day	Returns the day of the month (1..31) from a Date value.
Weekday	Returns the day of the week, between 1 (Sunday) and 7 (Saturday), from a Date value.
Month	Returns the month (1..12) from a Date value.
Year	Returns the year part of a Date value (1753..2078).

- **Trigonometric functions** In this chapter you learned about the Sin (sine) and Cos (cosine) functions. Visual Basic also provides the Tan (tangent) and Atn (arc-tangent) functions.
- **Scale-related properties** When you set a custom scale, you can use the ScaleWidth and ScaleHeight properties to get the current width (in drawing units) and height of your form. You can also get the coordinates of the top and left edges using ScaleLeft and ScaleTop.

Summary

You covered a lot of ground in this chapter, but you should have a much better understanding of how to write programs. In Chapter 8, we'll start all over again with a new program. This program, however, will be larger, so you'll get a chance to learn how to write large programs. It will also be a useful program, and one you'll probably want to change to suit your own needs.

The following is what we've covered in this chapter:

✱ **Designing programs.** You learned more about writing programs using step-wise refinement and planning ahead. It's always a good idea to think about what you want your program to look like, and how you want it to work before you start programming. You also learned about using pseudo-code to design programs. Pseudo-code is a cross between English and Basic. Finally, you learned about boundary conditions, which are parts of your program where you need to handle a special case. You looked at the case where you wanted to erase the previous line, but there wasn't a previous line to erase.

✱ **Drawing inside icons.** You can draw inside an icon just as easily as you can draw inside a form. You can also change the caption below a minimized program by setting the Caption property to any string.

✱ **Timers.** You learned how to create a timer object, and to write code in the Timer event that will run every so many milliseconds. The timer interval is set by selecting the timer object on the form, then setting the Timer property using the Properties window.

✱ **Reading the time.** You can use the Time$ string to get a string that shows the current time in 24-hour format. You can also use the Format$ (Now, "h:mm AM/PM") to display a string with the time in 12-hour format. The functions Hour, Minute, and Second will break a Date value, returned by the Now function, into the hour, minute, and second part of the time.

✱ **WindowState and Form_Load.** The WindowState property allows you to minimize your program when you first start. You do this by setting WindowState in the Form_Load event handler, which runs once when your form first loads (and before it appears on the screen).

✱ **Const keyword.** The Const keyword allows you to define constants in your programs. These are like variables in that they have a name, but they have a single value and can't be changed.

✱ **Color.** The RGB function allows you to draw lines using any color. You provide a red, green, and blue component, and each component can be between 0 and 255 (0 is no color, and 255 is full color). RGB(0, 0, 0) is black, and RGB (255, 255, 255) is white.

✱ **DrawMode.** Setting DrawMode to 10 allows you to draw erasable lines. The normal drawing mode (13) writes non-erasable lines.

DESIGNING AND BUILDING PROGRAMS

- How to design programs
- Designing user interfaces
- Building programs

In this chapter you're going to start building a large Visual Basic program. By building a large program, you'll see firsthand how programmers go about designing and building real programs. You'll also learn a number of new techniques that you'll find useful in writing your own programs.

First, we'll spend some time talking about how you go about designing programs. As you'll see, there are a number of different approaches that you can take. We'll take just one approach in this book, which is the one that works best for us (but it may not be the best approach for you).

After several pages of philosophy and approaches, we'll get down to the actual work of designing a large program, which will be an Address Book program that you can use to keep track of names and addresses, and to print them out. Because we'll be building this program for the next few chapters, you'll be able to change anything you don't like, or add features you think are missing. Let's look at how you start to build a large program.

How to Design Programs

There are a number of schools of thought on the "correct" way to design and build programs. Some people believe that you should write very detailed specifications for any program before you write a single line of code, or spend any time at all behind your computer. Other people believe that programming is an incremental process that constantly evolves, and that you should start writing *something* as soon as you can. We'll spend a few paragraphs explaining these approaches in more detail, and then we'll present the approach we use, which is the approach that you'll use in the next few chapters.

We should mention that there is no one correct method for writing programs, although you're likely to run into programmers and managers who do believe there is one correct approach. What this really means is that each person has their own approach, and if you're working for someone else, you may have to use the approach they like, rather than using your own.

However, by understanding the different approaches to designing programs, you'll be able to use different techniques even if you have to follow the "one correct approach" to software design.

Detailed Specifications

The idea behind using detailed specifications is that you want to completely design your program before you write any code. This allows you to work out all of the complicated interactions in a program before you've worked yourself into a hole. If you just start writing the program, you may discover that you've headed off in the wrong direction, so it's important that you think things through first.

Design specifications vary considerably in the amount of detail you'll find, but they usually contain a description of what problems your program should solve, and how it should solve them. Specs also usually contain drawings of what the different screens in your program should look like. Really detailed specifications contain a list of all the modules (and sometimes even subroutines and functions) that will be in the program, along with a description of what they should do, and what conventions will be used to call the subroutines and functions.

Programming as Evolution

Other people believe that you only need the idea for a program before you start to work on the program. In this approach, you start writing something as soon as possible, and then you modify your design as you go along. In a sense, this is a very evolutionary approach. Your design will be very fluid. To managers, this is a scary approach because they won't know what they have until it's finished. But if you're working on a program for your own use, or if you're building the next great *fill-in-the-blank* all by yourself, this may be a good approach.

In-Between Approaches

In between these two basic approaches are many variations. When you're working with other people on a project, you'll need to have some type of design specifications. How detailed these specifications are really depends on a number of factors, including how many programmers are working on the program, how many other people are involved in the project, the philosophy of the managers involved, and so on.

Our preference, when working on commercial software rather than small programs for our own use, is to write a design specification that's about 5 pages long. This document usually lists features that should be in the finished program, with a short one- or two-paragraph description of each feature. We also spend some time talking about the general philosophy of the program and how the features should work together. John doesn't tend to include any screen designs, module lists, or any other details below the level of a feature list. This works well for his way of designing programs, which is closer to the evolutionary approach than the detailed design approach. Devra, on the other hand, tends to include small pieces of pseudo-code because it helps her to keep track of which arrays and variables she plans to use for testing conditions.

The Approach We'll Use Here

We both agree that if you go too far in writing specifications, you'll lock yourself into a design that may not work well. We've discovered that you often don't know the real problems you're trying to solve until you've tried out some of your ideas on the computer. There are times when we had a clear idea of "the best way" to solve a problem, only to discover that the solution had its own problems when implemented. If we had been compelled to keep the original approach, we would have ended up with a program that wasn't very easy to use, and wasn't very reliable. The moral of the story is that you often learn the real problems that you're trying to solve only after you've done a few experiments.

Designing the User Interface

Every program has a user interface, particularly Visual Basic programs. The user interface is the part of the program that you see on the screen, and the part that responds to your key presses and mouse clicks. Because of the way Visual Basic is designed (in other words, because of its user interface), designing the user interface for your own programs is quite different from the way it's done in other computer languages, so we'd like to spend a few paragraphs talking about these differences.

Most programmers don't start with the user interface (the look and feel of the screens) when they start to work on a program. Instead, they tend to start working on the code inside of the program that does the hard (and for many programmers, interesting) work.

For example, in the Address Book program, many programmers would start by writing the code that handles working with the disk file used to store names and addresses. Why would they start there? The answer has a lot to do with history.

If you look at most programming languages (and systems), they don't offer many tools for building the user interface. In other words, if you want a window with a button in it, you have to write quite a bit of code before you can get such a program to work. This is very different from Visual Basic. In Visual Basic you can build the same program in a matter of minutes (if that long) and have it running without writing a single line of code. That's why Microsoft calls it *Visual* Basic.

Because other languages require so much work to build an interface, programmers tend to tackle the "easy" part first—they would start with the "core" part of the project. But for a new programmer, this can be a very difficult approach. At this point you know enough to be able to write very simple programs, but you haven't learned yet how to read and write disk files. So even though we could start this project by working with disk files, it may not be the best approach.

One problem with leaving the user interface for last is that it tends to get the least amount of attention. Most programmers start to run out of energy by the time they get to the end of a project. If they save the user interface until the end, they don't have much energy (or interest) left for creating a good user interface.

But there are other reasons why it's not a good idea to leave the user interface for last. The first idea and design you have for a user interface may not be a very good one. Often you'll find that you have to actually try out your ideas before you discover how they feel. You may discover that other people have problems using a design you come up with. If this happens, the best thing to do is try to figure out why other people have problems with your design, and then try some other ideas. Leaving the interface until the end won't give you time to experiment.

Other parts of your program may also need to change if you change your idea of the interface. In other words, if you work on the interface first, you can design the rest of your program to fit the interface. But if you design the interface last, you're really designing the interface to fit the rest of your program, which isn't a very good solution.

All that said, people who start a new program by working on the user interface generally tend to design better programs than people who leave the user interface until last. Visual Basic makes designing the user interface first much easier.

So for the Address Book project, let's start by thinking about the user interface—what it should look like, and how people will interact with it.

The Initial Design

One final comment before we start to design the Address Book program: Anytime you create a design for a program, you should consider the design to be a preliminary design (as we've mentioned before), and you should allow yourself the freedom to change the design as you learn more about your program through building it.

Let's take a look at what we want the Address Book program to do, and how we want it to work. When we design a program, the very first thing we do is to come up with a short list of features we want in the program. In a sense, these are a set of objectives we have for the finished program. We also come up with some initial ideas for the user interface; these are usually sketches drawn on paper and filed away in a folder that we create for each program we have in mind.

For a simple program like an address book, it may not seem like there are many features you'll need in the program. After all, you just want to keep a list of names and addresses. But computer programs, unfortunately, aren't as simple as the paper analogies we're accustomed to. With a paper address book, there are a number of features already built in.

First of all, a typical address book has a number of pages that are divided into sections corresponding to the letters of the alphabet. We all know from experience that these sections are based on last name (although some people actually use first names rather than last names). Each page is also divided into sections, usually with ruled lines in each address, plus some boxes for phone numbers. All these elements, in a sense, are features.

Now let's take a look at how we'll need to transfer these ideas over to the computer. But first, a word of warning. Computers work with information very differently than we do, and things that might work well on paper may not be the best solutions when we try to implement them in a computer program.

For example, with an address book program, it doesn't really make sense to implement individual pages, with a number of addresses on each page, which you have to flip through on the screen. What makes more sense is to use your computer's ability to search for and find names. So instead of flipping pages looking for a name, you could type in the name of the person you're looking for. The computer would then search for that person and display their address and phone numbers.

Writing a Feature List

We're going to create a new design that uses your computer's abilities to be its best. The first thing we'll do, as mentioned above, is write down a list of *features* we want in this program. These features are sort of a list of what we want our program to be able to do. Here's how we'll build this list. First, we'll talk you through the thinking process we followed to come up with a feature list.Then we'll present the final list.

When you're writing a feature list, you'll often need to write down things that may seem obvious. Even though they're obvious, someone else might not think about doing it in the same way. For example, it's clear that we need to be able to type in names and addresses. But it isn't clear how you enter this information. Most address book programs we've seen and worked with have a number of fields marked First Name, Middle Initial, Last Name, Address Line 1, Address Line 2, City, State, and Zip Code. Figure 8.1 shows an example of what this might look like.

You might be wondering, and rightly so, why you have to enter the parts of addresses in separate fields, instead of simply typing the following information:

```
Joe M. Smith
Great Software Company
238 Somewhere Lane
Imaginary, CI 12345-6789
```

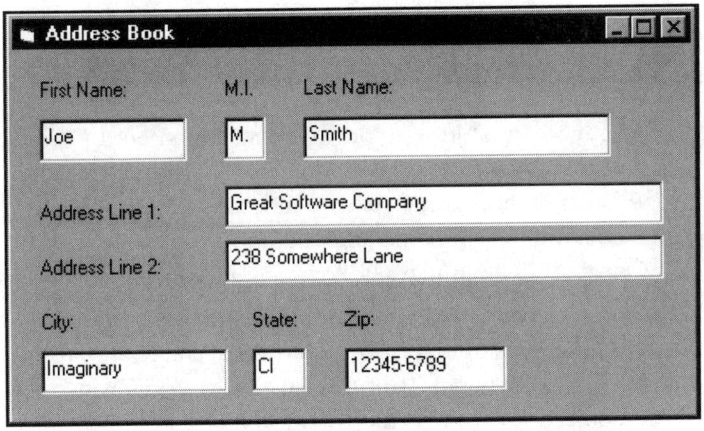

FIGURE 8.1 *Many address book programs require that you enter an address into separate fields.*

The reason most programs look like Figure 8.1, rather than the address above, is entirely historical. Most address book programs are built on top of *database programs*, which is a type of software designed specifically to store and retrieve data. By chopping addresses into separate fields, it's possible for the database to perform a number of functions such as sorting on last names, printing out address labels grouped by zip code (which gives you lower rates for bulk mail), listing people in a certain city, and so on.

In other words, the choice of a data entry form like the one shown in Figure 8.1 has much more to do with how a program's written than with how you interact with it. In the address book program we'll build here, we chose to take a very different approach to entering names and addresses. We wanted to be able to just type in names, so instead of having a number of text fields, we chose to have a single field for the entire name and address, that allows you to type in the address in any form. This is particularly useful for foreign addresses because they often have very different addresses, such as the following:

```
Joe M. Smith
"Hartley Cottage"
17 Beacon Place
Waymouth WA8 2ST
Dorset
ENGLAND
```

This address would be very hard, if not impossible, to type into the address form shown in Figure 8.1. So our first feature is that we want to be able to type in the entire address into a single field.

We'll also want to be able to type in phone numbers of different types. We've chosen to allow up to four phone numbers. Each phone number can be of a different type, such as fax, home, office, and car. We also like to be able to write notes that go along with a name and address, which is very useful for keeping track of information like birthdays, follow-up dates, or the purpose of a call.

For this address list to be really useful, however, you need to be able to use these names and addresses after you've typed them in. There are several ways you can do this. First, you might want to print out your address list so you can find names. Of course, you'll need these names to be in alphabetical order, so you'll need to make sure you have some way to sort the names. If you're working with your computer, rather than a printed list, you'll need to be able to type in a name (first or last or company) and have your computer search for the name, which is a lot easier than searching through a printed list.

Now that we've thought through the feature list, we can write it down as a bulleted list. The following is the list we used when we designed the address book program for you to use with this book. You can see that it's a sketch of we're where going to head, and it leaves a lot of details unspecified.

* **Name and address.** You'll use an input box that allows you to type multiple lines, which will allow you to type the address any way you want (Most programs require you to enter the first name, last name, middle initial, first address line, and so on in separate fields.)
* **Phone numbers (up to four).** You'll also want to keep track what each for number is for, such as fax, home, office, and car
* **Notes.** You should be able to write notes along with a name and address so you can remember small facts about a person (such as their spouse's or children's names)
* **Printing.** You'll want to be able to print out the address list so you can take it along in your briefcase.
* **Searching.** You should be able to search for any person by name or company name. For this feature you'll search the entire address information.
* **Sorting.** This may seem obvious, but you'll want to sort the names in alphabetical order. And as you'll see, this will actually take quite a bit of work.

Drawing the Screens

When we have a preliminary feature list put together, we will draw some sketches of what we want the screen to look like. Figure 8.2 shows the sketch John drew for the main screen, which is what you'll see most of the time when you're running the address book program.

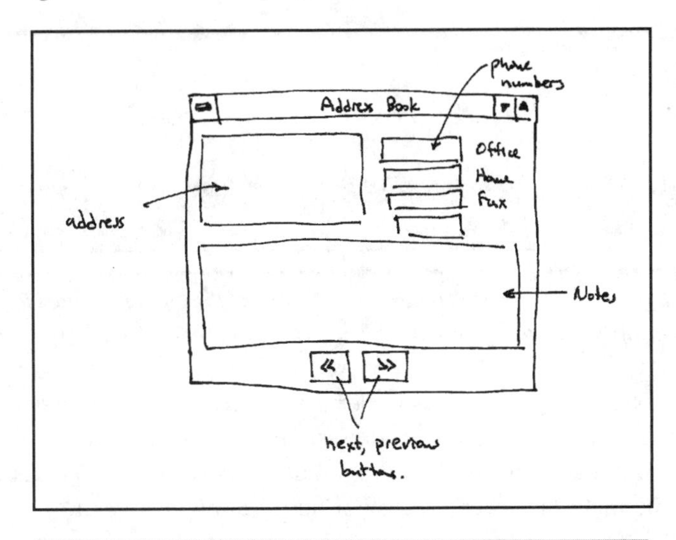

FIGURE 8.2 *Here is the pen sketch John drew for the address book program before starting to build the program on the computer.*

These sketches aren't exact drawings, so we usually end up making some small changes between the drawing and the actual program when we're finished. We also tend to change, remove, and add features to the program as we gain experience using the program. Often your best ideas will appear only after you've started to build a program, and they are usually triggered by something that happens when you're using what you've built so far. That's what happens to us when we're creating new programs. For example, Figure 8.3 shows the actual screen you'll end up with after the next few chapters.

As you can see, there are a few differences between this screen and the sketch in Figure 8.2. Most of the changes are rather small, and you'll see them appear as we build the program. But we'll say a few short words here about the changes. First of all, you'll notice a menu bar that wasn't in the sketch. This menu bar provides a number of small functions you'll be adding later on in the development process. Initially, you'll build the Address Book program without a menu bar.

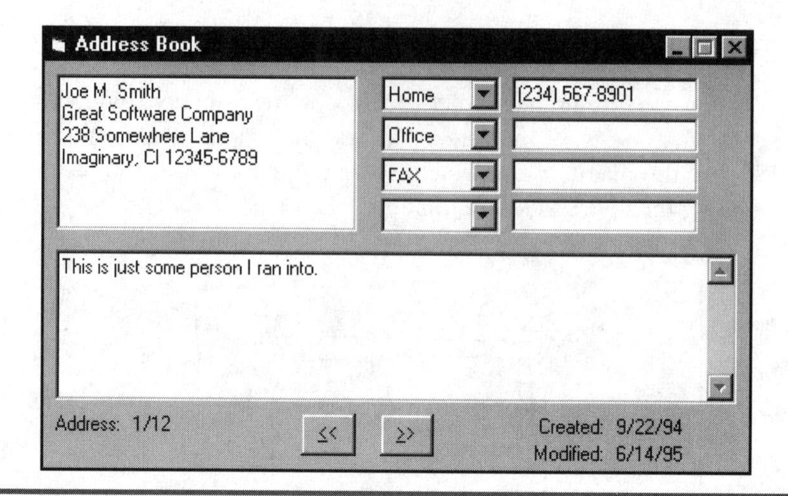

FIGURE 8.3 *The Address Book program you'll have at the end of the next few chapters. This is fairly close to the sketch in Figure 8.2, but there are some differences.*

You'll also notice a few text fields under the notes area. On the left side is a display that shows you how many addresses are currently in the file. The 12/11 means that you're adding a 12th address, but it hasn't been saved yet to the file. (It's saved automatically when you're finished making changes.)

There are also two dates on the right side. The top date shows the date that you initially created an address in the file. The lower date shows when you last changed an address. These dates are useful for keeping track of how old your information is, and is especially useful when you have two addresses for someone and you're not sure which is more current.

Building Programs

Just as there are a number of ways to design programs, there are also a number of ways to go about building large programs. We'd like to spend a few paragraphs talking about the different approaches.

Add Features First, Test Later

Most software companies start with a detailed design specification and then hand it over to a team of programmers. This team of programmers writes code to implement all of the features in the program. When all of the features are implemented, the software goes into a testing phase called *alpha* testing. In alpha testing, most of the features are implemented, more or less, but many of them aren't working correctly. The idea is that the program will be far enough along that you can start to work with it and identify any problems with the design.

The problem, however, is that alpha testing starts fairly late in the development cycle, so by the time you get to alpha testing, it's hard to make any major changes in your design. If you do have to make major changes, you may have to throw out large chunks of the program that will cause major delays in the release of your software. Not good.

The next stage of testing is called *beta* testing. During this phase of testing all of the features should be working correctly, but there are usually a large number of bugs left in the program that keep it from working reliably. The last phase of development is a mad scurry to eradicate all the bugs in the program, and often takes several months. (Some companies have spent six months or more just trying to fix all the bugs in a program.)

The Origin of the Term Bug

One of the first modern-day computers to be built was the Harvard Mark I computer, which was built in the early 1940s. One hot day in the summer of 1945, the Mark I computer mysteriously failed. After a careful search, the programmers found the remains of a moth blocking an electrical relay inside the circuitry of the computer. They extracted the remains with a pair of tweezers and taped it into the logbook that they kept for their work on the Mark I computer for the U.S. Navy. Grace Hopper (who found the bug) recalled, "From then on, when the officer came in to ask if we were accomplishing anything, we told him we were 'debugging' the computer."

The term stuck, and today a bug is some type of failure in a computer program. Programmers *debug* programs by looking for the problem and fixing it. A program that has a large number of design and/or reliability problems is said to be a *buggy* program.

Add, Test, Redesign

In contrast (many programmers and managers don't agree with us on this one), we believe you should start alpha testing as soon as possible, usually within a few months of starting development (as opposed to a year or more down the line). We also believe that each alpha release of the program should be very reliable. The only difference between an alpha release and the final program (in our scheme) is that all the features won't be implemented yet. But any features that are implemented should be reliable.

When we're building a program, we start by implementing some core features. As each feature is implemented, we carefully test each one so that we'll have a debugged and reliable program when we finish the first part. This initial program won't be very useful because it won't have many features implemented, but it will allow us to start using the program as quickly as possible.

Then we start to add other features. Each time we add a feature, we test it both to make sure it works correctly under all cases, and that it "feels" right. In other words, we start usability testing very early on in the development. The earlier you start such testing, the easier it is to change your mind about how you want your program to work.

Oftentimes we'll partly implement a feature so we can get a sense for how it will feel and work. This is before we've invested much time handling all of the special cases that will make the feature general-purpose and reliable. By doing our testing early on, we can easily make major changes to the design without affecting the final schedule. More importantly, because we're doing all the reliability testing as we're writing the program rather than during the beta test period, we're doing all the work on each problem while it's still fresh in our minds.

John used this very approach when he was developing the *Norton Commander*, which is a program designed to make DOS easier to use. After about a month, he had a program that he could work with, but it didn't do very much. After about two or three months, he had a program that was actually somewhat useful, and he put it into alpha testing and had several other people using the program in their normal work. The final program wasn't finished until about a year later, so he had a full year to do reliability and usability testing, and he got valuable feedback on his design very early on, when it was still easy to make changes.

What's most interesting about this approach, however, is that there really wasn't much of a beta-test period. The total beta-test period for the Norton Commander lasted about one month, which is very short in this industry. But the best part is that there were no major bugs in the Norton Commander. Version 3.0, which is the last release John worked on, was on the market for over two years without any major bugs being reported.

Allegory I

We've had many opportunities to beta test software for a number of companies (they almost never let outsiders see alpha software). We've reported some problems and made lots of suggestions, but so often the response is, "That's a really good idea! But at this point, it's too late for us to make any changes like that." In other words, even though the beta test period should allow you to change your design, in reality it's almost always too late.

Devra likes to follow a similar approach when designing interactive multimedia titles. Such titles tend to be information rich and quite complex, but by asking potential users to try out the interfaces early on, she can make changes and incorporate suggestions before it's too late.

Allegory II

When John was a junior in college, he was taking a Plasma Physics exam, and partway through the exam his professor came over and said, "Stop. You're writing too quickly and making too many mistakes. Slow down and do everything slowly and carefully. You'll finish sooner and make fewer mistakes." He was right.

John has remembered the professor's words of advice ever since and believes they're true for almost everything you do. They are certainly true for programming.

What is Good Design?

There is no single answer to this question. In many ways, good design is a matter of opinion, which means that it's very important that you test your designs out on other people. Unless your program's designed for other programmers, you should try out your programs on real users—people who don't have any programming or technical experience, but who would use the program you're writing.

When you do test your programs on users, you'll probably be frustrated. They won't understand how to use your program the way you do, and they'll make mistakes. When they do make mistakes, don't correct them. If you correct them and explain the right way to do things, you're not really testing your program, you're simply teaching someone how to use it.

So when a user has problems with your program, resist the urge to teach. Instead, try to ask questions so you can understand why they're having problems with your design. This is very hard to do because you first have to admit that the design you worked so hard on may have some flaws. But if you do open your mind and try to find out why someone is having problems with your design, you can learn a lot. And then you'll be able to think about how you could improve your design to make it easier to learn and use. The thing to remember is that any design, no matter how good, can be improved.

There are several ways to learn good design. One way is to work with as many different Windows programs as you can, so you can learn from other programmers. Programs written by Microsoft are considered by many to be the *de facto* standard for user interface design, but even Microsoft doesn't always do a good job. But, they're spending a lot of time and effort on testing and redesigning the programs in usability labs, so you'll probably learn a lot from their programs.

Another good source of information is books. There are many books about user interface design, and about program design in general. We have our own favorites, which we've listed below.

- Norman, Donald A. *The Design of Everyday Things.* New York: Basic Books, 1988. If you only read one book from this list, read this one. It should open your eyes to the problems that ordinary people have with common, everyday designs. And it should give you some insight into how to build designs that get around these problems.
- Heckel, Paul. *The Elements of Friendly Software Design.* Second edition. Alameda, CA: Sybex, 1991. This useful book can help you gain a better understanding of the things you should think about when you're designing user interfaces.
- Laurel, Brenda. *The Art of Human-Computer Interface Design.* Reading, MA: Addison-Wesley, 1990. This book is a collection of papers and articles published on user interface design and is a very good book to have around. It has much more information about graphical environments (like Macintosh and Windows) than the other two books, and covers far more ground.
- Brooks, Frederick P. Jr. *The Mythical Man-Month.* Reading, MA: Addison-Wesley, 1975. Anyone developing computer software should read this book. You'll learn a lot about why it's difficult to use classical management techniques with software projects.

✷ Microsoft Corp. *Microsoft Windows User Interface Style Guide.* Seattle, WA: Microsoft.

Summary

Chapter 8 has been more philosophical than other chapters in the book, but it's good to know more about designing programs. The following is a quick review of the material in this chapter:

✷ **Specification.** You'll probably want to write some type of design specification for any programs you write, except for very small programs. Such documents can be anywhere from a page or two to 100 pages (although we believe there is such a thing as a spec with too much detail).

✷ **User interfaces.** Learning how to design good user interfaces is very important, and it's something not everyone can become an expert at. And you certainly can't become an expert in a vacuum. Talk with other people and see how they interact with your programs. Ask questions, and don't succumb to the temptation to explain to your testers how to use your program. You should also read some books like the ones we listed above.

✷ **Building programs.** Just as there are many opinions on how you should design a program, so too are there many opinions on how you should build your programs once you have a design. We tend to view a program as a living entity that has a soul of its own. Our job (and yours, should you choose to accept it) is to learn what that soul is and redesign and write the program to best bring out that soul. This is a very evolutionary process, rather than a straight-forward coding task.

✷ **Testing.** It's very important that you test your programs, and we'll have much more to say about this in Chapter 10, where you'll really get down to the work of building the Address Book program. There is an art to testing your programs, which begins with being skeptical about whether your program really works correctly.

✷ **Address Book design.** We spent some time in this chapter writing a short design specification for the Address Book program you'll be building in the next few chapters.

BUILDING ADDRESS BOOK'S INTERFACE

* Creating controls
* Creating a Program Manager icon for your projects
* New controls: text boxes, labels, command buttons, and combo boxes
* Controlling tab order
* Methods—subroutines defined as part of a control
* Setting up combo boxes

In this chapter, you're going to start building the Address Book program we designed in the last chapter. As you'll recall, we sketched a design for Address Book and wrote down a short list of features that you'll put into the program. In this chapter you'll work mainly on the user interface, the part of the program that you see. You'll start by drawing all the controls on the form and setting their properties. When you have all the controls, you'll start bringing Address Book to life by adding some code. You'll continue this process in the next few chapters by bringing more and more of Address Book to life.

Creating the Controls

The way you go about building a program in Visual Basic is really quite different from the way you would do it in any other language. In Visual Basic, you start by drawing controls on a form, which can take quite a bit of work, but doesn't involve writing a single line of code. In most other languages, creating the user interface is something programmers do much later because it requires writing quite a bit of code. In other words, drawing the user interface in Visual Basic is a *lot* easier than writing code to create the same interface.

As you can see in Figure 9.1, you'll draw a total of 18 controls on this form, not including the menu bar, that you'll add in a later chapter.

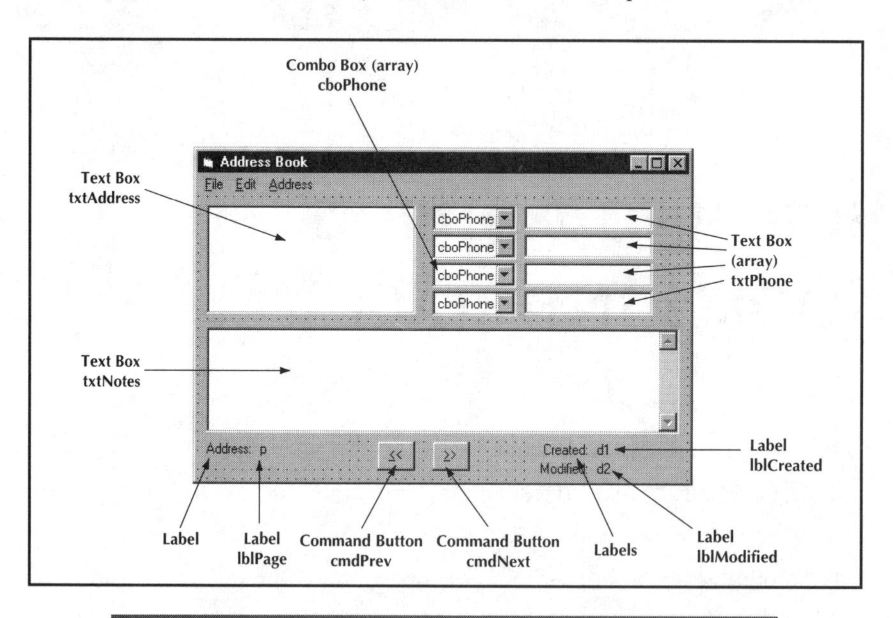

FIGURE 9.1 *These are all the controls you'll add to the main form. Notice the names for each control (expect for the labels that won't change).*

There are a number of ways you can go about drawing the controls on a form to match the design in Figure 9.1. First, you could just draw all the controls on the form, and then align them and set their sizes later. Or, you can draw each control in place, and set its size before you draw the next control. We tend to do a little of both, and we keep moving the controls around on the form until everything looks nice. In other words, we do a lot of experimenting.

It's a good idea to experiment so that you can get an idea of what works and what doesn't work. But it's also a little frightening. What happens if you have a nice design, and then you start changing it? How can you get back to a previous design you preferred? The way we solve this problem is to save a copy of the form whenever we have a design we like. You can use the File Manager in Windows to make a copy of the .FRM file. If you decide later that you really want to go back to a previous design, you'll still have a copy of the .FRM file you liked.

You'll probably settle on an approach to drawing controls that works best for you after you've worked with Visual Basic for a while. Here you're going to go through the steps of drawing each control and setting its size and location before you go on to the next control. You can do this because you've already spent some time experimenting with the size and locations of the controls.

NOTE

You're free to make your controls any size you want and place them wherever you want on your form—Address Book will work correctly no matter where the controls are or how large they are. So feel free to redesign the look of Address Book. The only thing you'll need to ensure is that all of the control names and other properties (except Left, Top, Width and Height) match the ones in Table 9.1 later in this chapter.

A Step-by-Step Approach

In the detailed instruction below, we'll include the size and location of each control so you can make these controls the same size as in Figure 9.1. All of these sizes will be in twips, because that's the default measurement scale used by Visual Basic.

There are two ways that you can set the location and size of a control. First, you can use the information shown in the Tool bar (see Figure 9.2). When you drag controls around on the form and resize them, the Tool bar tells you the size of the control and the location of its top-left corner.

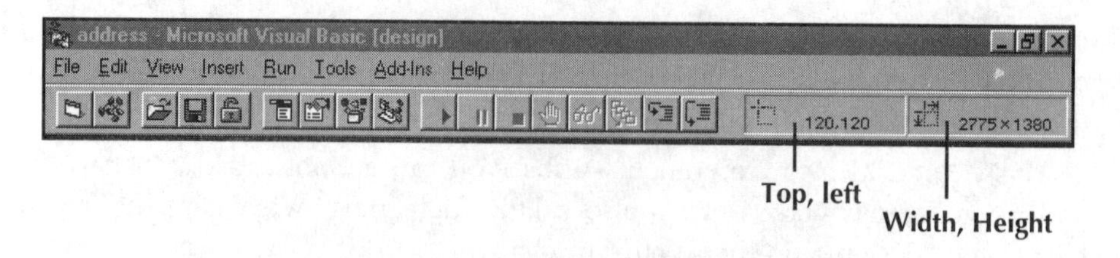

FIGURE 9.2 *The Tool bar showing the Top, Left, Width, and Height values for the selected object txtAddress.*

Your other option is to directly set the Top, Left, Width, and Height properties of a control. Doing so will change the size and location of a control to match the numbers you type in.

Both of these methods work very well, so which one you choose really depends on your own preference.

KEYBOARD SHORTCUTS IN THE PROPERTIES WINDOW

There are a number of very useful keyboard shortcuts you can use to help you navigate the Properties bar (these are documented in the on-line help, but because they're hard to find we've summarized them as follows):

Ctrl+Shift*alpha*	**Select property.** Select the property that starts with the letter alpha in the Properties window. Pressing Ctrl+Shift*alpha* again selects the next property that starts with the same letter.
alpha	**Change Setting**. Typing any character when the form is active will change the value in the Settings box. For settings like Caption, pressing a key inserts that character and activates the Properties window. If the Settings box is a combo box, typing a letter selects the first option that starts with the letter (or number) you typed.
Esc	**Cancel changes.** Cancels changes you've made to the setting.
Enter	**Accept Setting.** Accepts the changes in the Settings.
F4, Alt +	**Drop combo box.** Pulls down the active combo box. If the Settings box has a **...** button at the end, pressing one of these keys is the same as pressing the **...** button.

As you'll recall from Chapter 7, you draw controls on a form by clicking first on the control in the Toolbox (see Figure 9.3) that you want to draw. Then click and drag inside the form to tell Visual Basic where, and how large, you want the control.

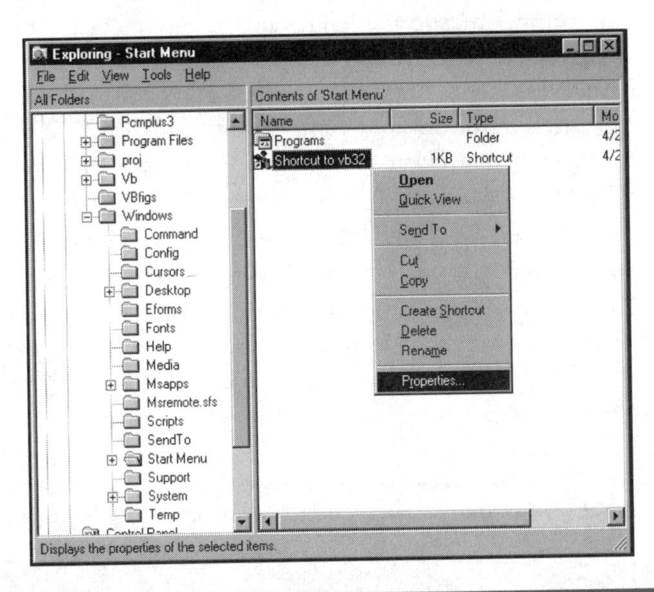

FIGURE 9.3 *Visual Basic's Toolbox allows you to add controls (objects) to your forms.*

Creating Control Arrays

Before you draw any controls on the form, we need to say a few words about control arrays. As you'll recall from Chapter 5, control arrays are groups of controls that all have the same name, and you use the Index property to distinguish between each control in the array. The Address Book program uses two control arrays: One for the Phone combo boxes (which tell you whether a number is a home, office, fax, or car phone) and one for the phone number text boxes.

To create a control array of combo boxes, all you have to do is give each control the same control name and assign a value to the Index property for each control. That's all there is to it. In Figure 9.1 you'll find all the information you need to create control arrays, but we've removed a lot of the redundant information. For example, in the entries for the Combo boxes, the first seven lines list all of the properties you'll need to set for the first control in the array, as well as the other three controls in this array. The next six lines list the properties that are different for the last three controls in this array. When you create the controls in an array, make sure you set all the properties for all the controls in the array.

There's also a simpler way you can do this. Create the first control in an array and set all its properties to the values in Table 9.1. Then click on this control and press **Ctrl+C** (or select **Copy** from the Edit menu) to copy this control to the clipboard. Next press **Ctrl+V** (or select **Paste** from the Edit menu) to paste a copy of this control on your form. Finally, move this new control from the upper-left corner (where pasted controls appear) into place (or set the Top property) and set the Index property.

Now you'll need to create all of the controls shown in Figure 9.1. You can use the information in Table 9.1 to create a form that looks exactly like the one shown in Figure 9.1, or you can try to create the form yourself, without using any of the information in Table 9.1. If you forget which control is which in the Toolbox, go back and look at Figure 9.3. You'll be using the Text Box, Label, and Command controls.

TABLE 9.1 *Properties for Each Control in the Address Book program.*

Object	Property	Setting
Form	Appearance	1-3D
	BorderStyle	1 – Fixed Single
	Caption	Address Book
	Height	4020
	MaxButton	False
	Name	Address
	Width	6615
Text Box	Height	1380
	Left	120
	Height	1380
	MultiLine	True
	Name	txtAddress
	Top	120
	Width	2775

continued

Object	Property	Setting
Combo Box (array)	Index	0
	Index	0
	Left	3120
	Name	cboPhone
	Style	2 – Dropdown List
	Top	120
	Width	1095
	Index	1
	Top	480
	Index	2
	Top	840
	Index	3
	Top	1200
Text Box (array)	Height	300
	Height	300
	Index	0
Text Box	Left	4320
	Name	txtPhone
	Text	
	Top	120
	Width	2055
	Index	1
	Top	480
	Index	2
	Top	840
	Index	3
	Top	1200

continued

Object	Property	Setting
Text Box	Height	1335
	Left	120
	Height	1335
	MultiLine	True
	Name	txtNotes
	ScrollBars	2 – Vertical
	Top	1680
	Width	6255
Label	Caption	Address:
	Height	255
	Left	120
Label	Top	3120
	Width	615
Label	Caption	p
	Caption	p
	Height	255
	Left	840
	Name	lblPage
	Top	3120
	Width	1095
Label	Alignment	1 – Right Justify
	Caption	Created:
	Height	255
	Left	4440
	Top	3120
	Width	735

continued

Object	Property	Setting
Label	Caption	d1
	Caption	d1
	Height	255
	Left	5280
	Name	lblCreated
	Top	3120
	Width	1095
Label	Alignment	1 – Right Justify
	Caption	Modified:
	Height	255
	Left	4440
	Top	3360
	Width	735
Label	Caption	d2
	Caption	d2
	Height	255
	Left	5280
	Name	lblModified
	Top	3360
	Width	1095
Command Button	Caption	&<<
	Height	375
	Left	2400
	Name	cmdPrev
	Top	3120
	Width	495

continued

Object	Property	Setting
Command Button	Caption	&>>
	Height	375
	Left	3120
	Name	cmdNext
	Top	3120
	Width	495

When you're all finished creating these controls, there is one last thing you'll want to do. You'll notice that all six text boxes currently contain the text *Text1*, which is the default text you'll see in each text box when you run Address Book. This initial string isn't very useful, and you'll probably want all the text boxes to be empty. What you'll need to do is set the Text property of each control to nothing. How do you do this?

The easiest way to clear the default text in a text box is as follows. First, click on a text box and select the Text property in the Properties window; and then press the **Spacebar**, **Backspace**, and **Enter**. This has the effect of setting the default text to nothing. You can also use the mouse to select the property value in the Properties window, and then press **Backspace** to delete it. Finally, press **Enter** to accept this change.

Make sure you set the Text property for all six text boxes to nothing. You'll see the default text inside each text box, so it's easy to tell when you've cleared the default text.

Save Your Work

Make sure you save your project, by choosing **Save Project** from the File menu, after you've created all of these controls (or even before that). When Visual Basic prompts you for the project and form name, use ADDRESS.MAK and ADDRESS.FRM.

Creating a Start Menu Item

Because you'll be working a lot with this project in the next few chapters, you may want to create an item on your desktop Start menu that will launch Visual

Basic and automatically load your Address project. Setting up such a menu item isn't very hard, but it may not be obvious how you do so.

First, using the Windows Explorer window, double-click on your Windows folder so that you can see all of the files and other folders that it contains. Then find the directory to which you installed Visual Basic 4.0 (on Devra's system that's the vb folder), find the vb32 application file, and drag it over to the Start Menu folder that is inside the Windows folder, as shown in Figure 9-4. (Don't worry, you're not moving the file. This process just creates a Windows 95 Shortcut object.)

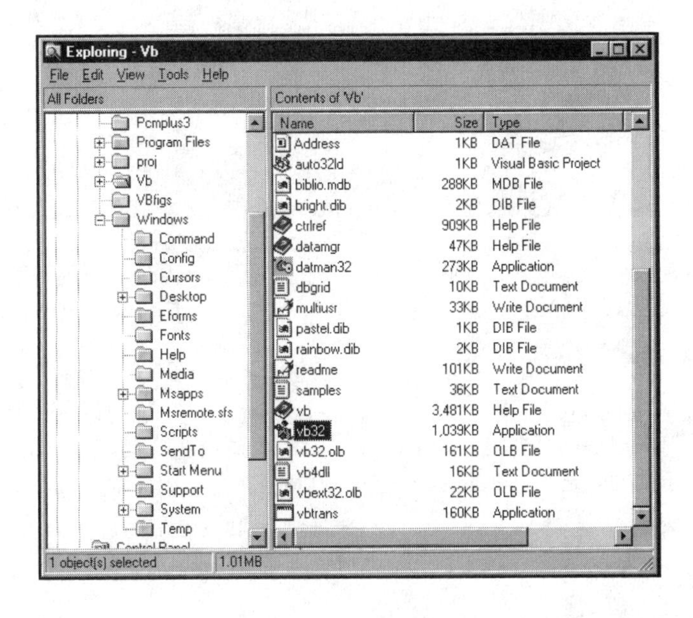

Figure 9.4 *In this Explorer window you can see the vb32.exe file in the VB folder, as well as the folders inside of the Windows folder.*

Next, navigate to the Start Menu folder so that you can see its contents. Click once to select the Shortcut to vb32 object, and then right-mouse click to display the pop-up menu as shown in Figure 9-5. Choose the Properties... menu item, and when the window appears, select the Shortcut page. This is where you can define the settings that will not only run Visual Basic, but will load your project file.

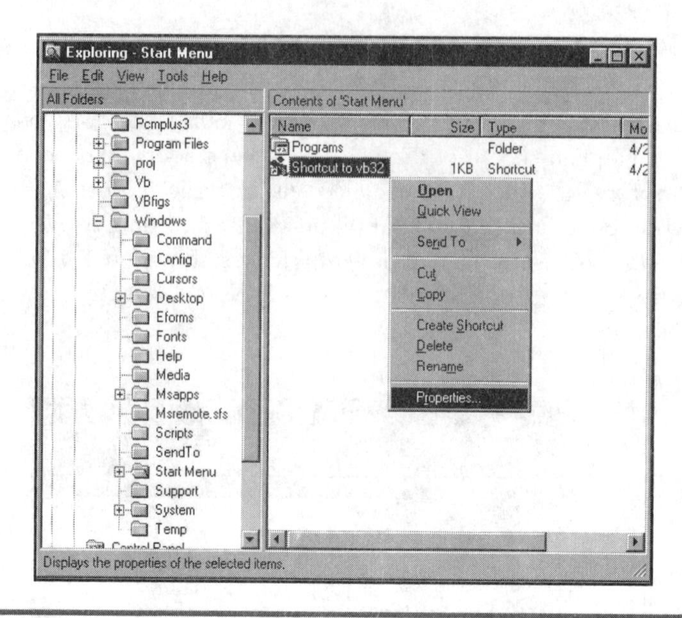

Figure 9.5 *In this Explorer window you can see the Shortcut to vb32 object inside the Start Menu folder. The object's pop-up menu is displayed with the Properties... item highlighted.*

For example, let's say you installed Visual Basic into the folder C:\VB and your saved your project in a folder called C:\PROJ\ADDRESS1. You would enter the following information, as shown in Figure 9-6:

Target `c:\vb\vb32.exe c:\proj\address1\address.vbp`

Start in `c:\proj\address1`

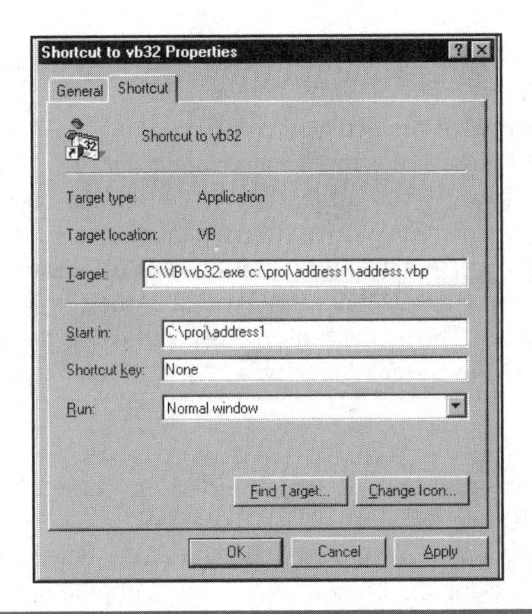

Figure 9.6 *The Shortcut page of the Shortcut to vb32 Properties dialog window.*

Target specifies what program will run when you click on the icon. In this case it will run VB32.exe, and it will tell Visual Basic 95 to load the Address project file (ADDRESS.VBP) into it after Visual Basic starts.

Start in allows you to secify which directory will be the current directory when the program first starts. Because Address Book will be creating files, it's really better to have the current directory be the same as your project's directory so any files Address Book creates will be in its, rather than Visual Basic's, directory.

When you run a program, Windows always sets the current directory to that program's directory unless otherwise specified. So the current directory for projects you run from within Visual Basic would use Visual Basic's directory as the current directory. On the other hand, any programs you turned into EXE files, and then run as EXE files, will see their directory as the current directory. In other words, programs will have one of two current directories, depending on whether you run them from within Visual Basic or as stand-alone EXE files. This is the reason we need to use the Start in option to change the current directory.

If you want, you can also change the icon. Click on **Change Icon...** to bring up a dialog box from which you can select a new icon. As you'll see in a moment, we chose the letter A icon usually used for Write files. When you're done selecting an icon, and making the other changes discussed, the new icon will appear in you Explorer window.

There's one more thing to fix. The object is still named Shortcut to vb32, so we suggest that you rename it. Once again, select the object, right click and select **Rename** from the pop-up menu, type in Address Book, and press **Enter** to save the new name.

Now the point of all of this was to create an expedient way to launch your Address Book project. Close your Explorer window now, and take a look at your desktop Start menu. It should look something like he one in Figure 9-7.

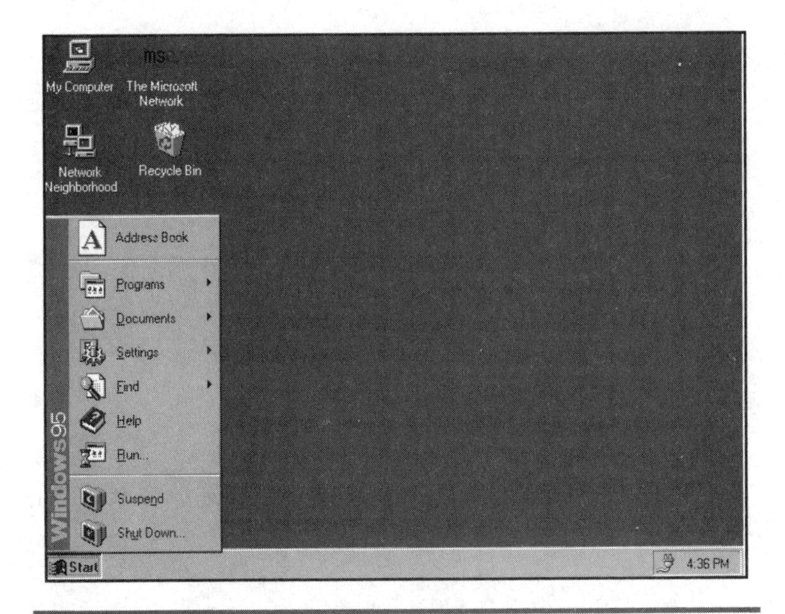

Figure 9.7 *A Windows 95 desktop with the Start menu extended to show the new Address Book menu item.*

Overview of Controls and Properties

Address Book contains several controls we haven't discussed before, so we'd like to take some time to cover these new controls, and the meaning of some of the properties connected with these controls.

Text Boxes

The first new type of control is the text box, which provides a simple text input field. You can type any text into such fields, but you can't change the font, style, or size of individual characters—all of the characters in a text box share a single font, style, and size. So you can't use a text box to implement a word processor, but you can use it to edit simple text.

Address Book uses two variations on the text box: single- and multiline. The single-line text boxes allow you to type in only one line of text. If you press Enter inside a single-line text box, Visual Basic will beep. This is the default behavior for Visual Basic's text boxes.

You can also create multiline text boxes by setting a text box's MultiLine property to True. After you make this change, your text box will support many lines of text. You can even add a scroll bar to a text box by setting the ScrollBars property to a value other than 0 – None. For example, the txtNotes text box has the ScrollBars property set to 2 – Vertical to add just a vertical scroll bar to the text box (you can also add a horizontal scroll bar, or both vertical and horizontal scroll bars).

If your text box doesn't have a horizontal scroll bar, Windows automatically word-wraps long lines just as a word processor does. Text boxes are really quite powerful, and you'll probably use them in many of your own projects.

Labels

Any time you want to display text on a form without the ability to edit it, you'll need to use a label control. Address Book contains a total of six labels: three act as titles and the other three are used to display information, such as the date that you created an address-book entry. In a later chapter, you'll write some code that sets the Caption property of lblCreated and lblModified to show the dates that each address was created and last modified.

Labels have a property called Alignment that allows you to control how text will be formatted inside of its box. You can choose between flush left (the text starts at the left side), centered (the text is centered left to right inside the box) and flush right (the lines of text touch the right, rather than left, side of the label box). All Visual Basic labels are left-aligned when you first create them. If you used the settings in Figure 9.1, you've set the Created and Modified labels to right justified.

Command Buttons

You'll use two command buttons to show the previous and next address in your address book. Each command button has a Click event that you'll use in a later chapter. For now, setting the Caption property and the Name is enough. As with menu items, you can place an & in a command button's caption to create a mnemonic access character. When you set the caption of cmdPrev to &<<, pressing Alt+< is the same as clicking on this button.

Combo Boxes

Address Book has four combo boxes that allow you to select the type of phone number that appears in each of the txtPhone text boxes. These combo boxes allow you to choose from a list of options, that you'll set to Home, Office, fax, Direct, and Car because these are the common types of telephone numbers. You'll be able to add your own types of phone numbers if you want.

The names in these combo boxes are names that you add to a list with lines of code you write. You can't set up a list of names as you design your program. Instead, you have to write some code that will set the names in each combo box when Address Book first starts. You'll learn how to do this later.

One of the combo box settings listed in Figure 9.1 is the Style property, which you set to 2 — drop-down list. There are actually three types of combo boxes you can use in your programs, but you'll only use the drop-down list style here.

Form Properties

There are also several new properties you'll use in the form. Before version 4.0, we used Visual Basic's BackColor property to changes the color used for the background (as opposed to the foreground, which is the color used for the characters and lines). While the BackColor property is still available, we like the nice recessed 3-D effect afforded by the new Auto3D property, and when that is set to True, Visual Basic ignores BackColor setting. (When 3-D is not appropriate for the look you want, use BackColor.) The settings suggested in Figure 9.1 sets the background color to light gray, which is more appealing than the standard all-white background. It also means that the white areas show you quite clearly where you can make changes. Any text with a gray background provides information, and can't be changed.

If you follow the settings suggested in Figure 9.1, you may or may not end up with a light gray background. Why? Because when Auto3D is set to True, Visual Basic looks at your Windows system Control Panel and adopts whatever color you set for Button Face.

The standard border for Visual Basic's forms allows you to change the size of a form. In this case, however, our design doesn't allow you to change the size of the form when Address Book is running. We designed Address Book to be one, and only one size. When you set BorderStyle to 1 — Fixed Single, you made it so the border won't have resizing corners.

Whenever you change the border style so you don't have resizing corners, you'll probably want to remove the maximize button as well, which is exactly what the MaxButton property controls. Following our settings, you've set MaxButton to False so you won't have a maximize button (this also removes the Maximize option from the control menu.

New Properties

There are several new properties that Address Book uses:

Control	Property	Meaning
Form	Appearance	Gives the form a recessed 3-D look, and automatically sets the background color to the match the Windows system Button Face color setting.
	BackColor	Sets the background color used for the form.
	BorderStyle	Controls what type of border your window will have; whether it's fixed or resizable, and whether it's a thin or wide line.
	MaxButton	Determines whether or not your form will have a Maximize button.
Combo Box	Style	Controls which type of combo box you'll get—there are three types.

Command Button	Caption	The name you'll see on the button. You can include an & in the name to create a mnemonic access character.
Labels	Alignment	Controls how the text inside a label is aligned: Left justified, centered, or right justified.
	Caption	The text you see inside the label.
Text Box	MultiLine	Controls whether text boxes can have more than one line of text.
	ScrollBars	Allows you to add scroll bars to multi-line text boxes.
	Text	This property contains all the text you type into a text box. We'll use it later to get and set the text for each address.

Bring Address Book to Life

You should now have an Address Book program you can run, but it doesn't do very much. Go ahead and run your program and experiment with typing text into the text fields. You'll notice you can type multiple lines of text into both the txtAddress and txtNotes text boxes, and you can use the Enter key to start new lines in these text boxes. On the other hand, Visual Basic beeps whenever you press Enter inside one of the phone number text boxes.

Controlling the Tab Order

Now try using the Tab key to move between the different controls. Each time you press the Tab key, a different control in your program will receive the *focus.* The control with the current focus is the control that responds to keys you press on your keyboard. In other words, the focus refers to which control has the keyboard's focus of attention.

For example, when a text box has the current focus, anything you type will appear inside that text box. When a command button has the focus, pressing the Spacebar has the same effect as clicking on that control with the mouse button.

Not all controls are capable of receiving the focus from the keyboard. Labels, for example, can respond to mouse clicks, but *not* to keyboard events, so labels will never receive the current focus. The controls in Address Book that can receive focus are the text boxes, the combo boxes, and the command buttons.

Each time you press the Tab key, Visual Basic uses a property called TabIndex to determine which control should receive the focus next. Whenever you create new controls on a form, Visual Basic assigns TabIndex values to each one, starting with 0 and counting up. If you created the controls in the order shown in Table 9.1, you'll probably notice that the Tab order is fairly reasonable.

But what if you decide you want to change the Tab order? How can you do this? All you have to do is change the TabIndex property for each control.

Reference: TabIndex Property

Visual Basic uses the TabIndex property to determine which control will receive the focus next when you press the Tab key. Here's how it works. Every time you press the Tab key, Visual Basic looks at the value of TabIndex for the control that currently has the focus, and then it scans through the controls looking for the next highest TabIndex number. If this new control can accept the keyboard focus, Visual Basic moves the focus to this control. Otherwise it looks for the next higher TabIndex value, until it finds a control with a higher TabIndex value.

When there are no more controls with higher TabIndex values, Visual Basic starts over again with 0 and looks for the first controls with a TabIndex of 0 or higher that can accept keyboard input.

When you first load a form, the control with the lowest TabIndex (usually 0) that can accept keyboard input will receive the focus.

Here's how you would set up a tab order. Click on the control you want to receive the focus when your program first starts, and set its TabIndex property to 0, and then click on the next control and set its TabIndex property to 1, and so on. Visual Basic will automatically adjust all the other TabIndex values if some control already has the TabIndex value you assign to a control. The TabIndex order we suggest for Address Book is as follows:

Name	TabIndex
txtAddress	0
txtPhone	1–4
txtNotes	5
cmdPrev	6
cmdNext	7
cboPhone	8–11

You'll notice we set the cboPhone combo boxes so they're last in the list. This order will make it easy for you to type in address and phone numbers using the default phone types (which will be Home, Office, and fax for the first three combo boxes). If you don't like this tab order, you can easily change it to anything you want.

Setting up the Combo Boxes

The combo boxes you'll be using here are called *drop-down lists* because whenever you click on the down-pointing arrow you'll see a list of options; these are the only options that you can choose from (the other two types of combo boxes allow you to type in any text you want).

We mentioned before that the phone combo boxes will have the following options: Home, Office, fax, Direct, and Car. As it turns out, it's also a nice idea to include a sixth option: a blank entry. Why do you want to include a blank entry? So you can have no label at all next to lines that will be blank. If you look at Figure 8.3 again (which shows what Address Book will look like when you're finished writing it) you can see that the bottom-most combo box is blank, which is possible because the last option is a blank.

Figure 9.8 shows what the phone combo boxes will look like when you have the list dropped down. As you can see, all six possibilities are in this combo box, in the order we wrote them above. You can put these entries in any order: We chose to put them in the order that made the most sense to us. But you may decide, for example, that you want the Office, Direct, and fax numbers to appear before the Home number. It's entirely up to you.

FIGURE 9.8 *The cboPhone combo boxes will look like this when you click on the down-pointing arrow.*

Let's look at how you can create this list in a combo box. Each combo box has a list of items you can select from. But when Visual Basic first creates a combo box (when it first loads a form), there are no entries in this list. So you, the programmer, have to add these items to the list.

When do you add items to the list? In this case the items will never change, so you can load the items into the list whenever your form is loaded into memory. As you saw in Chapter 7, the Form_Load event is called by Visual Basic every time a form is loaded. This is the best place to write code that will fill in the combo box's list, which you'll do next.

Method of Methods

But first, we need to cover another piece of jargon. Visual Basic has a number of commands you can apply to its objects. For example, you write Form1.Line to draw a line on the form called Form1. Form1 is an object, and the Line "command" is actually called a *method*. Many other objects also have methods, and the reason they're called methods has to do with a branch of computer science called *object-oriented programming* (no, you don't have to remember this part), or OOP as it's often known. In the world of OOP, functions that act on objects are called methods, rather than subroutines. They're called methods so it's clear that they're connected with a specific object instead of being a general-purpose subroutine.

WHAT ARE METHODS?

Methods are very much like subroutines, only different. Each object defined by Visual Basic (such as timers, text boxes, and so on) have a set of properties, events, and methods that are defined as part of the object. So in a sense, a method is really a subroutine attached to an object by a period. You call a method as follows:

```
object.method
```

Run the "subroutine" called *method* on the control (or form or printer) called *object.*

For example, to add an item called "Red" to a combo box called myCombo, you would write

```
myCombo.AddItem "Red"
```

Enough theory. Combo boxes, like any other object in Visual Basic, have a number of methods you can use to control them. One of these methods is called AddItem. The AddItem method adds a single item to your combo box. For example, if you have a combo box called myCombo and you want it to have two choices: Red and Green, you can write the following two lines of code to add these two items to the combo box's drop-down list:

```
myCombo.AddItem "Red"
myCombo.AddItem "Green"
```

THE ADDITEM METHOD

The AddItem Method allows you to add items to a combo box's list of possibilities (which you'll see when you click on the down-pointing arrow).

```
control.AddItem item$ [, index%]
```

Adds the item in *item$* to the control (which can be a combo box or a list box, which you haven't used yet). The optional parameter, *index%,* allows you to control where the item will be added in the list. Without this parameter, Visual Basic always adds the item to the end of your list.

You use the RemoveItem method to remove items.

Initializing the cboPhone Combo Boxes

The Address Book program has four different combo boxes you need to initialize using the AddItem method, and each combo box needs to have six items added to it. You need code that looks something like the following:

```
cboPhone(0).AddItem "Home"
cboPhone(0).AddItem "Office"
cboPhone(0).AddItem "FAX"
cboPhone(0).AddItem "Direct"
cboPhone(0).AddItem "Car"
cboPhone(0).AddItem ""
cboPhone(1).AddItem "Home"
cboPhone(1).AddItem "Office"
  .
  .
  .
```

The problem with this approach is that you need a total of 6 x 4 = 24 lines of code to add six items to each of the four combo boxes. That's a lot of code!

Fortunately, you can use the For..Next command you learned in Chapter 6 to reduce these 24 lines of code to just 8, as you can see here:

```
Sub Form_Load ()
  For i = 0 to 3
    cboPhone(i).AddItem "Home"
    cboPhone(i).AddItem "Office"
    cboPhone(i).AddItem "FAX"
    cboPhone(i).AddItem "Direct"
    cboPhone(i).AddItem "Car"
    cboPhone(i).AddItem ""
  Next i
End Sub
```

Add this code to the Form_Load event handler in your form and run Address Book. You should now have four combo boxes, each with a list of these six items.

It's a good idea to save your program before you run it in case your computer should crash (it happens) when you're running your program. It can be really frustrating to lose work, even if it's only five minutes' worth. One way to save your project is to press **Alt+F V**. An even easier way is to set Save Before Run (an Environment Option accessed from the Tools menu) to Save, Don't Prompt. That way the Save will be automatic and require no further action on your part. If you prefer, you can choose Save, Prompt to give you the option of bypassing the Save.

There is one small problem: All four combo boxes are initially empty, even though they now have the correct list of items. Fortunately, combo boxes have a property, called ListIndex, that you can set to tell it which item each combo box should currently have selected. When you first create a combo box, ListIndex is set to –1, which means that no item is currently set in the combo box.

LISTINDEX PROPERTY

The ListIndex property of a combo box allows you to select which entry in the drop-down list will be used in the combo box. Combo boxes start with ListIndex = –1, which means that no entry is currently selected. You can set it to any value between 0 and the number of items in the list – 1 as long as you have at least one item in the list.

Value	Meaning
–1	No item selected
0	The first item will be selected
1	The second item will be selected
n – 1	The last item will be selected, when there are *n* items in the list.

If you look in the Properties combo box when you have one of the cboPhone objects selected (in design mode), you'll notice there's no ListIndex property. Why not?

ListIndex is missing because it's a property that you can only read and set at run-time, and not at design time. All of the properties you've work with up till now were properties you could set at design time, and many of them, but not all, you could also set at run time. But, as you've just discovered, there are some properties you can only set at run time.

The reason you can only set ListIndex at run time is actually very simple. ListIndex can never be set to a value larger than the number of items in the list. And as you've discovered, the list is empty until your code adds some items to the list during the Form_Load event handler. In other words, the only allowed value for ListIndex is –1 (nothing selected) until you add some items to the list. At design time it doesn't really make sense to assign a value to ListIndex;, this is why Microsoft defined ListIndex as a run-time-only property.

Add the last four lines of code below to your Form_Load event handler so they appear *after* the For..Next loop:

```
    ...
    Next i

    cboPhone(0).ListIndex = 0     ' Set these combo boxes to
    cboPhone(1).ListIndex = 1     ' Home, Office, FAX, and blank
    cboPhone(2).ListIndex = 2
    cboPhone(3).ListIndex = 5
End Sub
```

These lines must appear after the For..Next loop so the combo boxes will have entries that you can select. If you put these lines before the For..Next loop, you'll get an Invalid property value error message from Visual Basic because the only ListIndex value that's valid for an empty list is –1.

Your program should look like Figure 9.9. Address Book's looking more and more like a real program. And you really haven't done that much work yet (believe it or not).

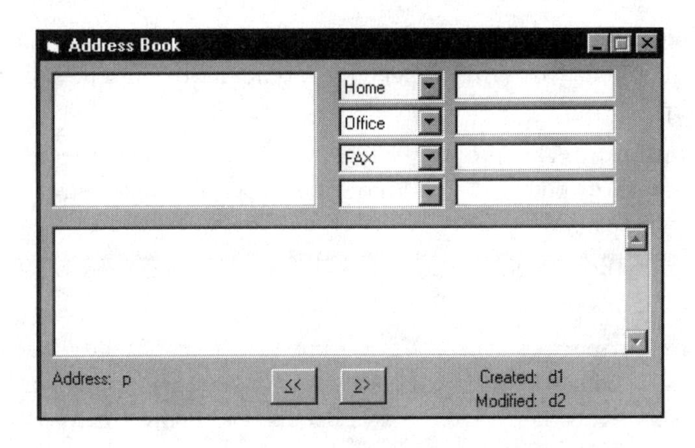

FIGURE 9.9 *Your version of Address Book should now look like this. Notice the combo boxes show the correct titles.*

You'll notice that the three information labels haven't been filled in yet (the ones that read p, d1, and d2). You won't start to use these labels until a later chapter, after you start to read and write addresses to disk.

Actually, when we originally designed and started to write Address Book programs, we didn't even have these labels in the program. We didn't add these labels until later. You may recall that they're not shown in John's pen sketch, shown in Figure 8.2. As you begin to write your programs from your initial specifications, you'll often have new ideas about what you want your program to do. You'll almost always find yourself adding or changing features in your program, as is the case with the three labels, that will report information on the current address.

Related Tools

✱ **RemoveItem.** The RemoveItem method allows you to remove items from combo or list boxes that you added with AddItem.

✷ **ListCount.** You can use the ListCount property (read-only, and only available at run time) to get the number of items in a combo box's drop-down list.

✷ **MinButton.** This property allows you to control whether your form has a Minimize button (it also controls whether the Control menu has a Minimize item).

✷ **ControlBox.** You can remove the control menu (and box) entirely by setting this property to False.

✷ **Font Properties.** There are a number of font properties, who's names all start with *Font,* that you can use to control the appearance of characters in text boxes, combo boxes, labels, and many other controls.

✷ **TabStop.** If you don't want the Tab key to be able to move to one of your controls (such as the cboPhone combo boxes), you can set TabStop to False. This property is called TabStop because it controls whether the focus can stop on a control when you press the Tab key.

Summary

At this point you have a user interface that is functional, but the Address Book program doesn't do very much right now. The next step, which you'll take in the next chapter, is to read and write all the information to a file on your disk.

The following is what you've learned in this chapter:

✷ **Drawing controls.** The Toolbar provides size read-outs that you can use to set the size of your controls. You can also set the Height, Width, Left, and Top properties using the Properties window.

✷ **Program Manager icon.** You learned how to create a Program Manager icon for your project, which is an easy way to start your projects.

✷ **Text boxes.** The text box control allows you to create text-entry sections in your forms. These text boxes can be limited to a single line of text, or you can allow multiple lines by setting the MultiLine property to True. You can also use the ScrollBars property to add scroll bars to any text box.

✱ **Labels.** These controls are useful anytime you want some text on your form that you don't need to be able to edit. You can use labels for static labels, and for information read-outs. Address Book has three read-out labels you'll use later to show information about the current address.

✱ **Command buttons.** Visual Basic makes it very easy to add command buttons to your programs.

✱ **Combo boxes.** These controls are the controls that you spent the most time on in this chapter. You learned how to add items to the lists attached to combo boxes using the AddItem method, and you learned how to select an item in a combo box using the ListIndex property.

✱ **Tab order.** The TabIndex property allows you to determine which control will receive the keyboard focus when you press the Tab key. Visual Basic looks for the control with the next-highest TabIndex that can accept keyboard input and sets the focus to that control. Shift+Tab moves the focus backwards through the same list.

✱ **Methods.** Methods are like subroutines, but they're defined as part of an object. In other words, a method is a predefined subroutine that you call using the *control.method* convention we used here.

✱ **AddItem method and ListIndex property.** The AddItem method allows you to add items to a list box's drop-down list. You can use the ListIndex property to select one of these items into the list box, but only at run-time. The ListIndex property can't be set until you run your program.

READING AND WRITING ADDRESS BOOKS

* Creating, reading, and writing disk files
* Random-access files
* User-defined variable types
* The global module
* Fixed-length strings
* Using on-line help
* Creating new subroutines
* When variables are visible

The next step in building the Address Book program is to write addresses to a disk file, and reading back later. To do this, you'll need to learn several new concepts. Rather than cover everything all at once, we'll go one step at a time so you can try out each new concept before you move on.

Here's the basic plan. First, we'll look at how you read and write disk files. You'll see that it's fairly easy to do. But it won't be easy to write all of the data Address Book needs because Visual Basic can only write a single type of data (Integer, String, etc.). So what you'll have to do is create a new type that packages all of this data into a single, new variable, which you'll then be able to read and write.

At the end of Chapter 10, you'll have a program that can save a single address to the disk. Each time you start Address Book, it will show this address. But you won't be able to add more than one address. For that, you'll need to do some more work, which you'll do in Chapter 11.

Working with Disk Files

If you know anything about working with disk files from other languages, the first thing you should do is forget everything you know. Visual Basic works with disk files a little differently than many other programming languages. In some ways, Visual Basic is simpler than other languages, and in some ways it's more confining.

The best way to understand Visual Basic's approach is to think about arrays of variables. You used arrays of variables in Chapter 6, where you used the array *saveX* to save the points in Sketch. It was defined like the following:

```
Dim saveX(1000) As Single
```

This statement defines *saveX* as an array of 1,001 elements of type Single. You refer to these elements using an index (or offset). So saveX(9) refers to the 10th element of this array (because saveX(0) is the first element).

When it comes to disk files, Visual Basic has a number of ways it can work with the files. You'll be using the *random-access* method that allows you to treat a disk file as an array. You'll be able to write elements to this file and read them back in any order by providing the index for the element you want to read or write.

Random Access Files

Visual Basic provides a number of *modes* for reading and writing disk files. The mode called *random-access* allows you to treat the disk file as if it contains an array of *records*.

There are a couple of differences between variable arrays and random-access files. First, variable arrays have elements, and random-access files have records. They're really the same idea, but Microsoft gave them different names. Second, variable arrays usually start with element number 0, while the first record in a random access file is record 1. Third, random-access files can grow to any length—you're limited only by available disk space, and you don't have to define the size of a random-access file ahead of time. Variable arrays, on the other hand, are limited in size to about 32,000 elements.

If these concepts seem a little confusing, hang in there. It's not that difficult, and a couple of examples should make it clear. You'll start with a small test program that doesn't do very much. When you're trying to learn some new concepts, it's often easier to write a small test program than it is to try your new ideas in a program you're currently writing.

You could start to add some test code to Address Book, but there are a couple of problems with doing so. First, if you're writing a test program, the simpler the program, the easier it is to understand everything that's happening. If your program doesn't work the way you expect, you won't have much code to understand, so it should be easier to understand what's going wrong. Second, your ideas of what kinds of changes you want to make to your program often change after you've learned the new concept. If you start to change your program before you know, for example, how disk files work, you may discover later that there are better ways that you could have changed your program. For these reasons, you'll work first with a very small test program.

Creating a Disk File

The first thing you'll need to do is create a disk file. When you've created the file, you'll want to *open* the file so you can read from it, or write to it. As you'll see, Visual Basic handles both of these functions with a single command: **Open**.

Save any changes you've made to Address Book, and then select **New Project** from the File menu to start a new project. Next open the Code window and enter the following two lines into the Form_Load event handler:

```
open "\test.dat" as #1
beep
end
```

You'll notice that Visual Basic shows the code you just typed into Form_Load as follows:

```
Sub Form_Load ()
  Open "\test.dat" For Random As #1
  Beep
  End
End Sub
```

Visual Basic added the "For Random" to the Open command. We'll look at what all this means in a minute. For now, suffice it to say that Open will open a file called \TEST.DAT, or create it if it doesn't already exist. We chose to use the root directory for the new file so this file will be easy for you to find. If you don't put a \ in front of the name, it may not be clear where Visual Basic will create the file (we'll look at this in more detail shortly).

COMMAND REFERENCE: OPEN AND CLOSE

The Open command allows you to open files on your disk.

```
Open file$ [For mode] [Access acc] [lock] As
           [#]filenumber% [Len = reclen%]
```

Opens a file called *file$*, or creates the file if it doesn't exist (new files always have a length of 0). There are a number of optional parameters you can use to control how Visual Basic will open a file, but we'll only use a few of them as follows:

```
For Random
```

We'll use the random-access mode for read/writing files that will treat disk files as an array of records (the first record is always 1).

```
As [#]filenumber%
```

Specifies which file number you'll need to use to refer to the file after you open it. In this chapter you're using #1, but the best way to assign a file number (as you'll see later) is with the FreeFile function).

```
[Len = reclen%]
```

Specifies how long each record is in the random access file. The default is 128 bytes; we'll change it later to be the size of the address book type.

Whenever you open a file, you should also close that file when your program finishes with it by using the Close command.

```
Close [[#]filenumber%]] [,[#]filenumber%]] ...
```

Closes a file that you opened with Open. If you don't provide any file numbers, Close will close all the files you opened in your program. However, it's usually better to explicitly close each file you opened.

Run this program. It will start, create the file \TEST.DAT, beep, and finally exit (we put the Beep command in this program so you would have some feedback that it ran). You should now see a new file in your root directory called TEST.DAT (use the Explorer to check this out, as in Figure 10.1), and this file should have a length of zero, because you haven't written anything to it yet.

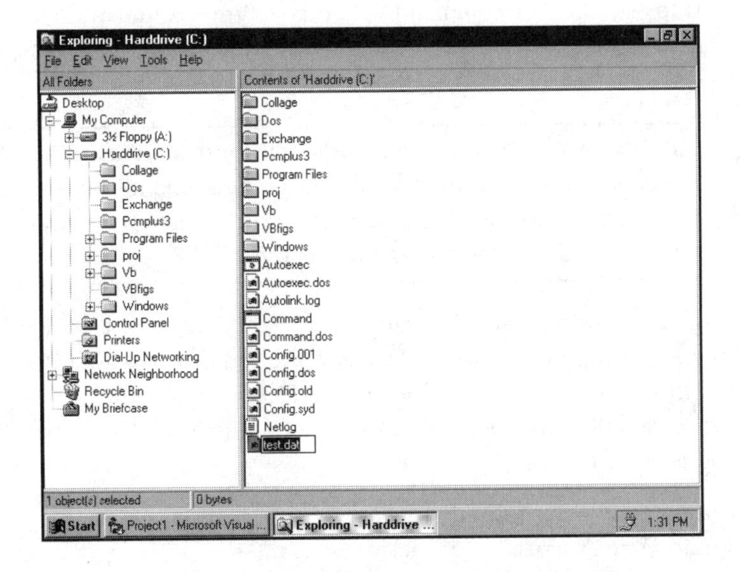

FIGURE 10.1 *The Open command creates an empty file in your root directory called TEST.DAT.*

Before we move on, let's take a closer look at the Open command. The name of the file you want to open is a string, which means that it must be enclosed in double quote marks. Next is the "For Random" that Visual Basic added to the Open command. What this means is that you'll be able to read or write any element in the disk file. In other words, you can read or write elements in any order, which is usually called *random access* by computer scientists.

Finally, the "As #1" is an element that Visual Basic needs for some bookkeeping. When you open a file, you'll need to be able to refer to the file you opened. Because you can open more than one file at a time, Visual Basic needs to assign a *file number* to any file you open. In this case you simply used 1 (later we'll show you a better way to assign file numbers). The # in front of the file number is optional—we've included it because it's easier to tell that this number is a file number, which will be more important later.

Writing to a File

Now that you've managed to open a file, let's see how you can write to this file. You'll need to use the Put command (there is a Write command, but it doesn't work for random access files). The Put command writes a single element to a disk file.

By the way, computer scientists call these *records* rather than elements. A record is exactly like an array element, but it refers to the "elements" in disk files. In other words, memory arrays have elements, and disk file arrays have records.

The Put command writes variables, rather than raw data, to a disk file. Put can't directly write a string or a number. Instead, you need to create a variable first, then write this variable. So you'll need to add two commands to Form_Load: one to set a variable, and one to call the Put command. The new version of Form_Load is as follows:

```
Private Sub Form_Load ()
  Open "\test.dat" For Random As #1
  test$ = "This is a test file."
  Put #1, 1, test$
  Beep
  End
End Sub
```

Run this program now. Your TEST.DAT file should be 22 bytes long (you can verify this using the File Manager). How can we see what's inside this file? By using DOS, of all things.

Reference: Put Command

The Put command writes a record to a file you've opened for random access (using For Random).

```
Put [#]filenumber%, [recordnumber&], recordvariable
```

Writes a single variable to a record in the disk file. The first parameter *filenumber%* is the file number that you used in the Open command. The *recordnumber&* variable specifies which record you want to write (the first record is always 1). Finally, *recordvariable* is the variable you want to write to the file.

Start a DOS window and use DOS's Type command to display the contents of the file as follows:

```
D>type \test.dat
¶ This is a test file.
D>
```

You can see the string you created, "This is a test file." is in the file. But there are also two characters that appear before the string. Why are they there? After all, you didn't put them there. The reason is quite simple.

Visual Basic keeps two bytes (characters) at the start of each string so that it can keep track of how many characters are in each string. The paragraph mark, ¶, is a DOS character with a value of 20 (every character you see has a value associated with it called it's *ASCII value*) and the space is actually a character with value zero. If you count the characters in "This is a test file." you'll find there are 20 characters. So the ¶ followed by a space tells Visual Basic that the string has 20 characters in it.

Characters and ASCII Values

Every character you see on your screen has a number associated with it, between 0 and 255 (the range of values you can represent with a single byte). The way numbers are assigned to characters is specified by a document called the American Standard Code for Information Interchange, or ASCII for short (pronounced *askee*).

ASCII really only defines the values for letters, number, and the standard punctuation marks and symbols you find on U.S. keyboards, and uses the numbers between 32 and 127. Special characters such as ¶ and foreign-language characters such as ü are defined as *extended ASCII* characters. There is no broad standard for how numbers are assigned to these characters. IBM PC-compatible computers have one standard, and Windows has a different standard (Windows has some functions that convert strings of characters between the DOS standard and the Windows standard). So the assignment of 20 to ¶ was defined by IBM.

Let's now take a closer look at the Put command. The first two parameters refer to the file and record and numbers, respectively. In other words, the #1 means that you're writing to file number 1. The second 1 means you're writing the first record in the file. If you think back to Chapter 6 where you worked with arrays, the first element in an array was element 0. But here, the first record in a file is record 1. Why did Microsoft use 0 in one case and 1 in the other? Who knows? There are a number of such inconsistencies in Visual Basic.

Reading Files

Now that you have a disk file with some data in it, let's look at how you can read this data back into your program. But first, let's think about what you'll want to do. What will you do with the data when you read it back into your program? Right now, this program writes some data, and then quits immediately.

One solution, which nicely heads back to the Address Book program, is to use a text box to display the data you read back into your program. You can also add some code that will write any changes you make in this text box back to your \TEST.DAT file. You'll rewrite this test program so you can type in text that will be saved to the disk, which is exactly the way you'll want Address Book to work.

Once again, instead of making all these changes immediately, you'll need to make one small change at a time, then test the change. If you try to change too much at once, you may find yourself getting lost. Or worse, you may forget to test some changes you make. Good programmers test everything they write very carefully; you can never test your program too much.

The first thing you should do is remove the Beep and End commands from the Form_Load event, and then run your program again. Instead of running only briefly, now it will show an empty form on your screen. Double-click on the Control box in the upper-left corner to close the form and return to design mode.

Now add a text box to your program. This text box can be any size you want, and it can be anywhere on your form. The only thing that's important about this text box is its name property, which should be Text1.

Finally, you'll need to change the code in Form_Load so it reads, rather than writes, data to the test file, which you do using the Get command. But how do you get this string into the text box?

All text boxes have a property called Text that refers to any string inside a text box. You can read this property to get the current string from a text box. And you can change the text inside a text box by assigning a string to this property.

This new version of Form_Load will read the first record in \TEST.DAT and assign the string to your text box, as follows:

```
Private Sub Form_Load ()
  Open "\test.dat" For Random As #1
  Get #1, 1, test$
  Text1.Text = test$
End Sub
```

Run this new program and see what happens. You should see something like Figure 10.2, and you'll be able to make any changes to the text inside the text box. But this test program won't save any of these changes back to the disk file.

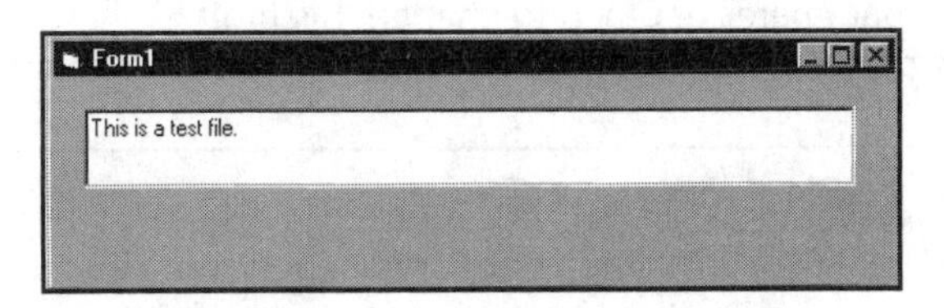

FIGURE 10.2 *Notice how the program read the string back from \TEST.DAT.*

Reference: Get Command

The Get command reads a record from a file you've opened for random access (using For Random).

```
Get [#]filenumber%, [recordnumber&], recordvariable
```

Reads a single variable from a record in the disk file into a variable. The first parameter *filenumber%* is the file number that you used in the Open command. The *recordnumber&* variable specifies which record you want to read (the first record is always 1). Finally, *recordvariable* is the variable you want to read from the file.

Let's make another small change to this program so it will save any changes you make in the text box, which is easy to do using the Form_Unload event handler. This event is called whenever your form is *unloaded* from memory, in other words, whenever you double-click on the Control box (or select **Close** from the Control menu). By calling Put in the Form_Unload event handler, you can write the Text property of the text box back to your \TEST.DAT file, as follows:

```
Private Sub Form_Unload (Cancel As Integer)
  test$ = Text1.Text
  Put #1, 1, test$
End Sub
```

That's all there is to it. Now your test program should save any changes you make to the text box, and load the modified string back into your program when you run it again.

NOTE

Using this technique for reading and writing files, the length of your strings is limited to 126 characters. Later you'll see how to use the Len parameter of Open to change this limit.

Reference: Form_Unload Event

The Form_Unload event handler will run whenever you unload a form from memory. For simple programs with just one form, this happens whenever you quit your program.

```
Private Sub Form_Unload (Cancel As Integer)
```

Runs whenever you quit your application, or otherwise unload a form.

Cancel

Set this parameter to True (–1) to prevent your form from being unloaded. This is useful when you display a dialog box asking if the user wants to quit without saving changes. If they say no, set Cancel = –1 and your program will continue to run.

Closing Files

You're now almost ready to add reading and writing to the Address Book program. But first, there is one small detail that we should cover. In all of the tests that you've done so far, you've been opening a file, but you may have noticed that you never closed the file. Consider what would happen on your desk if you kept opening file folders, but you never closed them and put them away. Pretty soon your desk would become very cluttered. (Maybe that's what John's problem is!) So you need to close file folders and put them away when you're done with them. (Of course, some people have assistants to clean up after them.)

In the same way, you should close Visual Basic's files after you're done with them. If you don't, Visual Basic will clean up for you when your program finishes. But it's better to explicitly close the file rather than rely on Visual Basic to clean up after you. So add a Close #1 to your Form_Unload event handler as follows:

```
Private Form_Unload (Cancel As Integer)
  test$ = Text1.Text
  Put #1, 1, test$
  Close #1
End Sub
```

This closes file number 1, which is the file number you opened in Form_Load.

Reading and Writing the Address Book

If you think about this simple test program and what you want Address Book to do, they're fairly close. (Big surprise, right?) The test program allows you to save any changes in a text box, which is the same type of thing that you need Address Book to do. The difference, of course, is that Address Book will be able to read and write more than a single address. It will also save more than a single text box (it needs to save the phone numbers, the notes, and so on for each record).

We'll add all these features in sections later in this chapter. For now, though, let's modify Address Books so it remembers the contents of the address text box.

But first, let's think about where the address book file should be. You certainly don't want to keep it in your root directory, as your test program did; it's a good idea to place as few files as possible in your root directory. So where can you keep it? The best place to keep the address book file is in the same directory as your program, which is usually the *current directory.*

Whenever you create a file without a path name in front of it, such as ADDRESS.DAT, the file will be created in the current directory. But the question (and problem) is: Which directory is the current directory?

In the last chapter we had you set up a Start menu item for your Address Book project. At that time we mentioned that you should fill in the StartIn field of the object's Properties dialog window with the directory that contains your ADDRESS.VBP project file. When you set this field, you tell Windows that you want this to be the current directory when you start your project.

If you don't use this field (or if you open your project with the Open Project... item from the Visual Basic File menu), the current directory probably won't be the same as your ADDRESS.VBP file; it will probably be the same directory as VB.EXE, but it could be the same as the last project you worked on if it had a different current directory.

The bottom line is that you should always open your Address Book project using it's icon to make sure it will always look in the same place for it's files.

Now that we have that out of the way, let's modify Address Book so it saves the contents of the txtAddress text box. You'll need to quit Visual Basic, and then double-click on your Address Book program to start Visual Basic again with your project loaded. Before we show you the code, can you guess how you need to modify Address Book? Go ahead and make the changes.

OK, now that you've given it a try, here's the code that we wrote to modify Address Book. First, let's look at the changes you'll make to Form_Load. Rather than show you the entire Form_Load subroutine, we'll just show you the changes with ellipses (**...**) to represent previous code that we're not showing again, as follows:

```
...
  Next i

  Open "address.dat" For Random As #1
  Get #1, 1, temp$               ' Read text from disk file
  txtAddress.Text = temp$        ' Set address to first record

  cboPhone(0).ListIndex = 0     ' Set these combo boxes to
...
```

Then you'll need to add three lines to Form_Unload to save anything you type into the txtAddress text box, as follows:

```
Private Sub Form_Unload (Cancel As Integer)
  temp$ = txtAddress.Text       ' Get the new text
  Put #1, 1, temp$              ' Save it back to the file
  Close #1                      ' Close the data file
End Sub
```

Is this what your code looked like? How does your Address Book program work? It should now remember anything you type into the address text box—but it won't remember anything you type into other text boxes. If your program doesn't work this way, check your changes and see how they compare to our changes.

When you have your program working, you'll be ready for the next step (but save your project first). We're going to show you how you can write records that include all parts of the address: The address, phone numbers, phone number types, notes, and creation and modification dates.

Packaging Data: User-Defined Types

You're probably wondering how you can write multiple variables into each record. It would be really simple if you could write Put #1, 1, address$, notes$ and so on. But that doesn't work; the Put command only writes one variable in each record.

You have to use another approach. The approach that works best is to use something called a *user-defined type*, that allows you to "package" several variables into a single new variable. You do this by creating a new variable type (in Chapter 2 you learned that Visual Basic has six types of variables: five numeric types plus strings).

Defining New Types

Here's how it works. Visual Basic has a keyword called *Type* that allows you to define new types of variables. You'll use Type, for the most part, to create "compound" variables, where each variable actually contains several pieces. Because this can be a little confusing, let's look at an example.

In Chapter 6 you created two arrays to hold the X and Y parts of lines you wanted to remember in Sketch. Using the Type command, you can instead create a single, compound variable that contains both the X and Y part in a single variable. These "parts" are known as *elements*, and you get to each element by using the following notation:

```
variableName.elementName
```

For example, if you have a variable called *save* that's defined as a compound type with an x and y element, you can set each element like the following:

```
save.x = 10
save.y = 20
```

Now let's look at how you go about creating compound variables. The first thing you'll need to do is create a *user-define type*. This is a description of what you need to be inside each of your compound variables. The Type description includes the name you need to use for your new type, as well as one line for each element in the type, as you can see in the following example that defines a Point type:

```
Type Point
  X As Single
  Y As Single
End Type
```

The first line says you're defining a type called Point, and the second and third lines define the elements that will be in the type. You can have any number of elements, and they can all be different types, as you'll see below.

When you've defined such a type, you can use this new type name (Point in the example above) to declare new variables. For example, you can declare an array called save with the following statement:

```
Dim save(1000) As Point
```

The only question left is: Where do you put the Type declaration? Do you put the Type statements into the (declarations) section of your form? No. For some reason, Visual Basic is very picky about where you define new types, and you can't define new types inside forms. Instead you must define new types in a *module.*

Modules are somewhat like forms because they can contain code, but they don't have a form attached to them—they're just used for holding code and definitions for new types of variables. In Chapter 11 you'll be using a new module, and will see firsthand why they're so useful.

All the projects you've worked with so far have used a single form file. More complex and larger Visual Basic programs use a number of forms, as well as a number of modules to keep the code well organized; you'll probably use modules for all but the smallest programs. Later in this chapter you'll create a module so you can define a new variable type (for some reason, type definitions must be in modules, rather than forms).

REFERENCE: TYPE STATEMENT

The Type statement allows you to define new types for creating compound variables (variables with one or more components inside).

```
Type typeName
  elementName As type
     .
     .
     .
End Type
```

Defines a new variable type, with the name *typeName*. Every variable of this type will have at least one element, *elementName*. You can have any number of elements in a user-defined type.

You create variables of new types using the Dim statement, just as with regular types like Single or Integer. To read the value of an element, or change its value, you use the variable name followed by a period and the element name as follows:

```
varName.elementName
```

Use this syntax to read or write any element in a compound variable that you create with a user-defined type.

Designing an AddressInfo Type

You're almost ready to define an AddressInfo type that will package all the data Address Book needs to save and read for each record (address) in the file. Before you actually define the type, let's take a look at all of the pieces that you'd like to save.

The Address Book form has a total of 10 input fields you'll need to save: the address, the four phone types, the four telephone numbers, and the notes. You'll also need to save the creation and modification dates for each record in your file, so there are 12 pieces of information that you'll need to save.

Now let's look at what types of information you'll need to save (String, Integer, etc.). The address and notes will obviously be strings, so you'll need to String types. But what about the telephone numbers? Do you want to save them as strings or numbers?

We've chosen to save telephone numbers as strings for a very good reason. We have a number of friends in Europe, and the telephone numbers there look very different than numbers here. But even here in the United States, there are some variations in how you'll write telephone numbers. Here, for example, are some numbers you might write:

(310) 555-1212	A telephone number without an extension
(800) 555-1212 x123	A telephone number with an extension
011 49 2134 33 44 55	A telephone number in Germany

As you can see, saving these numbers as strings is a lot easier than saving them as numbers. So you'll save the four telephone numbers as strings, for a total so far of six strings.

You have a couple of choices about how you save the type (Home, Office, etc.) in the phone-type combo boxes: You can save them as numbers (the value of the ListIndex property) or you can save them as strings. There are advantages and disadvantages to each approach. Saving them as numbers is very easy, but if you later change your mind about the order of items in the phone type's list, you'd also have to change all of the numbers in your address book file. On the other hand, if you save the types as strings, and then later change the names of some of the strings, you'd have to change all the affected names in your address book file. So it's really not clear which approach is best. Therefore, because saving the ListIndex property is a little easier, you'll use this approach. Add four integers to the list of elements in the AddressInfo type.

Finally, you'll need to save the creation and last modification dates. These are the numbers that you'll get from the Now() function you used in Chapter 7, which you'll recall returns a number of type Date. So add two Dates to the list.

The following list is a summary of all the data types you'll need in your AddressInfo type:

Type	How Many	What for
String	1	Address text
Integer	4	Phone type combo boxes (ListIndex)
String	4	Telephone numbers
String	1	Notes text
Date	1	Creation date
Date	1	Last modification date

You might expect, then, that you can write something like the following to define the type:

```
Type AddressInfo
  address As String
  types(4) As Integer
  phones(4) As String
  notes As String
  created As Date
  modified As Date
End Type
```

But this doesn't work for a subtle reason.

Fixed-Length Strings

All of the string variables you've worked with so far have been variable-length strings. They could be almost any size you want, large or small (strings can never be larger than 65,533 bytes long, however). But this presents a problem when you're writing records to a disk file (or reading them back).

Visual Basic doesn't allow you to read or write compound variables that contain variable-length strings (for an explanation, see the sidebar *Random-Access Files and Variable-Length Strings*). Instead, you have to use what's known as a fixed-length string. Fixed-length strings are strings that always have the same length, and they're defined like the following 20-character long string:

```
Dim fixedString As String * 20
```

The "* 20" identifies the string as a 20-character long string. Remember before how the string you wrote to the test file began with a 2-byte length count? Fixed-length strings don't have a length count. Instead, you define their length when you define the string. Because each string has no length count, any "empty" slots at the end of the string will be filled with spaces. For example, setting fixedString = "Word" will set the variable *fixedString* to "Word" followed by 16 spaces (20 – 4).

RANDOM-ACCESS FILES AND VARIABLE-LENGTH STRINGS

Visual Basic isn't always consistent, and it certainly isn't consistent in the way it handles variable-length strings and random-access files.

As you saw earlier in this chapter, Visual Basic makes it very easy to read and write variable-length strings (in other words, strings you define As String). But this is only true as long as such strings are shorter than a record (which is 128 bytes, unless you use the Len parameter in Open).

On the other hand, you can't create a user-defined type that has a variable-length string, and then write variables of this new type to random-access files. If you try it, you'll get an error message from Visual Basic saying: "Record with variable-length String not allowed."

Why this restriction? Well...it's not really a restriction. Instead, this "restriction" is a result of the way computer scientists often view database files. In the database world, non-relational databases have a number of records in them. Each record is divided into one or more fields, and the length of each field is fixed. This is exactly how Visual Basic's Put and Get commands work with random-access files and user-defined types. To fit the standard database model, you'll need to define the strings in your records as fixed rather than variable-length strings.

There are a couple of other issues about fixed-length strings we'll need to cover later. But you now know enough to modify your Address Book program so it reads and writes more information than before.

Type the following into the (General) (declarations) section of your Address form code window:

```
Private Type AddressInfo
  address As String * 160      ' The address
  notes As String * 300        ' Notes field

  types(3) As Integer          ' Four telephone types
```

```
    phones(3) As String *25       ' Four telephone numbers

    created As Date        ' Date record was created
    modified As Date       ' Date record last modified
  End Type
```

Notice the order in which we wrote these elements? The order you use really isn't important, as long as you don't change it after you start to create an address book file. The data on the disk will be stored within each record in exactly the same order as you write it (see Figure 10.3), so if you later change the order of the elements, your data won't be read back in correctly.

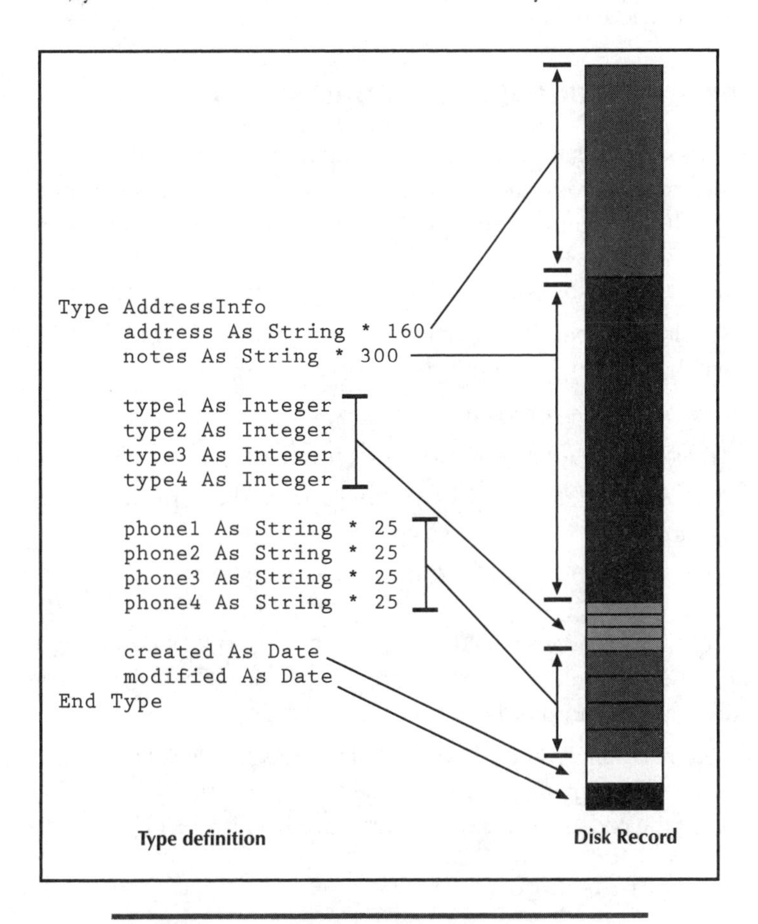

FIGURE 10.3 *Variables created by user-defined types are written directly to a disk record, byte-for-byte.*

In case you're wondering where the strings lengths came from, they're really just arbitrary numbers. We chose 160 for the length of the address field because the longest address John has in his files (including the company name, division name, and the person's title) is about 130 characters long. We added an extra 30 characters just to be safe. In the same spirit, the longest telephone number in his files was 20 characters long, so we set the length of these fields to 25.

Finally, the 300-character length on the notes field is really arbitrary. We wanted to keep it small to keep the size of the address-book file small (since each notes field will use 300 characters, even if you leave it blank). Setting the size to 300 characters allows about three full lines of text, or a number of shorter lines, which is enough for our needs.

Writing and Reading Compound Variables

Let's take a look at what you'll need to change in Form_Load and Form_Unload to read and write compound variables. The following list is a summary of the changes you'll need to make, that we'll describe in more detail below:

1. Define a variable called *addr* that has the type AddressInfo.
2. Specify the length of a record in the Open command so Visual Basic will know how long your records are.
3. Read in the *addr* record.
4. Transfer the values from *addr*'s elements to your form's controls.
5. In Form_Unload, transfer the values from the form back into the *addr* variable.
6. Write the *addr* record back to disk.

Each one of these changes is actually fairly simple, so let's go through them one at a time. (We'll present the new Form_Load and Form_Unload subroutines in their entirety at the end of this section.)

The very first thing you have to do is define a variable called *addr* that has the type AddressInfo. Define this variable in the Form_Load subroutine (later we'll think about how all the code should really be organized) so it looks like the following:

```
Dim addr As AddressInfo
```

Next you'll want to modify the Open statement in Form_Load so it defines the length of each record, which you do like the following:

```
Open "address.dat" For Random As #1 Len = Len(addr)
```

The Len parameter tells Visual Basic how large each record is in the file you're opening. Here the function Len(addr) calculates the size, in bytes, of the variable *addr*, which means you don't have to calculate the size of each record yourself. In fact, it's better not to calculate the size yourself—letting Visual Basic do it for you is much safer, because Visual Basic won't make a mistake. It's also a lot easier to let Visual Basic do all of the work.

REFERENCE: LEN() FUNCTION

The length function tells you how large a variable is, in bytes. For string variables, it tells you how many characters are in the string.

```
Len(strVar$)
```

Reports the number of characters in the string *strVar$*. Note that this isn't the size of the variable in bytes; rather, it's the number of characters in the string.

```
Len(varName)
```

Reports how many bytes are used to store the variable called *varName*. This is very useful when used with variables of user-defined types in the file Open command.

Be careful not to use Len with a type name, as this won't give you a correct value. You need to define a variable of that type, then use Len on the variable.

Next you'll need to modify the Get statement along with the statement that sets the Text property of text boxes (you'll want to make sure you remove any lines that refer to the variable *temp$*). The new Get statement, along with statements to read the address and the first telephone number as follows:

```
Get #1, 1, addr                      ' Read first record from file
txtAddress.Text = addr.address       ' Transfer the address field
txtPhone(0).Text = addr.phones(0)    ' Transfer first phone num
```

You've written code to read only two fields of the record, as test code. The idea is to keep your code as simple as possible until you have something that works.

Only then should you add all of the remaining code. This approach makes it much easier to track down problems, because you'll tend to discover them soon.

You'll need to make one last change to Form_Unload, before you try these changes in your program. Replace the first two lines in Form_Unload (the assignment and the Put statements) with the following lines:

```
Dim addr As AddressInfo

 addr.address = txtAddress.Text
 addr.phones(0) = txtPhone(0).Text
 Put #1, 1, addr           ' Save changes back to file
```

Now try your new program. Does it work correctly? It should save anything you write in the address field and the first telephone field. Does it work this way? If not, check your Form_Load and Form_Unload subroutines to make sure they're correct. The correct versions are as follows:

```
Private Sub Form_Load ()
  Dim addr As AddressInfo

  For i = 0 To 3
    cboPhone(i).AddItem "Home"
    cboPhone(i).AddItem "Office"
    cboPhone(i).AddItem "FAX"
    cboPhone(i).AddItem "Direct"
    cboPhone(i).AddItem "Car"
    cboPhone(i).AddItem ""
  Next i

  Open "address.dat" For Random As #1 Len = Len(addr)
  Get #1, 1, addr                        ' Read first record
                                         ' from file
  txtAddress.Text = addr.address         ' Transfer the
                                         ' address field
  txtPhone(0).Text = addr.phones(0)      ' Transfer first
                                         ' phone num.
```

```
    cboPhone(0).ListIndex = 0            ' Set these combo
                                         ' boxes to
    cboPhone(1).ListIndex = 1
    cboPhone(2).ListIndex = 2
    cboPhone(3).ListIndex = 5
  End Sub

  Private Sub Form_Unload (Cancel As Integer)
    Dim addr As AddressInfo

    addr.address = txtAddress.Text
    addr.phones(0) = txtPhone(0).Text
    Put #1, 1, addr               ' Save changes back to file
    Close #1                      ' Close file before exit
  End Sub
```

Removing Trailing spaces

There is one small problem that's very easy to fix. Run your program again, and then use the cursor keys to move within the address or the first phone number text box. You'll notice there are a number of spaces at the end of each field. Why? Because all of the strings in the *addr* variable are fixed-length fields, assigning the following:

```
txtAddress.Text = addr.address
```

This places all of the trailing spaces into the text box. Wouldn't it be nice if there were a simple way to remove all of these spaces? Well, there is. Visual Basic has a number of functions for working with Strings, and one of them, called RTrim$() removes trailing spaces from a string. So you can remove the trailing spaces in your program by changing two lines in Form_Load as follows:

```
txtAddress.Text = RTrim$(addr.address)
txtPhone(0).Text = RTrim$(addr.phones(0))
```

Now run your program again and you'll notice that there are no trailing spaces.

Using On-Line Help

You're probably getting to the point where it's hard to remember all of the statements and functions that you've learned, much less the syntax for each instruction. Fortunately, there's a very quick way to get information on these commands. To see how it works, switch to the Form_Load subroutine in your Code window, then position the insertion point anywhere inside the RTrim$ function you just added. Next, press **F1**. This will bring up a Help window that shows information on the command (see Figure 10.4).

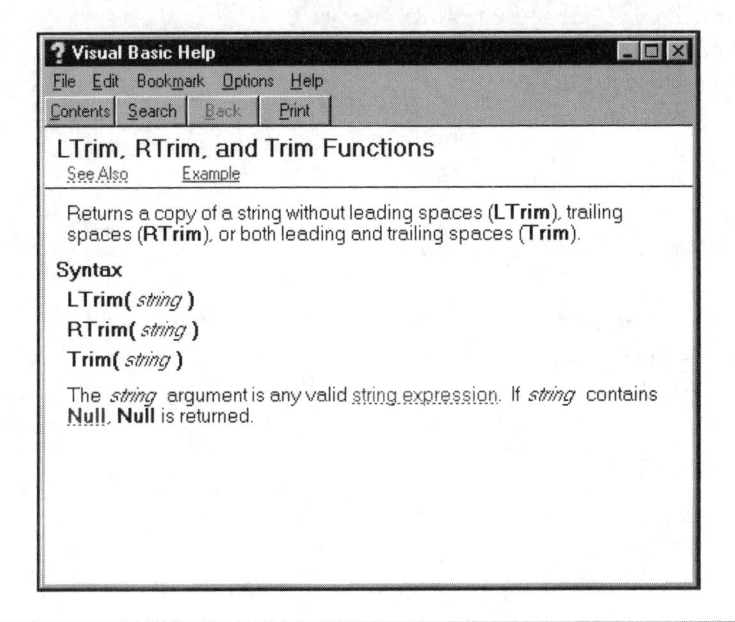

FIGURE 10.4 *Pressing* ***F1*** *at any time will display Visual Basic's on-line help, which is a quick way to refresh you memory on how a command works.*

There are a couple of useful shortcuts that you can use when you have the Help window visible. First, Help allows you to jump between related items very easily. You'll notice an underlined string in Figure 10.4: example. If you click on this item, Help will show you information on this item.

You can also search for keywords in the help file. To do this, press on the Search button at the top of the help screen, and then start typing a word that you need to look for. Help will show you the first keyword that matches what you've already typed. Click on the **Show Topics** button to see the related topics. For example, to find the help screen on the Open statement, do the following:

1. Click on the **Search** button.
2. Type **open**.
3. Click on the **Show Topics** button.
4. Double-click on the **Open Statement** item in the lower list.

As you can see, the on-line help can be much faster than looking commands up in your Visual Basic *Language Reference Manual*, especially if you don't remember (or know) the name of a command.

Creating New Subroutines

You now have an Address Book program that remembers just two fields, out of a total of ten different fields. Remembering the other text fields is really quite simple. See if you can write the code yourself before we present our solution. Remembering the ListIndex property for each of the phone-type combo boxes is also very simple. Try adding this code as well.

The changes we suggested you make so far are a little different from the ones we're going to suggest next. If you've added all the code in Form_Load and Form_Unload to load and save a single record, you'll notice that these two subroutines are becoming rather long. And the Form_Load subroutine is also doing a number of tasks. It's initializing the combo boxes, opening the database file, reading in the first record, and setting the fields in your form.

In general, it's best to keep your subroutines short, and to have each subroutine perform a single function. But how do you do this? By using a feature of Visual Basic that you haven't explored yet. You can create new subroutines, with your own names and your own parameters.

Start by creating a new subroutine called DBOpen, which stands for Database Open; programmers often use DB as an abbreviation for *database*. To create this new subroutine, first make sure your Code window is visible and active. Then choose the Procedure... item from the Insert menu, and type **DBOpen** in the Name text box of the dialog box that appears (see Figure 10.5).

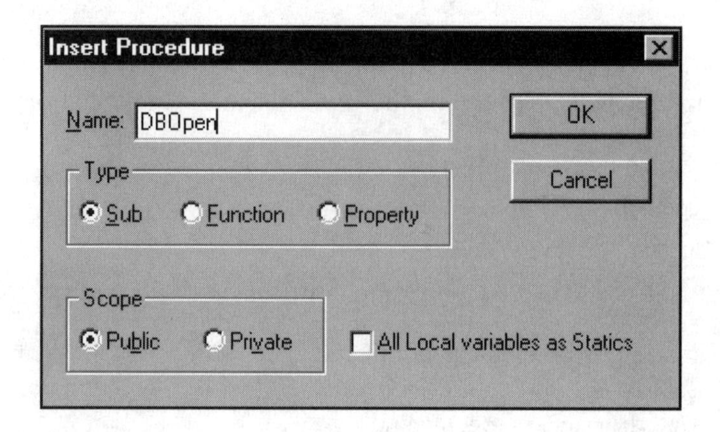

FIGURE 10.5 *Define new subroutines by choosing the* ***New Procedure...*** *item from the Code menu to display this dialog box.*

Your code window should now show a new, empty subroutine called DBOpen. Enter the following code into this subroutine:

```
Private Sub DBOpen ()
  Dim addr As AddressInfo

  Open "address.dat" For Random As #1 Len = Len(addr)
End Sub
```

Finally, switch back to the Form_Load event (select the **Form** object from the Object combo box, then select the **Load** event from the Proc combo box) and change the Open command in Form_Load to the following line:

```
  DBOpen                 ' Open the database file
```

This line looks very simple, and it is, but it's something new: a command that calls the subroutine DBOpen that you just created. DBOpen then runs until it's finished doing all its work, at which time Visual Basic continues to run the code in Form_Load. In other words, you can move code into a subroutine, and then run that code by writing the name of the subroutine, with a small caveat that we'll talk about shortly.

To view your own subroutines inside of the Code menu, first select the (general) section from the Object combo box in the Code window. Next pull down the Proc combo box and you'll see a list of all the subroutines you created yourself. Selecting any of these subroutines will take you to its code. Figure 10.6 shows the Proc combo box with four new subroutines—only one of which you've created so far.

Why did we have you create such a short subroutine? The answer is that we have some ideas about how we like to organize programs, based on our experience writing commercial software. And we're heading toward reorganizing Address Book along these lines. Here's a quick overview of what we have in mind, and where we're headed.

We usually like to organize our programs into different modules that each perform a different function. All the subroutines in any module are related in terms of the type of function they provide. In the case of Address Book, you can draw a fairly clear distinction between the database side of the program (the part that works with the disk file) and the user-interface (of form) part of the program. What we plan to do is have you separate these two areas of the program into two distinct modules.

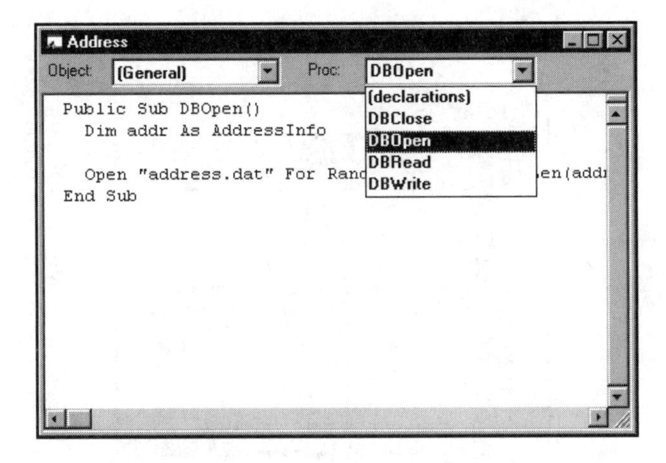

FIGURE 10.6 *The Proc combo box showing the four new subroutines you'll create in this chapter.*

Creating the DBOpen function was the first step toward creating such a module. You'll also need several other subroutines in the module, namely DBClose, DBRead, and DBWrite. You'll notice we put a DB in front of each of these names. Programmers often like to put a short two- or three-letter mini-description in front of all the subroutines and functions in a module; this makes it easy to tell that these functions all belong to the same module.

By the way, by the time you're finished writing DBOpen in Chapter 11, it will be a little longer than what you see here.

Subroutines and Variables

There is one small detail about subroutines that can be a little confusing when you're first getting started. You'll notice that we used the Dim keyword to define the variable *addr* in the DBOpen subroutine, even though it was already defined in Form_Load. Why did we do this? Because any variable you define inside one subroutine won't be available to any other subroutine.

The best way to understand this is with an illustration, showing when variables are available, and when they're not. For example, let's say you have a form-level variable called *someVar*, and you have two subroutines, Form_Load and DBOpen, that each defines a variable: *addr1* and *addr2* respectively (see Figure 10.7). Let's take a look at where each of these variables will be visible.

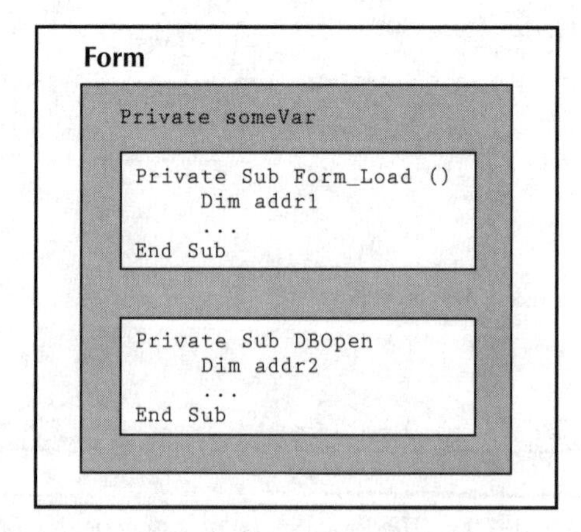

FIGURE 10.7 *Form-level variables are available to all subroutines. But subroutine-level variables are only available to the code within the subroutine where that variable is defined.*

The variable *someVar* is visible to any code inside both Form_Load and DBOpen, because it's defined as a form-level variable. As you'll recall from Chapter 6, any variables defined in the (declarations) section of a form will be visible in every subroutine and function inside of the same form.

On the other hand, the variables *addr1* and *addr2* are each defined inside a subroutine. What this means is that these variables are visible only to the other statements inside the same subroutine. So if Form_Load calls DBOpen, none of the code inside DBOpen will see the variable *addr1* because this variable was defined in Form_Load, not DBOpen. The following is a chart that summarizes which variables will be visible in each subroutine as follows:

Subroutine	someVar	addr1	addr2
Form_Load	✔	✔	
DBOpen	✔		✔

The thing to remember is that what determines whether a variable will be visible is not what happens when you run your program, but where you write the lines of code.

Creating the DBClose Subroutine

Any module with an Open subroutine should also have a Close subroutine to balance the Open subroutine. Move the Close command from the Form_Unload event handler into its own subroutine as follows:

1. Replace the Close #1 statement in Form_Unload with DBClose.
2. Create a new subroutine called DBClose (use the Procedure… item from the Insert menu) that contains Close #1.

You should now have a new version of Address Book that uses subroutines to open and close the database file. Save your project, then try this new program. Does it work correctly? If it doesn't, check your work carefully.

Creating DBRead and DBWrite Subroutines

The last thing you'll do in this chapter is move the code that reads and writes individual records into separate subroutines. This new code will read and write all the text and combo box data, so you'll have an Address Book program that remembers all of the fields. The only thing it won't remember yet are the creation and modification dates.

At this point you probably have a pretty good idea about what the DBRead and DBWrite subroutines should look like, so we'll simply show them here along with the new versions of Form_Load and Form_Unload as follows:

```
Private Sub Form_Load ()
  For i = 0 To 3
    cboPhone(i).AddItem "Home"
    cboPhone(i).AddItem "Office"
    cboPhone(i).AddItem "FAX"
    cboPhone(i).AddItem "Direct"
    cboPhone(i).AddItem "Car"
    cboPhone(i).AddItem ""
  Next i

  DBOpen                 ' Open the database file
  DBRead                 ' Get the first record
End Sub

Private Sub Form_Unload (Cancel As Integer)
  DBWrite                 ' Write record back to file
  DBClose                 ' Close the file
End Sub

Private Sub DBRead ()
  Dim addr As AddressInfo

  Get #1, 1, addr          ' Read first record from file
  txtAddress.Text = RTrim$(addr.address)
  txtNotes.Text = RTrim$(addr.notes)

 For i = 0 to 3
    txtPhone(i).Text = RTrim$(addr.phones(i))
    cboPhone(i).ListIndex = addr.types(i)
  Next i
End Sub
```

```
Private Sub DBWrite ()
  Dim addr As AddressInfo

  addr.address = txtAddress.Text
  addr.notes = txtNotes.Text

  For i = 0 To 3
    addr.phones(i) = txtPhone(i).Text
    addr.types(i) = cboPhone(i).ListIndex
  Next i

  Put #1, 1, addr           ' Save changes back to file
End Sub
```

When you make all of these changes and run Address Book, you'll notice one slight anomaly: All the phone-type combo boxes now say Home. How did this happen? When you wrote out records before, you never set any values into the addr.type(*n*) fields, which means they were all 0 (all new variables have their values set to 0). Because cboPhone(i).ListIndex = 0 shows the first item in the list (Home in this case), all the combo boxes will say Home.

This, by the way, falls under the heading of boundary conditions. Later when you write code that allows you to add new addresses to the database, you'll have to write code that sets the initial values for the four phone-type combo boxes.

Related Tools

- **Deleting and renaming files.** Visual Basic has two commands for deleting and renaming files. The *Kill* command deletes a file (or a group of files) and the *RmDir* command deletes an empty directory. The *Name* command renames a file or a directory.
- **File information.** There are several functions that you can use to obtain information on files. The LOF function returns the size of an open file, in bytes. You'll use it in the next chapter to determine how many records are stored in a file. Another function, Loc, returns your current location in the file. This is the number of the last record you read or wrote.

- **Binary and sequential files**. Visual Basic provides two other modes for opening files: binary and sequential. Binary access mode allows you to read and write groups of bytes anywhere in the file. This mode gives you the most control over a file, but requires a lot of work. Sequential files allow you to read a file from start to finish, one line at a time. This is useful if you want to read lines of text, but you don't need to go backward through the file.
- **Sequential file functions.** Print # or Write # allows you to write lines, and Input # or Line Input # allows you to read lines.
- **Binary files.** You use the Get and Put statements to read and write data to a binary file.
- **Unload command.** The Unload command allows you to unload a form from within your program. This is very useful when your program uses multiple forms and you need to remove a form as a result of pressing an OK or Cancel button in a form.
- **LTrim$.** This function allows you to remove leading spaces from a string, just as RTrim$ removes trailing spaces. (Trim$ removes both.)

Summary

You've learned a lot in this chapter and made a number of changes to Address Book. In the next chapter you'll continue to work on Address Book. You'll modify Address Book so it can read and write more than one record. In the process you'll also make some more changes to the organization of Address Book so it will be nicely modularized.

The following lists what you learned in this chapter:

- **Open and close.** You used the Open command to create a new address book file, and then to open it so you could read and write to the file. You should always close any files you open.
- **Random-access files.** The type of file you worked with in this chapter is a random-access file, which is like an array of records in a disk file. This "array" starts with record 0, and can grow to any size.
- **Put and get.** These commands allow you to read and write single records in any disk file.

✱ **User-defined types.** The Type command allows you to define new variable types. These new types are compound types, because they contain one or more elements. In other words, you can create a variable that "packages" a number of pieces of information into a single variable. This is very useful for reading and writing records, where each record contains all of the information you want to store, along with an address.

✱ **Modules.** All Type declarations must appear in a module.

✱ **Fixed-length strings.** Whenever you create a user-defined type with strings that you want to write to a disk file, all the strings must be fixed-length strings. This restriction is a result of the way records are defined.

✱ **On-line help.** If you want help on a command or function, place the cursor on that command in your Code window and press F1. This will display a Help screen with information on that function. You can also search help for keywords by clicking the Search button near the top of the Help window.

✱ **Creating new subroutines.** You can create your own subroutines by selecting Procedure… from the Insert menu whenever you have a Code window visible and active. Then type in the name you want to use for your new subroutine (or function).

✱ **Subroutines and variables.** Any variables you define in a subroutine will only be visible to lines of code that appear inside that same subroutine. For example, if subroutine A calls subroutine B, any variables inside subroutine A won't be visible to code inside subroutine B. The best way to understand this is to think of boxes within boxes. Any variable defined inside a box is only visible to code written inside the same box. (Figure 10.7 shows this.)

WORKING WITH MULTIPLE RECORDS

- ✱ Using modules
- ✱ Using parameter subroutines you create
- ✱ Creating a separate database module
- ✱ Debugging and testing programs
- ✱ Creating new functions
- ✱ Reading and writing multiple address records
- ✱ Adding a menu bar to Address Book
- ✱ Cut, Copy, Paste, and Undo in text boxes

We're going to change the approach somewhat in this chapter and in Chapter 12. You're almost finished reading the tutorial part of this book. The remaining parts contain more advanced information and hints and techniques you can use in your own program. What we'd like to do in this and in Chapter 12 is give you as much information and show you as much code as possible. So instead of taking you through all the steps of adding the rest of Address Book's features, we're going to present the code, and then describe how it works.

By taking this approach we'll be able to show you more examples of code. The best way for you to learn how to program is to see examples of other people's programs. It's also useful to see the techniques people use in building larger programs. By adding new features to Address Book, you'll gain insight into how we go about writing larger programs. (You may find that other programmers use different approaches.)

In this chapter you're going to continue building Address Book. First, you'll extend Address Book so it can work with more than one record. In the process, you'll fill out some of the other details, such as saving the creation and modification dates, and displaying information on which record you're looking at.

Creating Modules

In Chapter 10, you created a set of four subroutines as part of Address.frm, and as a group, these subroutines are sort of like a module of their own. Visual Basic, however, also has its own type of module, which is a file that contains nothing but code. You're about to create such a module, and when you're done, your project will have two files in it: the Address Book form (Address.frm) and the Database module (DATABASE.BAS). You can also add other forms to your project, as well as other modules.

New modules are also somewhat like forms without any objects—they contain subroutines you create as well as module-level variables. They can also contain type definitions (as you saw in the last chapter), and a few other things we'll get into later. What we're going to do here is make a greater separations than we already have between the form code and the DB module.

This approach is called *modular design,* and the idea is that it's much easier to write a larger program if you divide it into modules. Each module should be self-contained, and its connections to other modules should be as simple as possible. The database module you'll build will have just four subroutines (DBOpen, DBClose, DBRead, and DBWrite) and one function (DBLen). All the rest of the work will be handled internally by the database module.

To add a module to your project, select **Module** from the Insert menu. This will create a new module in your project, called *Module1.bas.* It will also display a Code window with the caption Module1. Then, select Save Project from the

File menu to save these changes. You'll see a File Save As dialog box asking your where you want to save the new Module1.bas file. Type **database** and then press **Enter** to save this file as DATABASE.BAS. You'll add code to this module in the next chapter to read and write to the disk file (or *database*), which is why we've called it DATABASE.BAS.

Now that that's done, you can move the DB routines from your form to your database module. Click on **DATABASE.BAS** in your Project window, and then click on the **View Code** button. This will bring up the code window for your database module. Now do the same for the ADDRESS.FRM module to make its Code window visible as well. You may want to move one of your windows so the Address.frm and Database.bas Code windows don't overlap.

Next, use the mouse to select all the text from each of the four DB subroutines (see Figure 11.1), and then choose Cut from the Edit menu. Finally switch back to the Database Code window, and select Paste from the Edit menu. These steps first remove the DB subroutines from your form, and then put it into the Database module.

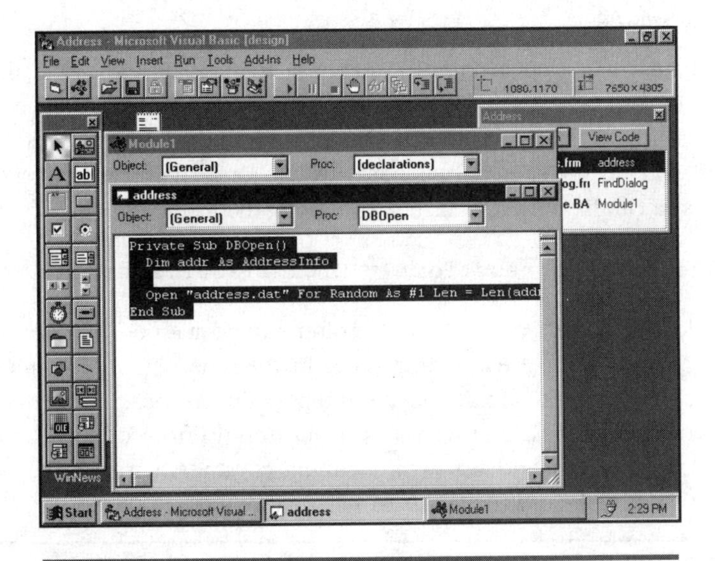

FIGURE 11.1 *Your project should look something like this after you create a new module, then select the DB subroutines in your form.*

At this point your form should no longer have any DB subroutines: Instead, they're now in your Database module, and they have automatically become Public subroutines. That was easy, but before you can test your changes, you'll need to move one more piece of code—the Type definition. Unlike moving private subroutines that automatically become public, you'll have to manually change the Type definition from Private to Public once you place it in the Database module. Private types are allowed, but the Address program needs to use the Type in both the form and database modules.

Finally, select **Save Project** from the File menu to save these changes. Now run your program and make sure it still works correctly.

Does it still work? Nope. (See how important step-by-step testing can be?) Visual Basic displays an Element not defined dialog box and then shows the DBRead subroutine in the Code window. What's going on?

The problem is with the following line in DBRead:

```
txtAddress.Text = RTrim$(addr.address)
```

Here's what's happened. Visual Basic knows that *txtAddress* must be either a control or a variable with a user-defined type. It knows this because of the *.Text* after the name *txtAddress*. But it couldn't find a variable or control called *txtAddress*. Why not?

Any time you create a control in a form, such as txtAddress in the Address form, that control belongs to the form where you created it, and it won't automatically be visible anywhere outside that form. To make the control accessible outside the form, you need to tell Visual Basic which form that control resides in. For example, you can fix the previous line by adding the form name like the following:

```
Address.txtAddress.Text = RTrim$(addr.address)
```

This would work, but it's not the only solution, and it's not the one we want to suggest so you won't use this approach in this chapter. As we mentioned a moment ago, modules should be as independent as possible from the other parts of your program. If you were to put *Address.* in front of each control name in this module, you'd end up with a complex, rather than simple, connection between this module and the form. So what can you do?

Referencing Controls Inside Other Forms

As mentioned in the text, you can gain access to any control inside any form by writing the form's name, a period, and the control's name as follows:

```
formName.controlName
```

Refers to a control called *controlName* inside the form called *formName*.

Note that this only works for controls or properties inside a form. You can't reference form-level variables inside other forms.

The best solution is to keep the interface between form and module as simple as possible by making some changes to DBRead and DBWrite, and adding two new subroutines to your form: GetRecord and SaveRecord. The idea is that DBRead and DBWrite should read or write information into a variable of type AddressInfo. The statements that transfer information between this variable and the controls of your form should be in the subroutines GetRecord and SaveRecord in your form.

Rather than go into all the details of how you make these changes (you've learned all of these methods already), we'll present the finished subroutines. First, the new subroutines you should create in your form (Address.frm) are as follows:

```
Private Sub GetRecord ()
  Dim addr As AddressInfo

  DBRead addr           ' Read one record

  txtAddress.Text = RTrim$(addr.address)
  txtNotes.Text = RTrim$(addr.notes)

  For i = 0 To 3
    txtPhone(i).Text = RTrim$(addr.phones(i))
    cboPhone(i).ListIndex = addr.types(i)
  Next i
End Sub
```

```
Private Sub SaveRecord ()
  Dim addr As AddressInfo

  addr.address = txtAddress.Text
  addr.notes = txtNotes.Text

  For i = 0 To 3
    addr.phones(i) = txtPhone(i).Text
    addr.types(i) = cboPhone(i).ListIndex
  Next i
```

```
  DBWrite addr          ' Write record back to file
End Sub
```

When you Insert a Procedure into a form module, the default selection in the dialog box is Public. The GetRecord and SaveRecord routines, however, will only be used internally within the form module, so you should change the setting to Private.

These two subroutines should be fairly clear. The only new twist we've added is in the calls to DBRead and DBWrite. You'll notice that you're providing the variable *addr* as an argument to each of these functions. DBRead and DBWrite will use and set the information in this variables. (We'll describe how this works in the next section.)

The following new definitions for DBRead and DBWrite (subroutines of your Database module), which show how you define parameters for subroutines that you create:

```
Public Sub DBRead (addr As AddressInfo)
  Get #1, 1, addr        ' Read first record from file
End Sub
```

```
Public Sub DBWrite (addr As AddressInfo)
  Put #1, 1, addr       ' Save changes back to file
End Sub
```

As you can see, these two subroutines are now quite simple (you'll add more to them later to support more than one record in the file).

Finally, moving back to Address.frm again, change the line with DBRead in Form_Load to the following:

```
GetRecord               ' Get the first record
```

And change the DBWrite in Form_Unload to the following:

```
SaveRecord              ' Write record back to file
```

Save your project, and then try to run this new program. Does it work correctly? If it doesn't, check your work carefully to make sure you've made all of the changes.

Your program now has a database module that is cleanly separated from the rest of your program. We'll use this fact, after a short detour, to make some changes to the way your database code works. The amazing thing is that these changes won't affect the rest of your program. By modularizing your program, you can make major changes to the way a module works without having to rewrite any other code.

Using Subroutine Parameters

The two subroutines DBRead and DBWrite each use a parameter to pass information back and forth. Whenever SaveRecord writes a record to your file, it first sets all the information in the *addr* variable, and then passes this information to the DBWrite subroutine as a parameter. Simple enough.

Now let's look at what happens when you call GetRecord. This subroutine "passes" the *addr* variable to DBRead; DBRead then sets the values in its *addr* variable. But what does this mean? Will the changes DBRead makes to *addr* change the *addr* variable in the GetRecord subroutine? Yes they will, but it may not be obvious why.

Using subroutine parameters to pass information back and forth can seem complicated, so if you find yourself feeling somewhat confused, finish reading this section, and then put the book aside for a while. After a of couple hours, try reading this section again and see if it makes any more sense. Sometimes you just need time to let ideas percolate.

To give you a better idea of exactly what's happening, let's look at a very simple example, using two subroutines called GetInfo and SupplyInfo:

```
Sub GetInfo ()
  Dim info As AddressInfo

  SupplyInfo info
End Sub
```

```
Sub SupplyInfo (addr As AddressInfo)
  addr.address = "My Address"
End Sub
```

These two subroutines are actually using two separate names (*info* and *addr*) to refer to the same variable. The reason for this is very simple. Subroutines you create, such as SupplyInfo, need to be able to work with any variables you send to it, no matter what you call these variables. You can write "SupplyInfo info" to tell SupplyInfo that it should work with the *info* variable. Inside SupplyInfo, any statements that reference *addr* actually use the variable *info*.

This method of passing a variable to a subroutine is called *passing by reference* because it passes a reference to a variable, rather than a copy of the variable's data. So, any changes you make to the value of *addr* inside SupplyInfo change the value of *info*.

Visual Basic also allows you to pass parameters *by value*. In this case you're sending a copy of the variable to the subroutine, which means that the subroutine can't change the value in your main program (see Figure 11.2). To send a copy of a variable, rather than a reference to the variable, you need to place the ByVal keyword in front of the parameter definition. In other words, if you wanted a copy of *info* sent to SupplyInfo, you would define SupplyInfo like this:

```
Sub SupplyInfo (ByVal addr As AddressInfo)
```

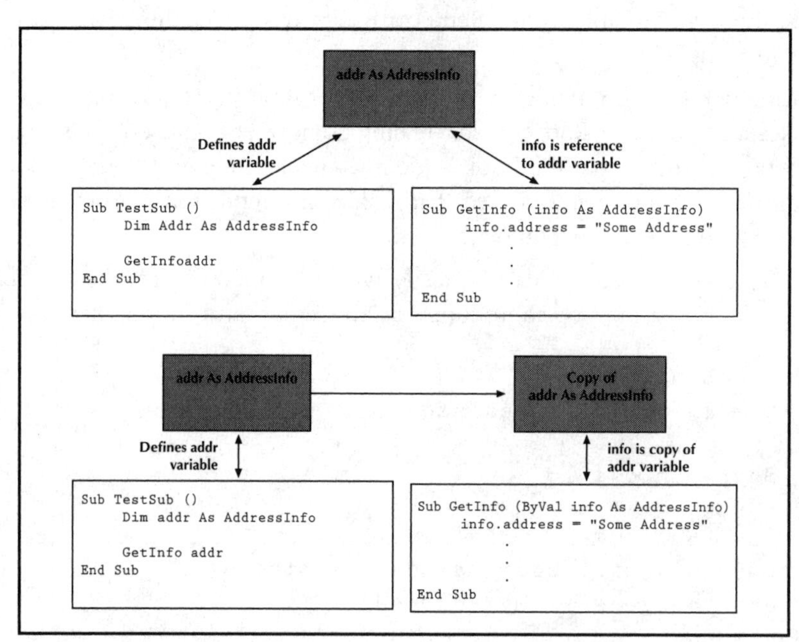

FIGURE 11.2 *The top part shows passing a variable by reference (the default) and the bottom part shows passing by value (which requires that you place ByVal in front of the parameter definition).*

REFERENCE: SUBROUTINE PARAMETERS

Whenever you create new subroutines in your forms and modules, you can also define parameters that you can pass to these subroutines. You define parameters in the following way:

```
Sub SubName(param1 [As typeName] [,param2
            [As typeName]] ...)
```

Defines parameters that you can pass to a subroutine. This is a simplification of the real definition which allows more options.

By default, variables are passed to subroutines by reference. That means your subroutine can change the values of variables you pass to them.

If you don't want your variables to be modified, you can place the ByVal keyword in front of the parameter definition to tell Visual Basic that you want a copy of variables passed.

Modifying the Database Module

Now that you have a better understanding of subroutines and parameters, let's get back to working on the database module. We mentioned earlier that you can often rewrite a module without affecting any of the code that uses it. Right now your database module does a very simple job. But there is one assumption you should change. If you look again at the DBOpen, etc. subroutines in your database module, you'll notice that they all have the file number hard-coded as #1. This isn't a good idea. What happens if you try to use another module that also uses file number #1? Not good.

These subroutines should not have a fixed file number. Instead, they should use a function in Visual Basic called FreeFile, which will return a file number that's not being used.

Here are the changes you'll need to make to use FreeFile. First, you'll need to create a module-level variable to keep track of the file number. A module-level variable works just like a form-level variable works: you define it in the (declarations) section of your module and it will be visible to all of the subroutines in your module.

Add the following line to the (declarations) section of your module (either before Public Type AddressInfo statement or after End Type statement, but not in between):

```
Private fileNum As Integer        ' The file number used
                                  ' in DB subs
```

Make two changes: Add a new statement that uses FileFree, and change the #1 to #fileNum in the Open statement. Your DBOpen subroutine should look like the following:

```
Public Sub DBOpen ()
  Dim addr As AddressInfo      ' Used to calc record size

  fileNum = FreeFile           ' Get next file number
  Open "address.dat" For Random As #fileNum Len = Len(addr)
End Sub
```

Finally, change all of the #1s in the other three subroutines to #fileNum. Now try your program again to make sure it works correctly. You've changed the way the database subroutines work, yet you've only changed code inside the database module. Dividing the code into modules really makes it easy to make changes, because you're working with separate and distinct pieces. As you make changes in this and the next chapter, you'll see this modular approach in action, and you'll see how it simplifies the process of writing Address Book.

Modifying DATABASE.BAS for Multiple Records

In this section we'll present the code that will allow your Address Book program to read and write multiple records. As we mentioned at the start of this chapter, we'll present the code and explain how it works, rather than show you all of the steps you would take to write it.

First, let's look at the changes to the Database module to support multiple records.

Adding Multirecord Support to DBOpen

Modifying Database to work with multiple records is actually quite simple, as you'll see in the following below. The first thing you'll need to do is add another form-level variable to keep track of how many records are in the database file. Strictly speaking, this variable isn't really necessary because you can use the LOF (length of file) function to calculate the number of records in the database. But using a variable instead will speed up your programs.

Add the definition of numRecords to the (declarations) section of DATABASE, so it looks like the following:

```
Private fileNum As Integer       ' The file number used
                                 ' in DB subs
Private numRecords As Integer    ' Number of records in
                                 ' database
```

Next, modify DBOpen so it sets the following variable to the number of records in your file:

```
Public Sub DBOpen ()
  '
  ' This subroutine opens the database file for reading one
  ' record at a time. The length of each record is simply
  ' Len(addr), which is why we've defined the variable addr
  ' below.
  '
  Dim addr As AddressInfo          ' Used to calc record size

  fileNum = FreeFile               ' Get next file number
  Open "address.dat" For Random As #fileNum Len = Len(addr)

  numRecords = LOF(fileNum) / Len(addr)
End Sub
```

You'll notice we also added a comment at the start of DBOpen. It's a good idea to put comments at the start of your subroutines that describe what each subroutine does. As you modify each subroutine in DATABASE, we'll suggest comments for the start of the subroutine.

There are two reasons these types of comments are important. First, comments that tell why you're doing something, not just what you're doing (which you can often figure out by looking at the code) make it much easier for other people to understand how your program works. And second, if you're writing a larger program and you don't work on it for, say, a year, you might not remember yourself why you wrote your program the way you did. By including comments that explain why (as well as what) each subroutine does), it will be much easier for you to go back to your own code several years later. John learned this lesson writing three versions of a commercial product called *The Norton Commander*, a DOS product that he worked on over a period of six years. The longer he worked on this product, the gladder he was that he had written detailed comments (and the more comments he added).

Testing Your Code

We've mentioned before that it's a good idea to test each part of your code as you write it. But how do you check the changes you've made to DBOpen to calculate the number of records?

Visual Basic has a debugger built into it, which you haven't used so far. Debuggers are programs, or part of environments like Visual Basic, that allow you to run your program one line at a time. This is known as *stepping* through your program. The easiest way to use the debugger in Visual Basic is to set a *breakpoint.* A breakpoint is a line of code in your program that you mark to tell Visual Basic that you want it to stop running (and enter Break mode) whenever it tries to run this line. Let's look at an example, using the new DBOpen subroutine.

Make sure DBOpen is visible in your Code window. Then move the insertion point to the last line, which sets the *numRecords* variable. Next, select **Toggle Breakpoint** from the Debug menu (or press **F9**). This last line of code will now be in bold, red text (see Figure 11.3) to indicate that it's a breakpoint.

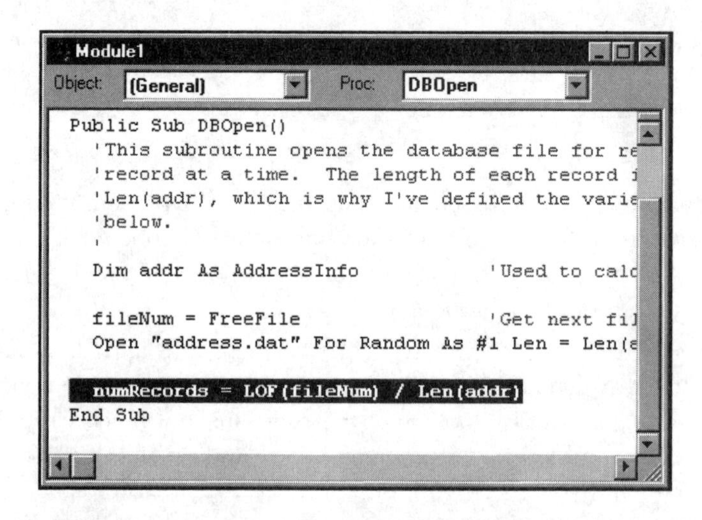

FIGURE 11.3 *Lines marked as breakpoints appear in inverse red type.*

Now press **F5** to run your program. Visual Basic will run your program until it encounters a breakpoint, stopping just before running the breakpoint line itself.

Next press **F8** or select **Single Step** from the Debug menu. This command runs a single line of code at a time. In this case it will run the code that sets *numRecords*.

After you've run this line of code, you can use the top part of the Debug window to display the value of the *numRecords* variable. Make sure the Debug window is active (select the Debug Window item from the Window menu if necessary), and then type the following line into the window:

```
?numRecords
 1
|
```

Visual Basic reports that there is just one record in the database, which is exactly what it should report (it will report 0 if you delete the ADDRESS.DAT file).

To "remove" this breakpoint, click on the line in your Code window that sets *numRecords* and press **F9** again. The F9 key *toggles* a breakpoint on and off. So pressing **F9** again will turn a breakpoint off if it was turned on.

You can continue running your program at any time by pressing **F5** again. Using breakpoints to stop your program (along with the F8 key to run your program one line at a time and using the Debug window to see the values stored in variables), is extraordinarily useful. From time to time you'll find your programs don't work the way you expect them to, and you won't be able to figure out why they don't. This is when using breakpoints and single-stepping (the F8 key) is really useful. You can see exactly what lines of code your program runs, and you can see the values of the variables your program uses.

There is another debugging technique that is also very useful, but not used as often by Visual Basic programmers, simply because they're not familiar with it. Add the following line to the end of your DBOpen subroutine, just before the End Sub statement:

```
Debug.Print "numRecords = "; numRecords
```

The Debug object actually refers to the Debug window, so this line of code displays text in the Debug window. Run your program again (make sure you don't have a breakpoint set). Then select Debug Window from the Window menu after your program starts. You should see a line like the following one in your Debug window:

```
numRecords = 1
```

Using the Debug object to send output to the Debug window is a very useful method for debugging your program. You can easily track exactly what changes your program makes to variables, and when they're made.

Remember to remove the Debug.Print statement before you continue. If you leave it in, your program will continue to work correctly, but because you don't need this statement anymore, it's a good idea to remove it.

Creating a DBLen() Function

Now that you know DBOpen is correctly calculating the number of records in a file, let's finish making the changes to support reading and writing multiple records.

Several of the modified subroutines, which you'll see below, use a new function called DBLen(). This function returns the number of records in your database file. You create functions in a module just as you create subroutines (select Procedure from the Insert menu), except that you need to click on the option button called Function in the Insert Procedure dialog box.

The following function is called DBLen():

```
Public Function DBLen () As Integer
  '
  ' Returns the number of records currently stored in
  ' the database.
  '
  DBLen = numRecords          ' Return number of records
End Function
```

Notice how Functions begin and end with the word "Function," just like subroutines begin and end with the word "Sub." And notice also the use of As Integer that appears after the function name, telling Visual Basic that this function returns a number of type Integer. "DBLen = numRecords assigns a value to the DBLen function, which is the value that will be returned by DBLen.

REFERENCE: FUNCTIONS

You can create functions just as easily as you can create subroutines. The only difference is that you'll want to define the type of value your function will return.

```
Function funcName ([parameters]) [As typeName]
  [statements]
  [funcName = value]
  [Exit Function]
  [statements]
  [funcName = value]
End Function
```

Defines a function called *funcName* that returns a value with the type *typeName*. The default return type, if you don't provide one, is As Variant.

```
funcName = value
```

Sets the return value for the function.

```
Exit Function
```

This statement stops running the function and returns the current value stored in *funcName*.

When you have this function in your DATABASE.BAS module, you can test DBLen to make sure it works as follows: Run your program, and then press **Ctrl+Break** to stop your program and display the Debug window. You can then call this function directly to see what number it returns by typing the following line:

```
?DBLen()
 1
|
```

DBLen() reports that there is one record in the database file, which is what it should return. When you're done with the Debug window, press **F5** to continue running your program.

There is one thing about using functions that's different from using subroutines. You'll notice the two parentheses after the function name. Visual Basic distinguishes between functions and subroutines by requiring parentheses for functions, but not for subroutines.

Modifying DBRead

The DBRead subroutine, as you can see here, has a lot more code than before, which we'll describe below:

```
Public Sub DBRead (num As Integer, addr As AddressInfo)
  '
  ' Retrieves a single record from the database. Records
  ' range from 1..DBLen().
  '
  ' On entry:   num   Number of record to read
  ' Returns:   addr  The record just read
  '
  Dim i As Integer             ' Actual record number

  i = num                      ' Record number requested
  If i < 1 Then i = 1          ' Make sure i >= 1.
  If i > DBLen() Then          ' Is i too large?
    i = DBLen()                ' Yes, use the last record
  End If

  Get #fileNum, i, addr        ' Read record i from the file
End Sub
```

When you modify DBRead in your program, make sure you add the *num* parameter to the first line, and don't forget the parentheses that follow DBLen.

Most of this new code checks and handles boundary conditions. As we mentioned before, boundary conditions are special cases you need to check in your programs. Here, for example, the Get command doesn't allow record numbers less than 1, so you need to make sure you don't pass it a number less than 1. That's why you added code that sets the variable *i* 1 if *num* is less than 1. It's also a good idea to check for numbers that are larger. The Get command can never read records past the end of the file, so you set *i* to the number of records if *num* is too large.

When you've made these changes, you should test your program to make sure these changes work correctly. You can do that by changing the call to DBRead in the GetRecord subroutine of Address.frm as follows:

```
DBRead 1, addr               ' Read one record
```

Run your program to make sure it works correctly. You can also easily test to make sure DBRead handles the boundary conditions correctly. Here's how. Change the 1 in the line above to a 0. Does your program still display the first record correctly? Then change this number to 2, which is larger than the number of records in your file. Does your program still work correctly? Make sure you set it back to 1 when you're done testing.

It's a good idea to perform such simple tests whenever you make changes to your program. We know we've said this before, but it's so important that we wanted to mention it again.

Modifying DBWrite

The changes to DBWrite look very much like the changes to DBRead, except for one small difference: DBWrite allows you to create a new record, which requires writing a record past the end of the file. In other words, you need to be able to write a record number equal to DBLen() + 1 as follows:

```
Public Sub DBWrite (num As Integer, addr As AddressInfo)
  '
  ' Writes a single record to the database file. The
  ' record number ranges from 1 .. DBLen() + 1
  '
  Dim i As Integer                ' Number of record to write

  i = num                         ' Record you want to write
  If i < 1 Then i = 1             ' Make sure i >= 1.
  If i > DBLen() Then             ' Is this past end of file?
    i = DBLen() + 1               ' Yes, add new record to file
    numRecords = numRecords + 1 ' Keep track of num records
  End If

  Put #fileNum, i, addr           ' Write record to file
End Sub
```

Again, you'll need to make sure you add the *num* definition to the first line above.

All of this code should be clear after the description above of DBRead, except for the small change we already mentioned that allows you to add a new record to the file.

To test these changes, you'll need to modify the call to DBWrite in the SaveRecord subroutine of Address.frm as follows:

```
DBWrite 1, addr         ' Write record back to file
```

Your program should now run correctly (but remember that SaveRecord won't run until you quit your program). You can test the boundary conditions by changing the 1 here to a 0 or a 2. Remember to set it back to 1 when you're finished testing boundary conditions.

By the way, when you test this with the record number set to 2, you should discover that your file size grew from 584 bytes to 1,168 bytes because you just added a second record to your database.

Adding Comments to DBClose

Finally, the DBClose subroutine doesn't require any changes to support multiple records, but we've added the following comments to the start of this subroutine:

```
Public Sub DBClose ()
   '
   'You should call this subroutine when your program is
   'finished using the database (usually just before it
quits).
   '
   Close #fileNum
End Sub
```

These are all the changes you'll need to make to the DATABASE.BAS module. All the other changes will be to the form itself.

Adding Multiple Records to the Form

The form actually needs much more code to support multiple records than you've written in the DATABASE.BAS module. Why is this? Many Windows programs you write will have more code to handle the user interface than to do the actual work. Reading and writing multiple records is actually quite easy, but providing the support behind the user interface is not so simple.

Think about this: There are a lot of functions you'll need to have available when you're viewing or changing records in your database. For example, you'll need to be able to find addresses, sort them, delete them, and so on. The reading and writing of a record is just one small part of the picture. All of the other functions are built on top of the database functions.

In this section you'll modify the form so all of the basic user-interface functions work, such as adding new records. (We'll leave printing, searching, and sorting for the next chapter.)

Adding Form-Level Variables

Right now your form only reads and writes a single record, and it doesn't remember the creation or modification dates for records. We've used four form-level variables to keep track of information on the current record: Whether you've changed it, the number of the current record, and the modification and creation dates. Add the following definitions to the (declarations) section of your form:

```
Private recChanged As Boolean      ' True when record's changed
Private currentRec As Integer       ' Current record number
Private createDate As Date          ' Date record was created
Private modifyDate As Date          ' Date record last modified
```

You've defined *currentRec* as an Integer, which means you won't be able to have more than 32,767 records in your file. We didn't think this would be a problem, but if you do want to allow more records, you should redefine all numbers that refer to record numbers As Long rather than As Integer. And both *createDate* and *modifyDate* are defined as Variant—that is what you want because this is the type of number returned by the Now() function.

Modifying GetRecord

Next you'll modify the GetRecord and SaveRecord subroutines so that they'll have a record number parameter, allowing them to read and write any record number. Right now they're both hard-coded to read record number 1. These subroutines contain all the other code you'll need for the rest of this chapter. The new version of GetRecord (make sure you add the parameter *num* in the first line) is as follows:

```
Private Sub GetRecord (ByVal num As Integer)
  '
  ' Reads a record from the database and sets all the
  ' controls in this form.
  '
  ' On entry:   num   Number of record, 1..DBLen()
  '
  Dim addr As AddressInfo

  If num > DBLen() Then       ' Is this past end of file?
    num = DBLen()             ' Yes, set to last record
```

```
    ElseIf num < 1 Then          ' Is it before first record?
      num = 1                    ' Yes, set to first record
    End If
    currentRec = num             ' Remember current record num

    If DBLen() = 0 Then          ' Are there any records?
      ClearRecord                ' No, return a clear record
      UpdateStatus               ' Update the status info
      Exit Sub                   ' We're all done here.
    End If

    DBRead num, addr             ' Read one record

    '
    ' Finally we need to set all the controls based on the
    ' values of this record.
    '
    txtAddress.Text = RTrim$(addr.address)
    txtNotes.Text = RTrim$(addr.notes)

   For i = 0 To 3
      txtPhone(i).Text = RTrim$(addr.phones(i))
      cboPhone(i).ListIndex = addr.types(i)
    Next i

  createDate = addr.created      ' Get creation date into
global
    modifyDate = addr.modified ' Get last modify date
    UpdateStatus                 ' Update record number display
    recChanged = 0               ' Record hasn't changed yet
  End Sub
```

Before you can try this new subroutine, you'll need to make three other changes. First, you'll need to change the call to GetRecord in Form_Load so it supplies a record number:

```
    GetRecord 1                 ' Get the first record
```

Second, you'll need to create an empty subroutine called ClearRecord. You'll fill this subroutine in later, but for now you need to create it so you'll be able to test the new version of GetRecord.

Finally, you'll need to define the subroutine UpdateStatus, which will update the labels at the bottom of your form to show the record number, creation date, and modification date. The subroutine UpdateStatus is as follows:

```
Private Sub UpdateStatus ()
   '
   ' Updates the status information, which includes the
   ' current record counter and the create/modify date
   ' at the bottom of the input window.
   '
   lblPage.Caption = Format$(currentRec) + "/" + _
   Format$(DBLen())
   lblCreated.Caption = Format$(createDate, "ddddd")
   lblModified.Caption = Format$(modifyDate, "ddddd")
End Sub
```

This last subroutine should be clear, because you've worked with Format$ and the Caption parameter before. There are just a couple of new items. First, the formatting string "ddddd" tells Format$ to format a Date value as a short date. For the United States, a short date is a date like 12/25/92. It may be 1992-12-25 if you have the country setting in Windows set to Sweden. Also, you used the plus operator to combine three strings in the first assignment statement. As you learned in Chapter 2, plus concatenates strings.

Because the new GetRecord is rather long, let's take a quick look at what it does, and how it works. First, you'll notice we had you put a ByVal keyword in front of the definition of the *num* parameter. Why did we do this? For a couple of reasons. First, defining *num* as ByVal means GetRecord gets a copy of *num*, so you can change the value inside GetRecord without affecting the original number—in other words, without changing the variable used in any subroutine that calls GetRecord. But the real reason is a little more subtle.

Whenever you call a subroutine or function, every parameter has a specific type. In the case of GetRecord, that type is Integer. Without the ByVal keyword, all parameters are passed by reference, which means that the parameter in your subroutine refers to the original variable. This can only work if both the variable and the parameter have the same type.

But if you use a variable, such as *i*, that you haven't defined with a Dim statement, its type will be Variant. If you try to pass a Variant variable by reference to a subroutine that expects an Integer parameter, Visual Basic will stop your program and display an alert box that says "Parameter type mismatch." Passing a variable by value eliminates this problem.

Parameters defined as ByVal receive a copy of the variable, rather than a reference to the original variable, so the variables don't have to be the same type—provided both the variable and the parameter are numbers (Byte, Integer, Long, Single, Double, or Currency type).

The first few lines of code make sure *num* has a valid record number: Between 1 and DBLen(). Then GetRecord saves this record number in the form-level variable *currentRec*. This variable keeps track of what record you're looking at, and it's used by several subroutines, including UpdateStatus.

Next you'll notice five lines of code that start with If DBLen() = 0. When you run Address Book for the very first time, the address book file will be empty. In this case, you need to make sure that you have a new, empty record with all of the values set correctly, which is what the ClearRecord subroutine does. UpdateStatus makes sure all the status displays are correct. The Exit Sub statement exits from the subroutine without running any more commands in the subroutine; you don't need to run the rest of GetRecord after you create an empty record.

Reference: Exit Sub Statement

The Exit Sub statement allows you to control when your program will finish running a subroutine.

```
Exit Sub
```

Stop running the subroutine, just as if Visual Basic had encountered the End Sub statement.

GetRecord then calls DBRead to read one record from the file, and the rest of the code transfers the values from the *addr* variable to the controls on the form. The very last line sets the *recChanged* variable to False (0), to mark this record as unchanged. Other subroutines will set this value to True whenever you make changes to the record, which allows SaveRecord to save a record only when you've made changes to it.

Now run your program to see if it works. The status line at the bottom of your program should now show a record counter as well as the creation and modification dates. What you'll notice, however, is that the dates are blank. This is because you haven't added any code yet to set them. The creation date will be set correctly by ClearRecord whenever you create a new record, but right now ClearRecord has no code in it.

Creating Empty Records

New records are records that have all of the text fields blank, the phone-type combo boxes set up correctly, and the creation date set to the current date. The easiest way to set these fields is with ClearRecord, which clears all of the fields on the form. Add this code to the empty ClearRecord subroutine you created in the last section.

```
Private Sub ClearRecord ()
  '
  ' This subroutine clears all the fields in the data entry
  ' screen, which you'll need to do for a new record.
  '
  txtAddress.Text = ""          ' Clear the Address field
  txtNotes.Text = ""            ' Clear the Notes field
  For i = 0 To 3                ' Clear the telephone numbers
    txtPhone(i).Text = ""
  Next i

  cboPhone(0).ListIndex = 0   ' Set 1st type to Home
  cboPhone(1).ListIndex = 1   ' Set 2nd type to Office
  cboPhone(2).ListIndex = 2   ' Set 3rd type to FAX
  cboPhone(3).ListIndex = -1  ' Set 4th type to blank

  createDate = Now              ' Set creation date to today
  modifyDate = createDate

  recChanged = 0                ' Mark as unchanged.
End Sub
```

You can test this subroutine by first deleting the DATABASE.DAT file. Then run Address Book again. This time Address Book will notice there are no records in the file, so it will call ClearRecord to create a new record. You should now see a correct creation and modification date appear at the bottom of your form. However, when you close Address Book and run it again, you'll notice the dates are 12/30/99. This is because SaveRecord isn't saving this information (the date for a Date value of 0 happens to be 12/30/99), so you'll need to modify SaveRecord, which you'll do next.

Modifying SaveRecord

The changes to SaveRecord are really quite simple. It has some extra lines to save the creation and modification dates, as well as a couple of lines that check and set the *recChanged* variable. The new SaveRecord is not short, but it should be fairly clear as follows:

```
Private Sub SaveRecord ()
  '
  ' Saves the current record if it's been changed.
  '
  Dim addr As AddressInfo

  If Not recChanged Then      ' Did you change record?
    Exit Sub                  ' No, we're all done
  End If

  '
  ' This code sets all the fields in the variable addr
  ' to reflect the values stored in the controls.
  '
  modifyDate = Now          ' Set modify date to today

  addr.address = txtAddress.Text
  addr.notes = txtNotes.Text

  For i = 0 To 3
    addr.phones(i) = txtPhone(i).Text
    addr.types(i) = cboPhone(i).ListIndex
```

```
    Next i

    addr.created = createDate
    addr.modified = modifyDate

    DBWrite currentRec, addr  ' Write record back to file

    recChanged = False        ' We just saved the record
End Sub
```

Testing this code requires some changes you'll make below. If you delete the DATABASE.DAT file, and then run your program, it will show the correct date when you exit, then run again. But this is a result of the file being empty; SaveRecord won't save any changes because the *recChanged* variable will always be False. You need some code to set *recChanged* to True.

Noticing Changes to Records

The way that you can keep track of any changes you make is by using an event in text boxes called *Changed.* Visual Basic calls this event handler whenever you type any characters into a text box, so you can set the *recChanged* variable to True in these event handlers. Add the following code to track such changes:

```
Private Sub txtAddress_Change ()
  recChanged = True
End Sub

Private Sub txtNotes_Change ()
  recChanged = True
End Sub

Private Sub txtPhone_Change (Index As Integer)
  recChanged = True
End Sub
```

Now when you run Address Book, it should correctly save your record whenever you change the text in any of your text fields.

Reference: Change Event

The Change event is called anytime you change any of the text in a text box.

```
Sub ctlName_Change ()
```

This event handler is called whenever the text in a text box is changed.

There are other controls that also support the Change event (combo boxes, directory list boxes, drive list boxes, scroll bars, labels, and picture boxes), and the meaning is a little different for each control. See the *Language Reference Manual* for more details.

You'll also need to set the *recChanged* flag whenever you change any of the phone-type combo boxes. But you can't use the Change event for combo boxes because this event doesn't apply to the drop-down list style of combo boxes you're using here. Instead, you'll need to use the Click event, which is called whenever you select one of the items from the drop-down list. Add the following code to your form:

```
Private Sub cboPhone_Click (Index As Integer)
  recChanged = True
End Sub
```

Those are all the changes you'll need to keep track of when you modify the address information in your form.

Creating the Menu Bar

To add new records to the database, you'll need some way to ask for new records. So the next thing you'll want to do is create a menu bar for your program, with a menu item for adding new records to your file. Table 11.1 shows all the menus, items, and control names for the menu. Add this menu to your program.

TABLE 11.1 *Menus Used by Address Book*

Caption	CtlName	Accelerator
&File	menFile	
&Print…	miPrint	Ctrl+P
P&rint Setup…	miPrintSetup	
—	miFileLine	
E&xit	miExit	
&Edit	menEdit	
&Undo	miUndo	Ctrl+Z
—	miEditLine1	
Cu&t	miCut	Ctrl+X
&Copy	miCopy	Ctrl+C
&Paste	miPaste	Ctrl+V
—	miEditLine2	
&Find…	miFind	Ctrl+F
&Go to…	miGoto	F5
&Address	menAddress	
&New	miNew	Ctrl+N
&Delete	miDelete	
&Sort	miSort	
—	miAddressLine1	
Ne&xt	miNext	F4
&Previous	miPrevious	F3

Most of these menu items use a number of Ctrl+*key* shortcuts that may or may not be familiar to you. With the introduction of Windows 3.1, Microsoft changed some of the standard keyboard shortcuts that new programs should use (see Table 11.2 for a list of recommended and suggested shortcuts). You set these *accelerator* keys with the Accelerator combo box inside the Menu Design window.

TABLE 11.2 *Keyboard Shortcut Standards*

Function	Key
Recommended Ctrl+*letter* Shortcuts	
Undo	Ctrl+Z
Cut	Ctrl+X
Copy	Ctrl+C
Paste	Ctrl+V
Suggested Ctrl+*letter* Shortcuts	
New	Ctrl+N
Open	Ctrl+O
Print	Ctrl+P
Save	Ctrl+S
Bold	Ctrl+B
Italic	Ctrl+I
Underline	Ctrl+U
Double underline	Ctrl+D
Small caps	Ctrl+K
Word-by-word underline	Ctrl+W
Remove char formatting	Ctrl+space

Before Windows 3.1, the standard shortcut keys for Undo, Cut, Copy, and Paste were Alt+Backspace, Shift+Del, Ctrl+Ins, and Shift+Ins, respectively. We don't know about you, but we found these hard to remember, and often chose the wrong key. Microsoft's new shortcuts are much easier to work with.

Your program should not use any of the shortcut keys in Table 11.2 for functions other than the ones listed. In other words, don't use Ctrl+N for Next record—only use Ctrl+N for New.

How to Choose Keyboard Shortcuts

Microsoft has a number of suggestions on how to choose keyboard shortcuts for different functions. When you have a choice between a function key or a Ctrl+letter, the Ctrl+letter combination is often better because it's easier to remember than a function key. Below you'll find suggestions for the use of shifted and unshifted function keys:

- **Unshifted function keys.** Assign simple function keys, like F3, to small tasks that you might perform frequently. For example, in the Address book program you've assigned F3 and F4 to Previous and Next record, so you can switch records easily.
- **Shift+key combinations.** Use for actions that either extend, or are complimentary to actions that have an unshifted function key assigned to them. For example, if you assigned find to F5 (rather than Ctrl+F), you might use Shift+F5 for search again.
- **Ctrl+key combinations.** Use for infrequent, larger tasks that are similar to the task provided by the unshifted function key. For example, Ctrl+F5 might be searched again backwards when F5 is search, and Shift+F5 is searched again. Also use Ctrl+cursor-movement keys to move in larger increments. For example, Ctrl+left arrow moves back by an entire word.
- **Alt+key combinations.** Microsoft generally recommends against using any Alt+key combinations. All Alt+letter keys are reserved for use with mnemonic access characters for selecting menus and or controls. Some of the Alt+function keys have assignments already in the control menu.

Adding New Records

You now have all of the pieces you need to be able to add new records to your database, and the code to do this is very simple. Add the following code to the miNew_Click event handler:

```
Private Sub miNew_Click ()
    '
    ' Create a new record at the end of the file. This
    ' record will be saved only if you type something into it.
```

```
    '
    SaveRecord                ' Save changes to current record
    currentRec = DBLen() + 1  ' Add record to the end
    ClearRecord               ' Clear the current record

    UpdateStatus              ' Update record counter display
    txtAddress.SetFocus       ' Put insertion point in address
End Sub
```

This subroutine took only five lines of code! When you've written the right tools, you'll find that you can write some very powerful subroutines by calling several existing subroutines. Let's take a quick look at how this works. First, miNew_Click calls SaveRecord to save any changes you may have made to the current record. Next, it changes the form-level variable *currentRec* so it points to an empty slot at the end of the database file. The call to ClearRecord initializes all the controls in the form for an empty record. UpdateStatus updates the status information at the bottom of the form.

The last statement uses a new method, SetFocus, that allows you to change which control has the current keyboard focus. The txtAddress.SetFocus statement moves the insertion point back to the address text box. Without this statement, the keyboard focus remains wherever it was before, which isn't the most natural place for it to be. Whenever you ask to create a new record, you'd expect to be able to start typing a new address in immediately. In other words, you expect the insertion point to be in the address text box, and this is why you included the txtAddress.SetFocus statement in this subroutine.

Reference: SetFocus Method

The SetFocus method allows you to change which control has the current keyboard focus. In the case of text boxes, the control with the focus is the control that will have the insertion point visible and active.

```
controlName.SetFocus
```

Causes the keyboard focus to shift to the control named *controlName*.

You can test this out, but you won't be able to look at any of your new records until you make the next set of changes.

Navigating through Records

In this section we'll show you the code we wrote to get Address Book to move between records, using the next and previous buttons at the bottom of the form. The first thing you'll need is a subroutine called NextRecord, which can move forward or backward through the records in your file. Add the following subroutine to your form:

```
Private Sub NextRecord (delta As Integer)
  '
  ' This subroutine moves between records, either forwards
  ' or backwards. NextRecord saves any changes to the
  ' current record before it shows a different record.
  '
  ' On entry:
  '   delta   +1   Show the next record
  '           -1   Show previous record
  '
  Dim num As Integer

  SaveRecord                    ' Be sure to save changes

  num = currentRec + delta      ' Move to "next" record
  If num < 1 Then               ' Are we past start?
    num = DBLen()               ' Yes, wrap to last record
  ElseIf num > DBLen() Then     ' No, are we past end?
    num = 1                     ' Yes, wrap to first record
  End If

  GetRecord num                 ' Show this new record
End Sub
```

Then you'll need to add code to the cmdNext_Click and cmdPrev_Click event handlers so clicking on these buttons will move you forward and backwards one record at a time. Add the following code to each event handler:

```
Private Sub cmdNext_Click ()
  NextRecord 1              ' Show next record in database
  txtAddress.SetFocus       ' Put insertion point in address
End Sub
```

```
Private Sub cmdPrev_Click ()
  NextRecord -1             ' Show previous record in dbase
  txtAddress.SetFocus       ' Put insertion point in address
End Sub
```

All three of these subroutines should be clear. Notice the txtAddress.SetFocus statement in each Click event handler. These statements put the insertion point into the address text box. Without these statements, the keyboard focus will remain in the next or previous command button, which probably won't feel as natural.

If you followed the values in Table 11.1, you also defined two menu items for moving to the next and previous records, called Next and Previous on the Address menu, and attached the keyboard shortcuts to these menu items, F3 and F4 respectively. Now you need to add the following code so you'll be able to move between records using either the keyboard or the mouse. The two event handlers for these menu items are as follows:

```
Private Sub miNext_Click ()
  cmdNext_Click
End Sub
```

```
Private Sub miPrevious_Click ()
  cmdPrev_Click
End Sub
```

Each of these event handlers simply calls the event handler for the next or previous button. Any code inside your form can activate a Click event handler simply by writing it's name, as shown here. Now try your program to see how the Next and Previous menu items work.

Enabling the Exit Menu Item

Let's take a look at what code you need to write for the miExit_Click event handler, which handles the Exit menu item on the File menu. You might expect that you'd need to put an End statement here. But you don't. An End statement will exit your program immediately, without ever running the Form_Unload event handler. But you need this event handler to run so it will save changes you've made to the current record.

You could duplicate the call to SaveRecord in miExit_Click, but there's a better way. Enter the following code into miExit_Click:

```
Private Sub miExit_Click ()
  Unload Address
End Sub
```

The Unload command *unloads* a form from memory. What this means is that the form will be removed from your screen, and Visual Basic will run its Form_Unload event handler. Your program will exit automatically as soon as all its forms have been unloaded from memory. So you should always be careful not to use the End command when any of your forms have a Form_Unload event handler, because calling Unload *form* will both run Form_Unload and exit your program.

Reference: Unload Command

The Unload command allows you to unload any form from memory, which causes that form's Form_Unload event handler to be called. Your program will quit when all its forms have been unloaded.

`Unload formName`

Unloads the form called *formName* from memory, which results in the Form_Unload event being called.

You can use the Load command to load a form back into memory, and the Show command to both load and show a form on the screen.

Supporting Cut, Copy, Paste, and Undo

At this point you have a fully functional address book program that you can start to use. You might want to delete the ADDRESS.DAT file before you continue, which will remove all of your test records. You'll be able to enter addresses and move between them. But you won't be able to delete them yet (you'll handle that in Chapter 12).

Any real Windows program should support the Cut, Copy, Paste, and Undo items on the Edit menu. Many programs that people write for themselves don't support these functions. But as you'll see here, it's very easy to add an Edit menu to any program that includes text boxes. Add the following code below to the four event handlers for the Edit menu:

```
Private Sub miUndo_Click ()
  SendKeys "%{BACKSPACE}" ' Send Alt+Backspace
End Sub
```

```
Private Sub miCut_Click ()
  SendKeys "+{DELETE}"    ' Send Shift+Del
End Sub
```

```
Private Sub miCopy_Click ()
  SendKeys "^{INSERT}"    ' Send Ctrl+Ins
End Sub
```

```
Private Sub miPaste_Click ()
  SendKeys "+{INSERT}"    ' Send Shift+Ins
End Sub
```

Here's how these subroutines work. Visual Basic has a command called SendKeys that sends keystrokes to whichever control has the current keyboard focus. To allow you to send special keys, such as Alt+Backspace, this command uses some special characters: % for Alt, + for Shift, and ^ for Control. Also, any characters between curly braces, such as {BACKSPACE}, refer to a key, and SendKeys will send this keystroke rather than the text inside the braces.

REFERENCE: SENDKEYS COMMAND

The SendKeys command allows you to send any keystrokes to the control with the current keyboard focus.

```
SendKeys "string" [,wait%]
```

Sends the characters in *string* to the active control.

wait%

Determines whether SendKeys waits until the keystrokes are processed before returning control. Set it to True (–1) to wait or False (0) to return immediately. By default, SendKeys returns immediately.

All text boxes support the keyboard combinations as follows:

Undo	Alt+Backspace
Cut	Shift+Del
Copy	Ctrl+Ins
Paste	Shift+Ins

All the code has to do is send these keystrokes to the edit boxes.

A few pages ago we told you that with the introduction of Windows 3.1, Microsoft changed its standard keyboard shortcuts, and now uses Ctrl+Z for Undo, Ctrl+X for Cut, Ctrl+C for Copy, and Ctrl+V for Paste. However, not everyone has adopted the new standard. Those who have adopted it support the old and new keystroke combinations. Visual Basic is no exception in that it, too, supports both, so don't be confused. We did tell you to use the Ctrl+Z, X, C, and V keystrokes, and we did tell you to put them on your Edit menu, but this is in no way a conflict with the use of the code in the event handlers shown above; rather, it is a safeguard.

You now have an Address Book program that actually works. In Chapter 12 you'll finish Address Book by adding three new functions: Print, Search, and Sort.

Related Tools

- **GotFocus and LostFocus events.** You can use these two events to tell when a control gains or loses the keyboard focus. The control receiving the focus will have it's GotFocus event handler called, and the control that just lost the focus will have it's LostFocus event handler called. Don't rely on the order of the GotFocus and LostFocus method calls: sometimes LostFocus will be called before GotFocus, and sometimes after GotFocus. In other words, the old control won't always be notified that it's lost focus *before* the new control is notified that it's gained the focus.
- **Debugging.** Visual Basic has almost an entire menu of commands you might find useful for debugging. They're on the Debug menu in four groups: one for setting and clearing breakpoints, one for stepping through your program, one for watching the values of variables and expressions as you step through your program, and one for setting and

showing the next statement. You might want to read the sections of your manual on these commands to learn how they work. The Debug window is also very useful for debugging, because you can run any subroutine or function from this window. You can also change the values of variables.

- **Show and Load commands.** The Show command allows you to load a form into memory and make it visible. You'll need to use this command when your program has more than one form (you'll see how this works in Chapter 12). The Load command loads a form into memory without showing it first, which is useful if you need to make some changes to the form before you show it on the screen, such as centering the form. You can then call Show after you've made your changes.
- **Sending keys to other programs.** You can send keystrokes to other programs by using the SendKeys command along with AppActivate, which allows you to activate another program. SendKeys will send keystrokes to whatever program is the current application.

Summary

You learned a lot in this chapter.

- **Modules.** You learned how to add new modules to your programs. Modules can contain subroutines and module-level variables, but not forms or controls. Modules are very useful for containing a group of related subroutines, such as the ones in the database module.
- **Controls in other forms.** You can read and write the properties of controls in other forms by putting the form name in front of the control: *formName.controlName.property.*
- **Defining parameters.** The subroutines you create can have any number of parameters in them. You define the parameters between the parentheses in the first line of the Sub or Function definition.
- **Passing parameters.** Parameters can be passed either by reference (the default) or by value. Whenever a parameter is passed by reference, any changes you make to the value of the parameter inside the subroutine will change the original value. Also, the type of the variable that you're passing to the subroutine must be the same as the parameter in your subroutine.

Parameters passed by value (you put the keyword ByVal in front of the parameter definition) have a copy of their value passed to the subroutine, so any changes that you make in the subroutine will not change the original value. Also, variables passed by value don't have to have the same type as the parameter, as long as both values are numbers (Integer, Long, Single, Double, Currency, or Variant).

- **FreeFile.** This function returns the first available file number. You should call this function rather than hard-coding a file number into your programs. Remember to retain this file number in a form- or module-level variable so you can use it in Get, Put, and Close calls.
- **LOF.** The LOF function returns the length, in bytes, of a file that you've opened with the Open command.
- **Breakpoints.** Visual Basic allows you to set breakpoints in your programs. These are lines you mark (they appear in inverse red) using the F9 key. Visual Basic will stop running your program whenever it gets to one of these lines. You can then use the Debug window to display the values of variables, to change values, or to run subroutines and functions. You can also use F8 to run your program one line at a time and F5 to continue running your program until the next breakpoint.
- **Debug.Print.** Another way to debug your programs is to use the Debug.Print command to display information in the Debug window while your program runs.
- **Functions.** You can create new functions just as easily as you create new subroutines. The only difference is that you'll need to define what type of value your function returns, which you do by placing an As *typeName* at the end of your function definition. You then set the value that this function will return by assigning a value to a special variable with the function's name.
- **Formatting dates.** The string "ddddd" tells the Format$ function to format a time serial number as a short date—for example, 12/30/92. The actual format used is determined by the country setting in Windows, and could be something like 30.12.92.
- **Change event.** Every text box has a Change event handler that's called whenever you change any of the text in the box. Combo boxes also have a Change event, but the Change event doesn't apply to the Dropdown List style of combo box; for these you need to use the Click event to tell when you select an item from the drop-down list.

- **SetFocus method.** You can set which control has the current keyboard focus by calling the SetFocus method for that control. For example, you used txtAddress.SetFocus to set the focus back to the address text box after you press the Next or Previous button.
- **Unload command.** You can remove forms from the screen, and memory, by using the Unload command. The Unload command causes the Form_Unload event handler to run. Your program will end after all forms have been unloaded from memory.
- **SendKeys command.** This command allows you to send keystrokes to the control with the current keyboard focus. You can even use this command to send keystrokes to other programs, by using the AppActivate command.

SEARCHING, PRINTING, SORTING, AND DELETING

* Searching for strings
* Printing the address book
* Sorting addresses
* Deleting records

In Chapter 12, we're going to take a very different approach from previous chapters in this book. All of the changes you'll find described in this chapter are in the final version of Address Book on the included disk. But because we don't have room for detailed explanations, Chapter 12 will be a very brief overview of the changes we've made.

The source code on the disk has comments, so along with the descriptions you'll find here, you should be able to figure out what's going on. If you can't, experiment with the source code. Make some changes, and see what happens. Doing this kind of experiment is the best way to learn more about programming; it's how we first learned to write software.

Searching

The *Find...* item in the Edit menu will allow you to search through your names and address for any text. For example, you can search for the word "Great" to find the following address:

```
Joe M. Smith
Great Software Company
238 Somewhere Lane
Imaginary, CI 12345-6789
```

The Address Book program will allow you to search for any string that appears inside any of the text fields in an address record. If it finds the string, it will simply display that address record for you; otherwise it will beep to let you know it couldn't find the string. The only problem with searching in Address Book is that it is case-sensitive, so searching for "great" won't find the word "Great."

Searching the database isn't very difficult. Most of the work is done using Visual Basic's InStr function, which tells you whether a string is inside another string. For example, if you're searching for "Great" in the address above, you can use the InStr function to see if the string "Great" appears inside the address field, the notes field, or any of the telephone-number fields.

There are a couple of other things that you'll need. First, when you select the Find... item from the Edit menu, you'll need to display a dialog box that allows you to input a search string, such as the one shown in Figure 12.1.

To create this dialog box, you'll need to create a new form, using the Form item from the Insert menu. Then you'll want to add a text box and two command buttons to this form. We've created what's called a modal form (no resizable borders, no minimize or maximize buttons, no control menu, and a 3-D look) by setting the following properties:

Property	Setting
Appearance	1 – 3D
BorderStyle	3 – Fixed Dialog
ControlBox	False
Caption	Find
Name	FindDialog

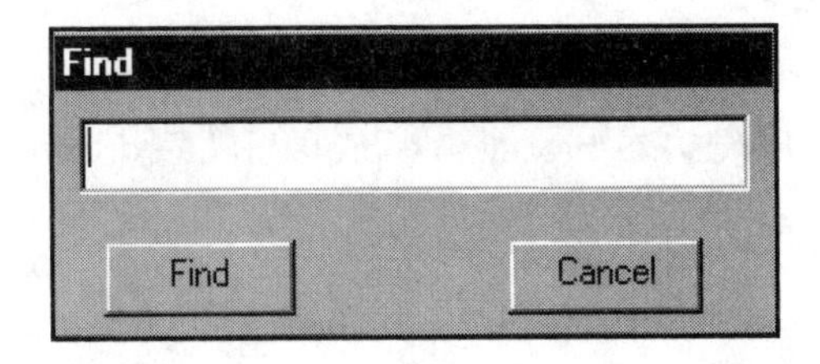

FIGURE 12.1 *This is what Address Book's Find dialog box looks like.*

You might have thought that the Common Dialog Custom Control on the Toolbox would do the trick here. After all, Find is a common function. Unfortunately, the Common Dialog Custom Control (in the standard edition of Visual Basic 4.0) only includes Open, Save As, Print, Color and Font. (The third-party custom control files from Crescent Software Inc. and MicroHelp Inc. support additional functions such as Find and Search-and- Replace. See Appendix B for more information.)

You'll also need to set the Default property to True for the Find button, and the Cancel property to True for the Cancel button. This will allow the Enter key to be the same as clicking on Find, and the Escape key to be the same as clicking on the Cancel button.

Now that you have two forms, there are a couple of questions that might occur to you. First of all, if you have two forms in your program, how does Visual Basic know which form to use when you run your program? Each project you create has a *Startup Form*, which is the form that Visual Basic will load and run when your program starts. You can actually change this form (you don't want to right now) using the Project Options dialog box, which you get to by selecting Project Options... from the Tools menu.

The other question, which is more relevant to what we're trying to do here, is how do you use a new form that you've added to your project? So far, you've used only one form in each of the projects you've built while reading this book. In turns out that you need to *load* a form into memory and then *show* the form. Loading the form triggers an event in the form called Form_Load, which you've already used in other programs, but it doesn't actually cause a form to become visible on the screen. You display a dialog box using the Show method (which will load a form if it isn't already loaded into memory:

```
FindDialog.Show          ' Load and display dialog box
```

When you display this dialog box, you'll probably need to make it a Modal dialog box. Modal dialog boxes always stay in front of the main window until you click on the Find or Cancel button. To display this dialog box as a Modal dialog box, you use the Show method of a form with a 1 after it, as follows:

```
FindDialog.Show 1        ' Display modal dialog box
```

Putting a 1 after Show tells Visual Basic that you want the form displayed as a Modal dialog box, so the subroutine that calls Show won't continue to run until the new form is no longer visible on the screen (you can hide a form using the Hide method).

Next, you'll need some way to communicate information between the Find dialog box and the code that called it. Prior to Visual Basic 4.0, there was no direct way to communicate between two forms, so you had to use a somewhat back-door approach. We'll show you the old method for two reasons: first, you might sometimes see code written by other programmers that uses this back-door approach, and second, the old method will allow us to show you some aspects of working with other forms.

Here's what to do. In the Click event handler for the Cancel button, set the **Text** field of the text box to an empty string: " ". Then in the Click event handler for both buttons, hide the form as follows:

```
Private Sub cmdFind_Click ()
  Hide                    ' Return to Address Book
End Sub
```

```
Private Sub cmdCancel_Click ()
  txtFind.Text = ""       ' Indicate cancel
  Hide                    ' Return to Address Book
End Sub
```

When you hide the Find dialog box, the code in Address Book that called FindDialog.Show will continue to run, so most of the work is done in the miFind_Click event handler. In this event handler you can look at the text in the txtFind button using a statement like the following:

```
If FindDialog.txtFind.Text = "" Then
  ' The Find dialog box was canceled
Else
  ' Do the find...
End If
```

When you hide the Find dialog box, the code after the call to FindDialog.Show 1 will continue to run, so most of the work is done in the miFind_Click event handler. In this event handler you can look at the text in the txtFind text box using a statement like the following:

```
FindDialog.Show 1

findStr$ = FindDialog.txtFind.Text
Unload FindDialog

If findStr$ Then
    ' The find dialog box was canceled
Else
    ' Do the find...
End If
```

This code retrieves the string from the Find dialog box. The next line, Unload FindDialog, removes the FindDialog form from memory, which you should do when you're done using the dialog box. If you leave the form in memory, your program won't actually quit when you unload the Address form. Visual Basic will continue to run your program as long as at least one form is loaded in memory (or until your code runs an End statement).

The actual searching for an address is reasonably simple. All you have to do is call DBRead to read each address, and InStr to search each field until you find a match. Then call GetRecord to retrieve and show the record you found. You'll find all the details in ADDRESS.FRM under miFind_Click and FINDDIAL.FRM.

Public Functions—Object-Oriented Programming

There is a much easier, cleaner way to use the Find dialog box that was introduced in Visual Basic 4.0. You can create a function in the FindDialog form called GetString() that will do all the work we just described. By creating this new function as a Public instead of a Private function, you will be able to call this function from any other form.

To create a new procedure, open the code window for the FormDialog form, then select **Procedure...** from the Insert menu. In the resulting dialog box, you'll want to type **GetString** and then click on the **Function** button before you press **Enter** (you'll notice that Public is already selected at the bottom of this window, see Figure 12.2). You have the choice of making any new function either Public or Private (private functions can only be called by code inside the same form or module as the function you're calling).

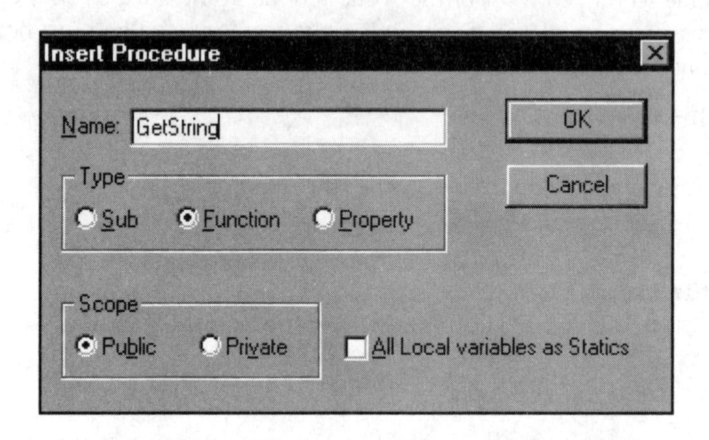

FIGURE 12.2 *This dialog box allows you to define new subroutines and functions.*

Here is the final code for the FindDialog form:

```
Dim findStr$                            ' Keep track of last
                                        ' string


Private Sub cmdCancel_Click()
    txtFind.Text = ""                   ' Indicate cancel
    Hide                                ' Return to GetString
End Sub

Private Sub cmdFind_Click()
    findStr$ = txtFind.Text             ' Remember the search
                                        ' string
    Hide                                ' Return to GetString
End Sub
```

```
Private Sub Form_Load()
    txtFind.Text = findStr$          ' Show previous search
                                     ' string
    txtFind.SelStart = 0             ' Select entire string
    txtFind.SelLength = 32767
End Sub

Public Function GetString() As String
    PositionDialog Me                ' Center over Address
    Show 1                           ' Show as modal dialog
    GetString = txtFind.Text         ' Get the final string
    Unload Me                        ' Can now remove from
                                     ' memory
End Function
```

Once you have the function GetString defined in this form, using the form is really simple, and you don't need to know anything about loading or unloading forms. In order to call a function defined inside a form, add the function name to the form name with a period in between:

```
findStr$ = FindDialog.GetString()
If findStr$ Then
    ' The find dialog box was canceled
Else
    ' Do the find...
End If
```

As far as your code is concerned, you're calling a Single function that belongs to the FindDialog form—the GetString function takes care of all the details of displaying and unloading the form from memory.

You'll find more examples of using Public functions in the version of Address Book on the disk included with this book. Using Public functions like we've done here allows for much simpler cleaner programs.

About Object-Oriented Programming

In this section we'd like to give you an overview of some of the features offered in Visual Basic 4.0 that we don't have room to cover in this book.

We've just introduced you to a very powerful programming technique, which we won't cover in any more detail in this book. If you're planning to write real programs in Visual Basic, however, this is a technique you'll want to learn and become proficient at. The time you spend learning about this technique will buy you vast returns on your investment. John owns a company that writes commercial software and they use these techniques all the time—they would not want to go back to the old way.

This type of programming has a couple of names. The first one is *object-oriented programming* (OOP for short). The idea of object-oriented programming is that you work with separate *objects*, and each object is completely self-contained. This last concept is called *encapsulation*, and it means that the inner workings of the object (such as the FindDialog form) are hidden from the rest of your program. For example, the FindDialog object has a single Public function that you can call to get a string from someone using your program. When you call this function, you don't have to know anything about how to use the FindDialog form—that's all taken care of by the GetString function. Using OOP and encapsulation is very powerful because it allows you to build lots of small objects that have very simple *interfaces* to the rest of your program.

Another word, less frequently used, to describe this type of programming is the *component object model* (COM), which coincidentally is very much like the model used for a piece of Windows that you might have heard about: OLE. OLE used to be called *object linking and embedding* a couple of years ago, but today that really isn't an accurate acronym. A more accurate acronym might be *object leveraging environment.* In other words, the OLE parts of Windows provide a way for different objects to be linked together to build custom programs.

For example, you might want to build a program that needs a spreadsheet for part of the program. Instead of writing an entire spreadsheet object, which is a lot of work, you could borrow Microsoft Excel's spreadsheet. Excel can be used inside other programs as an OLE object, and your program can control Excel using much the same type of code that you used with the FindDialog form. The following line of code reads the cell at 10, 1 and puts this value into the variable *i*:

```
i = excel.Cels(10, 1)
```

You can even use Visual Basic 4.0 to make your own OLE objects that you can use in other programs. For more details on all these techniques, you'll need to consult the manuals that come with Visual Basic.

Creating Properties

In addition to being able to create methods (Public Subs and Functions), Visual Basic 4.0 allows you to create your own properties. There are two ways you can create a property. The simplest way is to declare a variable as Public, like this:

```
Public varName
```

If you've defined this variable on a form called MyForm, you can read and write this value from anywhere in your program using the following type of code:

```
MyForm.varName = newValue        ' Set the value
i = MyForm.varName               ' Read the value
```

This type of property behaves exactly like a variable, except that you have access to this variable from outside the code in the form.

Another way to create a property is through property procedures. The idea here is twofold. First, sometimes setting a value requires that you actually run some code to handle changing the value. For example, when you set the Visible property of a control, this causes some code to run that actually hides the control. Simply changing the value of a Visible variable wouldn't cause the control to disappear. Second, there are times when the value of a property will need to be calculated when you ask to get its value. There may also be times when you want a property to be available only for reading or only for writing.

When you're creating a property that uses code instead of simply being a variable, you'll need to define either or both of the Property Let or Property Get subroutines. The Property Get subroutine reads the value of a property, while the Property Let subroutine sets the value.

Why is this last subroutine called Property Let instead of Property Set? Both types of procedures actually exist, but the Property Set is reserved for dealing with objects, which is an even more advanced topic that you may not get to for a while. In other words, for properties that use simple values such as numbers, strings, or dates, you'll want to use Property Let. (Many years ago, you had to use Let instead of = to assign values to variables, and this syntax is still supported in Visual Basic.)

As an example, let's say that you want to create a property that will return a number, and each time you ask for the value of this property it will return a higher number. (We can't think why you'd want a property to work this way, but it's a very easy example to write.) You can create such a property using the following code (notice that we've defined a variable where we keep the value inside the form):

```
Private myValue

Public Property Get Value()
    If IsEmpty(myValue) Then
        myValue = 0
    End If
    Value = myValue
    myValue = myValue + 1
End Property
```

In this example, the first line uses the IsEmpty function to determine if this is the first time the Value property is being read. Any variables that you define as Variant will be empty until you assign a value to them. The last two lines of this Property Get subroutine return the current value of myValue, which will be zero the first time, and then adds one to myValue.

The Property Set subroutine looks very much the same, except that it has a single parameter (or two if the property is part of an array), which is the value being assigned to the property:

```
Public Property Let Value(vNewValue)
    myValue = vNewValue
End Property
```

Property subroutines are another nice tool available to you for building object-oriented programs. These concepts take a little time to get used to, but as we said before, they're worth the effort.

Printing Addresses

Printing the address book doesn't take a lot of work, but we've used a few new concepts and techniques. You'll notice from the menu you created earlier that there are two menu items to support: Print... and Print Setup.... The Print... menu item allows you to print all of the addresses in your address book, and most Windows programs show a standard Print dialog box that lets you confirm your choice before the printing actually starts. The Print Setup... dialog box, on the other hand, allows you to change which printer you'll use or switch between portrait and landscape modes on your printer.

Both the Print and the Print Setup functions in Address Book use a set of dialog boxes provided by a *dynamic link library* (DLL) in Windows called COMMDLG.DLL, along with an OCX (*OLE Custom Control*) provided with Visual Basic 4.0 called COMDLG16.OCX for 16-bit Windows or COMDLG32.OCX for 32-bit Windows (Windows NT or Windows 95). The COMMDLG.DLL file is part of Windows (3.1 and later). In order to use the Visual Basic OCX, you'll need to select the **Custom Controls...** item from the Tools menu. Then check the item in the Custom Controls dialog that says Microsoft Common Dialog Control. Once you check this item, you'll see a new control appear on the tool bar. If you move the mouse over a control in the tool bar and pause, a small yellow window will appear with a name in it. The control you want will display the name CommonDialog.

Implementing the Print and Print Setup dialog boxes is actually very simple, as you can see in the file PRINT.BAS on the disk included with this book. The only tricky part is setting the correct flags before you call the ShowPrinter method. Fortunately, Visual Basic predefines all the constants that you'll need.

The actual work of printing records takes a little work, but it's not really difficult. Each address consists of a single string, which has to be broken up into individual lines so that they can be printing exactly where you want. The output from the Print routines looks something like the following:

```
Joe M. Smith                Home:      (800) 555-1212
Great Software Company      Office:     same
238 Somewhere Lane
Imaginary, CI 12345-6789
```

The left side contains the address (with a one-inch margin), and the right side contains any phone numbers you've filled in. We also draw a line between each address. You'll find all of the details in the PRINT.BAS module, as well as in ADDRESS.FRM.

Sorting Addresses

The Address Book program we developed in this book stores the addresses in the database in exactly the same order you typed them in, which isn't very useful. A real program should automatically sort addresses as you add them. The Address Book program included with this book, however, takes a slightly simpler approach. Each time you add a new address, it will be added to the end of the list. You'll then need to select the Sort item from the Address menu to explicitly ask Address Book to resort all of the addresses.

We took this approach because it's easy and fast. It's a little simpler (in terms of the code needed) to sort the addresses only on request. And by not having the program sort addresses as you add them, Address Book is a lot faster.

There are actually many different approaches to sorting names, so we chose the one that works best for us. The sorting program you'll find on the disk, in SORT.BAS, uses a sort method that John has used for years in a commercial product: *The Norton Commander.*

The idea behind this sort is that you want to compare two names in the address list, and if they're out of order, you want to "swap" them. You swap two addresses by reading one address, copying the second address to where the first address was, and then writing the first address to where the second address was. Again, you'll find all the details on how this works on the disk.

Deleting Addresses

We chose a very simple method for deleting addresses, but it's not very fast. The first thing we did was change the way the database works so we could use the first record in the file to keep information about the file itself. The first real address in the file will be in the *second* record.

The reason we did this is very straightforward. Visual Basic allows you to increase the size of a file, but it doesn't provide any way to decrease the size. In other words, you can't make a file shrink if you remove an address.

The problem is that DBLen uses the size of the file to calculate how many addresses are in the file, so it won't know that you've deleted records. By using the first record to keep track of how many addresses are actually in the file, you can remove addresses from the end of the file and then just update the count in the first record to keep track of the number of addresses.

Now when you remove an address from the file, the program moves all of the records after the deleted record down in the file by one record. For example, if you delete record number 10 from the file, the program copies record 11 to record 10, record 12 to record 11, and so on. Unfortunately, when you delete a record early in the file, the process is slow because each and every record following the deleted one must be moved down one at a time. On the other hand, because most people don't delete addresses very often, we decided to use this very simple approach.

You'll find all the details in the miDelete event handler. You'll also notice that we modified the DATABASE.BAS module to use the first record to keep track of how many files are in the address book.

Summary

You should now have enough of an understanding of programming and Visual Basic to start working on your own programs. In the next chapter we'll show you how you can use Data Manager and the Data control from the Toolbox to create Address Book in a different way. That will conclude Part II of this book. Part III contains some general-purpose subroutines and functions you can use in your own programs and as a source of inspiration in writing new programs.

Accessing Data: Data Manager and Data Control

In the last four chapters, you learned a great deal about interface building, reading and writing files to disk, working with multiple records, even searching, printing, sorting, and deleting records, all while building an address book application. Now we're going to show you a different approach to creating an address book application. In this chapter you'll use the Data Manager to create a database, and build your interface using a Data Control to access the database fields.

When you created your first Address Book program, you began with the interface design. This time, because you're already familiar with the design, you'll begin with the database itself. Also, until you decide how you want your data stored in the database, you won't be able to finalize the property settings for the form. For example, you know that your database will contain people's names and addresses, but until you decide whether you want to keep a person's name separate from his or her address or together as one field, you won't know whether to place one or two text controls on your form. Sometimes experimenting with the placement of controls on the form can help you to make these database decisions, but you will not be able to actually work with the data control and test your program step by step until you have created your database. Luckily for you, we have already made those decisions for the new Address Book application.

NOTE

The data control in the Standard Edition of Visual Basic 4.0 works with Microsoft Access databases (versions 1.0, 1.1, and 2.0), as well as with the following external databases: dBASE, Paradox, FoxPro and Btrieve.

Creating Your Address Book Database

You don't have Microsoft Access, or any of the other compatible database programs? No problem! You can use Visual Basic's Data Manager to create a database. Data Manager uses the same database engine used by Microsoft Access, so the Access database format is native to Visual Basic as well. But before you jump right in to the Data Manager program, let's define a few terms.

What is a Database?

A *database* is a collection of information (data) stored in one or more tables. Database tables, just like tables in word processing, are made up of columns and rows. In database lingo, columns are usually referred to as fields, and each row is a record. In your new Address Book sample application, each row/record will represent a person and you'll have columns/fields for name, address, phone numbers and other information.

Of course by now you're used to the fact that in Visual Basic lingo all these components are also referred to as objects—so you have database objects, table objects, field objects, even *index* objects. An index is one or more fields that you specify to make it easier and faster to find the information in your database. When you create an index, Visual Basic creates what is known as an *internal pointer*. Instead of reading entire records to find information, the pointers reference the chosen key field(s). You can also use indexes for sorting records and checking for duplicates.

A database object has properties that define such things as the Name of the database, the Connect string used to open the database, the CollatingOrder indicating the sort method to be used, whether or not the database is Updatable, and whether or not it supports Transactions.

Each database also has a collection of table definitions (TableDef objects) that define the fields and indexes for each table—one TableDef for each table in your database. TableDef properties include: Name, DateCreated, LastUpdated, and Updatable.

Each TableDef, in turn, maintains a collection of field objects to define each field—one field object for each field/column in a table. And (surprise!) field objects have properties too, including: Name, data Type, and maximum Size.

Another part of the TableDef object is its collection of Indexes. Four of the Index properties that will be most important to you at this time are: the index Name, the field or Fields that make up the index, whether or not the value in the index must be Unique for each record (thereby prohibiting duplicates), and whether the index in question is the Primary index for the table.

Many of the properties mentioned above are not available at design-time, and some of them you will not need to set, accepting instead the default settings. For example, not only is the CollatingOrder property of a database object not available at design-time, it is set by the language argument when the database is originally created. You can look up the valid setting for each of these properties in the *Microsoft Visual Basic Language Reference*. If you do check out the descriptions of these properties, you'll also find that some of them, for example, the Connect property, apply to more than one object (both the Database and TableDef objects have a Connect property).

Planning Your Database

The first thing you'll need to do is decide what tables and fields you'll need in your database. The new sample Address Book program uses only one table named Addresses. When it comes to defining the fields, we're going to maintain the approach you used in the earlier Address Book program, opting for one field that will contain the name and address information. Many database designers usually take a different approach, breaking fields down into smallest logical chunks of information, so that names, for example, are usually separated into first, middle, and last. Similarly, addresses are usually split into street1, street2, city, state, and zip code. We've chosen instead to show you a different way to handle the data—a way that includes a routine to select the last word from the first line of the address field, place it in a field called *Last Name*, and use it for sorting.

WARNING

Think your choices through carefully, because when you use the Data Manager to create your database, there's one catch: You can't alter the fields after they are defined. Nor can you delete an individual field, thinking to redefine it later. If you need to make a change to the database field definitions, you'll have to delete the whole table and start over. So make every effort to be sure of your fields, types, and lengths before you get started.

We've prepared a complete field listing, along with the type and size settings for the Addresses table (see Table 13.1). In the next section you'll use this listing to create your table fields.

TABLE 13.1 *Fields for the Address Table*

Field Name	Field Type	Field Size
Address	Text	160
Last Name	Text	25
Notes	Memo	
Phone 1	Text	25
Phone 2	Text	25
Phone 3	Text	25
Phone 4	Text	25
Phone Type 1	Integer	
Phone Type 2	Integer	
Phone Type 3	Integer	
Phone Type 4	Integer	
Date Created	Date/Time	
Date Modified	Date/Time	

Using the Data Manager

Okay, now you're ready to create your Address Book database. If you haven't done so yet, start Visual Basic. Then select **Data Manager** from the Add-Ins menu. The Data Manager application has two menus of its own: File and Help. Select **New Database** from the File menu. When the New Database dialog box appears, type in the database file name **ADDRESS.MDB** (the extension must be .MDB), and select the desired directory where you want this file to be located. When you click on **OK**, the Database: ADDRESS.MDB window appears as shown in Figure 13.1.

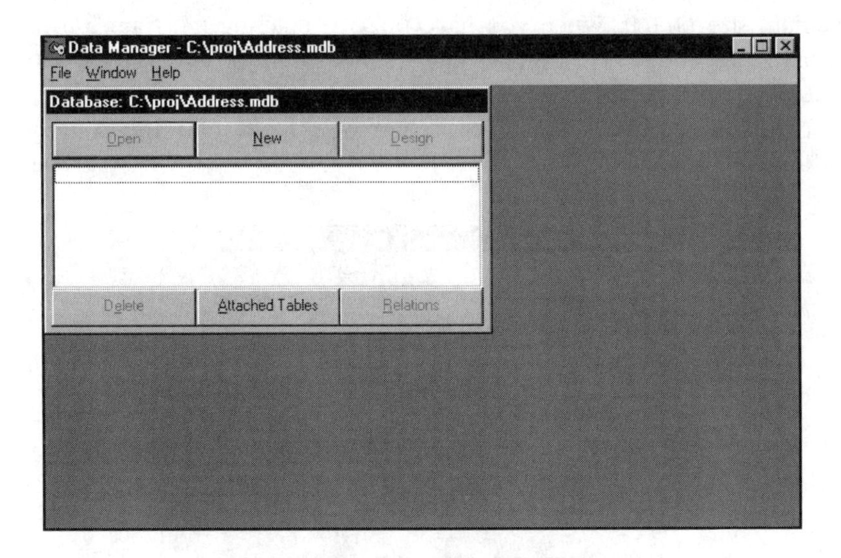

FIGURE 13.1 *Data Manger Database window.*

The main portion of the Database window is empty, because you have not yet created any tables. The window contains six buttons: Open, New, Delete, Design, Attach, and Relations. Because these actions apply to tables, and because you can't open, design, create relationships, or delete a table that doesn't exist, only the New and Attach buttons will work right now.

The ADDRESS database only needs one table, which we'll call Addresses. Click on the **New** button to bring up the Add Table dialog box where you will not only name the table, but also define all the fields. When the dialog box appears, enter the table name in the Table Name text box as shown in Figure 13.2.

Now use the **Tab** key or your mouse to move to the Field Name text box. Type your first field name, which is **Address**. Next, select **Text** from the Data Type combo box.

NOTE

You can also use the up and down arrow keys to move through the combo box selections, or if you type in a letter that is the first letter of one of the available Type choices, that type will automatically be selected.

Field Size is required for all Text fields, and your Address field should have a maximum size of 160. When you have finished entering the Name, Type, and Size, click **OK** and watch the field name show up in the box on the right (see Figure 13.2). Size applies only to text fields. When you define fields with other data types, as you'll see in a moment, N/A (not applicable) appears automatically in the Size box.

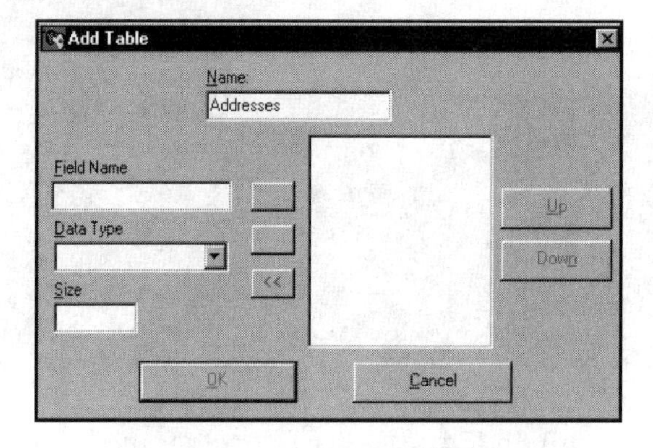

FIGURE 13.2 *Add Table dialog box.*

Now you can go ahead and create the rest of your Addresses table fields using the information in Table 13.1. As the field names appear in the box on the right, don't worry about running out of space. When you get to the Date Created field, vertical scroll bars will automatically appear, allowing you to scroll up and down. When you're done, click **OK** to close the Add Table dialog box. Then you'll be ready to create your table index.

Adding an Index

Now that your table definitions are complete, you can select the appropriate fields to create the indexes. You'll do this using the Table Editor. If you've been following instructions, the Data Manager windows should be open, the Addresses table should be listed in the box, and all except the New and Attach buttons are still gray. Once you select Addresses, the Design and Delete buttons also become accessible as shown in Figure 13.3.

When the Table Editor appears, as shown in Figure 13.4, click on the Indexes button to bring up the Indexes window. Then select Add to bring up the Add Index dialog box as shown in Figure 13.5.

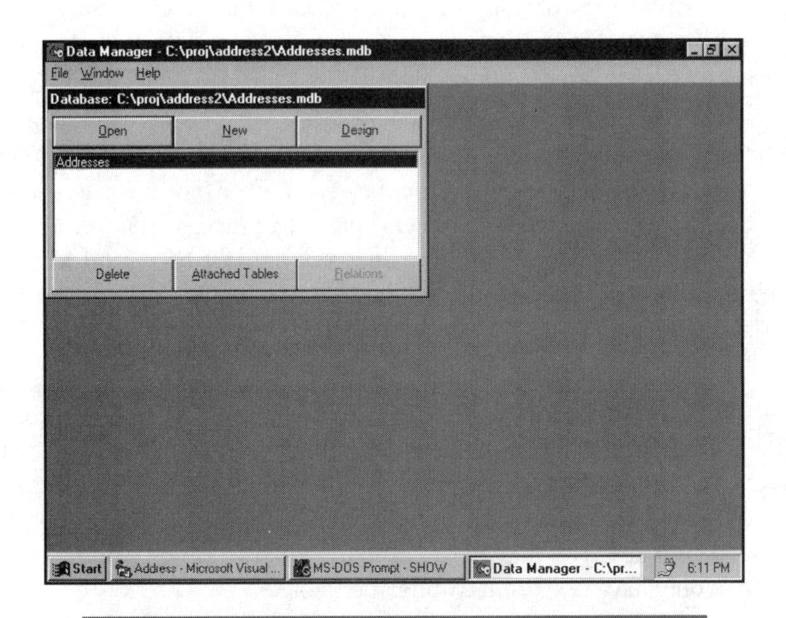

FIGURE 13.3 *Data Manager with the Addresses table selected.*

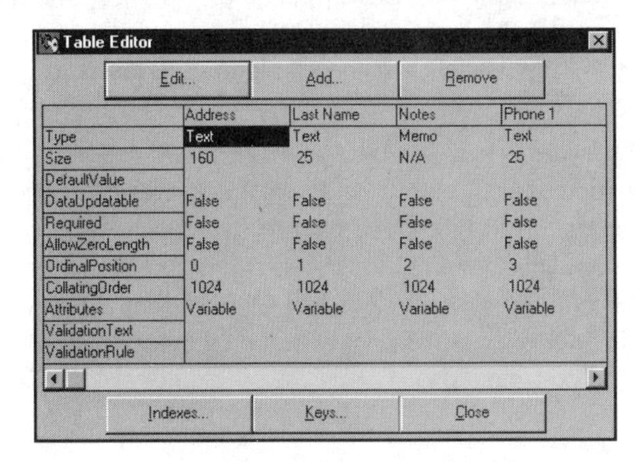

FIGURE 13.4 *Table Editor.*

You're going to have two indexes, one called Address and the other called Last Name. The Last Name index will be derived from the Address field using code we'll write for a function also called Last Name. This is the index that will be used for sorting the records in your database. Chances are pretty good that you will occasionally have more than one record with the same Last Name—either two records for one person, each with a different address, or two people with the same last name. For this reason, the Last Name index should not be defined as Unique. (Remember that Unique is the way to prohibit duplicate entries).

While it's not required, it is generally desirable to have a Primary index. A Primary index is one that uniquely identifies each record for the purpose of generating internal pointers. These pointers make data access quicker and easier. Because duplicate last names are to be allowed, the Last Name index cannot be Unique, and therefore it cannot be a Primary index either. Instead you will use the Address field as your Primary index.

When defining an index, you may combine as many fields as you like, providing the names of the fields (including +, –, and ; characters that separate field names) do not add up to more than 254 characters. Memo and Binary object fields, however, may not be used in an index. You may create as many indexes as you want, but you can only have one Primary index per table.

When the Add Index dialog box first appears, the Index Name text box will be blank. You'll see a list of all the fields in the box marked Fields in Table. The box marked Fields in Index will also be blank, and all the buttons except Cancel will be grayed out.

First, type **Last Name** in the Index Name box. Then select the **Last Name** field from the list. As soon as you select a field, you'll notice that the Add (Asc) and Add (Dec) buttons become available. These refer to sequencing: ascending (as in ABCD or 1234) and descending (as in DCBA and 4321). Because you'll want your names sequenced alphabetically, click on the **Add** (Asc) button. The field name moves from the Fields in Table list to the Fields in Index list, and is now followed by (ASC). If you had selected descending, the field name would be followed by (DEC).

NOTE

In our example, the index names happen to be the same as the field names. When the index is made of only a single field, this is often simpler. However, this is not a requirement. You can name your indexes anything you want.

Now that you've selected a field for the Index, the OK button has become available. Your dialog box should now look like the one shown in Figure 13.5. If you wanted this index to check for and prevent duplicate entries, you would select the Unique check box in the lower left of the window. For the Last Name field, however, you'll allow duplicate entries, so the check box should remain blank. Now you can click **OK**, if you haven't done so already.

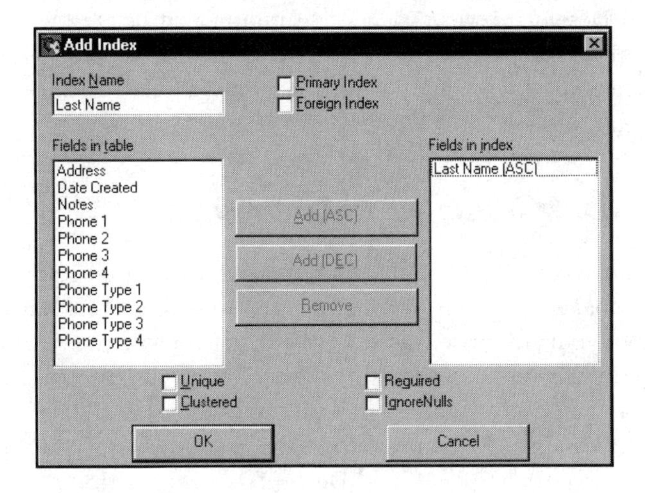

FIGURE 13.5 *Add Index dialog box with settings for Last Name index.*

Next you'll need to create the Address index, so click on **Indexes** to bring up the Add Index dialog box again. This time type **Address** in the Index Name box, select **Address** from the list of fields, and click on the ascending. Don't forget this is going to be your Primary index, so before you click OK, be sure to select the **Primary Index** check box on the upper-right side of the window (a checkmark in the box indicates that it's selected). Now you can click **OK**.

NOTE

When you're creating a Primary index, you must check the Primary Index box. You might also want to select the Unique box because a Primary index must be unique. If you forget, don't worry. The Data Manager will automatically assign the Unique property to a Primary Index. Another Data Manager safeguard worth noting: you can't create a second Primary Index. If you try to, you'll get the Error creating index VB: Primary key already exists message.

Close the Table Editor dialog box and the Indexes window, revealing once again the Database: ADDRESS.MDB window. As you saw a moment ago, now that you have a table, five out of the six buttons will work. You're already familiar with the New and Design buttons. The Delete button will delete the selected table, but you will be prompted for confirmation first. The Attach button Open will open the selected table, bringing up a window similar to the one shown in Figure 13.6. And that's what you're going to use next.

Using the Data Manager to Enter Data

Before you move on to creating the form, you're going to take advantage of one more Data Manager function. You are going to use the Data Manager to enter some data into your Addresses table. If you didn't do so a moment ago, click on **Open** to open your Addresses table (as described in the previous section). You should see a window similar to the one shown in see Figure 13.6. At the moment, your database is empty. However, now that the table is open, you have the ability to Add, Update, and Delete records as indicated by the buttons in this window. You can also use Find to search for records, and Refresh to repaint the form.

FIGURE 13.6 *Data Manger window for Addresses table data entry.*

To add a record, click on the **Add** button and then fill in the fields. You can add your own data or use the values provided in Table 13.2. You can use the Tab key to move from field to field, or use your mouse and the scroll bar. As you might guess by looking at that table, it is not required that you fill in all the fields. You may leave any field blank, except for the Primary Index, which in this application is the Address field.

If you use the data from Table 13.2, you'll notice that for the Address field we listed only the company name instead of the entire name and address. This is because you cannot enter multiple lines when using the Data Manager. The Data Manager is expedient for some purposes, but using a Form to design your own interface affords greater flexibility—such as allowing you to select the Multiline property for a text box.

TABLE 13.2 *Data for new Address Book Sample Records*

	Field Name	Value
Record 1	Address	Crescent Software Inc.
	Notes	Free software with "Teach Yourself Visual Basic 4.0" book.
	Phone 1	203-438-5300
	Phone Type 1	0
	Date Created	01/01/95
Record 2	Address	MicroHelp Inc.
	Notes	Free software with "Teach Yourself Visual Basic 4.0" book.
	Phone 1	404-516-0899
	Phone Type 1	0
	Date Created	01/01/95
Record 3	Address	Sheridan Software Systems Inc.
	Notes	Free software with "Teach Yourself Visual Basic 4.0" book.
	Phone 1	516-753-0985
	Phone Type 1	0
	Date Created	01/01/95

When you have filled in all the data for the first record, click on **Add** again to save the first record and clear the fields for the next set of values. When you finish entering the data for the final record, click on **Update**. This will save the data for the last record entered (once you confirm that you want the record saved) and then automatically display the table's data beginning with the first record.

You can move through the database using the left and right arrow buttons at the bottom of the window. If you spot any mistakes that you'd like to correct, type in the correction and press **Update**. You will be prompted to confirm your desire to "commit changes." You should also try changing a field and then pressing the **Refresh** button. Notice how your changes disappear, leaving only the original record. This is because as the form is redrawn, the data is reread from the table and you had not yet Updated the field (i.e., saved it back to the table). When you're all done, close the Table: Addresses and the Tables windows, and then close the Data Manager (double-click on the box in the upper left corner of the window) to return to the Visual Basic application.

Creating a Form with Data-Aware Controls

If you're not already running Visual Basic, double-click on the Visual Basic icon on your desktop to start the program. If you are already running Visual Basic, be sure that you do not have another project open at this time. If you do have another project open, select **New Project** from the File menu so you can start with a clean slate.

To create a form with data-aware controls, you'll need to add a data control to your form. Then you'll make the other controls (such as Text and Labels) "data-aware" by setting their DataSource and DataField properties, which we'll discuss in a moment. Figure 13.7 shows what the form will look like when you're done.

What is a Data Control?

Data controls are used in conjunction with other controls to display, add, modify, and delete data from a database. To make the connection between a form and a database, you place a data control in the form and set its properties to identify the name of the database and table that you want to access. If your form contains data from more than one table, you will need to use more than one data control—one for each table.

Some programmers allow the data control to remain visible and take advantage of its simple built-in functionality. Other programmers, like John, prefer to make the data control invisible (setting its Visible property to False), using instead their own command buttons and menus. This approach gives the programmer far greater flexibility, not just with the visual interface, but in terms of writing code that does more than the data control's built-in functions would do alone. Later in this chapter we'll talk about the extra code that makes Address Book more like a Rolodex and the ResortRecords routine that maintains your current position in the database. But first, let's talk a little more about data controls and get your form set up.

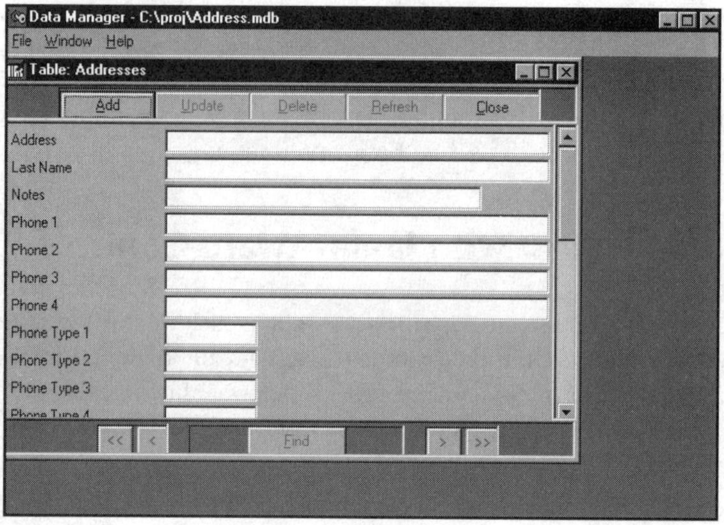

FIGURE 13.7 *The completed form for the database version of Address Book.*

Before you add the data control to your form, we suggest that you save your project; be sure to save it in the same directory that contains the ADDRESS.MDB file that you just created. After you save the project (call it ADDRESS.MAK), exit from the Visual Basic program. What we want you to do then is use the Windows' File Manager, locate the ADDRESS.MAK file, and double-click on it to launch Visual Basic with the newly saved project already loaded. This makes the directory that contains ADDRESS.* the current directory when VB starts.

Why should you do all this? Because this will allow you to refer to the ADDRESS.MDB file without a path or drive letter in front of the name, and that means that the location of the file won't be hard-wired into the program. If you use a full path name, any program you create using Make EXE will always look for the ADDRESS.MDB file only in the exact directory you wired into the program. This is bad programming practice. The best solution is to look in the same directory as the program for your data files when you're only using one data file. So all this work allows you to use a local file name.

To add the data control, click on the data control button in the Toolbox window (it's the third one from the bottom on the right side in Figure 13.?). When the crosshair appears, drag out an area on the form. You can place it by eye or let Visual Basic place it for you according to the Top and Left property settings. The data control should have handles around it, indicating that it is selected. (If it doesn't, click once on the control.) Now press **F4** to bring up Data Control's Properties window, and set the following properties:

Caption	dbAddress
DatabaseName	address.mdb
EOFAction	2 - Add New
Height	270
Left	120
Name	Data1
RecordSource	Addresses
Top	3180
Visible	False
Width	1140

As you might have guessed, the DatabaseName property identifies the name of the database, and the RecordSource property identifies which table in the database (the Address database only has one table) is to be managed by this Data control. As you'll see in a moment, the data control's Name property is also important because it will identify the data control to each of the other controls, making them *data-aware*.

NOTE

Setting the RecordSource property for a Data control is only an option when Visual Basic can open the data file referred to in the DatabaseName property. This also means that you must set the DatabaseName property first.

What are Data-Aware Controls?

Now that you have defined your data control and named it Data1, you will make your other controls data-aware by *binding* them to the data control. The term binding refers to making a connection between the data control (in this case Data1) and the other controls on the form. This connection, which you'll define in a moment using the Properties window, will tell each control where to find the data. In other words, each of the other controls will look to the data control for the name of the database, table, and field where the corresponding data are stored.

This really isn't as complex as it might sound. Try creating the text control for the Address field. Click on the **Text** control in the Toolbox and drag out an area for it on the form. Make sure the text box is still selected, press **F4** to bring up the Properties window, and set the following properties as follows:

DataField	Address
DataSource	Data1
FontBold	False
Height	1380
Left	120
Multiline	True
Name	txtAddress
Top	120
Width	2775

Now press **F5** and see what happens. Your program should run and you should see the Crescent Software Inc. address displayed in the text box. Select **End** from the Run menu to stop your program. It's that easy. Now that you've got the hang of it, you can create the rest of the form using the settings shown in Table 13.3. We suggest you save your Form periodically while working, in case you encounter any disk or memory problems. You should also test your program as you go along. When you're finished creating the interface, you'll move right along to navigating through the database and updating records. In fact, as you'll soon see, that part will be effortless.

TABLE 13.3 *Properties for Each Control in the New Address Book Application (Database Version)*

Object	Property	Setting
Form	Auto3D	True
	BorderStyle	1 – Fixed Single
	BackColor	&H00C0C0C0&
	Caption	Address Book
	Height	4020
	MaxButton	False
	Name	Address
	Width	6600
Text Box	DataField	Address
	DataSource	Data1
	Height	1380
	Left	120
	Multiline	True
	Name	txtAddress
	Text	
	Top	120
	Width	2775
Text Box	DataField	Notes
	DataSource	Data1
	Height	1335
	Left	120
	Multiline	True
	Name	txtNotes
	Scrollbars	2 – Vertical
	Text	
	Top	1680
	Width	6255

continued

Object	Property	Setting
Text Box (array)	DataField	Phone 1
	DataSource	Data1
	Height	300
	Index	0
	Left	4320
	Name	txtPhone
	Text	
	Top	120
	Width	2055
txtPhone(1)	DataField	Phone 2
	Index	1
	Top	480
txtPhone(2)	DataField	Phone 3
	Index	2
	Top	840
txtPhone(3)	DataField	Phone 4
	Index	3
	Top	1200
Label (array)	Caption	lblPhone(0)
	DataField	Phone Type 1
	DataSource	Data1
	Height	195
	Index	0
	Left	6420
	Name	lblPhone
	Top	180
	Visible	False
	Width	855

continued

Object	Property	Setting
lblPhone(1)	Caption	lblPhone(1)
	DataField	Phone Type 2
	Index	1
	Top	540
lblPhone(2)	Caption	lblPhone(2)
	DataField	Phone Type 3
	Index	2
	Top	900
lblPhone(3)	Caption	lblPhone(3)
	DataField	Phone Type 4
	Index	3
	Top	1260
Combo Box (array)	Index	0
	Left	3120
	Name	cboPhone
	Style	2 – Dropdown List
	Top	120
	Width	1095
cboPhone(1)	Index	1
	Left	3120
	Top	480
cboPhone(2)	Index	2
	Left	3120
	Top	840
cboPhone(3)	Index	3
	left	3120
	Top	1200

continued

Object	Property	Setting
Label	Caption	lblCreatedDb
	DataField	Date Created
	DataSource	Data1
	Height	195
	Left	3600
	Name	lblCreatedDb
	Top	3120
	Visible	False
	Width	915
Label	Caption	lblModifiedDb
	DataField	Date Modified
	DataSource	Data1
	Height	195
	Left	3600
	Name	lblModifiedDb
	Top	3360
	Visible	False
	Width	915
Label	Alignment	1 – Right Justify
	Caption	Created:
	Height	255
	Left	4440
	Name	Label2
	Top	3120
	Width	735
Label	Alignment	1 – Right Justify
	Caption	Modified:
	Height	255

continued

Object	Property	Setting
Label	Left	4440
	Name	Label3
	Top	3360
	Width	735
Label	BackColor	&H00C0C0C0&
	Caption	d1
	Height	255
	Left	5280
	Name	lblCreated
	Top	3120
	Width	1095
Label	Caption	d2
	Height	255
	Left	5280
	Name	lblModified
	Top	3360
	Width	1095
Label	Caption	lblLastName
	DataField	Last Name
	DataSource	Data1
	Height	195
	Left	1320
	Name	lblLastName
	Top	3240
	Visible	False
	Width	915
Command Button		
Caption	&<<	

continued

Object	Property	Setting
Command Button		
	Height	375
	Left	2400
	Name	cmdPrev
	Top	3120
	Width	495
Command Button	BackColor	&H00C0C0C0&
	Caption	&>>
	Height	375
	Left	3120
	Name	cmdNext
	Top	3120
	Width	495

Creating the Menu Bar

Now that your form has all the controls it needs, the only thing left to do before we get to the code is create the menu bar. Table 13.4 shows all the menus, items, and control names for the menu. Add this menu to your program the same way you did in Chapter 11 for your first Address Book program. The only difference between the two menu bars is that this Edit menu will not have a Go To item, and the Address menu will not have a Sort item.

TABLE 13.4 *Menus Used by Address Book (Database Version)*

Caption	CtlName	Accelerator
&File	menFile	
&Print...	miPrint	Ctrl+P
P&rint Setup...	miPrintSetup	

continued

Caption	CtlName	Accelerator
–	miFileLine	
E&xit	miExit	
&Edit	menEdit	
&Undo	miUndo	Ctrl+Z
–	miEditLine1	
Cu&t	miCut	Ctrl+X
&Copy	miCopy	Ctrl+C
&Paste	miPaste	Ctrl+V
–	miEditLine2	
&Find...	miFind	Ctrl+F
&Address	menAddress	
&New	miNew	Ctrl+N
&Delete	miDelete	
–	miAddressLine1	
Ne&xt	miNext	F4
&Previous	miPrevious	F3

Writing the Code

The new Address Book application contains four forms and lots of code. For the rest of this chapter, we'll focus on the main functions and subroutines that drive the database activity for this program. We will not repeat discussions about functionality that we've covered elsewhere, such as the cut, copy, paste, and undo code presented in Chapter 11, or the printing concepts touched on in Chapter 12.

Since your sample database already contains three records, we can start by examining the issues related to navigation.

Navigating and Automatic Updating

The data control has built-in functionality for moving forward and backward through the database. This functionality includes moving one record at a time and the ability to jump directly to the first or last record in the database. Also, whenever you use the data control to move forward or backward, any changes made to the current record will be saved. However, as we mentioned earlier, we have chosen to use our own command buttons and write our own code.

In the Address Book program, you have two ways to navigate. You can click on the **&>>** button to move forward and the **&<<** button to move back one record, or you can use the **Next** and **Previous** items from the Address menu. Since the desired actions are the same, the code for the two menu item click events will simply call the corresponding command button click events. The code for the miNext, miPrevious, cmdNext, and cmdPrev click event subroutines is as follows:

```
Sub miNext_Click ()
     cmdNext_Click
End Sub
```

```
Sub miPrevious_Click ()
     cmdPrev_Click
End Sub
```

```
Sub cmdNext_Click ()
     NextRecord 1                 ' Show next record in database
     txtAddress.SetFocus          ' Put insertion point in address
End Sub
```

```
Sub cmdPrev_Click ()
     NextRecord -1                ' Show previous record in dbase
     txtAddress.SetFocus          ' Put insertion point in address
End Sub
```

As you can see, each of the menu item click events calls the corresponding command button click event. The command button click events only contain two lines of code: one to call the NextRecord subroutine, passing to it a variable value; and the other to set the focus so that the insertion point will be in the Address text box when the next record appears.

Like the standard data control, the NextRecord subroutine also moves between records and performs the automatic save when the current record has changed, but it approaches the task a little differently. First NextRecord calls the ResortRecords subroutine. If the current record has changed, ResortRecords will save the changes, re-sort the database, and make that changed record the current record again, before returning to the NextRecord subroutine. (We'll talk more about saving records in the Saving a Record section.)

When the NextRecord subroutine is back in control, it uses the delta variable to determine whether to move forward or backward (the value of delta was passed from the click event). If delta = 1, you move forward. If delta = –1, you move backward. The code for moving between records is very simple. You use the data control name with the RecordSet property (representing the table name), and the MoveNext or MovePrevious method, as follows:

```
Data1.RecordSet.MoveNext
Data1.RecordSet.MovePrevious
```

Now you might wonder what would happen if you wanted to move to the next record but you were already looking at the last record in the table. If you were using the standard data control, nothing would happen. You'd click on the forward arrow and nothing would appear to happen. Our NextRecord routine checks to see if you have reached the end of file (EOF) or beginning of file (BOF). If you are already at the end of file when you choose to move next, you will instead find yourself at the first record in the table. This wraparound effect is what makes this Address Book sort of like a Rolodex. It becomes circular. If you are already at the first record and you choose to move to the previous record, you will instead find yourself at the last record in the table. This is accomplished by using the MoveFirst and MoveLast methods. The code for the NextRecord subroutine is as follows:

```
Sub NextRecord (delta As Integer)
    '
    ' This subroutine moves between records, either forwards
    ' or backwards.  NextRecord saves any changes to the
    ' current record before it shows a different record.
    '
    ' On entry:
    '     delta     +1       Show the next record
```

```
    '                -1      Show previous record
    '
    Dim num As Integer

     ResortRecords            ' This resorts the records
     If Data1.Recordset.RecordCount = 0 Then
          Exit Sub            ' No records.
    End If

    '
    ' First move to the previous or next record.
    '
    If delta = 1 Then
        If Not Data1.Recordset.EOF Then
            Data1.Recordset.MoveNext
        End If
    Else
        If Not Data1.Recordset.BOF Then
            Data1.Recordset.MovePrevious
        End If
    End If

    '
    ' The following code wraps around.  So if we moved
    ' past the end of the file, it will move to the first
    ' record in the database.  And if we move before the
    ' start of the file, we'll move to the last record.
    '
    If Data1.Recordset.BOF Then
       Data1.Recordset.MoveLast
    ElseIf Data1.Recordset.EOF Then
       Data1.Recordset.MoveFirst
    End If
End Sub
```

You should now be able to run this program and move between the three records you created using the Data Manager. You'll also notice that you can change any of these records and Address Book will automatically save all your changes. This automatic saving of your changes is handled by the data control whenever you change records (using MoveNext or MovePrevious, for example), as well as when you quit Address Book. (By the way, you'll notice that we commented out the call to ResortRecords. We did this so you can run the program now. You'll uncomment this line later, once you've written the ResortRecords subroutine.)

Speaking of quitting Address Book, you might want to add the following code to bring the Exit menu item to life:

```
Sub miExit_Click ()
    Unload address
End Sub
```

For the other two menu items in the File menu (Print... and Print Setup...), you'll find the code in the ADDRESS2 directory on the floppy disk included with this book.

Adding New Records

Adding a new record is handled by the New item on the Address menu, so you'll need some code for the miNew_Click subroutine. To add a new record you will use the AddNew method with the data control and RecordSet property. However, instead of placing that code in the menu item's click subroutine, you're going to save it for the NewRecord subroutine. Can you guess what code you'll need to put in the miNew_Click subroutine? That's right, you need to call the other subroutine, so your code should read as follows (which is exactly the same code we used in Chapter 11):

```
Sub miNew_Click ()
    '
     ' Create a new record at the end of the file. This
     ' record will be saved only if you type something into it.
    '
    NewRecord
End Sub
```

The NewRecord subroutine not only uses the AddNew method, which automatically updates the current record before creating a new one, but also contains code to bypass certain error conditions, set the Date Created, and preset the

Address form's combo boxes to the default values. The code is pretty straightforward, as you'll see in a moment. What you should take special note of, however, is the handling of the Created Date field and its display in the form. In this subroutine you are setting the lblCreatedDb control to the current date using Now. This label control is invisible on the Address form, but it is connected to the Date Created field in the database, so that's where the Now value, including the time portion, will be stored. However, just as in the first Address Book application, you'll use a second control to format the value of Now, so that only the date portion is shown in the lblCreated control on the form. This second step is handled in the lblCreatedDb_Change subroutine. The code for both routines is as follows:

```
Sub NewRecord ()
   '
   ' This procedure adds a new record to the database,
   ' default values for the Phone type fields.
   '
   On Error Resume Next
   Data1.Recordset.AddNew        ' Add a new record
   On Error GoTo 0

   lblCreatedDb = Now            ' Remember when we created

   lblPhone(0) = 0               ' Set 1st type to Home
   lblPhone(1) = 1               ' Set 2nd type to Office
   lblPhone(2) = 2               ' Set 3rd type to FAX
   lblPhone(3) = -1              ' Set 4th type to blank

   txtAddress.SetFocus           ' Put insertion point in
                                 ' Address
End Sub
-----------------------------
Sub lblCreatedDb_Change ()
   If lblCreatedDb <> "" Then
      lblCreated = Format$(DateValue(lblCreatedDb),
                           "ddddd")
   End If
End Sub
```

You should now be able to add new records to your database. Whenever the application starts, you'll see the first record—in this case the Crescent Software address. Select New from the Address menu and see all the fields go blank, clearing the way for a new record entry.

Did you notice that when the fields cleared, the combo boxes did not contain any preset values? Before we go on, this would be a good time to fill in the code for the Form_Load subroutine, as well as some code to save and restore the values in the combo boxes. That will not only take care of the combo box problem, but will also make sure that the database is properly sorted when it appears, and if no records exist in the table, it will call the NewRecord subroutine. The code for the Form_Load, cboPhone_Click and lblPhone_Change subroutines are as follows:

```
Sub Form_Load ()
    '
    ' Set up the combo box with the correct names.
    '
    Dim i

    For i = 0 To 3
        cboPhone(i).AddItem "Home"
        cboPhone(i).AddItem "Office"
        cboPhone(i).AddItem "FAX"
        cboPhone(i).AddItem "Direct"
        cboPhone(i).AddItem "Car"
        cboPhone(i).AddItem ""
    Next i

    '
    ' The next line of code causes the database to be
    ' sorted by the hidden Last Name field. This field
    ' is updated in the Data control's Validate event.
    '
    Show                            ' Make this form visible

    Data1.RecordSource = "“SELECT * FROM Addresses ORDER
                                    BY [Last Name]"
    Data1.Refresh
    If Data1.Recordset.RecordCount = 0 Then
        NewRecord               ' Add new record to database
    End If
End Sub
```

```
Sub cboPhone_Click (Index As Integer)
    Dim i

   '
   ' We need to make sure we don't set the
   ' lblPhone(Index) value when it doesn't change.
   ' Without this If statement, reading the value of
   ' lblPhone(Index) from the database triggers
   ' lblPhone_Change, which sets the ListIndex value
   ' for this combo box, which in turn would set the
   ' value in lblPhone.  Setting the value in this case
   ' tells the database that we've change the value,
   ' when in fact we haven't.
   '
   i = cboPhone(Index).ListIndex
   If Val(lblPhone(Index)) <> i Then
      lblPhone(Index) = cboPhone(Index).ListIndex
      recChanged = True
   End If
End Sub
```

```
Sub lblPhone_Change (Index As Integer)
   cboPhone(Index).ListIndex = Val(lblPhone(Index))
End Sub
```

The lblPhone labels (there are four in an array) are connected, or bound, to the Phone Type fields in the database. Whenever you change the value of the label, the value in the database will change. And reading in a new record (with Data1.RecordSet.MoveNext) will modify the value in the label. You then need to transfer these values between the labels and the combo boxes, which the lblPhone_Change and cboPhone_Click events do. You use the Click with a combo box because the click event of a combo box is fired whenever you select a different value. (The Change event is reserved for combo boxes that allow you to type values directly into the combo box.)

There is one line in the Form_Load subroutine that is probably a little bit of a mystery:

```
Data1.RecordSource = "SELECT * FROM Addresses ORDER BY
```

```
[Last Name]"
```

This line of code tells the data control that we want to select all the records (hence the *) from the table Addresses and we want to sort them by the Last Name field. This code is written in a language called *SQL*, which stands for Structured Query Language and is pronounced like "sequel." SQL is very important in the relational database world. Visual Basic's Access engine provides a great deal of power via the use of SQL. If you plan to do a lot of database work with Visual Basic, we strongly recommend that you learn more about Microsoft Access and SQL.

At this point we'll just mention one item about SQL statements. In most cases, a short bit of SQL code will be much faster (sometimes 10 times or more) than the same code written in Visual Basic using the database commands and methods.

Saving Records and Re-sorting the Database

You already know that moving from one record to another forces an automatic save, or in Visual Basic terms, an update, if any of the data have been changed. If you were using the standard data control alone, you would not need to write any code, as this functionality is built in. The Address Book program takes advantage of this automatic function. That's why you do not need to write code to save the current record before adding a new one. However, the NextRecord subroutine calls the ResortRecords subroutine, and this is where you will need to add some update code, as we'll explain shortly.

The update method is used with the name of the data control and the RecordSet property, as follows:

```
Data1.RecordSet.Update
```

The ResortRecords subroutine serves a couple of purposes. Its primary purpose is to re-sort the table before displaying the next record (either previous or next). Why would this be necessary? Because new records are initially added at the end of the database, rather than in alphabetical order. The records won't be put into alphabetical order until we tell the data control that we want to update, or *refresh*, the view of the database. Refresh is the method used for sorting the database, because of the SELECT statement you attached to the data control in Form_Load, as follows:

```
Data1.Refresh
```

The problem is that in addition to re-sorting the database, Refresh also moves back to the very first record. What we want is to re-sort the database and keep our current position. Let's take a look at the code to see how that's done:

```
Sub ResortRecords ()
    '
    ' Saves the current record if it's been changed.
    ' Then we resort the database and set the current
    ' record back to this same address.
    '
    Dim address                   ' Address we just added

    If Not recChanged Then        ' Did we change record?
        Exit Sub                  ' No, we're all done
    End If

    address = txtAddress          ' Save the current address
    If address <> "" Then         ' Is there something here?
       Data1.Recordset.Update     ' Yes, save changes to database
    End If

    Data1.Refresh                 ' Resort the recordset
    Data1.Recordset.FindFirst "Address = """ & address & """"
End Sub
```

NOTE

Before you can use this new procedure, there are some other additions you'll need to make. First, you'll need to add the recChanged variable in the (declarations) section of your form. You'll also need to add code to all the text boxes to set the recChanged variable to True. You'll find the details in Chapter 11, or better yet, the floppy disk that comes with this book has all this code included in the ADDRESS2 directory. We've saved the form as a text file (by checking the Save as Text check box in the Save As dialog box) so you can copy and paste code from this file. We find the NOTEPAD program that comes with Windows very useful for copying and pasting code from form files. Also make sure you uncomment the line in NextRecord so it calls ResortRecords.

The first step is to define a variable, called address, that we can use to save the Address from the current record. Then we check to see if the current record has been changed. The recChanged variable is set to False each time a new record becomes active (this code is handled in a data control subroutine called Data1_Reposition). Whenever a change is made to the txtAddress, txtNotes, or txtPhone controls, Visual Basic automatically runs the corresponding Change subroutines (txtAddress_Change, for example), and there we have added code to set the recChanged variable to True. Changes made by selecting a combo box item trigger the corresponding Click event; in our case the cboPhone_Click subroutine where we also added code to set the recChanged variable to True.

Getting back to the ResortRecords subroutine, if recChanged is False, there's no need to re-sort the database, and we exit the subroutine. If a change has occurred, then we save the current Address in the address variable and then update the database (provided the Address field isn't empty). Then after using Refresh to resort, we use another method, FindFirst, to search the database for the record we just added. This retrieved record then becomes the current record, and you're back in position on the record you just added. This allows the NextRecord routine to move relative to the new record once it's been placed in proper alphabetical order.

Extracting Last Name from the Address

In the previous section, we mentioned that a Validate subroutine is also automatically triggered by moving from one record to another. It is also triggered before an Update, Delete, or Close operation. For the purposes of the Address Book program, you'll use this subroutine to save the modified date and call the LastName function, which sets the Last Name field used by Address Book to sort records in the database.

The Modified Date code is similar to the Created Date code. If recChanged is True, the lblModifiedDb field in the database is set to the value of Now. The change to this field triggers the lblModifiedDb_Change subroutine that displays the date portion of Now in the lblModified control on the form.

The Data1_Validate subroutine actually calls the LastName function before getting to any of the Modified Date code. After checking to see that txtAddress is not empty, the Function LastName code kicks in. In this Address Book program, Last Name will be the last word on the first line of the Address text box, with one exception—if there is a comma (,) on the first line, Last Name will be the last word preceding that comma. This exception solves the problem of names like John Doe, Jr. by returning “Doe, Jr.” as the last name. Later, we'll say more about why we didn't remove the part after the comma.

After determining where the first line ends and finding the comma if one exists, a Do-Loop searches for spaces, resetting the Start position each time a space is found before the end of the line or comma. In the John Doe, Jr. example, the first space is found between John and Doe; because that space occurs before the comma, the Start variable is set to the position following that space, i.e., on the letter D. The next space found is the one between the comma and Jr., but this time the Start variable is not reset, because that space appears after the comma. When no more spaces can be found, the characters beginning in the Start position and ending at the end of the first line make up the value of LastName. Program control then returns to the Validate subroutine, which handles the Modified Date as described earlier in this section, and the recChanged variable is reset to False.

The reason we didn't remove the part of the name after the comma is that we were lazy. Removing this extra text would have required extra code, albeit not much. But it wasn't really important in this case to remove this extra text because sorting will work even with the extra text. However, if it bothers you, you should be able to rewrite LastName so it removes any text after the comma.

Finally, program control returns to whatever event it was that triggered the Validate subroutine in the first place. In addition to the Validate subroutine, you need to add code to the data control's Reposition event. The Reposition event will be triggered after a record becomes visible. The sole purpose of Data1_Reposition in Address Book is to set the recChanged variable to False when a record becomes visible. The code for the Validate, lblModifiedDb_Change, and Reposition subroutines and LastName function is as follows:

```
Sub Data1_Validate (Action As Integer, Save As Integer)
    '
    ' This method gets called whenever an action
    ' requires saving changes to a record.  We use this
    ' method to save the date of last modification.
    ' Also, it saves the last name in a hidden Last Name
    ' field, which we use to sort the database.
    '
    If txtAddress <> "" Then
       lblLastName = LastName()
    End If
```

```
   If recChanged Then        ' Did we make changes?
      lblModifiedDb = Now    ' Yes, remember when modified
   End If
   recChanged = False
End Sub
```

```
Sub Data1_Reposition ()
   '
   ' This method gets called after a new record becomes
   ' active.
   '
   recChanged = False           ' Nothing changed yet
End Sub
```

```
Sub lblModifiedDb_Change ()
   If lblModifiedDb <> "" Then
      lblModified = Format$(DateValue(lblModifiedDb),
                            "ddddd")
   Else
      lblModified = ""
   End If
End Sub
```

```
Function LastName () As String
   '
   ' This subroutine finds the last name in the address
   ' text box.
   '
   ' Last names, in this case, are the last word in the
   ' first line of an address. The only special case I
   ' handle is when you have a comma in the name, such
   ' as "Name, Jr.". In this case I use the word before
   ' the comma as the last name.
   '
   ' Note:  This subroutine does not handle names that
   '        include a number, such as "Some Name III".
   '
   Dim aName$, theLine$
   Dim crlf$
```

```
Dim lEnd, comma, start
Dim I

crlf$ = Chr$(13) + Chr$(10)
aName$ = RTrim$(txtAddress)

'
' First we'll get a string that contains the first
' line of text from the address. This text will be
' put into theLine$.
'
lEnd = InStr(aName$, crlf$) - 1    ' Look for end of
                                   ' line
If lEnd < 1 Then                   ' Is there only 1 line?
   lEnd = Len(aName$)              ' Yes, use whole line
End If

theLine$ = Mid$(aName$, 1, lEnd) ' Get first line of
                                 ' addr

'
' Next, extract the last name from this string.
'
comma = InStr(theLine$, ",")  ' Look for a comma
If comma = 0 Then             ' Is there comma in name?
   comma = 32767              ' No
End If

start = 1                     ' Start of last name
i = 1                         ' Start with first char
Do
   i = InStr(i, theLine$, " ") ' Look for space
   If i < 1 Then               ' Are we out of
                               ' spaces?
      Exit Do                  ' Yes, we're all done
   End If
   While Mid$(theLine$, i, 1) = " "
     i = i + 1                ' Skip over spaces
   Wend
   If i < comma Then
```

```
            start = i                    ' Remember word start
        End If
    Loop

    LastName = Mid$(theLine$, start)
End Function
```

This new code will apply only to new records you add since none of the records you've added so far will contain values in the Last Name field. You can force Address Book to update the Last Name field for existing records by making changes to any of the fields in a record, which will trigger the Validate code with recChanged = True.

Searching for a Record

In the first version of the Address Book program, the code for finding a record based on a search string was limited to case-sensitive searches using the InStr function. The version on the disk, however, uses the Like operator to case-insensitive searches. In the database version of Address Book you'll use the FindNext method of the data control to find a record using a search string that includes the Like keyword with a search string pattern, making it possible to do searches that are not case-sensitive.

The search begins with the miFind_Click subroutine. Here you'll create some variables, place a bookmark on the current record, display the Find dialog box (FINDDIAL.FRM), and then add an asterisk to the beginning and end of the search string to create a *pattern*. A pattern is a string that contains wildcard characters—in this case the *, representing any characters.

The code in this subroutine requests a search first of the Address field, calling upon the FindField function to actually perform the search. If nothing was found, another search is requested, this time in the Notes field. Again the FindField function is called. If still nothing is in the Notes field, the routines are repeated until each of the four Phone fields are searched. If the search is successful, the found record is retrieved and displayed. If the search is not successful, and no matches were found, the bookmark is used to return to whatever record was current before the search.

The syntax for the FindNext method is Data1.RecordSet.FindNext *criteria*, where Data1 is the name of the data control and criteria is the name of the variable containing the search string. In the Address Book program, the criteria turns out to be a variable called *searchStr* that uses the Like operator to compare two string expressions—in this case comparing the string inside the specified field with the pattern made by adding the asterisk to the string entered in the Find dialog box. The following is the full code listing for the miFind_Click subroutine and the FindField function.

The string expression in the call to the FindFirst method is actually a snippet of SQL code. In this case it is just the part of SQL known as the WHERE clause (without the word WHERE actually in the string). If you search for the string Smith, for example, the string that miFind_Click and FindField build to search the Address field looks like this:

```
Address LIKE ["*Smith*"]
```

This searches for a record that has the word Smith (or SMITH, or SmItH, etc.) anywhere in the Address field. There are other forms you can use for other types of searches, and you can find more information in Visual Basic's on-line help: From the Help menu select Search For Help On... and enter *where*. Press **Enter**, then in the lower list box click on WHERE Clause (SQL Only) and click the **Go To button**.

```
Sub miFind_Click ()
    '
    ' This subroutine finds displays the Find dialog box,
    ' then looks for a record that contains the text you
    ' typed in.
    '
    ' Note: this subroutine *does* ignore case because of
    '       the LIKE expression in FindFirst.
    Dim findStr$            ' String to search for
    Dim oldRecord           ' Record that we were looking at
    Dim result, i

    '
    ' I've added a * to the front and end of the find
    ' string to make it a pattern for the Like operator,
```

```
' so you can do case-insensitive searches.
'
findStr$ = FindDialog.GetString()
If findStr$ <> "" Then
    findStr$ = """*" + findStr + "*"""
End If

Screen.MousePointer = 11  ' Set to hour glass cursor

If findStr$ = “” Then       ' Is there a search string?
Exit Sub                    ' No, we’re all done here
End If

'
' The following code looks for a match in all of the
' text fields: Address, Notes, and 4 phone numbers.
'
oldRecord = Data1.Recordset.Bookmark

result = FindField("Address", findStr$)
If Not result Then
   result = FindField("Notes", findStr$)
End If
i = 1
While (Not result) And i <= 4
   result = FindField("Phone " & i, findStr$)
   i = i + 1
Wend

'
' Show the old record if we didn't find a match.
' We need this code because otherwise the Data control
' shows the first record in the database after a
' failed search.
'
 If Not result Then
   Data1.Recordset.Bookmark = oldRecord
   Beep
```

```
    End If

    Screen.MousePointer = 0
End Sub
```

```
Function FindField (findStr, fieldName)
    '
    ' This function searches a specific field for a match.
    '
    Dim searchStr

    searchStr = fieldName & " LIKE [" & findStr & "]"
    Data1.Recordset.FindNext searchStr
    If Data1.Recordset.NoMatch Then
       Data1.Recordset.FindFirst searchStr
    End If

    FindField = Not Data1.Recordset.NoMatch)
End Function
```

In order to use these new subroutines, you'll need the FINDDIAL.FRM form, which is theFindDialog form, as well as PRINT.BAS, which contains the PositionDialog code. You'll find both of these files in the ADDRESS2 directory on the floppy disk that comes with this book.

Deleting a Record

The only major thing still missing from the new Address Book program is some code to handle deleting records. The following code, which contains some nice features worth noting, belongs in the miDelete_Click subroutine:

```
Sub miDelete_Click ()
    '
    ' This subroutine deletes the current record from
    ' the database.
    '
    Dim record
    Dim doDelete
```

```
    If Data1.Recordset.RecordCount = 0 Then Exit Sub


    doDelete = DeleteDialog.DeleteOK(txtAddress.Text)
    If Not doDelete Then Exit Sub   ' Nothing to do.

    Screen.MousePointer = 11        ' Show wait cursor

    '
    ' Now actually delete the record.
    '
    If Data1.Recordset.RecordCount > 0 Then
       '
       ' These two lines of code handle the case where
       ' you delete a record that hasn't been saved yet.
       ' First we save the record.  The we move back to
       ' this record.
       '
       Data1.Recordset.Update      ' Save any changes
       Data1.Recordset.LastModified
       Data1.Recordset.Delete
    End If

    If Data1.Recordset.RecordCount > 0 Then
       NextRecord 1
    Else
       NewRecord                   ' Start a new record
    End If

    Screen.MousePointer = 0
 End Sub
```

After making sure that you're not trying to delete a nonexistent record (the subroutine exits if there are no records in the database), you are given the opportunity to confirm your intention to delete the record or change your mind. We use a delete dialog (DELETE.FRM) to display the Address field of the current record to be deleted. That form contains an invisible label control called *lblFlag*. When you choose the Cancel button, the click event changes the value in the lblFlag

Caption property from "flag," it's default value, to "" (i.e., nothing). The miDelete_Click event checks the value of this property and if it is empty, the Delete subroutine exits.

Another feature to note is the inclusion of two lines of code that make sure you can delete a record that has not yet been saved in the database. Such a circumstance could arise if you were to add a new record, type in the information, and then choose to delete the record before the update occurred. This would cause an error in Visual Basic because there is no current record until you save the new record. As explained in the code comments, you should save the record just in case, then return to that record and delete it.

Finally, the last If..Then..Else statement checks to see if there are any records left in the database. If there are, it calls for NextRecord to show the next record after the one you deleted. If, on the other hand, you just deleted the last record, there is no next record to move to, so instead it calls NewRecord. These are the types of considerations you must take into account when you are programming programs that other people will use.

Summary

You should now have enough of an understanding of programming and Visual Basic to start working on your own programs. Part III of this book contains some general-purpose subroutines and functions that you can use in your own programs and as a source of inspiration in writing new programs.

OVERVIEW OF ADVANCED TECHNIQUES

In this chapter, we'll give you a quick overview of more advanced techniques that you can use in the Visual Basic programs you write. These techniques generally fall into three categories: Visual Basic–only techniques, custom controls, and dynamic link libraries (DLLs) and Windows API functions. We'll describe each category briefly and then give you an idea of how you can put these techniques to use in your own projects.

Visual Basic–Only Techniques

Visual Basic is a very rich language and environment, which provides many possibilities without ever leaving the environment. We were only able to touch on a few of Visual Basic's abilities in the first two parts of this book, so in Chapters 14 through 19 you'll find a number of techniques, subroutines, and functions that you can use in your own programs. Some of these are written entirely in Visual Basic, and some use even more advanced techniques. To name just a few examples from these chapters, you'll find a subroutine for creating progress bars like you see in most install programs, you'll learn how to draw shadows around controls, and you'll learn how to center forms on the screen before they become visible.

We suggest you browse through these chapters to see what's there, and if you find anything that looks useful, try it. Some of the functions and subroutines from these chapters use very advanced techniques, but you don't need to understand all of the code details in order to use the functions or subroutines.

Custom Controls

There are a number of commercial add-on packages for Visual Basic that include *custom controls.* These are new types of controls that appear in Visual Basic's toolbox when you add a special file to your project. These files usually have the extension VBX. Visual Basic 4.0 adds the ability to use OLE-custom controls. In fact, the 32-bit version of Visual Basic is restricted to these controls. You'll have to use the 16-bit version of Visual Basic to use the VBXs on the disk.

Three of the top custom-control companies have provided some custom controls on the disk that comes with this book. These controls will give you an idea of what kinds of custom controls you'll find in commercial add-on products. The controls included with this book are real fully functional controls—not crippled demos—so you'll be able to use them in any programs you write.

To add a custom control file to your project, select the **Add File...** item from the File menu, and double-click on the name of the VBX file that you need to add to your project. After you add a VBX file to your project, you'll see some additional control icons appear in Visual Basic's Toolbox (see Figure 14.1).

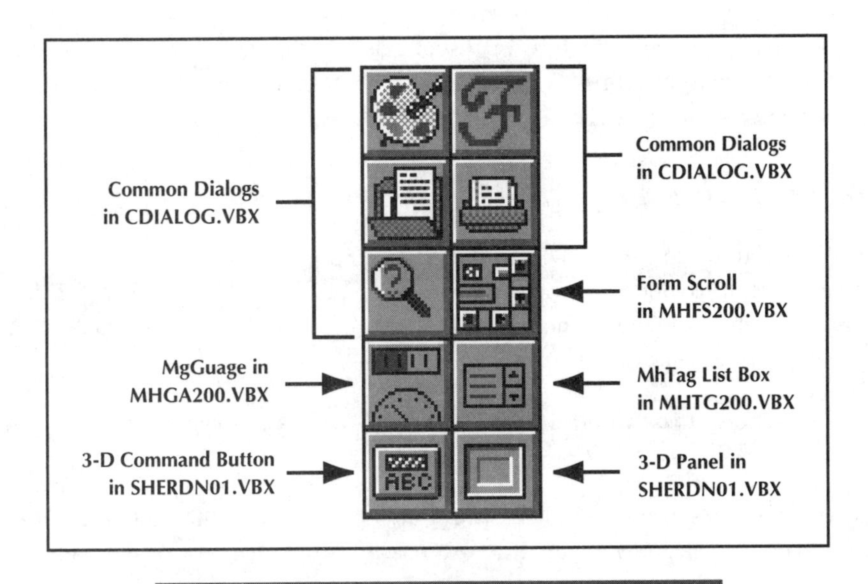

FIGURE 14.1 *The icons added to Visual Basic's Toolbox when you include the VBX files from this book's disk in a project.*

DLLs and Windows Functions

Behind every Windows program is the Windows system. Windows provides hundreds of functions and subroutines that programs can call to create windows, menus, controls, to do drawing, and so on. Any Windows program calls a number of these functions and subroutines. Visual Basic programs you write call these subroutines and functions indirectly. For example, Visual Basic's Line command is converted into a call to the Windows LineTo command that draws lines inside of a window.

All of these Windows functions are provided through a mechanism known as a *DLL*. This is an abbreviation for *dynamic link library*, which is a code library that's loaded into memory and connected to your program *on demand*. Windows comes with a number of DLLs to provide all the subroutines and functions Windows programs can call, or you can write your own DLLs in languages like C or Pascal (but not Visual Basic).

One really powerful feature in Visual Basic is the ability to call almost any DLL function or subroutine, both in Windows' DLLs and in other DLLs that you or someone else might write.

The Declare Statement

To call a routine inside of a DLL, the first thing you have to do is define the function or subroutine that you want to call. You do this by using the Declare statement, which defines a number of pieces of information. The basic syntax for Declare is as follows:

```
Declare Sub subName Lib libName$ [Alias aliasName]
([argument list])
```

This defines the subroutine called *subName* located in the DLL called *libName$*. **Note:** You don't need to include the extension for the DLL, just its file name.

```
Declare Function functionName Lib libName$
        [Alias aliasName] ([argument list]) [As type]
```

This defines a function called *functionName* located in the DLL called *libName$*, which returns a value of *type*. **Note:** You don't need to include the extension for the DLL, just its file name.

In the following chapters, you'll find a number of examples on how to use and declare Windows functions and subroutines. *Windows API* is another name for these Windows functions and subroutines. API is short for *applications programming interface*; it defines the functions on top of which all Windows programs are built. The best place to start would be with the section in Chapter 18 called *Fast Line Drawing*, which shows how to use a Windows function called Polyline.

Translating Between C and Visual Basic's Types

Whenever you're working with Windows API calls or with other DLLs, the documentation on the routines will probably be written for C programmers, which means it will use a number of terms and abbreviations you may not be familiar with. Let's take a look at a simple example to see how this works. The following shows how the Windows Polyline function is defined in the Microsoft Windows Programmer's manuals:

```
BOOL Polyline(hdc, lppt, cPoints)

HDC hdc;              /* handle of device context */
POINT FAR* lppt;      /* address of array with points */
int cPoints;          /* number of points in array */
```

What does all this mean? The names in all uppercase letters, such as BOOL, are C's version of types. For example, BOOL is a Boolean type, which means it is an Integer that returns either –1 or 0 (in other words, True or False); and HDC and POINT are also types. The lowercase *int* is also a type that is exactly the same as Visual Basic's Integer type.

Because there can be so many different types in C and Windows, we've put together a table that shows how to translate between C types and Visual Basic's types. Tables 14.1 and 14.2 provide much of the information you'll need. If you have the Professional Edition of Visual Basic 4.0 you'll also find definitions of all the functions and subroutines available in Windows in the WINAPI.TXT.

TABLE 14.1 *Translating Between C and Visual Basic Types*

Windows Names	C	Visual Basic
BOOL	int	ByVal ... As Boolean
BYTE	int	ByVal ... As Byte
WORD	int	ByVal ... As Integer
DWORD	long	ByVal ... As Long
LPSTR	char FAR*	ByVal ... As String
BOOL FAR*	int FAR*	... As Boolean
BYTE FAR*	int FAR*	... As Byte
WORD FAR*	int FAR*	... As Integer
DWORD FAR*	long FAR*	... As Long

The Intel microprocessor treats bytes as words when you pass them to subroutines.

TABLE 14.2 *Other Types of Variables and Some Rules on How to Convert from Some Windows Types to Visual Basic's Types*

Windows	Visual Basic	Comments
Hxxxxx	ByVal ... As Integer	Any type of handle is an Integer
ATOM	ByVal ... As Integer	
struct	ByVal ... STRUCT	A user-defined type created with the Type statement.

The following lists some special notes:

* To pass both a string and a NULL pointer to a subroutine, define that parameter As Any. You can pass a NULL pointer by passing the value 0&.
* Define all strings as ByVal when you pass them to DLLs. Visual Basic will automatically convert them to C strings before calling the DLL, and it converts C strings back to Visual Basic strings when the DLL finishes.
* Regarding arrays, pass the first element in the range that you need to pass. For example, if you have an array of points called *points*, you could send part of this array to a DLL, starting with the fifth element, by using *points(4)* as the "value" you pass to the DLL. See the *Fast Line Drawing* section in Chapter 18 for an example.

When you're ready to start using Windows API calls on your own, you'll find a number of examples in Chapters 15 through 19. You'll also find more information in your *Visual Basic Programmer's Guide*, and there are a number of books that have some excellent examples of using the Windows API calls.

The important thing to realize about the Windows API is that there really is no limit to what you can do in Visual Basic.

How Different Displays Affect Your Programs

Did you know that your nicely designed program won't always look good? If you've designed it on a VGA screen and then run that same program on an EGA or 8514/a screen, you may discover it looks terrible.

In this chapter, we'll look at what can cause programs to change their appearance and how to write programs that work well with all kinds of display adapters. We'll start by looking at the issues *screen resolution* and *dot density*, which are at the root of screen problems. Then we'll move on to the specifics of how Visual Basic's controls change size between different screens. Finally, we'll provide some suggestions for how to write and design your programs so they'll look good on all displays.

Understanding Screen Resolution

The entire subject of screen resolution can be a little confusing for a couple of reasons. First, not everyone uses the term *resolution* in the same way. Second, Windows introduces a new term, *logical inches*, which further confuses the issue.

We spent some time looking for a good definition of resolution. Webster's dictionary, as it turns out, wasn't much help. None of the definitions were even close. So we looked at a number of computer books to see how they define resolution and found that there are two main definitions in use: one for printer resolution and a completely different one for display resolution.

Printer Resolution

The definition of printer resolution is quite simple and has to do with density. All of the characters you see on this page were generated by a computer-driven printer (usually called a photo-typesetter) using a number of very small dots. These dots are so small and close together that you can't see them.

Most book publishers use printers that can print 1200 or 2400 dots per inch. Laser printers, like the Hewlett Packard LaserJet printers, typically print 300 dots per inch. A printer's resolution is measured by the density in dots per inch density (*dpi*) of the characters it produces.

Display Resolution

The resolution of displays, on the other hand, is *not* a measure of dot density. Instead, a display's resolution is measured in terms of the total number of dots that it displays horizontally and vertically. A standard VGA display, for example, is 640 dots wide and 480 dots high. We call this *display resolution* 640 x 480.

A higher-resolution display simply has more dots on it. For example, the resolution of Super VGA displays is 800 x 600. The display resolution has nothing to do with the physical size of the screen (such as a 14-inch versus 17-inch diagonal screen)—it only refers to the total number of dots on the screen. This is in contrast to printer resolution, which refers only to the density of dots, and not to the total number of dots that a printer can print.

THE TWO FACES OF RESOLUTION

The following is a quick review of the definition of resolution for printers and displays:

Printers: Density of dots (measured as dots per inch, or dpi)

Displays: Total number of dots displayed horizontally and vertically, such as 640 x 480

How Screen Size Affects Density

Now that you've seen that display resolution is not measured by the density of dots, let's look at how the density changes as the resolution and screen size change. We'll look at examples using a 14- and a 17-inch diagonal monitor (many VGA screens are 14-inch diagonal screens) with several different resolutions (see Figure 15.1).

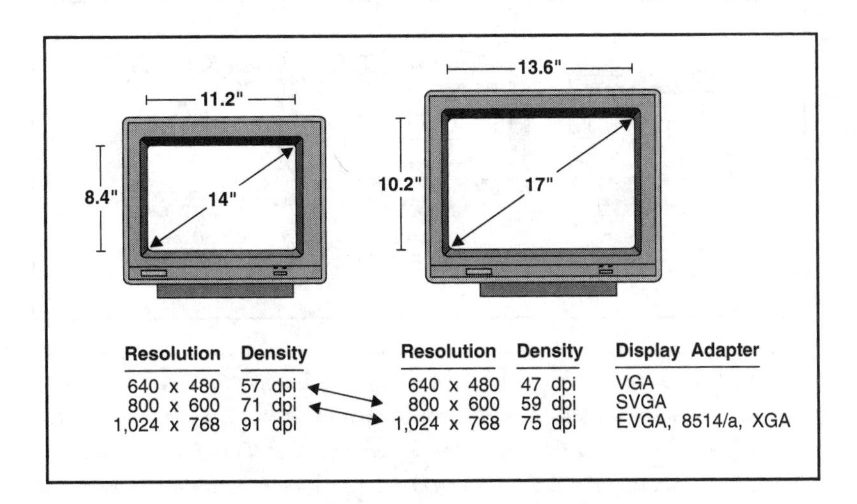

FIGURE 15.1 *This figure shows how the size of the screen and the display resolution affect the density of dots displayed on the screen, or dots per inch (dpi). The two arrows in the table show combinations of screen size and resolution that have similar dot densities.*

NOTE

The color you see on color screens is created by triplets of small phosphor dots. The size of these dots depends on your monitor and usually ranges from 0.28 mm for expensive monitors to 0.39 mm or larger for less expensive monitors. These dot sizes correspond to densities of 90 to 65 dpi.

You'll notice that the density of dots depends on the resolution (the total number of screen dots) and the screen size. If you increase the size of your screen without changing the resolution, you'll see a larger picture without any more detail, which is a result of spreading the same number of dots over a larger area. On the other hand, if you increase the resolution without changing the screen size, you'll see a smaller picture. (If you like the size of the images on your 14-inch screen at 640 x 480 but you'd like more room on your screen, you can upgrade to a 17-inch screen and change the resolution to 800 x 600 to obtain the same size images with a larger work space. See Figure 15.2.)

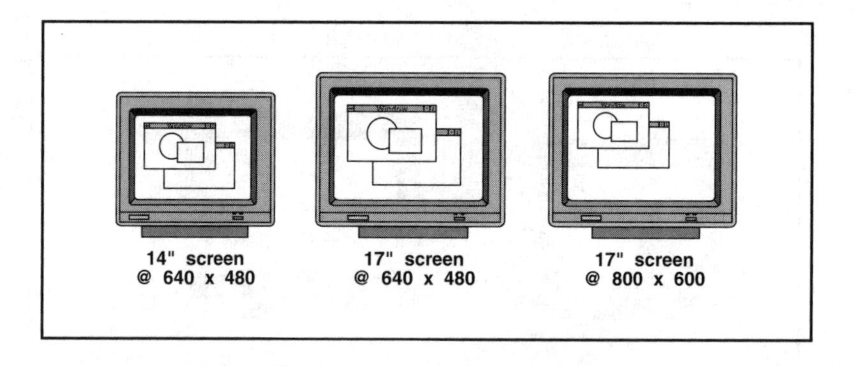

FIGURE 15.2 *How the screen size and resolution affect the image. The left two pictures show increasing the screen size from 14-to 17 inches, leaving the resolution at 640 x 480, which results in a larger image without more dots. The right-most picture shows increasing the screen size and the resolution to 800 x 600. Notice that the windows on the 17-inch screen at 800 x 600 are the same size as the windows on the 14-inch screen, but there are more dots.*

Magazine Advertisements: What Does It All Mean?

Magazine advertisements for monitors can also muddy the waters somewhat on the issue of resolution. Most companies advertise two numbers that they never define: *dot pitch* and supported modes.

Dot pitch is a measure of the smallest dot size that a color screen can theoretically display. The image you see on your screen is created by a large number of small phosphor dots grouped in triplets (called triads) of red, green, and blue. A shadow mask is used to make sure that the red, green, and blue electron guns only light up red, green, or blue phosphor dots (see Figure 15.3). The more expensive and higher-quality monitors used with Microsoft Windows have a dot pitch of 0.28 mm, which translates into a density of 90 phosphor triads per inch (less-expensive color monitors have dot pitches of 0.31 to 0.39 mm, which corresponds to densities of 81 to 65 dpi). This means that if you try to use a resolution and screen size that result in a density higher than these numbers, the image on your screen will be fuzzy because there aren't enough phosphor triads to show the image.

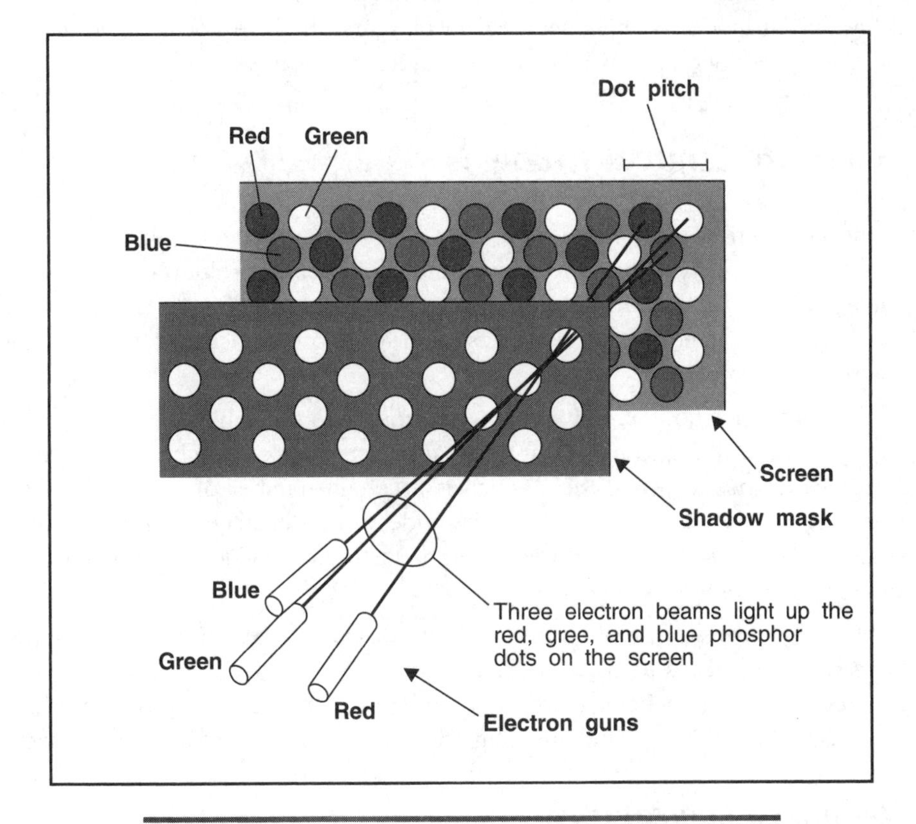

FIGURE 15.3 *The density of dots on a color screen is limited by the dot pitch, which is a measure of the smallest dot that you can display on the screen. Each dot is created by a combination of up to three colors from the red, green, and blue phosphor dots.*

On the other hand, even if you do have enough triads, your screen image may still be fuzzy. This is because the maximum screen resolution is dependent on more than just the density of phosphor triads. It also depends on how well the electronic circuitry inside the monitor is built.

For example, many 14-inch monitors have a dot pitch of 0.28 mm, but some 14-inch monitors with a dot pitch of 0.28 mm have a maximum resolution of 640 x 480, and other, more expensive 14-inch monitors with the same dot pitch might have a maximum resolution of 1024 x 768. It all has to do with the electronics and quality of the components used to build the monitor.

Even if a monitor is advertised as having a maximum resolution of 1024 x 768, it may not display clear images at this resolution. The supported display modes define which modes your monitor can display, but they are not an indication of the highest resolution that will be clear enough for your needs.

What are Logical Inches?

In the last section you saw that the size of an image depends on a combination of things, such as the screen size and the display resolution. But what if you're writing a program and you want an object to be 1 inch square? How does Windows handle this? Does it somehow know the size of the monitor you're using?

Windows has no idea how large your monitor is—it only knows the resolution. Instead of trying to make an image appear exactly one inch on the screen, Windows defines a *logical inch*, which is a certain number of pixels wide and high. Any object that is one logical inch wide will be exactly one physical inch wide when printed, but its physical width on the screen depends on the size and resolution of your screen.

If you're writing a program that needs to display a ruler, or anything else on the screen that needs to be measured in inches, the best thing to do is ignore the fact that logical inches are different from real inches. Simply program everything using logical inches and anything you print will come out the correct size.

Defining a Logical Inch

How many pixels should be in a logical inch? And how did Microsoft come up with a number? We'll answer both of these questions in this section. First, let's look at the number of pixels per logical inch.

Because Windows doesn't know the size of your screen (it only knows the type of display adapter and the resolution), Microsoft chose to define the size of a logical inch, in pixels, based solely on the screen resolution. Table 15.1 shows the numbers that Microsoft chose for various display adapters and resolutions.

TABLE 15.1 *The Logical Dot Densities that Windows Defines for Different Display Adapters and Resolutions*

Display Adapter	Resolution	x - dpi	y - dpi	Dot Aspect Ratio
CGA	640 x 200	96	48	2:1
EGA	640 x 400	96	72	1.33:1
VGA	640 x 480	96	96	1:1
SVGA	800 x 600	96	96	1:1
EVGA	1,024 x 768	96	96	1:1
8514/a	1,024 x 768	120	120	1:1

NOTE

These densities allow a logical display width of at least 6.5 inches, which is the width of the writing area on an 8.5- x 11-inch piece of paper with 1-inch margins. Notice that the dots are square (1:1 aspect ratio) rather than oblong on all display adapters except for the CGA and EGA adapters.

You'll notice that most of these screens have a logical dot density of 96 dots per inch. In order for a real VGA display to have a real (rather than logical) density of 96 dpi, it would have to be 6.7 by 5 inches, or 8.3 inches diagonal. On an 8.3-inch diagonal monitor, an object that was one logical inch wide would be *exactly* one physical inch wide on the screen. But most VGA screens are 14-inch diagonal with densities more like 60 dpi. So why did Microsoft define the density of logical inches to be 96 dpi instead of 60 dpi?

The reason for this has to do with readability. If the logical density is too small (like 60 dpi), you won't have enough dots in a 6- or 8-point font to be able to read it well. In other words, you need as high a density as possible so that small characters will be easy to read. A density of 300 dpi, for example is extremely readable, and this is the density used by most laser printers.

On the other hand, you don't want the density to be too high because this would limit the size, in logical inches, of documents you could see on your screen. For example, if you chose a logical density of 300 dpi, a 640 x 480 screen would be limited to a logical size of 2.1 x 1.6 inches, which is far too small for most programs, including word processors.

Here is where Microsoft's numbers came from. A standard sheet of paper is 8.5 inches wide with a 1-inch margin on each side. This means that we're using a printed area that's 6.5 inches wide (8.5 inches minus 2 inches). Microsoft wanted this print area to fit on the screen in any Windows program and wanted to include a vertical scroll bar. Because the width of a vertical scroll bar is 16 pixels, we can calculate the density needed to be able to display both 6.5 inches and a scroll bar as (640 – 16) / 6.5-inch = 96 dpi, which is the number Microsoft chose.

Once again, as long as you work just with logical inches in your programs, everything will print at the correct size. (Most users are used to the rulers on their screens showing inches that appear larger than a real inch.)

Can I Have Sharper Images?

Most people would like to have a sharper image on their screen in which Windows uses more dots to create the same image. Is there any way you can increase the logical density, and therefore the sharpness of your screen? The answer is yes and no.

As you'll recall from Table 15.1, the logical dot density is defined by the Windows display drivers, and different display adapters have different logical densities. In particular, notice that the logical density for an 8514/a display adapter is defined as 120 dpi, which is noticeably higher than the 96-dpi density for most other display drivers. So, yes, you can have a sharper display. But you, as the user, don't have control over this sharpness—the dot density is determined by the people who write the display adapters. Of course, in theory someone could write a display driver that allowed you to change the logical dot density, but we're not aware of any such driver. As you'll see in the next section when we talk about bit maps and icons, there is a good reason for not writing such a driver.

How Visual Basic's Objects Change Size

Now that you have a firm foundation in how Windows defines a logical inch, you're ready to learn how Visual Basic uses this information—in particular, how Visual Basic determines the size and locations of controls on different display adapters.

Twips and the Height of Text

The first thing you need to know is that Visual Basic uses twips (rather than pixels or inches or any other measure) to store the sizes and locations of all controls you place on a form. This allows Visual Basic to do a reasonable job of maintaining a form's appearance on different display adapters. But unfortunately, it can't do a perfect job, for reasons you'll see here.

To understand why Visual Basic has some problems, you need to take a closer look at how a twip is defined in terms of pixels and how this impacts the size of objects.

There are three logical dot densities that Windows 3.1† currently supports: 96 dpi (which is used for all VGA, SVGA, and EVGA displays), 72 dpi (which is used for EGA displays), and 120 dpi (which is used for 8514/a displays). We'll only look at the EGA, VGA, and 8514/a display modes for the rest of this chapter.

Table 15.2 shows the number of twips per pixel for each of these three displays (recall that a twip is 1/1440 inches). This table also shows the height of Visual Basic's default MS Sans Serif font, used for all controls unless you change the FontName, the FontSize property, or both.

TABLE 15.2 *Twips per Pixel and TextHeight for Displays*

Display	X Twips/Pixel	Y Twips/Pixel	TextHeight (Twips)
EGA	15	20	200
VGA	15	15	195
8514/a	12	12	192

Notice that the text heights are very close to each other, but they're not identical. Why? The font used to display characters on the screen (MS Sans Serif) is a bitmap font, which means its height is measured in pixels rather than twips. Each display mode (EGA, VGA, and 8514/a) actually has its own version of the font that it uses. Because these fonts have sizes measured in pixels, you can't get an exact match in the height of the font—you can only get close. This is why the TextHeight values are close but not exactly the same.

† Windows 95 allows you to change the logical dot density. In the Display control panel, under Settings, is a Font size area. The Small Fonts and Large Fonts entries correspond to 96 dpi and 120 dpi respectively. The Custom button allows you to select a custom font scale, which changes the logical dot density.

How the Heights of Controls Vary

What does this mean for your forms? It means that some controls will have different sizes, depending on the font and display adapter you're using. Table 15.3 tells most of the story, but requires a little explanation.

TABLE 15.3 *The Minimum Height for Each Control, Measured in Twips, for Each Type of Display Adapter*

Control Type	EGA	VGA	8514/a	Keeps Size	Fixed Height	Whole Lines
Combo Box	320	315	288		✔	
Drive Combo Box	360	315	288		✔	
List Box	≥ 240	≥ 255	≥ 216			✔
File List Box	≥ 240	≥ 225	≥ 216			✔
Directory List Box	≥ 240	≥ 225	≥ 216	✔		
Check Box	≥ 200	≥ 195	≥ 192	✔		
Command Button	≥ 200	≥ 195	≥ 192	✔		
Option Button	≥ 200	≥ 195	≥ 192	✔		
Text Box	≥ 300	≥ 285	≥ 288	✔		
Frame	any	any	any	✔		
Label	any	any	any	✔		
Picture Box	any	any	any	*	*	
HScroll Bar	≥ 240	same	same	✔		
VScroll Bar	≥ 240	same	same	✔		

*If AutoSize is False, the size of the picture box will remain the same, in twips, but the picture itself (bitmap or icon) will change in size because the size of a pixel will change. You can set AutoSize to True to keep the picture box the same size as the bitmap or icon inside it.

The first three columns show the minimum size for each type of control, measured in twips. Most of the controls have a minimum size that varies between the different display adapters. These variations are caused by the slight variations in the height of the default font. The last three columns give you an idea of how the height of the controls varies between the three display modes and requires further explanation as follows:

Keeps Size These controls will maintain their size, in twips, between the different display modes, as long as their initial height is greater than or equal to the minimum EGA heights.

Fixed Height You can't change the height for these controls, so they will change in height between the different display modes.

Whole Lines These controls increase and decrease in size by only a whole number of lines, which means they will vary in size between the different display modes. Table 15.4 shows how to calculate the height of these controls.

TABLE 15.4 *How to Calculate the Height of List and Dir Boxes*

Mode	Control Height (twips)
EGA	numLines * 200 + 40
VGA	numLines * 195 + 15
8514/a	numLines * 192 + 12

How to Adjust Your Programs

Now let's take a look at what all of this means for programs you write by concentrating on the items that can cause problems. If you look again at Table 15.3, you'll notice that there are only a few controls that can cause problems.

Combo Box	Directory List Box
Drive Combo Box	Picture Box
File List Box	Picture Property of a Form

You can group these controls into three groups: list boxes, combo boxes, and pictures. Of these three groups, the combo boxes tend to cause the fewest problems, and the pictures tend to cause the most problems. We'll look at each group and offer suggestions on how to write programs that work well on all displays.

By the way, we've said nothing about widths because, except for pictures, Visual Basic does an excellent job of maintaining the width of all controls. The only thing that you'll need to do is make sure all of your strings are visible on 8514/a displays. This is a concern because lines of text on 8514/a displays are often slightly wider (in twips) than the same string on a VGA (or EGA) display. The width of strings increases slightly because the widths of characters in the 8514/a display are a little different from the widths on a VGA display. As long as you check your programs on an 8514/a display, you shouldn't have a problem.

How to Work with Combo Boxes

You really have no choice about the height of combo boxes because the Height property is read-only (you can't change it). So all you have to do (and all you can do) is make sure you have enough room under each combo box so that they won't bump into other controls on an EGA display. In other words, drive combo boxes should have enough room to become 360 twips high on an EGA display, and regular combo boxes need enough room to become 320 twips high.

How to Work with List Boxes

List boxes are a little trickier. There are actually three types of list boxes you can use: List Box, File List Box, and Directory List Box. Only the first two really cause any problems. For reasons that aren't clear, a directory list box will keep its twip height as long as it's greater than 240 twips (the largest minimum size), because the last line in this list box is allowed to show a partial line. The other two list boxes can only change height by multiples of the line height, which means they can only show entire lines.

The result is that list boxes and file list boxes *will* have different heights on different displays, so here's what you have to do. If you want a directory list box and a file list box to have the same height, you'll need to put code like the following in your Form_Load subroutine:

```
Private Sub Form_Load ()
  Dir1.Height = File1.Height
End Sub
```

In other words, you can change the height of the directory list box to match the height of your file list box, but you can't do the reverse.

Because the height of a list box or file list box can change quite a bit (if you have many lines in the list), you may need to move any controls that appear below such list boxes to keep the list boxes from bumping into your controls. Again, the following code is the type of code that you can write in your Form_Load subroutine to move such controls (Command1 in this example):

```
Private Sub Form_Load ()
  Command1.Top = List1.Top + List1.Height + 150
End Sub
```

This code will move Command1 so its top is 150 twips below the bottom of List1.

How Pictures Change

Pictures have, by far, the most potential for creating problems when you're trying to write a program that will work with all display modes. The reason for this is quite simple (but the solution isn't). Bitmaps and icons are made out of pixels, which means that their actual size will always be measured in pixels rather than twips.

All controls other than picture boxes have the size measured in twips (it doesn't matter what ScaleMode you use, Visual Basic always remembers the size of objects in twips). This difference, then, between picture boxes and all other controls leads to several problems.

First, if you don't set the AutoSize property of a picture box to True, the picture box will stay the same size in twips, but the picture inside of a picture box will always keep its same size in pixels. For example, when you draw a picture box on a VGA display and then show it on an 8514/a display, the picture box will occupy more pixels on the screen (because the dot density is 120 dpi on an 8514/a display, versus 96 dpi for a VGA display), but the picture will use the same number of pixels. The picture will be smaller than the picture box.

On the other hand, if you set AutoSize to True, the picture box will always keep the same size in pixels. This means that its size in twips will change by a large amount. Let's say, for example, you have a picture box with an icon in it (which is 32 by 32 pixels), and you have set AutoSize = True and BorderStyle = 0 (no border). This picture box will have very different heights in twips for the three types of displays, as you can see in the following list:

Display	Height
EGA	640 twips
VGA	480 twips
8514/a	384 twips

To give you a better idea of what this means, Figures 15.4 through 15.6 show a form with a picture box and several controls. As you can see, the controls stay about the same size and remain in about the same location, but the bitmap changes considerably in size.

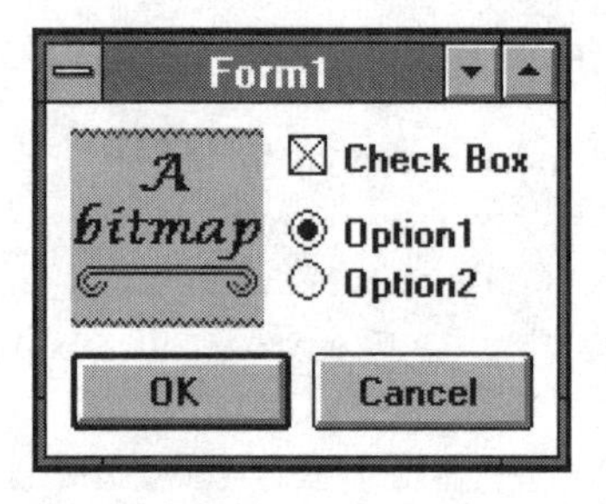

FIGURE 15.4 *The original form, designed and shown on a VGA display.*

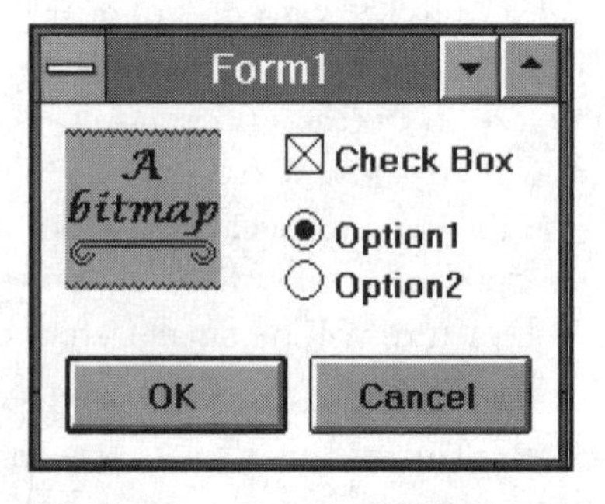

FIGURE 15.5 *The same form shown on an 8514/a display.*

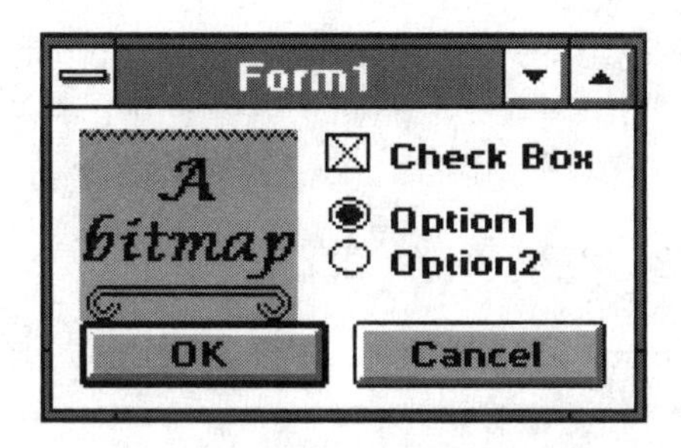

FIGURE 15.6 *The same form shown on an EGA display.*

Figure 15.4 shows the original form, designed and shown on a VGA display. Figure 15.5 shows the same form on an 8514/a display. The bitmap is noticeably smaller, compared with the other controls, than it was on the VGA display. Figure 15.6 shows the same form on an EGA display. Notice that the bitmap has the same width as on a VGA display, but now it's much taller and is cut off at the bottom by the OK button. Also notice how the gray in this picture is now shown as dark gray. This happens on an EGA display because it can't show light gray. But the button, which should have the same gray, uses a dithered pattern (alternating black and white dots) to show light gray.

How you solve this problem really depends on what you're doing with bitmaps and icons. If you're using a bitmap for a simple application, like displaying a logo, you really don't need to do much, except make sure you have enough room around your icon so that it won't bump into other controls on an EGA display.

On the other hand, if you're writing a program that uses a lot of bitmaps and the locations of these bitmaps are important, you'll definitely have to write some code that positions each bitmap and the controls around these bitmaps. Or you can have three sets of icons or bitmaps of different sizes: one for EGA displays, another for VGA displays, and the last for 8514/a displays. Then all you have to is write code to display the correct icon. The only hard part here is finding out which mode you're in.

The ChooseBitmap function shown below makes choosing an icon fairly simple. Let's say you have a four-element array of picture boxes, called *picLogo*. Element 0 is the one you'll show inside your form, and the other three contain the pictures for the EGA, VGA, and 8514/a displays, in that order. The first thing you need is a function that will tell you which bitmap to use, which might look something like the following:

```
Function ChooseBitmap () As Integer
    '
    ' This function returns the following:
    '
    '    1  Use 8514/a bitmap
    '    2  Use VGA bitmap
    '    3  Use EGA bitmap
    '
    Select Case Screen.TwipsPerPixelY
      Case 12
        ChooseBitmap = 1   ' Use 8514/a bitmap
      Case 15
        ChooseBitmap = 2   ' Use VGA bitmap
      Case Else
        ChooseBitmap = 3   ' Use EGA bitmap
    End Select
End Function
```

You'd use this function with some code like this:

```
Public Sub Form_Load ()
    i = ChooseBitmap()
    picLogo(0).Picture = picLogo(i).Picture
    picLogo(0).AutoSize = -1
End Sub
```

Here's how it works. The function ChooseBitmap gets the twips per pixel ratio from the Screen object's TwipsPerPixelY property. This ratio tells you exactly which type of display is being used. ChooseBitmap returns the array index for the bitmap you should use on the current display.

Text and Pictures

If you're mixing text and pictures—in particular, if you have text on top of pictures—you may need to adjust the size of your text to match the pictures. This is a real problem because pictures change in size (measured in twips) by a large amount between the different display modes, as mentioned in the last section. You'll probably want to adjust the font height so it keeps the same height in pixels, which takes a bit of work.

How do you set the size of a font in pixels? Can you simply supply the size of the font, measured in pixels or twips? The answer is no, for a couple of reasons. First, Visual Basic's FontSize property is *always* measured in points (1/72 inch or 1/20 twip), so you have to supply the size in points. To compound the problem, you can't always set the exact size of a font. For example, you might find that FontSize = 8.25 after you set it to 1.

There is still one other problem. The value you get back from TextHeight won't be the same as the font size you set because TextHeight and FontSize refer to different numbers that measure the size of a font. The FontSize property, as it turns out, sets the height of the characters in the font, whereas the TextHeight function reports this height *plus* the *leading* (extra spacing) between lines of text. This extra space, by the way, always appears above (rather than below) any text you display in a text box, label, or with the Print method.

The problem, then, is how to adjust the TextHeight of a font when all you can set is the FontSize property, and you don't have full control over that.

One solution is to write a small function that finds the closest font having a size (TextHeight) less than or equal to the height you need. Try using the FindFontSize function that John wrote to return the size of the closest font. You must pass a form to this function because it uses the FontSize property of a form.

```
Private Function FindFontSize (f As Form, ByVal high) As
Integer
   '
   ' This function returns the first font with a
   ' TextHeight <= high.
   '
   ' Note: If the smallest font has a TextHeight > high,
   '    this function will return a font larger than high.
   '
   Dim i, oldSize, size

   oldSize = f.FontSize          ' Remember old font size
   i = 1                         ' Start with 1 point font
```

```
    f.FontSize = i               ' Set first size
    size = f.FontSize            ' Keep track of best match

    While f.TextHeight("A") <= high ' Is font too large?
      size = f.FontSize          ' No, remember this size
      If f.FontSize > i Then     ' Is size larger than i?
        i = f.FontSize           ' Yes, adjust i to real size
      End If
      i = i + 1                  ' Try next higher size
      f.FontSize = i             ' Set font to this size
    Wend
    FindFontSize = size            ' Return size of found font

    f.FontSize = oldSize         ' Restore the old font size
  End Function
```

As you can see, this function starts by setting FontSize to 1, which will give you the smallest available font. Using Visual Basic's Helv font, this gives you an 8.25-point font with a TextHeight of 13 pixels. The While loop keeps increasing the FontSize value until TextHeight is greater than or equal to *high*. You now have the font size you want.

NOTE

This is not the same as the FindFontSize function included on the disk in the FONTTOOL file. That one is a slightly more complicated (and perhaps better) solution that we'll discuss in the Tool Box section of this book. That section also explains more about the difference between the TextHeight and FontSize values.

You'll notice that the FindFontSize function uses a form for calculating the size of a font that allows it to use the FontSize property and TextHeight method to do all of the work.

Colors

You may also need to think about how colors are used in your programs. For the most part, the colors you use in your programs will translate well between different displays. The light gray color, however, isn't available directly on EGA displays. How Visual Basic handles this is a little different for pictures and for colors set with the BackColor property.

All colors set to light gray using the BackColor property will be shown on the screen as a dithered pattern. Instead of showing a solid color, Visual Basic *simulates* a light gray color by setting alternate pixels to black and white (as you can see in the command buttons in Figure 15.6).

For pictures (bitmaps and icons), on the other hand, Visual Basic (actually, Windows) converts any colors in the bitmap or icon into the closest *solid* color that matches. Because light gray isn't available on an EGA display, you get dark gray instead (as you can also see in Figure 15.6).

As long as you don't use light gray in any bitmaps or icons, you won't have a problem. But if you mix the light gray in pictures with a light gray BackColor, you may want to set BackColor to dark gray on EGA displays so the BackColor gray will match the gray shown in bitmaps or icons.

Summary of Rules

The following list is a summary of the rules for writing programs that look good on all displays.

- **Widths of controls.** All controls, except some pictures, will keep the same width, in twips. The only thing to remember is that strings are sometimes wider on 8514/a displays because some of the characters in the font are wider.
- **Upper-left corner.** The top and left of all controls will stay the same, in twips, for all displays.
- **Combo boxes.** Make sure all drive combo boxes have enough space under them so they can be 360 twips high on an EGA display without bumping into other controls (320 twips high for regular combo boxes).
- **List boxes.** You normally don't have to do anything. But if you have a directory list box next to either a file list box or a regular list box, you'll need to change the height of your directory list box to match the other list box. You need to change the height of the directory list box, rather than the file list box, because the directory list box is the only one you can change by a partial line.
- **Pictures.** If you need other objects located at specific locations on top of the picture, you'll have to write code that moves controls to a specific position. You'll probably want to set ScaleMode = 3 (Pixel) and then set the location of controls using pixel values.

Setting ScaleMode = 3 (Pixel) when you're designing your program will *not* set the positions of controls to specific pixel locations. Visual Basic stores the size and locations of controls internally in twips, not in pixels, so their pixel location and size *will* change between different displays

- **Picture AutoSize.** You'll usually need to set the AutoSize property on a picture box to True to make sure the picture box will always be the same size as the picture or icon inside it.
- **Multiple pictures.** You can also have three bitmaps (or icons) for each picture you want to display, with each set tuned for EGA, VGA, and 8514/a displays. Then show the picture for the correct display (using code like that presented earlier in this chapter).
- **Colors.** If you're mixing the light gray color in bitmaps (or icons) with a light gray set by BackColor, you may want to set BackColor to dark gray whenever you program is running on an EGA display.
- **Testing.** There is no substitute for testing your programs. If your program uses a lot of bitmaps or icons, you'll need to do extensive testing on all three types of displays. The best way to do this type of testing is to have a card inside your computer that supports all three modes. John uses an ATI Graphics ULTRA card, and he can switch between the three modes using the Windows Setup program. Setup will change the drivers and then let you restart Windows in a new display mode. Devra has a similar setup that allows her to alternate between 640 x 480, 600 x 800, 1024 x 768, and 1280 x 960 and restart Windows using her Orchid Video Display Setup program in the Windows Control Panel. This process is reasonably fast under Windows 3.1 (it was quite slow under 3.0).

The ClockCal Example

When John was first learning Visual Basic, he wrote a program just for fun that displayed a clock and a calendar with the current date. He created an icon for each digit using Icon Works so the digits would look like the digits on a digital clock, and he put the current date on top of what looked like a calendar pad, which he created using PaintBrush. Everything looked really nice!

But then he got a new display adapter that allowed him to switch to 8514/a mode, and he discovered that his nice-looking program did not look as nice on it. The problem is that the bitmaps he used changed in size much more than anything else in his programs, as you can see in Figure 15.7.

John ended up rewriting his Clock/Calendar program by using the techniques outlined in this chapter, and as you can see in Figure 15.8, the final program looks very nice on all the different types of displays, although it does change in size quite a bit. In this section, we'll present the final program and show you how John rewrote ClockCal to resize all the objects connected with the bitmaps, which in this example is every object.

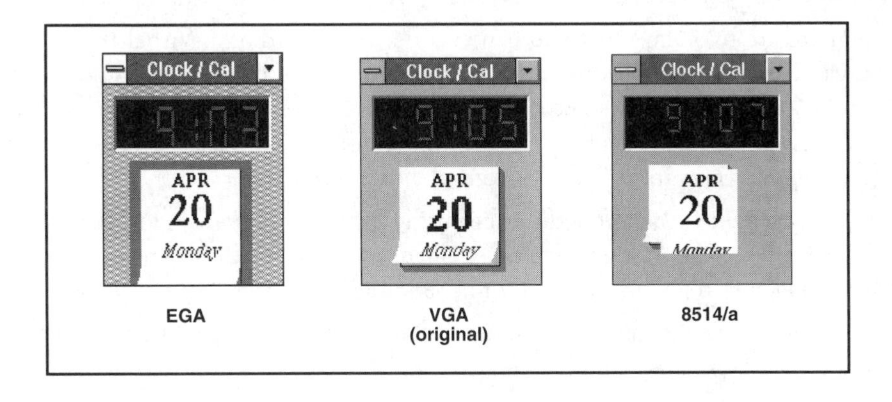

FIGURE 15.7 *The original program, designed on a VGA display, stays about the same size (in twips) on EGA and 8514/a displays. But as you can see, the bitmaps change considerably in size.*

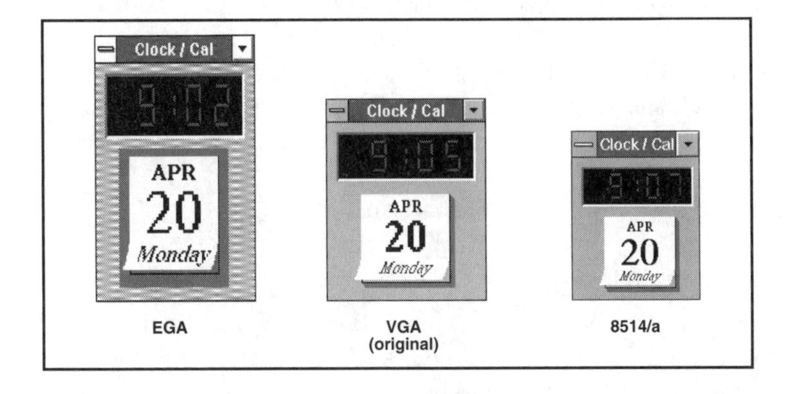

FIGURE 15.8 *The modified program that adjusts all the sizes to match the bitmap sizes. This program works well on all display adapters, even though it changes in size.*

Control Arrays

The ClockCal program makes heavy use of something called a *control*. Control arrays are groups of controls that all have the same name; you looked at them briefly in Chapter 5 where you used a control array for items in the menu bar. ClockCal uses two control arrays: one for the digits zero through nine, and the other for the digits in the clock. You can refer to any of the controls in the array by giving the index of that control. In other words, if you want to look at the digit 7 (which is the eighth element of the Digits array), you would write Digits(7).

There are two ways that you can create a control array in Visual Basic. First, you can assign a value to the Index property of a control. Second, you can create two (or more) controls and assign the same Name to both controls. As soon as you assign the same name to a second control, Visual Basic displays a dialog box asking if you want to create a control array. Just answer Yes.

John created a Digits control array using 10 controls with index values of 0 through 9. Then he loaded the correct icon into each of these image boxes so Digits(n).Picture refers to the icon for the *n*th digit.

Almost all of the other techniques used in ClockCal should be familiar to you after reading Parts I and II of this book.

How Resizing Works

Let's start by looking at the form in design mode. Figure 15.9 shows the ClockCal form with all the controls shown on it. You can see that there are 10 digits plus a colon and a blank icon near the lower part of the form. None of these controls will be visible while ClockCal is running because it resizes the form to a much smaller size. But we need these icons around so we can change the digits that will be visible, using a command like the following:

```
Digit(0).Picture = Digits(2)
```

This command will display a 2 in the leftmost digit on the screen.

There are really several parts to how ClockCal works. But because this chapter is about resizing objects as needed, let's look first at how ClockCal changes the size of its controls to match the bitmaps used.

There are three subroutines and one function that do all of the work: SetupSizes, SizeWindow, SizeCalendar, and FindFontSize. SetupSizes is called when ClockCal first starts by a single statement in the Form_Load event, as you can see in the program listings at the end of this chapter. SetupSizes does some work and calls SizeWindow and SizeCalendar.

First SetupSizes calls SizeWindow, which changes the size of the ClockCal form so its *inside* dimensions are 136 by 148 pixels. All the properties and methods provided by Visual Basic for changing a form's size work with the outside dimensions (which include the borders and the caption bar), so John wrote a special subroutine called *SizeWindow* that changes a form's size using inside, rather than outside, dimensions.

Let's take a quick look at the inner workings of SizeWindow. The first thing to do is calculate the size of the borders in the X and Y directions. You want to calculate these sizes in twips because the Move method used to change the form's size works only with twips. This is why the first statement changes ScaleMode to twips. The next four statements calculate the width and height of the borders, measured in twips. Next, you change the ScaleMode back to pixels and then calculate the twips/pixel ratio in both the X and Y directions: These values are stored in xScale and yScale. You need these values so you can convert the pixel dimensions into twips in the Move command. Finally, the last three statements calculate the new width and height, and then change the window's width.

Next, SetupSizes handles the sizes on the digital clock display. First you set the width and height of the colon place-holder, which is a picture box located between the first and last two digits inside the ClockFrame picture box. The For..Next loop handles setting the top left of each digit picture box, as well as setting the width and height. You need to set all of these values in pixels because Visual Basic tries to keep them constant in twips rather than pixels. Finally, you can set the left and top of the colon place-holder after you've positioned all the digits.

The next two lines set the width and height of the clock frame. Then you set the top of the DatePad picture box so it will be six pixels below the ClockFrame picture box.

Strictly speaking, John should also have set the left and top of the ClockFrame, but he didn't. If you look closely at Figure 15.8, you'll notice that the ClockFrame moves slightly to the right of center in the 8514/a display because he did not set the Left property. For the same reason, he should also have set the Left property on the DatePad picture box.

Finally, SetupSizes calls SizeCalendar, which handles all the resizing of the elements inside DatePad.

The code in SizeCalendar is rather simple. It sets the Top, Left, Width, and Height properties for each label inside the DatePad picture box. The last three statements are the really interesting part, because they're the ones that change the text sizes so they'll fit inside the labels. FindFontSize is used to calculate the correct FontSize to use for each label. but this FindFontSize function is slightly different from the one outlined previously. The one in ClockCal finds a font that is either the correct size or slightly larger, whereas the one presented earlier may find a font slightly smaller.

How ClockCal Works

Now that you've seen how ClockCal resizes all its controls, let's look at the rest of the program. First, let's examine a few cosmetic items. You may have noticed that there is a nice beveled edge on the inside of the ClockFrame. Where did this come from? The form, as well as most controls, have a property called Appearance that controls the 3-D appearance of a control. The default value is 1 – 3D, which for controls draws a nice bevel around the control. In other words, you get the nice beveled edges without doing anything.

However, there is one caveat. Since Visual Basic defaults to drawing a 3-D bevel around controls, the digits would look mighty strange with a bevel around each digit. John had to change the Appearance property for the Digit and ColonPlace picture boxes to 0 - Flat so the digits would not have a bevel around each one.

Both the clock and the calendar are updated by their own subroutine: UpdateClock for the clock, and UpdateCalendar for the calendar. Let's look at UpdateClock first.

UpdateClock is rather like the clock program you wrote in Chapter 7, but with a couple of differences. Instead of drawing hands on a clock, it shows individual digits. The way to do this, as mentioned earlier, is to assign the Picture property from the Digits array (which holds the digits 0 through 9) to the Picture property of a Digit (which is a control array that shows the digits in the form).

You can also use another one of John's small tricks to make the colon blink on and off. It will blink every half second, so it will be on for half a second and off for half a second. Here's how to do this. First, set the timer Interval to 500, which is half a second, so Ticker_Timer will be called (usually) every half-second. Then create a *Static* variable called showColon. A Static variable is like a form variable, because it keeps its value even after UpdateClock exits. But defining it as Static inside UpdateClock makes it visible only to the UpdateClock subroutine.

Every time UpdateClock is called, the value of showColon changes to Not showColon. In other words, if showColon was True, it gets set to False. If it was False, it gets set to True. The value of showColon determines which picture to show—the colon picture or the blank picture.

UpdateCalendar is also quite simple. The Format$() function does almost all the work of converting dates into names. The only extra thing is the UCase$() function, which converts the name of the month into all uppercase letters.

The ClockCal Form

The ClockCal form has a number of controls on it, as you can see from Figure 15.9. Most of the objects, including the form itself, are automatically sized correctly at run time, so these controls don't have to be placed very carefully. Table 15.5 shows the properties for the form, and Table 15.6 shows the controls on the form.

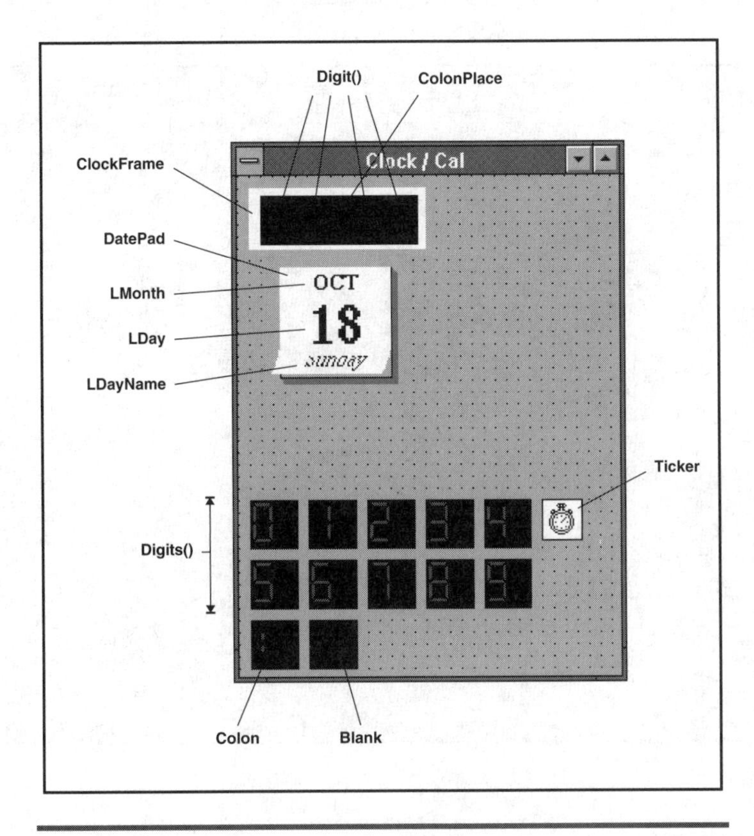

FIGURE 15.9 *The ClockCal form at design time, with all the controls.*

TABLE 15.5 *Properties for the Form*

Property	Setting
BackColor	&H00C0C0C0&
BorderStyle	1 - Fixed
Caption	Clock / Cal
FormName	ClockCal
MaxButton	False
MinButton	False
ScaleMode	3 - Pixel

TABLE 15.6 *Controls on the Form*

Control	Property	Setting
Picture Box	BorderStyle	0 – None
	Left	8
	Name	ClockFrame
	ScaleMode	3 – Pixel
	Top	8
Picture Box (4)	Appearance	0 – Flat
	BackColor	0
	Index	0, 1, 2, 3 — left to right.
	Name	Digit
Picture Box	Appearance	0 – Flat
	BackColor	0
	Name	ColonPlace

continued

Control	Property	Setting
Picture Box	Appearance	0 – Flat
	AutoSize	True
	BackColor	&H80000005&
	BorderStyle	0 – None
	Left	20
	Name	DatePad
Picture Box	Picture	(Bitmap) ...
	ScaleMode	3 – Pixel
Label	Alignment	2 – Center
	BackStyle	0 – Transparent
	FontName	Tms Rmn
	Name	LMonth
Label	Alignment	2 – Center
	BackStyle	0 – Transparent
	FontName	Tms Rmn
	Name	LDay
Label	Alignment	2 – Center
	BackStyle	0 – Transparent
	FontName	Tms Rmn
	Name	LDayName
Timer	Interval	500
	Name	Ticker

The Code for ClockCal

The following definitions are from the (declarations) area of the ClockCal form:

```
'
' These two variables are used to keep track of the
' last time we updated the clock so we won't flash
' the display when there are no changes.
'
Private lastHour
Private lastMin
```

The following code is code that initializes ClockCal:

```
Private Sub Form_Load ()
  ClockFrame.BackColor = 0   ' Set background to black
  lastMin = -1               ' Update minutes even if 0
  lastHour = -1              ' Update hour even if 0

  SetupSizes                 ' Set all the sizes

  UpdateCalendar
  UpdateClock
End Sub
```

Together, the following four subroutines take care of changing the size of all the nonbitmap items inside the window:

```
Private Sub SetupSizes ()
  '
  ' First we'll set the size for all the digits in the
  ' digital clock face.
  '
  SizeWindow 136, 148         ' Set form size, in pixels

  ColonPlace.Width = 16
  ColonPlace.Height = 33

  For i = 0 To 3
```

```
    Digit(i).Width = 24
    Digit(i).Height = 33
    Digit(i).Top = 5
    Digit(i).Left = 4 + 24 * i
    If i >= 2 Then
      Digit(i).Left = Digit(i).Left + ColonPlace.Width
    End If
  Next i

  ColonPlace.Left = Digit(1).Left + 24
  ColonPlace.Top = Digit(0).Top

  ClockFrame.Width = 120
  ClockFrame.Height = 41

  '
  ' Next we'll set the size and locations for the
  ' calendar.
  '
  DatePad.Top = ClockFrame.Top + ClockFrame.Height + 6
  SizeCalendar
End Sub
```

```
Private Sub SizeWindow (ByVal pWidth, ByVal pHeight)
  '
  ' This subroutine sets the inside dimensions of the
  ' window to 148 x 136 pixels.
  '
  Dim xScale, yScale              ' twips/pixel ratio
  Dim xBorder, yBorder            ' Size of border, in
                                  ' twips
  Dim newWidth, newHeight         ' New width, height of
                                  ' window

  ScaleMode = 1                   ' Set to twip scaling
  xBorder = Width - ScaleWidth    ' Size of x borders in
                                  ' twips
  yBorder = Height - ScaleHeight  ' Size of y borders in
                                  ' twips
```

```
  ScaleMode = 3                     ' Switch back to pixel
                                    ' scale

  xScale = Screen.TwipsPerPixelX ' x twips/pixel ratio
  yScale = Screen.TwipsPerPixelY ' y twips/pixel ratio

  newWidth = xBorder + xScale * pWidth
  newHeight = yBorder + yScale * pHeight
  Move Left, Top, newWidth, newHeight
End Sub
```

```
Private Sub SizeCalendar ()
  LMonth.Left = 16
  LDay.Left = 16
  LDayName.Left = 16

  LMonth.Width = 64
  LDay.Width = 64
  LDayName.Width = 64

  LMonth.Top = 7
  LMonth.Height = 16

  LDay.Top = 21
  LDay.Height = 42

  LDayName.Top = 58
  LDayName.Height = 16

  LMonth.FontSize = FindFontSize(LMonth.Height)
  LDay.FontSize = FindFontSize(LDay.Height)
  LDayName.FontSize = LMonth.FontSize
End Sub
```

```
Private Function FindFontSize (ByVal high) As Integer
  '
  ' This function returns the first font with a
  ' TextHeight >= high.
  '
```

```
    i = 1
    FontSize = i
    While TextHeight("Ay") < high
      FontSize = i
      If FontSize > i Then
        i = FontSize
      Else
        i = i + 1
      End If
    Wend
    FindFontSize = i
  End Function
```

The following set of subroutines handles the clock and calendar functions:

```
  Private Sub Ticker_Timer ()
    UpdateClock
    UpdateCalendar
  End Sub
```

```
  Private Sub UpdateClock ()
    Static showColon As Integer   ' True when colon visible
    Dim t As Double
    Dim h, m, s As Integer

    t = Now
    h = Hour(t) Mod 12
    If h = 0 Then h = 12
    m = Minute(t)
    s = Second(t)

    If h <> lastHour Then
      If Int(h / 10) = 0 Then
        Digit(0).Picture = Blank.Picture
      Else
        Digit(0).Picture = Digits(Int(h / 10)).Picture
      End If
      Digit(1).Picture = Digits(h Mod 10).Picture
      lastHour = h
```

```
    End If

    If m <> lastMin Then
      Digit(2).Picture = Digits(Int(m / 10)).Picture
      Digit(3).Picture = Digits(m Mod 10).Picture
      lastMin = m
    End If

    If showColon Then
      ColonPlace.Picture = Blank.Picture
    Else
      ColonPlace.Picture = Colon.Picture
    End If
    showColon = Not showColon
End Sub
```

```
Sub UpdateCalendar ()
    t = Now
    d = Day(t)
    LDay.Caption = Format$(d)
    LDayName.Caption = Format$(t, "dddd")
    LMonth.Caption = UCase$(Format$(t, "mmm"))
End Sub
```

TOOLBOX FOR CONTROLS

Progress Bars

File: CTRLTOOL.BAS

Purpose: Creates animated progress bars that show the current percentage as both a bar graph and a number.

Many programs display progress bars like the one in Figure 16.1 when they're doing a lengthy operation. It's actually quite easy to create progress bars, when you know how. You'll find a full explanation herein, in addition to a general-purpose progress bar subroutine that you can use in your own programs.

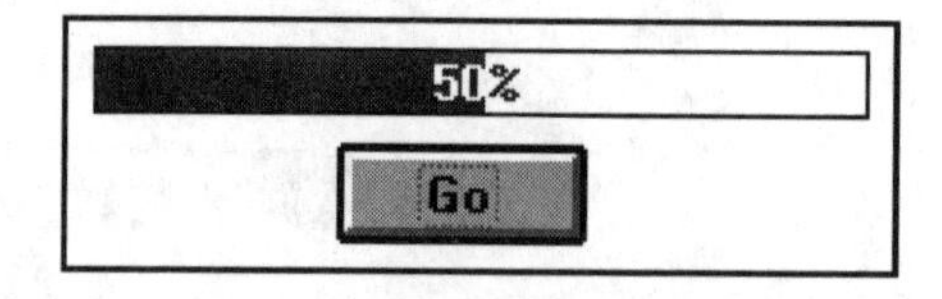

FIGURE 16.1 *A progress bar.*

How to Use UpdateProgress

If you want to create a progress bar in your own programs, the following shows what you have to do:

- Create a picture box on your form and give it a control name.
- Add the CTRLTOOL.BAS file to your project. You use the **Add File...** menu item from the File menu to select a file to add.
- Make a call to UpdateProgress in your program. You need to supply two parameters to this subroutine: the Name of the picture box and a number between 0 and 100.

Below is a sample program that shows you how to use UpdateProgress. John created a wide thin picture box called Picture1 and a command button called *Command1* with a caption "Go" as shown in Figure 16.1. When you click on Command1, you'll see an animation of the progress bar. You'll also notice that John changed the ForeColor property of the picture box to blue, which changes the color of both the bar and the text.

```
Private Sub Command1_Click ()
  Picture1.ForeColor = RGB(0, 0, 255)  ' Use blue
                                       ' progress bar
  For i = 0 To 100 Step 5
    UpdateProgress Picture1, i
  Next i
  Picture1.Cls                         ' Clear when
                                       ' we're done
End Sub
```

You might also want to set the Appearance property of the picture box to 0–flat if you don't want beveled edges around the progress bar.

How UpdateProgress Works

Visual Basic provides several features that make writing UpdateProgress particularly simple.

First, UpdateProgress sets the AutoRedraw property for the picture box to True. This creates an off-screen drawing image where all your drawing takes place. Any changes to this off-screen image are transferred to the screen in only three cases: when Visual Basic has some free time, as part of the Paint method, and when you explicitly call the Refresh method.

By using an off-screen image instead of drawing to the screen, the rest of UpdateProgress becomes much easier. For one thing, you can erase the image and redraw it from scratch without any screen flicker. If you want to see what we mean, remove the line that sets AutoRedraw to True. For another thing, you don't have to write any code for the picture box's Paint method, because Visual Basic will redraw the picture box using the off-screen image. Erasing the image first also makes it easy to draw the number on top of the progress bar and to handle cases where the percentage drops, causing the bar to become shorter.

After UpdateProgress erases the image, it sets ScaleWidth to 100. This allows you to draw a bar with the correct proportions without doing any calculations. Because the variable *percent* can range from 0 to 100, you draw the bar from 0 to percent.

Next, UpdateProgress changes the DrawMode to 10; that is, Not Xor Pen. In Chapter 7, we mentioned that this mode allows you to draw erasable lines on top of a white background. (You'd use mode seven for a black background.) Drawing a box over text in this mode inverts the text, which gives you the effect in Figure 16.1.

The next group of lines displays the current percentage as a number, centered in the picture box. After you've drawn the text, you can draw the bar on top. The Line command is quite simple because UpdateProgress already set up the coordinate so that 0 is at the left end and 100 is at the right end of the picture box.

Finally, the last line calls the Refresh method of the picture box, which forces Visual Basic to copy the new image to the screen right now. Without this method, you may not see your progress bar updated until much later.

There is one other small detail about UpdateProgress that we'd like to mention. The argument *percent* is defined to be ByVal. Without the ByVal in front of *percent,* you would only be allowed to pass numbers of type Single to UpdateProgress.

ByVal allows you to pass *any* number (including Integer and Single, as well as properties). It's a good idea to use ByVal in general-purpose subroutines so that you have the freedom to pass any type of number to your subroutine.

The Code

Here is the subroutine contained in CTRLTOOL.BAS. This is all the code you'll need to use progress bars in your programs (you'll find it on the disk at the back of this book).

```
Public Sub UpdateProgress (pb As Control, ByVal percent)
  Dim num$                      ' Used to hold percent string

  If Not pb.AutoRedraw Then     ' Do we have off-screen image?
    pb.AutoRedraw = True        ' No, set one up.
  End If

  pb.Cls                        ' Clear off-screen image
  pb.ScaleWidth = 100           ' Set for percentage
  pb.DrawMode = 10              ' Set for erasable drawing

  '
  ' Display the percentage, centered in the picture
  ' box.
  '
  num$ = Format$(percent, "##0") + "%"
  pb.CurrentX = 50 - pb.TextWidth(num$) / 2
  pb.CurrentY = (pb.ScaleHeight - pb.TextHeight(num$)) / 2
  pb.Print num$                 ' Display percentage

  '
  ' Draw box over the percentage.
  '
  pb.Line (0, 0)-(percent, pb.ScaleHeight), , BF
  pb.Refresh                    ' Show changes on screen
End Sub
```

Drawing Shadows Around Controls

File: CTRLTOOL.BAS

Purpose: Draws a drop shadow around any control on your form.

Have you ever wanted your controls to have drop shadows drawn around them, like the shadow around the text box in Figure 16.2? This is very easy to do and requires only a few lines of code.

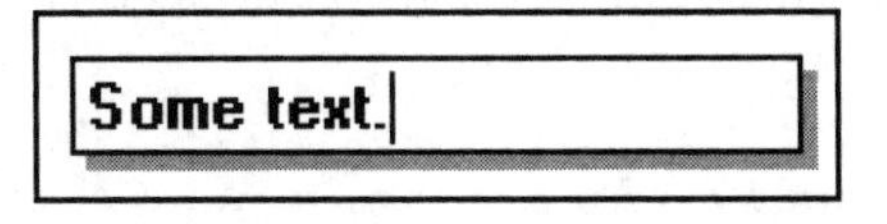

FIGURE 16.2 *The text box in this figure has a drop shadow drawn around it.*

Let's say you have a text box called Text1 on your form and you want to draw a drop shadow around your text box. How do you do it? Anything you draw on a form will be drawn behind all the controls on your form, so you can draw the shadow by drawing a gray rectangle behind your control. You can use this Shadow subroutine in any module, and it will do all the work of drawing shadows around controls.

To use this subroutine, place a call to it in your form's Form_Paint event handler, with two parameters: the name of your form and the name of your control. For example, if you have a form with a control called Text1, you write the following:

```
Private Sub Form_Paint ()
  Shadow Me, Text1
End Sub
```

By including both the form and the control as parameters, you can use this subroutine from any form. This allows you to put Shadow into a general-purpose module that you can add, without modification, to any form. This subroutine is also included in the CTRLTOOL.BAS module included on the disk that comes with this book.

If you use shadows, you should turn off the 3D appearance of any controls that have shadows (set the Appearance property to 0 - Flat).

By the way, you can change the color and width of the shadow by changing the *color* and *shWidth* constants at the start of Shadow.

The Code

Here's the subroutine that you can add to any module or include the CTRLTOOL.BAS module.

```
Public Sub Shadow (f As Form, c As Control)
  '
  ' This subroutine draws a gray shadow below and to
  ' the right of a control. This subroutine must be in
  ' one your form.
  '
  Const color = &H808080      ' Color of the shadow
  Const shWidth = 3           ' Width of the shadow
  Dim oldWidth As Integer     ' Saves old DrawWidth
  Dim oldScale As Integer     ' Saves old ScaleMode

  oldWidth = f.DrawWidth     ' Remember current DrawWidth
  oldScale = f.ScaleMode     ' Remember current ScaleMode

  f.ScaleMode = 3             ' Set to Pixel scaling
  f.DrawWidth = 1             ' 1-pixel wide lines
  '
  ' Draws the shadow around the control by drawing a
  ' gray box behind the control that's offset right and
  ' down.
  '
  f.Line (c.Left + shWidth, c.Top + shWidth)- _
          Step(c.Width - 1, _c.Height - 1), color, BF
```

```
    f.DrawWidth = oldWidth      ' Restore old DrawWidth
    f.ScaleMode = oldScale      ' Restore old ScaleMode
End Sub
```

Checking Text Box Input

File: CTRLTOOL.BAS

Purpose: Ensures that you can only type valid numbers or strings into a text box. This section includes subroutines that allow you to limit the input to simple floating-point numbers.

There are a number of cases where you'll need to be able to control what someone can type into your programs. For example, if you have a text box that should only accept numbers, you'll want to make sure you can't type letters into it.

In this section, we'll give you an idea of how to control what someone can type into a text box. We'll describe the techniques and show a few simple examples, but we won't provide any general-purpose subroutines because there are many possible types of input checking. (There are some commercial custom controls that provide very sophisticated input checking and formatting.)

Discarding Characters

The easiest type of input field is a numeric-only input field that accepts only integers. All you have to do in this case is throw out any characters that aren't numbers. But how do you do this? By using the KeyPress event handler.

Whenever you press a key that will be inserted into a text box, Visual Basic calls the KeyPress event handler *before* actually inserting the character into the text box. This event handler has a parameter, called KeyAscii, that contains the character code for this character. You can keep Visual Basic from inserting this character into a text box by setting KeyAscii = 0.

The following is a version of KeyPress for a text box called Text1 that only accepts the digits 0 through 9:

```
Private Sub Text1_KeyPress (KeyAscii As Integer)
  If KeyAscii < Asc(" ") Then    ' Is this Control char?
```

```
    Exit Sub                              ' Yes, let it pass
  End If

  If KeyAscii < Asc("0") Or KeyAscii > Asc("9") Then
    KeyAscii = 0                          ' Discard character
  End If
End Sub
```

Now the text box will accept any number of digits, but it won't accept any other characters.

There is a bit of extra code in the KeyPress event handler that is very important: Any keys with a KeyAscii less than Asc(" "), which has a numeric value of 32, are control keys, such as the Backspace key. If you don't keep these keystrokes, you won't be able to use Backspace to delete characters from your text box. KeyPress first checks to see if the characters are control characters, and if they are, it simply exits.

Limitations of Using KeyPress

There is one problem with using the KeyPress event handler that isn't easy to get around. Even though KeyPress gives you complete control over keys you type, it doesn't give you control over the Paste (Shift+Ins) keyboard combination supported by all text boxes.

With the previous example, you can insert *any* text into the text box by copying the text from another text box and pasting it in. The KeyPress event handler won't be called for any text you paste.

The easiest way to handle this situation, although perhaps not the best, is to disable the Shift+Ins key combination. If you want to do this, you can use the following code in KeyDown:

```
Private Sub Text1_KeyDown (KeyCode As Integer, Shift As
                          Integer)
  '
  ' Disable the Shift+Ins keyboard combination for Text1.
  '
  If KeyCode = 45 And (Shift And 1) = 1 Then
    KeyCode = 0
  End If
End Sub
```

This code looks for the Shift+Ins key combination. The KeyCode for the Ins key is 45 (note that unlike KeyAscii, KeyCode refers to actual key on your keyboard rather than to the character). The Shift parameter contains information on which shift keys are down (you can have, for example, both the Control and the Shift keys down at the same time). Checking to see if Shift And 1=1 checks lets you know whether the regular shift keys are down.

You'll also want to add some code to your KeyPress event handler to trap the Ctrl+V key combination, which is the new keyboard combination for Paste. Add the following code at the start of KeyPress to disable Ctrl+V:

```
If KeyAscii = 22 Then          ' Is this Ctrl+V?
  KeyAscii = 0                 ' Yes, discard character
End If
```

Checking Simple Floating-Point Numbers

Ensuring that the number in a text box is valid takes more work than simply ensuring that only digits can be entered. For example, let's say you need a numeric field where you can type in only valid floating-point numbers. In this case, you need to allow the decimal point as well as digits, but only one decimal point. You also need to support the minus sign, and the E notation for large numbers. How do you do this without knowing the exact format for all numbers?

You don't. You really have to know what numbers look like in order to check. But to give you an idea of how to go about checking more complex numbers, we've provided a very simple example that allows you to type in a floating-point number with a single minus sign and a single decimal point but no exponent. Below you'll find two general-purpose subroutines called *DoKeyPress* and *CheckPeriod* that do all the working of checking a floating-point number, as well as the *KeyPress* and *KeyUp* event handlers for a text box called Text1.

First, the KeyPress and KeyUp event handlers, along with the KeyDown handler that disables Paste as follows:

```
Private Sub Text1_KeyDown (KeyCode As Integer, Shift As
                           Integer)
  '
  ' Disable the Shift+Ins keyboard combination for Text1.
  '
  If KeyCode = 45 And (Shift And 1) = 1 Then
    KeyCode = 0
```

```
  End If
End Sub
```

```
Private Sub Text1_KeyPress (KeyAscii As Integer)
  '
  ' This code disables the Ctrl+V key combination for paste
  '
  If KeyAscii = 22 Then        ' Is this Ctrl+V?
    KeyAscii = 0               ' Yes, discard character
  End If

  DoKeyPress Text1, KeyAscii
End Sub
```

```
Private Sub Text1_KeyUp (KeyCode As Integer, Shift As _
                        Integer)
  CheckPeriod Text1
End Sub
```

You'll notice that these two event handlers rely completely on the DoKeyPress and CheckPeriod subroutines, which are shown as follows:

```
Public Sub DoKeyPress (t As Control, KeyAscii As Integer)
  '
  ' This subroutine discards any characters that can't be in
  ' a number. Here are the allowed characters:
  '
  '  0..9   All digits are allowed
  '    -    A minus, only if it's the first character
  '    .    Periods are allowed (they're checked in KeyUp)
  '
  If KeyAscii < Asc(" ") Then    ' Is this Control char?
    Exit Sub                     ' Yes, let it pass
  End If

  CheckPeriod t                  ' Remove excess periods

  If KeyAscii >= Asc("0") And KeyAscii <= Asc("9") Then
    ' keep digit
  ElseIf KeyAscii = Asc(".") Then
```

```
    ' keep .
  ElseIf KeyAscii = Asc("-") And t.SelStart = 0 Then
    ' Keep - only if first char
  Else
    KeyAscii = 0                     ' Discard all other chars
  End If

  '
  ' This code keeps you from typing any characters in front
  ' of a minus sign.
  '
  If Mid$(t.Text, t.SelStart + t.SelLength + 1, 1) = "-"
        Then
    KeyAscii = 0                    ' Discard chars before -
  End If
End Sub
```

```
Public Sub CheckPeriod (t As Control)
  '
  ' This subroutine makes sure your text box never has more
  ' than one period in it.
  '
  Dim i As Integer

  i = InStr(1, t.Text, ".")         ' Look for a period
  If i > 0 And InStr(i + 1, t.Text, ".") > 0 Then
    t.SelStart = t.SelStart - 1
    t.SelLength = 1                 ' Select new period
    t.SelText = ""                  ' Remove new period
  End If
End Sub
```

Let's take a look at how these subroutines work. Most of DoKeyPress should be clear. It makes sure you can only type digits, the minus sign, and periods. All other characters are discarded. The one new thing you'll notice is that DoKeyPress allows you to type a minus sign only if the SelStart property is 0, which ensures that the minus sign will only be allowed as the first character. The last three lines of DoKeyPress code keep you from typing any character in front of a minus sign.

The CheckPeriod subroutine makes sure that you don't have more than a single period in your text box. This subroutine is called in two different places. First, it's called in KeyUp to remove the last character, if it was a period. But CheckPeriod is also called in DoKeyPress to handle auto-repeat keys. When you hold a key down and it starts to repeat, this generates a number of KeyPress events without generating matching KeyUp events. You'll see the KeyUp event only when you release the period key. If DoKeyPress didn't call CheckPeriod, you'd be able to insert a number of periods into a text box just by holding down the period key.

Checking Other Types of Input

The techniques we've shown here should help you start to write your own input-checking routines. As you've seen, writing a set of input-checking subroutines takes a lot of work, but if you write them as general-purpose subroutines, such as DoKeyPress and CheckPeriod above, you can use them in any program.

Overtype Mode in Text Boxes

Purpose: Allows you to change a text box so it will work in overtype mode rather than insert mode, which is the default.

In this section, we'll show you how to change the way typing characters in a text box works. Normally when you type a character, Windows inserts that new character between two existing characters. But you can easily change this so that Windows will replace the character after the insertion point, rather than inserting your new character.

Add the following code to your KeyPress event handler for each text box that you want to support overtype mode:

```
If Text1.SelLength = 0 and KeyAscii >= 32 Then
  Text1.SelLength = 1
End If
```

You should have this code at the end of your KeyPress subroutine in case you do some other type of input checking on characters you type, in which case you might be setting KeyAscii to 0. This code works by selecting the character after the insertion point before Visual Basic inserts the character into your text box. In other words, by selecting the character after the insertion point, the character you typed will replace that character.

You need to make sure you change the selection length only if no characters are selected (hence the If Text1.SelLength = 0). And you also need to make sure you don't select a character if KeyAscii is less than 32. Such character codes are used for control characters, like the Backspace key, which erases characters.

An Example

Here is a simple example of using this technique, along with the techniques described previously for limiting the characters you can type to numbers only. The version of KeyPress that follows provides a numeric-input field that allows you to type only digits, and it supports the overtype mode:

```
Private Sub Text1_KeyPress (KeyAscii As Integer)
  If KeyAscii < 32 Then             ' Is this Control char?
    Exit Sub                        ' Yes, let it pass
  End If

  '
  ' Only allow digits in this text box.
  '
  If KeyAscii < Asc("0") Or KeyAscii > Asc("9") Then
    KeyAscii = 0                    ' Discard character
  End if

  '
  ' Use overtype mode to write over the character after
  ' the insertion point.
  '
  If Text1.SelLength = 0 and KeyAscii >= 32 Then
    Text1.SelLength = 1
  End If
End Sub
```

Password Text Boxes

Purpose: Builds a password text box that allows you to type in a password without the password appearing on the screen. Instead you'll see the • character.

When you want a text field to contain a password, you probably won't want the password itself to be visible. After all, if it were visible, someone looking over your shoulder could read your password as you typed it in. What you probably want your program to show is some character, such as •, for each character in the password field and to keep all the characters you've typed hidden. All you have to do is set a few properties, which will change any text box to a password input box. Figure 16.3 shows what a password field looks like in operation.

FIGURE 16.3 *A password input field used in a log-in dialog box. The actual text in the box is Hello, but all you see are bullets*

How to Create Password Fields

Text boxes have a property called PasswordChar that does much of the work, and it is normally blank. (In other words, it contains the empty string.) Setting this property to any character will change a normal text box into a password text box. In order to create a password field like the one in Figure 16.3, you need to set the following properties:

Property	Setting
PasswordChar	Alt+0183
FontName	Symbol
FontBold	False

The Alt+0183 character (hold down the **Alt** key and type **0183** on your numeric keypad with the Alt key still down and Num Lock on) produces a very nice bullet in the Symbol font. Or if you're a card player, you might want to use **Alt+0167**, **Alt+0168**, **Alt+0169** or **Alt+0170** to create clubs, diamonds, hearts, or spades, respectively.

Supporting an Edit Menu

Purpose: Allows you to support the Undo, Cut, Copy, and Paste menu items in a text box.

All Windows programs that use text boxes of any kind should support the standard Edit menu, with the items Undo, Cut, Copy, and Paste. Fortunately, this is extremely easy to do in Visual Basic.

Let's assume you have an Edit menu that's defined as follows:

Caption	Control Name	Accelerator
&Edit	menEdit	
&Undo	miUndo	Ctrl+Z
–	miEditLine1	
Cu&t	miCut	Ctrl+X
&Copy	miCopy	Ctrl+C
&Paste	miPaste	Ctrl+V

Then all you have to do to support these menu items is add the following event handlers:

```
Private Sub miUndo_Click ()
  SendKeys "%{BACKSPACE}"     ' Send Alt+Backspace
End Sub
```

```
Private Sub miCut_Click ()
  SendKeys "+{DELETE}"        ' Send Shift+Del
  recChanged = True           ' Record has changed.
End Sub
```

```
Private Sub miCopy_Click ()
  SendKeys "^{INSERT}"        ' Send Ctrl+Ins
End Sub
```

```
Private Sub miPaste_Click ()
  SendKeys "+{INSERT}"      ' Send Shift+Ins
  recChanged = True         ' Mark record as changed
End Sub
```

How It Works

Here's how these subroutines work. Visual Basic has a command called *SendKeys* that sends keystrokes to whatever control has the current keyboard focus. To allow you to send special keys, such as Alt+Backspace, SendKeys uses some special characters, such as % for Alt, + for Shift, and ^ for Control. Also, any characters between braces, such as {BACKSPACE}, refer to a key, and SendKeys will send this keystroke rather than the text inside the braces.

All text boxes support the following keyboard combinations:

Undo	↑	Alt+Backspace
Cut	↓	Shift+Del
Copy	→	Ctrl+Ins
Paste	←	Shift+Ins

All the code has to do is send these keystrokes to the edit boxes.

Table 16.1 lists the special symbols you can use in the SendKeys strings. You'll notice these symbols provide keys and actions.

TABLE 16.1 *Special SendKeys Strings*

Key	String
	{UP}
	{DOWN}
	{LEFT}
	{RIGHT}
Home	{HOME}
End	{END}
PgUp	{PGUP}
Break	{BREAK}
PrtScr	{PRTSC}
Num Lock	{NUMLOCK}
Scroll Lock	{SCROLLLOCK}
Caps Lock	{CAPSLOCK}
Help	{HELP}
Clear	{CLEAR}
Tab	{TAB}
Enter	{ENTER} or ~
Backspace	{BACKSPACE} or {BS}
Del	{DELETE} or {DEL}
Ins	{INSERT}
Esc	{ESCAPE} or {ESC}
F1 .. F16	{F1} .. {F16}
Shift	+
Ctrl	^
Alt	%

Keyboard Shortcuts

Incidentally, you'll notice we've used the Ctrl+Z, Ctrl+X, Ctrl+C, and Ctrl+V keyboard shortcuts for the Undo, Cut, Copy, Paste menu items. These are the new standard shortcuts that Microsoft suggests all programs use for these menu items; Table 16.2 lists all of them. This list has two parts. Recommended shortcuts should be used for all programs; the suggested shortcuts are keys that programs should support if they have a similar function.

TABLE 16.2 *Keyboard Shortcut Standards*

Function	Key
Recommended Ctrl+Letter Shortcuts	
Undo	Ctrl+Z
Cut	Ctrl+X
Copy	Ctrl+C
Paste	Ctrl+V
New	Ctrl+N
Open	Ctrl+O
Print	Ctrl+P
Save	Ctrl+S
Suggested Ctrl+letter Shortcuts	
Bold	Ctrl+B
Italic	Ctrl+I
Underline	Ctrl+U
Double underline	Ctrl+D
Small caps	Ctrl+K
Word-by-word underline	Ctrl+W
Remove char formatting	Ctrl+spacebar

TOOLBOX FOR FORMS

Centering Forms

File: FORMTOOL.BAS

Purpose: Centers a form on the screen.

When you're writing programs that use multiple forms, where some of your forms act as dialog boxes, you might want to center the forms on the screen when they're displayed. This is often better than using the positions you set during design time, because centered forms tend to stand out better. In fact, most commercial programs center dialog boxes on the screen.

Centering a form is really very simple; it takes a single line of code. But John has written a general-purpose subroutine that will do all of the work for you. By writing this code as a subroutine, it's much easier than typing in the code each time you want to center a form.

How to Use CenterForm

To use CenterForm all you have to do is make a call to it, and then show your form. For example, if you have a form called OpenDialog, you might use CenterForm like the following:

```
CenterForm OpenDialog   ' Center, but don't display form
OpenDialog.Show         ' Display the form on screen
```

You don't have to do anything special before you call CenterForm. In other words, you don't have to explicitly load the form by using the Load command. If you actually need to use the Load command, you can call CenterForm either before or after the Load command.

It is, however, a good idea to call CenterForm *before* you use Show to display the form for two reasons. First, if you display the form on the screen before you center it, you'll see your form move on the screen. Calling CenterForm before you call Show does all of the moving before you see anything appear on the screen.

Second, if you want to show your form as a modal form (using OpenDialog.Show 1), you'll need to center the form before you call Show because Visual Basic won't return to the next command following Show until your new form is removed from the screen.

Notes

Some notes on using CenterForm:

- **Center in Resize method.** If you want your window to always be centered, even when the user changes the size of your form, you can call CenterForm inside your Form_Resize event.
- **Center on Form_Load.** You have two choices about where you can put the code that centers a form: You can call CenterForm before you call the Show method, as described above, or you can put a call to CenterForm in your Form_Load event. This will cause your form to be centered each time it's loaded.
- **Note about CenterForm on Form_Load.** If you put the call to CenterForm in your Form_Load method and you hide the window by using the Hide rather than the Unload method, your form won't be centered automatically the next time it's shown using the Show method.

How It Works

The first two lines (x = and y =) calculate the new left and top values for the form. The number Screen.Width is the width in twips of the screen, and aForm.Width is the width, also in twips, of the form you want to center. The difference of these two numbers divided by two is the space you'll need between the left side of the screen and the left side of the form when the form is centered. The Move method does the work of actually moving the window to this new location.

The Code

The following subroutine centers a form:

```
Public Sub CenterForm (aForm As Form)
  Dim x, y                    ' New top, left for the form

  x = (Screen.Width - aForm.Width) / 2
  y = (Screen.Height - aForm.Height) / 2
  aForm.Move x, y             ' Change location of the form
End Sub
```

You can place this subroutine in any module or form. We suggest placing it in a module so that you can call it from anywhere in your program.

Sizing Forms Using Inside Dimensions

File: FORMTOOL.BAS

Purpose: Allows you to set the size of the inside of a form.

The only tools Visual Basic provides for changing the size of a form (the Height and Width properties and the Move method) refer to the outside dimensions of a form. If you want to resize a form to have specific inside dimensions, you need to know the size of the borders and the title bar, or you can use the ResizeInside subroutine presented here.

How to Use ResizeInside

Using ResizeInside is simple. Let's say you have a form called *Form1* and you want the inside dimensions of this form to be 2880 by 1440 twips (2 inches by 1 inch). You would then make the following call to ResizeInside:

```
ResizeInside Form1, 2880, 1440
```

There are only a couple of things you should be aware of when you use the previous subroutine:

- ResizeInside changes the ScaleMode of your form to 1 – Twips. If you want to use some other scale mode with your form, you'll need to change it when you're finished resizing the form.
- ResizeInside doesn't change the Top and Left properties of your form: it only changes the Width and Height properties. If you want to center the form, you can call CenterForm, also in **FORMTOOL.BAS**, *after* you call ResizeInside.

To use this subroutine, you must add the file FORMTOOL.BAS to your project or type the code shown here into any form or module.

Notes

Here are some notes on using ResizeInside:

- **ResizeInside in Form_Load.** A good place to call ResizeInside is in your form's Form_Load event, which allows you to change your form's size before it is shown on the screen.
- **ResizeInside in Form_Resize.** Be careful not to call ResizeInside from within your form's Form_Resize event handler. Doing so can result in an Out of stack space message from Visual Basic. The reason this happens is that any code that changes a form's size, which ResizeInside may do, results in Form_Resize being called again.

How It Works

ResizeInside is fairly simple—when you figure out how to write it, that is.

The secret behind ResizeInside is to calculate the size of the borders in both the X and Y directions. In the X direction, the borders will be the resize borders (or just lines if you've set the BorderStyle to Fixed). In the Y direction, the borders also include the height of the title bar, if you have one. In Figure 17.1, we have resize borders and a title bar with the caption Form1.

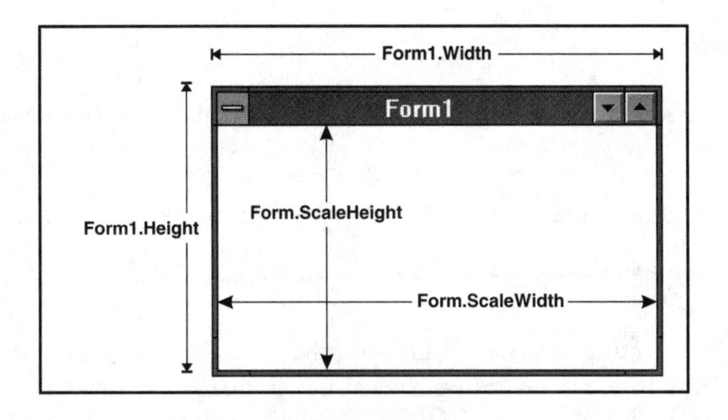

FIGURE 17.1 *The Height and Width properties refer to the outside dimensions of a form, in twips, and ScaleHeight and ScaleWidth refer to the inside dimensions when ScaleMode = 1 – Twips.*

Calculating the size of the borders requires some knowledge about how the Height, Width, ScaleHeight, and ScaleWidth properties work. You can see in Figure 17.1 that the Height and Width properties of a form *always* measure the outside dimensions of a form, and they measure these dimensions in twips. The ScaleHeight and ScaleWidth properties, on the other hand, measure the inside dimensions of the form, but not necessarily in twips. So in ResizeInside, the first thing to do is set ScaleMode = 1, which sets the units for ScaleHeight and ScaleWidth to twips.

Subtracting ScaleHeight from Height gives the height of the Y borders in twips, including both the top and bottom resize borders and the title bar. Similarly, subtracting ScaleWidth from Width gives the width, in twips, of the left and right resize borders.

Finally, using the Move method of the form to change the width and height of a form results in a snappier response on the screen because it changes both dimensions of a form at once. If you were to set Width and Height separately, rather than using Move, you'd see your form change in size twice, once for each dimension.

By the way, using the ByVal keyword in front of the *w* and *h* parameters lets you pass properties in calls to ResizeInside. Normally Visual Basic passes arguments by reference, which means you can change the values in variables you pass to a subroutine from inside that subroutine. But you can't change properties this way, so you have to use the ByVal keyword. ByVal tells Visual Basic to send a copy of the value to the subroutine, which works with properties, as well as any other value.

The Code

Here is the code you'll find in FORMTOOL.BAS. You can also type it into any module or form.

```
Public Sub ResizeInside (f As Form, ByVal w As Integer,
_
ByVal h As Integer)
  '
  ' This subroutine changes the size of a form so the
  ' inside of the form will be w twips wide, and h
  ' twips high.
  '
  '  Note: Sets ScaleMode = 1
  '
  Dim yBorders              ' Size of vertical borders
  Dim xBorders              ' Size of horizontal borders
  Dim x, y                  ' Location of the form

  f.ScaleMode = 1           ' Switch to twips
  xBorders = f.Width - f.ScaleWidth
  yBorders = f.Height - f.ScaleHeight
  x = f.Left                ' Get location of form
  y = f.Top

  f.Move x, y, w + xBorders, h + yBorders
End Sub
```

Limiting a Form's Size

Purpose: You need to limit how small a form can be resized or you want to fix the width of a form, but allow the height to change.

Suppose you have a program that has a window with a fixed width, but you need to be able to change its height by dragging on the size borders. The problem is that Visual Basic doesn't provide any way to put limits (either upper or lower) on the size of a form. So how do you do this?

It is not that difficult, and it doesn't require much code. You just have to know how to do it.

Keeping the Width Constant

Let's first look at how you'd keep the width of a form constant, letting the height be anything you want. All you have to do is change the Width property of the form inside of the Form_Resize event. For example, if you want a form to always be 4000 twips wide, put the following line into Form_Resize:

```
Private Sub Form_Resize ()
  Width = 4000           ' Set width back to 4,000 twips
End Sub
```

If you try this, you'll notice that your form's width is always the same and you can change the height to anything you want.

Setting a Minimum Size for a Form

The next example shows how to set a minimum size for a form. Let's say you need to make sure your form is never smaller than 4000 by 3000 twips, but it can be any size larger than this. The following Form_Resize code does just that:

```
Private Sub Form_Resize ()
  If Width < 4000 Then Width = 4000
  If Height < 3000 Then Height = 3000
End Sub
```

Try this and see how it works. You can also set upper limits for the width or height exactly the same way: just use an If..Then statement with the > operator, rather than the < operator used in this example.

Notes

Visual Basic calls the Form_Resize event *after* Windows changes the size of your form on the screen. This means that you'll see your form change its size twice when you use the methods in this section. Commercial programs, on the other hand, manage to limit the size of a window as you're dragging the new window size. The solution provided here is the best that you can do in Visual Basic.

Resizing a Form's Controls

Purpose: If you have a resizable form, you may have controls inside of the form that you want to move or resize when you change a form's size.

The best way to see how resizing works is with an example. Figure 17.2 shows a small program that has a single text box that takes up most of the window and has two buttons at the bottom of the window. You'll need to change the size of the text box whenever you change the size of this window. You'll also need to move the two buttons so they'll always be near the bottom of the window and nicely centered.

There are two ways that you can change the size of a control (or move it): Either change the properties (Width, Height, Left, and Top) or use the Move command. The Move command is best if you want to change more than one property, because Move will make all the changes at once. If you change the individual properties, you'll see your control redrawn at the new size or location each time you change a property, whereas Move will change all the values at one time.

Resizing a Text Box

In this example, the text box will always be 2 pixels wider than the width of the form. The reason for this is quite easy: text boxes have a 1-pixel-wide box drawn around them (unless you set BorderStyle to 0 – None), so you have to make the text box wider by 2 pixels if you want the left and right lines to be outside the form. The following code will change the width of a text box to fill the entire form:

```
ScaleMode = 3           ' Switch to pixel mode
Text1.Left = -1
Text1.Width = ScaleWidth + 2
```

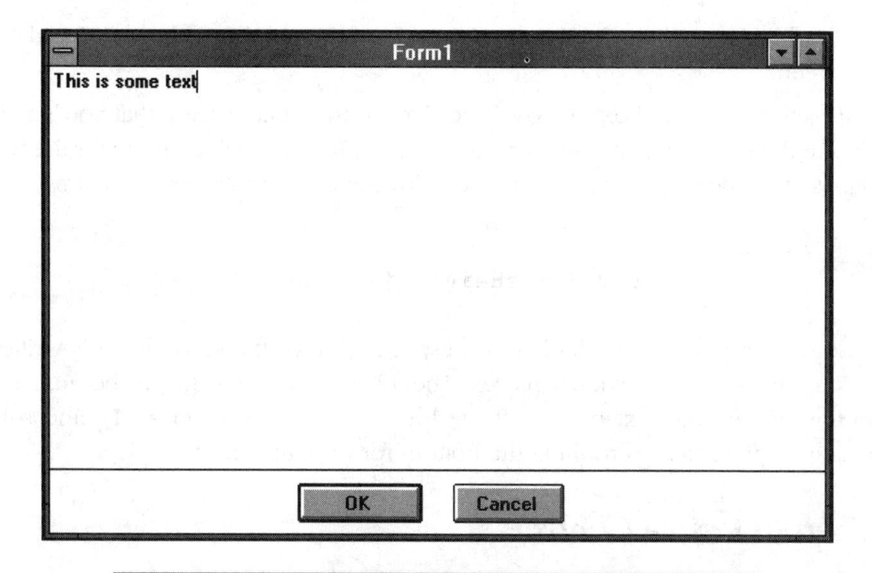

FIGURE 17.2 *For the sample program shown below, the text box will change in size whenever you resize this window, and the two buttons will always be centered at the bottom of this window.*

The first line sets the form so that the units will be pixels instead of twips. You need to do this to set Left to –1 pixel in the next line, which moves the line on the left side of the text box off the left side of the screen.

Some programmers use –15 twips rather than switching to pixel mode, but this won't always work. On VGA (and Super VGA) screens, 1 pixel is always 15 twips wide and high. But on an EGA screen, one pixel is 20 twips high and 15 twips wide, and on an 8514/a screen, a pixel is 12 twips wide and high.

The third line moves the line at the right side of the text box off the right side of the screen.

Changing the text box's height is very much the same, except that you'll want to make the text box a little shorter than the form so there will be room for the two buttons at the bottom of the screen. The following code shows how to do this:

```
Text1.Top = -1
Text1.Height = ScaleHeight + 1 - 30
```

These two lines should be fairly clear, especially since the second line is written so you can see the individual pieces: The +1 adds 1 to the height because the top line around the text box is off the top of the screen (Top = –1), and subtracting 30 pixels leaves room at the bottom for the buttons.

When to Resize Controls

Each time you change the size of your form, the form will receive a Form_Resize event. Putting your resizing code into this event handler will then allow your program to correctly resize your controls every time a form's size changes. This event will also be called the first time your program starts.

There is one small problem with sizing your controls only in the Form_Resize event. This event will be called the first time you run your program after all of the controls have been drawn on the form, so you'll see all the controls resize after your program starts. The easiest way to get around this, which we'll show you in the sample program section, is to also resize the controls in Form_Load, which is called before your program draws any of the controls.

Moving Controls

Now let's look at how you would move the two buttons in the window. The following commands move the cmdOK and cmdCancel buttons:

```
cmdOK.Top = Text1.Top + Text1.Height + 8
cmdCancel.Top = cmdCancel.Top
cmdOK.Left = ScaleWidth / 2 - cmdOK.Width - 10
cmdCancel.Left = cmdOK.Left + cmdOK.Width + 20
```

The first two lines move the buttons down so they'll be eight pixels below the bottom of the text box called Text1. Then the last two lines center these controls, with 20 pixels between the two controls.

Sample Program

The sample program shown here uses all of the methods described above, as well as the Move command, to make all the resizing as fast and unobtrusive as possible. You'll notice both Form_Load and Form_Resize call the same subroutine, MoveControls, to actually move the controls. The call in Form_Load resizes and moves all the controls before your window appears.

```
Private Sub Form_Load ()
  MoveControls
End Sub
```

```
Private Sub Form_Resize ()
  MoveControls
End Sub
```

Here is the MoveControls subroutine, which includes code to center the controls vertically in the gap left by the text box. Notice the use of the Move command instead of setting the properties, which is faster and doesn't cause as much screen flicker.

```
Private Sub MoveControls ()
  Dim newTop              ' The new Top for the buttons
  Dim center              ' Used to position the buttons

  ScaleMode = 3           ' Switch to pixel mode
  Text1.Move -1, -1, ScaleWidth + 2, ScaleHeight + 1 - 40

  newTop = Text1.Top + Text1.Height
  newTop = newTop + (ScaleHeight - newTop) / 2
  newTop = newTop - cmdOK.Height / 2
```

```
    center = ScaleWidth / 2
    cmdOK.Move center - (cmdOK.Width + 10), newTop
    cmdCancel.Move center + 10, newTop
End Sub
```

Showing a Startup Screen

Purpose: Your program takes a long time to load before you see the first form, so you'd like to display a startup screen while your program loads.

If you have a large Visual Basic program, or even a small one that has a complicated form, you may have noticed that your program takes a long time to load, which makes it seem very slow. Fortunately, there is a trick you can use to make your program *seem* like it's loading faster—you can display a startup screen while the rest of your program loads into memory.

Using a Startup Screen

There are several things you'll need to do in order to create a startup screen as follows:

1. **Create a form.** You'll need to create the form you'll display as the startup screen. This can be anything you want, but it's usually a form without a caption; with MaxButton, MinButton, and ControlBox all set to False; and BorderStyle set to 1 – Fixed Single.
2. **Create a Sub Main.** You'll find instructions for creating a Sub Main later. If you already have a Sub Main, you'll need to add the code here to this subroutine.
3. **Add Code to Sub Main.** You'll find a full description later of the code you'll need to add to Sub Main.
4. **Make Sub Main the Startup form.** Select **Options...** from the Tools menu, click on the Project tab, then click on **StartUp Form** and select **Sub Main** in the combo box.

Creating a Sub Main

If you don't have a Sub Main already in your project, you'll need to create one using the following steps:

1. Select **Module** from the Insert menu (or use an existing module if you have a .BAS module).
2. Click on the **View Code** button in your project window to display the Code window for this module.
3. Select **Procedure...** from the Insert menu.
4. Type **Main** into the New Procedure dialog box, then press **Enter**. This will create a subroutine called Main.

You should now see a blank Main subroutine, like the following one:

```
Public Sub Main ()

End Sub
```

Adding a Startup Screen to Sub Main

Now that you have a startup form and a Sub Main, you can add the lines of code that show the startup screen when your program loads. Let's say, for example, that your main form is called MainForm, and you startup form is called StartupForm. The simplest (but not best) way to display this startup screen when your program loads is as follows:

```
Private Sub Main ()
  StartupForm.Show           ' Show startup form
  StartupForm.Refresh        ' Force everything to draw
  MainForm.Show              ' Show program
  Unload StartupForm         ' Remove startup form
End Sub
```

The first line displays your startup screen, but without all of your form being drawn. It turns out that your form won't be redrawn completely until all your forms finish loading, unless you explicitly call the Refresh method, which explains the second line here. The third line then loads your main form. Finally, when your main form finishes loading, Main unloads the startup form from memory, because it won't be needed anymore.

This code works quite well, but there are a few extra touches you can add to make your program even more professional in the way it feels.

```
Sub Main ()
  Screen.MousePointer = 11    ' Set to wait cursor
  CenterForm StartupForm      ' Center startup screen
  StartupForm.Show            ' Show startup form
  StartupForm.Refresh         ' Force everything to draw
  MainForm.Show               ' Show program
  Unload StartupForm          ' Remove startup form
  Screen.MousePointer = 0     ' Restore mouse pointer
End Sub
```

The first line sets the mouse pointer to a wait cursor (an hourglass) while your program loads into memory. You set it back to its default shape at the end of Sub Main by setting ScreenMousePointer back to 0.

You'll also notice a call to CenterForm to center the startup screen. This is a nice touch, and you'll find the CenterForm subroutine described elsewhere in this chapter (it's also in the file FORMTOOL.BAS on the disk included with this book).

TOOLBOX FOR DRAWING

Fast Line Drawing

Purpose: A very fast way to draw lines (it's about six times faster than using Visual Basic's Line command).

There are times you'll find that the Line command is much too slow, for example, when you're drawing a complex graph or figure. In these cases, you can use a Windows API function called *Polyline.* The Polyline command draws a number of lines with a single call. All you have to do is create an array of points, and then send these points to Polyline.

To give you an idea of how fast Polyline can be, John wrote two programs, one using Polyline and one using Line –(x, y), to draw a spiral with 3000 points (see Figure 18.1). The Polyline function took approximately 0.5 second, and Line took 2.9 seconds. That means Polyline is about six times faster than using Basic's Line command.

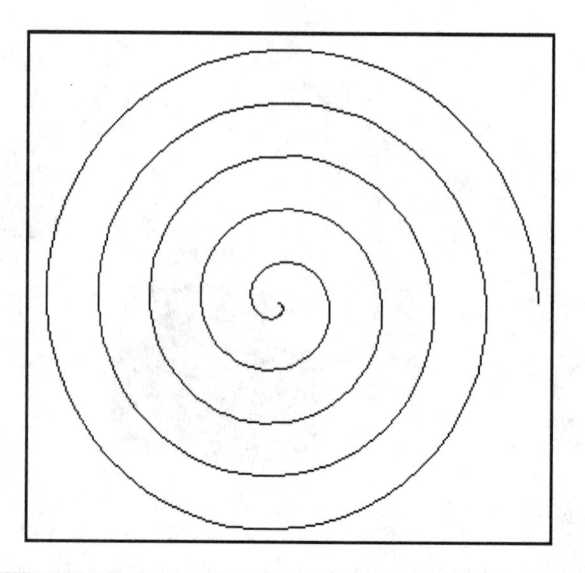

FIGURE 18.1 *This is the output you'll see from the Polyline sample program. Drawing this screen with 3000 line segments (which is more than you need) takes less than half a second.*

NOTE

The mapping mode used by default for all Windows API calls inside Visual Basic is the pixel-mapping mode. But if you also want to draw on a printer, the twip mapping mode is a better choice. The section on *Using Twip Scaling with API Calls* at the end of this chapter contains some subroutines that will allow you to use Polyline in the twip scaling mode, on both your screen and your printer.

You might also want to use Polyline if you're planning to draw a complex curve with a line style like *dashed*. In these cases, the Line command won't always produce very good results (see Figure 18.2), whereas Polyline always will.
The reason for this is quite easy: When you use a pattern with the Line command, it always begins at the start of the pattern. This means that you'll never get very far into the pattern if you have very short lines (like near the center of the spiral). Visual Basic applies the line pattern individually to each short line you draw, whereas Polyline applies the line style to the entire curve, not just one line segment.

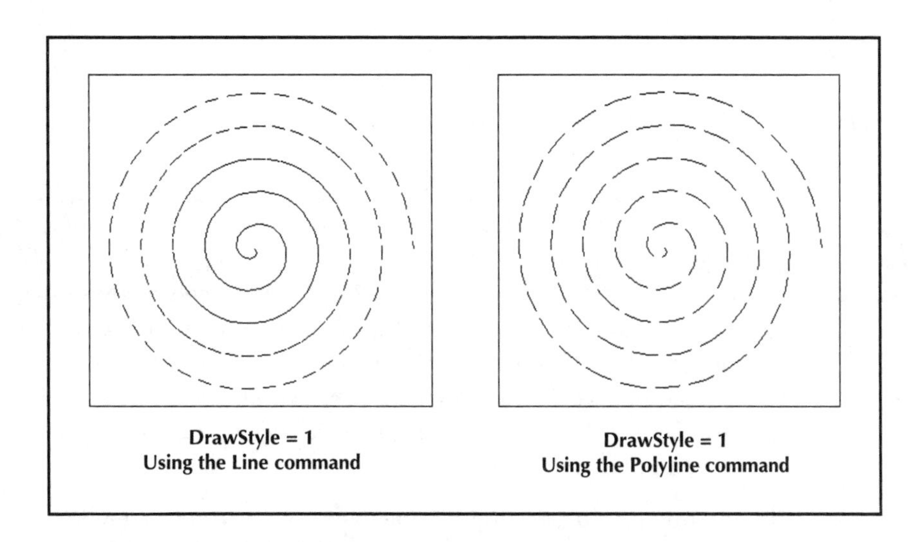

FIGURE 18.2 *This figure shows you the difference between using Line and Polyline with the dashed drawing style (DrawStyle = 1). You can see that Line doesn't do a very good job dashing a complex curve, whereas Polyline does.*

How Polyline Works

The Polyline routine draws a number of connected lines, where the points in the lines are in an array of type POINTAPI. You must have at least two points (one line) to use the Polyline routine. This API call uses three parameters, hDC, lpPoints, and nCount, with the following syntax:

```
Function Polyline (ByVal hDC As Integer, lpPoints As POINTAPI, _
ByVal nCount As Integer) As Integer
```

hDC A handle to the *device context* of the current form. API calls use the DC for permission to write on a form or picture control. Use the hDC property of a form, a picture box, or Printer.

lpPoints The points you want to display. This should be the first element of the array you want to send, such as points(0). Note that you can also start with the fifth element, for example, by writing points(4).

nCount The number of points in the array, which is one more than the number of lines.

returns 0 if no lines were drawn, some other number (Microsoft doesn't say what) if the lines were drawn.

The Polyline function shown above can only be used when you're using the 16-bit version of Visual Basic. If you're using the 32-bit version, in Windows '95 for example, you will need to replace all the Integer variables with Longs. The code shown below uses conditional compilation, which was first introduced in Visual Basic 4.0, to use the correct version of Polyline. Conditional compilation allows you to control which code will actually be included in your program when you build your project.

In the examples below, the #If statements allow you to include both the 16- and 32-bit code in your source files, but only one version in the program you're building. Win16 and Win32 are two constants defined by Visual Basic; only one can be true at a time. Win32 will be true only if you're building your project using the 32-bit version of Visual Basic.

Sample Program

Here is a small sample program that uses Polyline to draw a spiral using 300 line segments. The lines before the Form_Load Sub below should be in the (declarations) section of your form.

```
#If Win16 Then
    Private Type POINTAPI
        x As Integer
        y As Integer
    End Type

    Private Declare Function Polyline Lib "GDI" _
        (ByVal hDC As Integer, lpPoints As POINTAPI, _
         ByVal nCount As Integer) As Integer
#ElseIf Win32 Then
    Private Type POINTAPI
        x As Long
```

```
        y As Long
    End Type

    Private Declare Function Polyline Lib "gdi32" _
        (ByVal hDC As Long, lpPoints As POINTAPI, _
         ByVal nCount As Long) As Long
#End If
Private numPoints
Private points(3000) As POINTAPI

Private Sub Form_Load ()
  numPoints = 300
  dTheta = 3.14159 / numPoints * 10
  dR = 150 / numPoints
  For i = 0 To numPoints -1
    points(i).X = i * dR * Cos(dTheta * i) + 150
    points(i).Y = i * dR * Sin(dTheta * i) + 150
  Next i
End Sub

Private Sub Form_Paint ()
  j% = Polyline(hDC, points(0), numPoints)
End Sub
```

You'll notice that both the Type and the Declared are defined as Private. You can put Types and Declares into any form, provided you declare them as private. If you want a Type or Declare to be public, you must put the code into a module rather than a form.

You'll notice that this program jumps onto the screen when it finishes running Form_Load. If you minimize and then restore this screen, you'll see that it takes almost no time at all to redraw the screen. Figure 18.1 shows the output from this program.

Drawing on a Printer with Polyline

It's very easy to use Polyline to draw onto your printer. All you have to do is use Printer.hDC as the first argument as follows:

```
Printer.Print " "
j% = Polyline(Printer.hDC, points(0), numPoints)
Printer.EndDoc
```

The Printer.Print command makes sure Visual Basic starts the printing process so the Polyline command will work correctly. Without this Print command, Polyline may not work with all printer drivers.

There is one small problem, however. Because Polyline in this case is working with pixels, and since pixels are much smaller on printers, the image drawn on your printer will be much smaller than the one on your screen. But there is a solution. You can use twips, rather than pixels, with the Polyline command as explained next.

Using Nonpixel Scaling Modes

Polyline, like all other Windows API functions, uses the scaling mode that's being used underneath Visual Basic, which is usually the Pixel scaling mode (called MM_TEXT in Windows jargon). You have two choices: either use the pixel scaling mode for all your work (see the section *Printing Using the Screen Pixel Mode*), or use the twip scaling mode (see the section *Printing with API Calls Using Twip Scaling*).

Other Notes

Color You can change the color of lines drawn with Polyline by setting the ForeColor property to whatever color you want. Polyline, as it turns out, uses the current ForeColor when it draws.

Width The DrawWidth property changes the line width of the lines drawn by Polyline.

Dash/Dot If you need to draw dashed or dotted lines, the DrawStyle property works much better with Polyline than with Line. This is because Windows starts the dashing over for each new line drawn with Line, but not with Polyline. Thus, a number of very short lines drawn with Line will be solid, rather than dashed. To see how this works, add the line DrawStyle=1 in Form_Paint before the Polyline command. **Note:** DrawStyle applies only if DrawWidth=1.

Mode DrawMode has the same effect on Polyline as it does on lines drawn with the Line command.

Fast Ruler Drawing

Files: RULER.BAS and APISCALE.BAS (used by RULER.BAS)

Purpose: Drawing rulers, with inch marks, on the screen. (You can also modify the code to draw rulers with any mark spacing.)

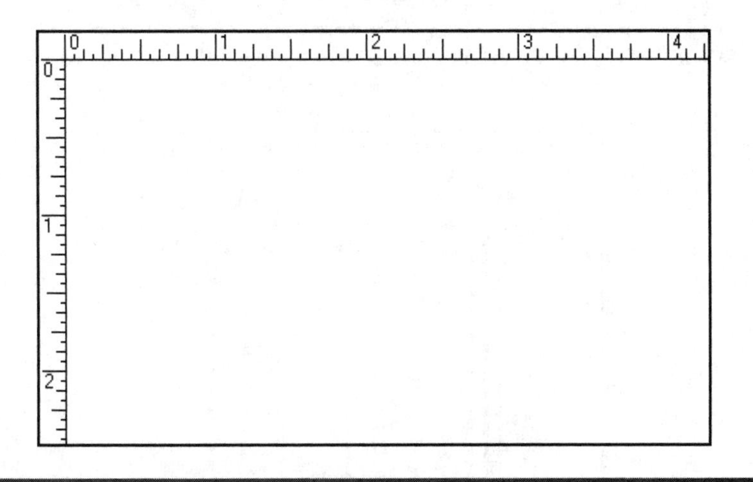

FIGURE 18.3 *The output of the Ruler sample program. These rulers are drawn almost instantaneously using Polyline to draw the lines. Writing the same program using the Line command, it takes about five times longer to draw the rulers.*

It's not hard to draw a set of rulers, like the ones shown in Figure 18.3, using Visual Basic's Line command. Such a program, however, will be somewhat slow at drawing the ruler. It takes about 1.5 seconds to draw both rulers for a full-screen form on a 16-MHz laptop. But if you use the Polyline function to draw the lines, you can cut this time to about a quarter of a second, which is nearly instantaneous!

How Ruler Works

The trick to using the Polyline function to draw the ruler is to turn the ruler into a list of lines that are all connected. But instead of defining the entire length of the ruler, you'll define just one inch (see Figure 18.4). This one-inch section, as you'll see shortly, requires a total of 51 points, or three points for each tick mark.

Figure 18.5 shows how to define the points that will draw this one-inch segment of the ruler. You'll notice that you actually need to draw two lines for each tick mark, one going up and the second returning to the base line, so that Polyline doesn't have to lift the pen when it is drawing the ruler.

FIGURE 18.4 *The algorithm stores 51 points—enough to define one inch.*

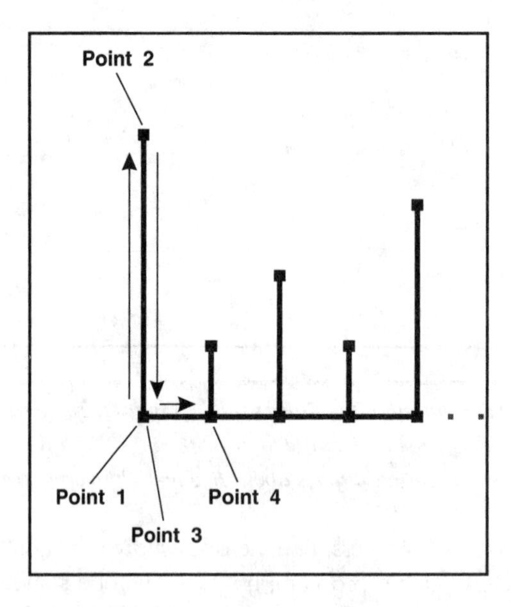

FIGURE 18.5 *To draw the ruler, you'll need to draw all the lines without lifting the pen. You can see how each tick mark consists of two lines: one going up and the second going back to the base line.*

The final trick is to use the SetWindowOrg function in Windows to change the starting point of the coordinate system. This will let you draw a one-inch section of the ruler anywhere inside a window without changing the points that define the ruler.

The Ruler.bas Module

The ruler-drawing code is actually in a Visual Basic module, called RULER.BAS. By putting this code into a module, you can add a ruler to any program by loading Ruler.bas and APISCALE.BAS and then calling DrawXRuler or DrawYRuler.

Here are the definitions and code in RULER.BAS:

```
#If Win16 Then
    Private Type POINTAPI
        X As Integer
        Y As Integer
    End Type

    Private Declare Function Polyline Lib "GDI" _
        (ByVal hDC As Integer, lpPoints As POINTAPI, _
         ByVal nCount As Integer) As Integer

    Private Declare Function SetWindowOrg Lib "GDI" _
        (ByVal hDC As Integer, ByVal X As Integer, _
         ByVal Y As Integer) As Long
#ElseIf Win32 Then
    Private Type POINTAPI
        X As Long
        Y As Long
    End Type

    Private Declare Function Polyline Lib "gdi32" _
        (ByVal hDC As Long, lpPoints As POINTAPI, _
         ByVal nCount As Long) As Long

    Private Declare Function SetWindowOrgEx Lib _
        "gdi32" (ByVal hDC As Long, ByVal X As Long, _
         ByVal Y As Long, lpPoint As Long) As Long
#End If

Private xPoints(51) As POINTAPI
Private yPoints(51) As POINTAPI
Private numPoints As Integer
```

```
Private validData As Boolean        ' True when we have points

Public Sub DrawXRuler(theForm As Form, X As Integer, _
Y As Integer, wid As Integer)

    If Not validData Then InitRuler
    SetFormToTwips theForm
    For i = 0 To wid
        #If Win16 Then
            l& = SetWindowOrg(theForm.hDC, _
                                  -X - 1440 * i, -Y)
        #ElseIf Win32 Then
            l& = SetWindowOrgEx(theForm.hDC, _
                                  -X - 1440 * i, -Y, 0)
        #End If
        j% = Polyline(theForm.hDC, xPoints(1), _
                        numPoints)
    Next i

    #If Win16 Then
        l& = SetWindowOrg(theForm.hDC, 0, 0)
    #ElseIf Win32 Then
        l& = SetWindowOrgEx(theForm.hDC, 0, 0, 0)
    #End If
    ResetFormScale theForm
End Sub

Public Sub DrawYRuler(theForm As Form, X As Integer, _
Y As Integer, wid As Integer)
    If Not validData Then InitRuler
    SetFormToTwips theForm
    For i = 0 To wid
        #If Win16 Then
            l& = SetWindowOrg(theForm.hDC, _
                                  -X, -Y - 1440 * i)
        #ElseIf Win32 Then
            l& = SetWindowOrgEx(theForm.hDC, _
                                  -X, -Y - 1440 * i, 0)
        #End If
```

```
        j% = Polyline(theForm.hDC, yPoints(1), numPoints)
    Next i

    #If Win16 Then
        l& = SetWindowOrg(theForm.hDC, 0, 0)
    #ElseIf Win32 Then
        l& = SetWindowOrgEx(theForm.hDC, 0, 0, 0)
    #End If
    ResetFormScale theForm
End Sub

Private Sub InitRuler ()
  Dim x As Integer, n As Integer

  n = 0                        ' No points yet.
  bot = 250
  For x = 0 To 1440 Step 90
    n = n + 1                  ' Next free point
    xPoints(n).x = x           ' Bottom of this line
    xPoints(n).y = bot
    yPoints(n).x = bot
    yPoints(n).y = x

    tick = 0                   ' Reset tick height
    If x = 1440 Then tick = tick + 1
    If (x Mod 720) = 0 Then tick = tick + 1
    If (x Mod 360) = 0 Then tick = tick + 1
    If (x Mod 180) = 0 Then tick = tick + 1
    If (x Mod 90) = 0 Then tick = tick + 1

    n = n + 1                  ' Next free point
    xPoints(n).x = x           ' End of tick mark
    xPoints(n).y = bot - tick * 45
    yPoints(n).x = xPoints(n).y
    yPoints(n).y = x
    n = n + 1
    xPoints(n).x = x           ' Back at bottom
    xPoints(n).y = bot
    yPoints(n).x = bot
```

```
    yPoints(n).y = x
  Next x
  numPoints = n
  validData = True          ' Now have points
End Sub
```

Sample Program

This simple program draws the rulers you see in Figure 18.3.

```
Private Sub Form_Paint ()
  Dim iWidth As Integer, iHeight As Integer
  Dim wid As Integer
  Dim i As Integer
  Const offset = 250

  iWidth = ScaleWidth / 1440    ' Size of form, in inches
  iHeight = ScaleHeight / 1440
  DrawXRuler Me, offset, 0, iWidth
  DrawYRuler Me, 0, offset, iHeight

  FontBold = False              ' Don't use bold
  wid = iWidth                  ' Set wid to widest dimension
  if iHeight > wid Then wid = iHeight
  For i = 0 To wid
    CurrentX = offset + i * 1440: CurrentY = 0
    Print i
    CurrentX = 0: CurrentY = offset + i * 1440
    Print i
  Next i
End Sub
```

See Also

SetFormScaling: The DrawRuler subroutines use the SetFormScaling subroutine, which you'll find in the APISCALE.BAS module, to change the scaling mode for the Polyline function.

Drawing Filled Polygons

Purpose: Draws polygons that can be filled with any color.

Visual Basic allows you to create filled boxes and ellipses, but not polygons, such as the one shown in Figure 18.6. For that, you need to use a Windows function called Polygon, which, as you'll see here, is very easy to use.

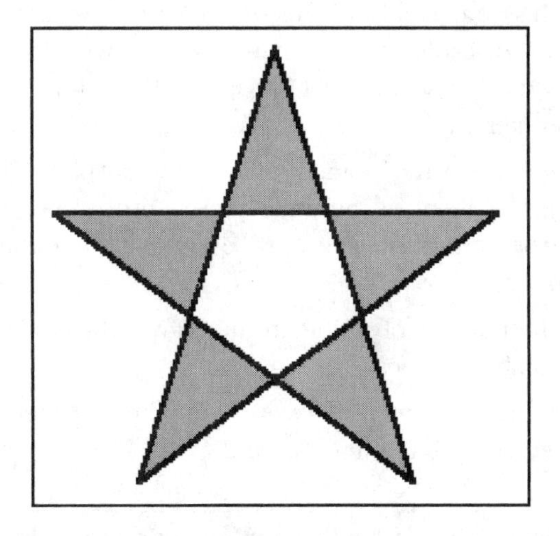

FIGURE 18.6 *A filled polygon drawn using the Polygon API call. Notice how the line width, color, and fill color are all set using Visual Basic properties.*

NOTE

The default-mapping mode used for all API calls inside visual Basic is the pixel-mapping mode. But if you also want to draw on a printer, the twip-mapping mode is a better choice. The section on *Using Twip Scaling with API Calls* later in this chapter provides some subroutines that will allow you to use Polyline in the twip-scaling mode, on your screen and your printer.

How Polygon Works

Similar to the Polyline routine discussed earlier in this chapter, the Polygon routine draws a number of connected lines, where the points in the lines are in an array of type POINTAPI. You must have at least three points (two lines, which will be connected automatically by a third, closing line) to use the Polygon routine. The three parameters to this API call are the same as those for Polyline: hDC, lpPoints, and nCount. These arguments mean the following:

```
Function Polygon (ByVal hDC As Integer, lpPoints As POINTAPI, _
ByVal nCount As Integer) As Integer
```

hDC This is a handle to the *device context* of the current form. API calls use the DC as a permission to write on a form or picture control. Use the hDC property for a form, a picture box, or Printer.

lpPoints Pointer to the points you want to display. This should be the first element of the array you want to send. Note that you can also start with the fifth element, for example, by writing points(4).

nCount The number of points in the array, which is one more than the number of lines.

returns 0 if no lines were drawn, some other number (Microsoft doesn't say what) if the lines were drawn.

NOTE

The declaration of the Polygon function shown here is for the 16-bit version. The 32-bit version, which you need for the 32-bit version of Visual Basic, is exactly the same, except that all the parameters declared as Integer become Longs instead (as you'll see below in the actual code).

Sample Program

Here is a small sample program that uses Polygon to draw a pentagon with a 2-pixel-wide black border and filled with light gray. The lines up to the sub should be in the (declarations) section of your form. Also, you'll want to set the form's Appearance property to 0 – flat so the background will be white.

```
#If Win16 Then
    Private Type POINTAPI
        X As Integer
```

```
        Y As Integer
    End Type

    Private Declare Function Polygon Lib _
        "GDI" (ByVal hDC As Integer, _
        pPoints As POINTAPI, _
        ByVal nCount As Integer) As Integer
#ElseIf Win32 Then
    Private Type POINTAPI
        X As Long
        Y As Long
    End Type

    Private Declare Function Polygon Lib "gdi32" _
        (ByVal hDC As Long, pPoints As POINTAPI, _
        ByVal nCount As Long) As Long
#End If

Private Sub Form_Load ()
  numPoints = 5
  dTheta = 4 * 3.1415926 / 5
  For i = 1 To numPoints
    points(i).X = 100 * Sin(dTheta * i) + 110
    points(i).Y = -100 * Cos(dTheta * i) + 110
  Next i
End Sub

Private Sub Form_Paint ()
  ForeColor = RGB(0, 0, 0)        ' Draw lines in black
  FillColor = RGB(192, 192, 192)  ' Fill with light gray
  FillStyle = 0                   ' Use a solid fill
  DrawWidth = 2                   ' Set line width to 2
  j = Polygon(hDC, points(1), numPoints)
End Sub
```

The code in Form_Load calculates the points for the polygon in Figure 18.6. Calculating these points at form load time allows redraws (Form_Paint) to be very fast.

Polygon Fill Modes

You may be wondering why there's a hole inside the star drawn by the sample program. By default, Polygon only fills areas that can be reached from outside the figure by crossing an odd number of lines. Consequently, the branches of the star are filled (you only need to cross one line), and the interior isn't (because you have to cross two lines).

Fortunately, as you can see in Figure 18.7, you can tell Polygon to fill the entire figure, using another Windows call. The SetPolyFillMode function tells Polygon which mode to use. The definitions are as follows:

```
Const ALTERNATE = 1
Const WINDING = 2

#If Win16 Then
    Private Declare Function SetPolyFillMode _
        Lib "GDI" (ByVal hDC As Integer, _
        ByVal nPolyFillMode As Integer) As Integer
#ElseIf Win32 Then
    Private Declare Function SetPolyFillMode _
        Lib "gdi32" (ByVal hDC As Long, _
        ByVal nPolyFillMode As Long) As Long
#End If
```

Add the following line just before the Polygon call to change the fill mode:

```
j = SetPolyFillMode(hDC, WINDING)
```

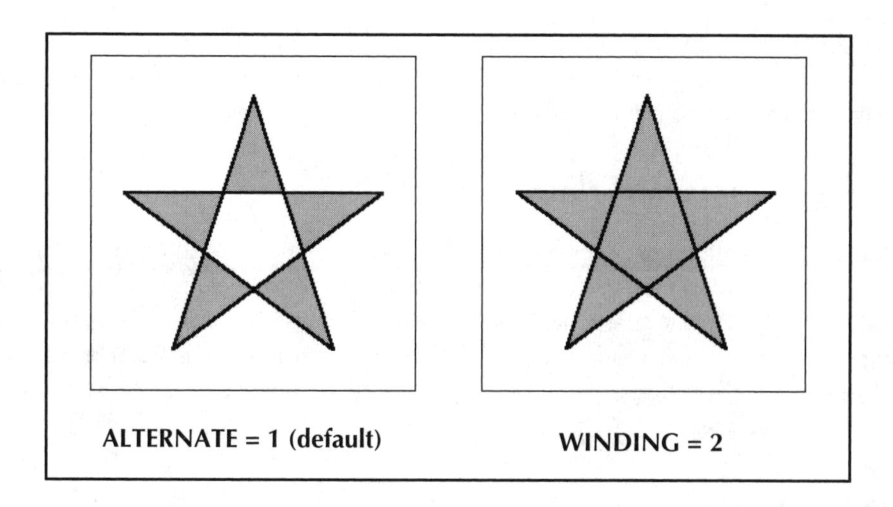

FIGURE 18.7 *The effects of setting the polygon fill mode. The ALTERNATE fill mode only fills areas that can be reached by crossing an odd number of lines, while WINDING fills the entire inside of a figure.*

Drawing on a Printer with Polygon

It's very easy to use Polygon to draw on your printer when your coordinates are in pixels. All you have to do is use Printer.hDC as the first argument:

```
Printer.Print " "
j = Polygon(Printer.hDC, points(0), numPoints)
Printer.EndDoc
```

The Printer.Print command makes sure Visual Basic starts the printing process so the Polygon command will work correctly. Without this Print command, Polygon may not work on all printer drivers.

Using Nonpixel Scaling Modes

Polyline, like all other Windows API functions, uses the scaling mode that's being used underneath Visual Basic, usually the pixel-scaling mode (called MM_TEXT in Windows jargon). You have two choices: Either use the pixel-scaling mode for all your work (and see the section *Printing Using the Screen Pixel Mode*), or use the twip-scaling mode (and see the section *Printing with API Calls using Twip Scaling*).

Other Note

FillColor The fill color for polygons is set by the FillColor property. You'll also need to set FillStyle to 0 (solid).

Color You can change the color of lines drawn with Polygon simply by setting the ForeColor property to whatever color you want. Polygon, as it turns out, uses the current ForeColor when it draws on the screen.

Width DrawWidth will change the line width of the lines drawn by Polygon.

Dash/Dot If you want to draw dashed or dotted lines, the DrawStyle property works much better with Polygon than it does with Line. This is because Windows restarts the dashing for each new line drawn with Line, but not with Polygon. In other words, a number of very short lines drawn with Line will be solid, rather than dashed. **Note:** DrawStyle applies only if DrawWidth=1.

Mode DrawMode has the same effect on Polygon as it does on lines drawn with the Line command.

Adjusting DrawWidth on Printers

Purpose: Allows you to draw lines on your printer that will have the same width as the lines you draw on your screen.

Some of Visual Basic's commands work with the current ScaleMode (such as twips or inches), but other commands don't. The DrawWidth property, for example, is *always* measured in pixels. But there are times where this presents problems. For example, when you're printing on a printer (where pixels are much smaller), you'll discover that the lines are narrower because pixels are smaller on a printer (see Figure 18.8).

You'll find two functions here to help you solve these problems. The first function returns a number that is the width of a pixel, as measured in twips, and the second function returns the ratio of the screen to printer-pixel size (which is 3 for a VGA screen and a 300-dot-per-inch printer).

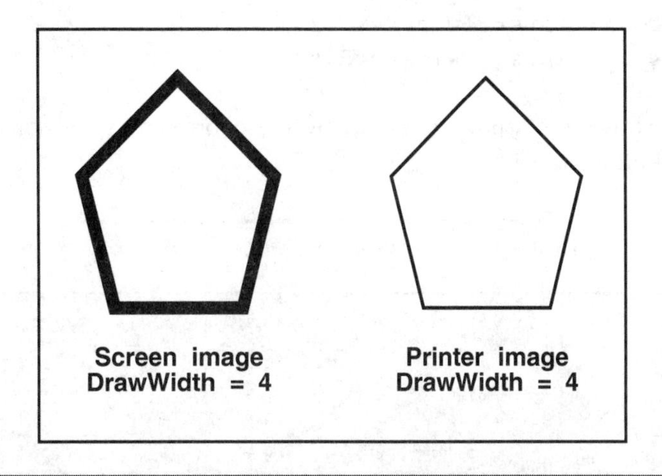

FIGURE 18.8 *Setting DrawWidth to 4 will result in nice, fat lines on the screen. But on a laser printer, these 4-pixel lines will be much narrower for the same size image, as you can see in the picture on the right.*

If you're using the pixel-scaling mode, another solution to this problem (which is actually easier) is to use the subroutines described in the next section: *Printing Using the Screen Pixel Mode.*

Calculating the Width of a Pixel

It's very easy to calculate the width or height a pixel, by using a single instruction for each as follows:

```
xUnits = Screen.TwipsPerPixelX ' Twips/pixel in X direction
yUnits = Screen.TwipsPerPixelY ' Twips/pixel in Y direction
```

These two instructions use two properties from the Screen object, which is a special object that provides a number of pieces of information about the screen, including the screen's height and width (measured in twips, of course). The two properties used here simply return the number of twips per pixel in the X and Y directions.

These two properties also work with the Printer object, to report the size of a pixel on the printer:

```
xUnits = Printer.TwipsPerPixelX
yUnits = Printer.TwipsPerPixelY
```

Table 18.1 shows the values returned by these properties for some common screens and printers.

TABLE 18.1 *Twips per Pixel on Common Devices*

Device	xUnits	yUnits
EGA screen	15	20
VGA screen	15	15
8514/a screen	12	12
300 dpi laser printer	4.8	4.8
2,400 dpi phototypesetter	0.6	0.6

Ratio of Screen to Printer Pixel Size

If you want to calculate the ratio of the width of pixels on your display and printer, you can use the following code:

```
Public Function PrinterToScreenRatio () As Single
   '
   ' Returns a multiplier that reports the number of
   ' printer pixels per screen pixel.
```

```
    '
    ' Usually 3.125 for a VGA screen and a 300 dpi printer.
    '
    xUnits = Screen.TwipsPerPixelX
    xUnitsP = Printer.TwipsPerPixelY

    PrinterToScreenRatio = xUnits / xUnitsP

End Function
```

Call this one time near the start of your program and assign the result to a global (or module) variable. Then use the variable (which equals the number of printer pixels per screen pixel) as a multiplier to calculate the printer DrawWidth as follows:

```
Printer.DrawWidth = PrinterToScreenRatio * DrawWidth
```

Printing Using the Screen Pixel Mode

File: APISCALE.BAS

Purpose: Allows you to draw on your printer using the pixel-mapping mode used by your screen. The subroutines given here adjust the size and spacing of your printer's pixels to match the size and spacing of your screen pixels.

If you've written programs using the pixel mapping mode on your screen, you've probably discovered that these images appear much smaller when you print them on your printer, and they use thinner lines. For example, if you're using a VGA screen and a laser printer with 300 dots per inch (dpi), anything you printed on your printer will be about one-third the size of your screen image. This happens because a VGA screen is defined as having a pixel density of 96 dpi, so a 100-pixel-long line will be about 1 inch on your screen and one-third of an inch long when printed.

You can easily reprogram any Windows printer so it will have larger pixels, which is what the SetPrinterToScreenPixels subroutine does. You can then draw anything you want, both on the screen and your printer, and it will be the correct size in both cases.

How to Use APIScale.bas

To use the subroutines described here, you'll first need to add the APIScale.bas file to your project, using the Add File... item from the File menu. Next, you'll need to call these subroutines at the correct times. There are two subroutines you'll need to use as follows:

```
SetPrinterToScreenPixels
```

This subroutine changes the size of pixels on your printer so that they will match the size of the pixels on your screen. After calling this subroutine, anything you draw in pixel mode will be about the correct size when printed.

```
ResetPrinterScale
```

This subroutine restores the pixel size on your printer so the pixels will be as small as possible. Call this subroutine after you have finished drawing in pixel mode on your printer.

How Pixel Scaling Works

The basic idea behind SetPrinterToScreenPixels is that you need to tell Windows to multiply each pixel coordinate by some scale factor. For example, if your screen has a dot density of 96 dpi and your printer has a density of 300 dpi, you have 3.125 printer pixels per screen pixel. So you want to multiply all coordinates by 3.125.

But there's a problem with this. For reasons of speed, Windows uses Integer numbers for coordinates and scaling factors, which means that you can't use the number 3.125. Of course, we have a solution for you. You can get around this by telling Windows to multiply by 3125 and divide by 1000. This is, in effect, what we'll do.

Let's take a look at the code to see how it actually does this. The code uses several Windows API calls that may be new to you. The first call, GetDeviceCaps, is a function that reports various pieces of information on a particular device (like the screen or printer). Here it's used to get the number of pixels per inch in the X and Y directions for both the screen and the printer. To get this information you use a *device context*, which is the hDC property of a form or the Printer object (this is why you must pass a form to the SetPrinterToScreenPixels subroutine).

The first three lines (after the Dim statements) calculate the printer-to-screen pixel ratio and save this number in *xRatio*. For the example above, *xRatio* would be 3.125 (notice that *xRatio* is type Single). The next three lines calculate this ratio in the Y direction. It's important to calculate the ratio independently in both directions because some devices have a different number of pixels per inch in the X and Y directions. (For example, an EGA screen has 96 dpi in the X direction, but only 72 dpi in the Y direction.)

The next line uses the SetMapMode API call to change the mapping mode on the printer. By default, the printer uses a mapping mode of MM_TEXT, which is its internal pixel-scale mode. Changing the mapping mode to MM_ANISOTROPIC allows you to define a custom scale.

The next four lines actually define the scale. The first call, SetViewportExt, sets the multiplier for the coordinates. Windows will multiply each coordinate by these numbers (one for X and one for Y), then divide by the numbers in SetWindowExt. Using a very large even integer for the multiplier (30,000) lets you keep as much information as possible in the divider. The divider is this number (30,000) divided by the printer-to-screen pixel ratio. For the example above, 30,000/3.125 = 9600.

The Code

Place these lines into the (declarations) area of the module where you'll put the following two subroutines.

```
Private Const MM_TEXT = 1          ' Pixel scale mode
Private Const MM_ANISOTROPIC = 8 ' Custom scale mode

Private Const LOGPIXELSX = 88      ' Logical pixels/inch in X
Private Const LOGPIXELSY = 90      ' Logical pixels/inch in Y

#If Win16 Then
    Private Declare Function SetMapMode Lib "GDI" _
        (ByVal hDC As Integer, _
         ByVal nMapMode As Integer) As Integer

    Private Declare Function SetViewportExt Lib "GDI" _
        (ByVal hDC As Integer, ByVal X As Integer, _
         ByVal Y As Integer) As Long
```

```
    Private Declare Function SetWindowExt Lib "GDI" _
        (ByVal hDC As Integer, ByVal X As Integer, _
         ByVal Y As Integer) As Long

    Private Declare Function GetDeviceCaps Lib "GDI" _
        (ByVal hDC%, ByVal nIndex%) As Integer
#ElseIf Win32 Then
    Private Declare Function SetMapMode Lib "gdi32" _
        (ByVal hDC As Long, _
        ByVal nMapMode As Long) As Long

    Private Declare Function SetViewportExtEx Lib "gdi32" _
        (ByVal hDC As Long, ByVal nX As Long, _
         ByVal nY As Long, lpSize As Long) As Long

    Private Declare Function SetWindowExtEx Lib "gdi32" _
        (ByVal hDC As Long, ByVal nX As Long, _
         ByVal nY As Long, lpSize As Long) As Long

    Private Declare Function GetDeviceCaps Lib "gdi32" _
        (ByVal hDC As Long, ByVal nIndex As Long) As Long
#End If
```

This subroutine does all the work of changing the size of pixels on your printer.

```
Public Sub SetPrinterToScreenPixels (f As Form)
  '
  ' This subroutine enlarges the pixels on your printer so
  ' they will match the size of your screen pixels. You
  ' can then use Windows API calls to draw on the printer.
  '
  Dim screenRes As Integer      ' Screen pixels/inch
  Dim printerRes As Integer     ' Printer pixels/inch
  Dim xRatio, yRatio            ' Printer/screen ratio
  Dim extX As Integer           ' X printer/screen ratio
  Dim extY As Integer           ' Y printer/screen ratio

  screenRes = GetDeviceCaps(f.hDC, LOGPIXELSX)
```

```
    printerRes = GetDeviceCaps(Printer.hDC, LOGPIXELSX)
    xRatio = printerRes / screenRes

    screenRes = GetDeviceCaps(f.hDC, LOGPIXELSY)
    printerRes = GetDeviceCaps(Printer.hDC, LOGPIXELSY)
    yRatio = printerRes / screenRes

    i = SetMapMode(Printer.hDC, MM_ANISOTROPIC)

    k& = SetViewportExt(Printer.hDC, 30000, 30000)

    extX = 30000 / xRatio
    extY = 30000 / yRatio
    k& = SetWindowExt(Printer.hDC, extX, extY)
  End Sub
```

Call this subroutine to restore the size of your printer's pixels to their normal size.

```
  Public Sub ResetPrinterScale ()
    '
    ' This subroutine restores the printer's scale so each
    ' pixel will be as small as possible.
    '
    i = SetMapMode(Printer.hDC, MM_TEXT)
  End Sub
```

Using Twip Scaling with API Calls

File: APISCALE.BAS

Purpose: Allows you to use Windows API calls to draw on the screen and/or printer in the twip-scaling mode. Also changes DrawWidth so it measures line widths in twips, rather than pixels.

All Windows API calls, such as Polyline, use the scaling mode that underlies Visual Basic, the pixel-scaling mode (Visual Basic does all the work of scaling itself, rather than using Window's scale modes). So if you want to use API calls with coordinates in twips, you'll need to use the subroutines in this section.

How to Use APISCALE.BAS

To use the subroutines described here, you'll first need to add the APISCALE.BAS file to your project, using the Add File... item in the File menu. Next, you'll need to call these subroutines at the correct times. There are two subroutines you'll need to use:

```
SetPrinterToTwips
SetFormToTwips formName
```

These subroutines change the underlining scale mode of a form or the printer to use twip scaling. After calling these functions, any API calls you make will use twip scaling.

```
ResetPrinterScale
ResetFormScale formName
```

This subroutine restores the underlying scale mode of a form or the printer to pixel mode, which is what Visual Basic uses (since it does its own scaling). Call this subroutine after you finish drawing with Windows API calls.

NOTE

The SetPrinter... and SetForm... subroutines have one small side effect, which may or may not be desirable. They both change the meaning of the DrawWidth property, which is the width of lines (normally measured in pixels). After you call SetPrinterToTwips or SetFormToTwips (and before you call one of the reset functions), DrawWidth will measure line widths in *twips*.

If you'd like to work with twips and always have both coordinates and line widths measured in twips (for Visual Basic commands as well), you can set the ScaleMode to Pixel, and then do all of your drawing by using coordinates measured in twips after calling SetFormToTwips.

How Twip Scaling Works

These subroutines allow you to tell Windows to multiply each pixel coordinate by some scale factor. For a standard VGA screen, which is defined by Windows to have 96 dots per inch, this scale factor will be 1440/96 = 15 (since there are 1440 twips per inch).

These two subroutines each take only five lines of code to do all the work. The first line, SetMapMode, sets the Windows mapping mode (which is similar to Visual Basic's scale mode)—in this case, to MM_ANISOTROPIC, which means that you can set the scaling to anything you want.

The next two lines of code (which use GetDeviceCaps) calculate 10 times the number of twips per pixel in the X and Y directions; multiplying by 10 increases the accuracy of the scaling. The actual scaling is done by multiplying the coordinates by 10 and dividing by *extX* or *extY*.

The line SetViewPortExt sets the multiplier for the X and Y parts of the coordinates, while SetWindowExt sets the divider. Windows uses these two numbers, rather than a single number of type Single, in the interest of speed—working with integers is much faster than working with numbers of type Single.

The Code

Place these lines into the (declarations) area of the same module where you'll put the following four subroutines.

```
Private Const MM_TEXT = 1         ' Pixel scale mode
Private Const MM_ANISOTROPIC = 8 ' Custom scale mode

Private Const LOGPIXELSX = 88     ' Logical pixels/inch in X
Private Const LOGPIXELSY = 90     ' Logical pixels/inch in Y

#If Win16 Then
    Private Declare Function SetMapMode Lib "GDI" _
        (ByVal hDC As Integer, _
         ByVal nMapMode As Integer) As Integer

    Private Declare Function SetViewportExt Lib "GDI" _
        (ByVal hDC As Integer, ByVal X As Integer, _
         ByVal Y As Integer) As Long

    Private Declare Function SetWindowExt Lib "GDI" _
        (ByVal hDC As Integer, ByVal X As Integer, _
```

```
        ByVal Y As Integer) As Long

    Private Declare Function GetDeviceCaps Lib "GDI" _
        (ByVal hDC%, ByVal nIndex%) As Integer
#ElseIf Win32 Then
    Private Declare Function SetMapMode Lib "gdi32" _
        (ByVal hDC As Long, _
        ByVal nMapMode As Long) As Long

    Private Declare Function SetViewportExtEx Lib "gdi32" _
        (ByVal hDC As Long, ByVal nX As Long, _
         ByVal nY As Long, lpSize As Long) As Long

    Private Declare Function SetWindowExtEx Lib "gdi32" _
        (ByVal hDC As Long, ByVal nX As Long, _
         ByVal nY As Long, lpSize As Long) As Long

    Private Declare Function GetDeviceCaps Lib "gdi32" _
        (ByVal hDC As Long, ByVal nIndex As Long) As Long
#End If
```

Here are the four subroutines that do all the work.

```
Public Sub SetFormToTwips (f As Form)
  '
  ' This subroutine sets a form to Twip scaling mode
  ' for all Windows API calls. You'll need to call
  ' ResetPrinterScale before you use any Visual Basic
  ' drawing commands.
  '
  i = SetMapMode(f.hDC, MM_ANISOTROPIC)
  extX = 14400 / GetDeviceCaps(f.hDC, LOGPIXELSX)
  extY = 14400 / GetDeviceCaps(f.hDC, LOGPIXELSY)
  l& = SetViewportExt(f.hDC, 10, 10)
  l& = SetWindowExt(f.hDC, extX, extY)
End Sub

Public Sub SetPrinterToTwips ()
  '
```

```
  ' This subroutine sets the printer to Twip scaling
  ' mode for all Windows API calls. You'll need to call
  ' ResetPrinterScale before you use any Visual Basic
  ' drawing commands.
  '
  Dim extX As Variant                ' Windows extent
  Dim extY As Variant

  i = SetMapMode(Printer.hDC, MM_ANISOTROPIC)
  extX = 14400 / GetDeviceCaps(Printer.hDC, LOGPIXELSX)
  extY = 14400 / GetDeviceCaps(Printer.hDC, LOGPIXELSY)
  l& = SetViewportExt(Printer.hDC, 10, 10)
  l& = SetWindowExt(Printer.hDC, extX, extY)
End Sub

Public Sub ResetPrinterScale ()
  '
  ' This subroutine restores the printer's scale so
  ' each pixel will be as small as possible.
  '
  i = SetMapMode(Printer.hDC, MM_TEXT)
End Sub

Public Sub ResetFormScale (f As Form)
  '
  ' This subroutine restores a form's API scale back to
  ' MM_TEXT (pixel) scale mode.
  '
  i = SetMapMode(f.hDC, MM_TEXT)
End Sub
```

CHAPTER 19

TOOLBOX FOR FONTS

Asking for a Font by TextHeight

File: FONTTOOL.BAS

Purpose: Find the largest font whose TextHeight is less than or equal to a given height.

Whenever you set the TextHeight property of a form or control, you're always setting the height of the font in points. But what if you want the height of the font to be a certain size in twips? How do you do that?

It turns out that you can't simply convert the height to points and use that number. This is because the size of a font (in points) never includes the font's *leading*, which is a measure of the extra space between lines. Although this may not seem like much of a problem, it is a little trickier than you might guess. To understand all these issues, let's take a short look at fonts and how the TextHeight and FontSize values relate. (They don't measure the same thing.)

A Brief Primer on Fonts

Any font includes some extra space above it that's used to separate lines. This extra space is also used for displaying diacritical marks on international characters, such as umlauts over characters, like *ü*.

What you can also see from this figure is that TextHeight and FontSize measure different sizes in a font. FontSize refers to the height of characters, without including the extra space for leading. TextHeight, on the other hand, includes the FontSize height *and* the leading between lines. So if you want a font to have a certain size including the leading, you can't just set FontSize to this number. Instead, you'll need some way to find a slightly smaller font having a TextHeight the height you need.

The FindFontSize function is just what you need.

How to Use FindFontSize

Using FindFontSize is really easy. Let's say, for example, that you have a form called Form1. Let's also say that you need to create a label (called Label1) no more than 18 pixels high. The kind of code you would use is as follows:

```
ScaleMode = 3             ' Set to pixel scaling
Label1.FontSize = FindFontSize(Form1, 18)
```

The first line makes sure that you're using pixel scaling in the form that you'll pass to FindFontSize (this function uses the form's FontSize property and TextHeight method to do all the work). The second line then calls FindFontSize to find the largest font size (in points) that has a TextHeight of no more than 18 pixels.

How It Works

How do you set the size of a font in pixels? Can you simply supply the size of the font, measured in pixels or twips? The answer is no, for a couple of reasons. First, Visual Basic's FontSize property is *always* measured in points (1/72 inch, or 1/20 twip), so you have to supply the size in points. To compound the problem, you can't always set the exact size of a font. For example, you might find that FontSize = 8.25 after you set it to 1.

There's still one other problem. The value you get back from TextHeight won't be the same as the font size you set because TextHeight and FontSize refer to different numbers that measure the size of a font. The FontSize property sets the height of the characters in the font, whereas the TextHeight function reports this height *plus* the *leading* (or extra spacing) between lines of text. This extra space always appears above (rather than below) any text you display in a text box, a label, or with the Print method.

The problem is how to adjust the TextHeight of a font when all you can set is the FontSize property, and you don't even have full control over that.

One solution is to write a function that finds the closest font having a size (TextHeight) less than or equal to the height you need. The FindFontSize function does this by first converting the height to points, then setting FontSize to this value. Finally, it looks for fonts smaller and smaller than this initial size until it finds one with a small enough TextHeight.

Let's take a closer look at the function. (The code is shown in the next section.) The first line of code saves the current FontSize so that it can be restored at the end. Next, this function converts the size from whatever units you're using to points, and it sets the initial FontSize value to this number. This number will be too large, since the actual text height includes some extra leading. Finally, Do-Loop looks for smaller and smaller fonts until it finds a font having a TextHeight less than or equal to the height you want. This is the number it returns to you.

You'll notice that this function uses a form for calculating the size of a font, which allows it to use the FontSize property and TextHeight method to do all the work.

The Code

Here is the code that you can put into a module or a form.

```
Public Function FindFontSize (f As Form, ByVal high)
  '
  ' This function returns the first font with a
  ' TextHeight <= high.
  '
  ' Note: If the smallest font has a TextHeight > high,
  '    this function will return a font larger than high.
  '
  Dim i, oldSize, size
  Dim oldScale
```

```
  oldSize = f.FontSize          ' Remember old font size

  '
  ' Convert starting height to points.
  '
  oldScale = f.ScaleMode        ' Remember scale mode
  CurrentY = high               ' Set Y to height we want
  ScaleMode = 2                 ' Switch to points
  f.FontSize = CurrentY         ' Set to size, in points
  f.ScaleMode = oldScale        ' Restore the scale mode

  i = f.FontSize                ' Size we'll start at
  Do
    If f.FontSize < i Then      ' Is size smaller than i?
      i = f.FontSize            ' Yes, adjust i to real size
    End If
    i = i - .5                  ' Try next smaller size
    f.FontSize = i              ' Set font to this size
  Loop While f.TextHeight("A") > high And i > 1
  FindFontSize = f.FontSize     ' Return size of found font

  f.FontSize = oldSize          ' Restore the old font size
End Function
```

TOOLBOX: MISCELLANEOUS

Multimedia Sound

Purpose: Playing the .WAV files that are supported by Windows.

With version 3.1, Windows added multimedia sound support to the system, allowing you to play recorded sound (**.WAV**) files on your computer. To use these features, your computer must have a sound board, such as the SoundBlaster, installed. If your computer makes a "symphony" sound when it first starts, chances are very good that your computer has a sound card.

The Windows function that plays .WAV files is called sndPlaySound, and it's very easy to use. All you have to do is make sure you're using Windows 3.1 (or a later version), which you can do by using the WindowsVersion function described later in this chapter.

How to Use sndPlaySound

The sndPlaySound command takes just two parameters: the name of the .WAV file and a flags value that gives you control over how sndPlaySound works.

The simplest call to sndPlaySound looks like the following:

```
i% = sndPlaySound("tada.wav", 0)
```

This will play the chord sound you hear when Windows 3.1 first starts.

If your computer doesn't have a sound device installed, this function will return 0, indicating that it was unable to play the sound.

Instead of using 0 for the second parameter, you can set a number of flags to control how sndPlaySound works. You set flags by using the Or operator to combine flags. For example:

```
flags = SND_ASYNC Or SND_LOOP
```

Descriptions for each of the flags you can use with the sndPlaySound function are as follows:

SND_SYNC Waits until the sound finishes playing before returning from the call to sndPlaySound function.

SND_ASYNC Returns immediately to your program; the sound plays when your program continues to run. You can stop the sound by calling sndPlaySound(0&, 0).

SND_NODEFAULT Tells sndPlaySound to remain silent if it can't find the sound file. Normally sndPlaySound will play the default sound if it can't find the .WAV file name you provided.

SND_LOOP Keeps playing the sound file over and over until you stop it. Call sndPlaySound(0&, 0) to stop playing the sound file. You must use the SND_ASYNC along with this flag.

SND_NOSTOP Returns False immediately if a sound is currently playing, rather than starting to play the new sound file.

This single line of code will play the chord.wav file over and over as follows:

```
i% = sndPlaySound("chord.wav", SND_ASYNC Or SND_LOOP)
```

You can then stop the sound with the following command:

```
i% = sndPlaySound(0&, 0)
```

The Definitions

The definitions for the sndPlaySound function and its constants, which you must put in the same form or module as the code that uses sndPlaySound, are as follows:

```
#If Win32 Then
    Declare Function sndPlaySound Lib "winmm" _
        Alias "sndPlaySoundA" (ByVal WaveFile As Any, _
        ByVal uFlags As Long) As Long
#ElseIf Win16 Then
    Declare Function sndPlaySound Lib "mmsystem.dll" _
        (ByVal WaveFile As Any, ByVal wFlags As Integer) _
        As Integer
#End If

Const SND_SYNC = 0
Const SND_ASYNC = 1
Const SND_NODEFAULT = 2
Const SND_MEMORY = 4
Const SND_NOSTOP = 16

Declare Function sndPlaySound Lib "MMSYSTEM.DLL" _
(ByVal WavFile As Any, ByVal wFlags As Integer) As Integer
```

NOTE

If you put these in a form, you must declare them as Private.

Running DOS Programs

File: MISCTOOL.BAS

Purpose: Runs a DOS command, and then allows you to continue with your Visual Basic program.

See Also: Checking the DOS and Windows Versions later in this chapter.

Visual Basic has a command called *Shell* that allows your programs to launch DOS programs. In this section we'll show you a few things about Shell that aren't documented. We'll also show you how to do more than you can do with the Shell command.

The Basics of Shell

The Shell command has two parameters (the second is optional): the command you want to run and how you want Windows to run the program (such as full screen or windowed). To run the Format command (for example, to format a floppy disk in drive A), you would use the following command:

```
i = Shell("format.com a:")
```

You need to include the extension .COM, because Shell needs the whole filename—the name of the command and its extension. This means that you can't use the Shell command to directly run any of DOS's internal commands, such as Dir or Del (use the Kill command to delete files instead).

Shell can run any type of program that has the .COM, .EXE, .BAT, or .PIF extension.

Running Special DOS Commands

There are cases where you can't run a command directly, for example, when you're using internal commands or using command redirection. Some DOS commands aren't programs on your disk. Instead, they're built into a file called *COMMAND.COM.* Also, you can't use the DOS redirection characters (<, >, and |) as the command line for most commands. How do you get around these limitations?

You can use the COMMAND.COM program to run *any* DOS command. All you have to do is run COMMAND.COM with a /c followed by your DOS command, as follows:

```
command.com /c any DOS command
```

The next section shows an example using the Format command with input redirection.

Waiting Until a DOS Program Finishes

Normally the Shell command returns to your program as soon as it has started the program you need to run. That means your program will continue running before your DOS program finishes. How can you have your program wait until the DOS program finishes?

It turns out to be fairly easy, thanks to some help from another Windows function. You can use GetModuleUsage to tell if a program is still running. The Shell command returns an ID (identification) number of the program that you started, and GetModuleUsage tells you how many copies of that program are running. The code below waits, using a Do...While loop, until GetModuleUsage returns 0. You'll notice that DoEvents() is called before the first call to GetModuleUsage. This is necessary to make sure Windows has a chance to finish starting the program before you see if it's still running.

```
Private Declare Function GetModuleUsage Lib "Kernel" _
(ByVal hInst As Integer) As Integer
```

```
Public Sub RunDOS(prog As String)
  Dim hInst As Integer

  hInst = Shell(prog, 7)
  Do
    i = DoEvents()
  Loop While GetModuleUsage(hInst) > 0
End Sub
```

Checking the DOS and Windows Version

File: MISCTOOL.BAS

Purpose: Sometimes you'll need to know under which version of DOS or Windows your program is running. For example, if you're using a Windows function or DOS command that is not available in all versions, you should make sure you're running under a recent-enough version before you use that command or function.

Every new version of DOS or Windows has some new commands or features you can use. But if you want your program to run under previous versions, you'll need to make sure that you can tell when you can and when you can't use these new commands. In this section you'll learn about two functions—DOSVersion() returns the DOS version number (such as 6.0 or 6.2) and WindowsVersion() returns the Windows version (such as 3.1 or 4.0).

Normally, you use these functions like the following:

```
If WindowsVersion() >= 3.1 Then
   ... do new stuff
Else
   ... do it the old way
End If
```

You might use this kind of test, for example, before you try to use any of the Multimedia functions in Windows such as the sound routines.

How It Works

Each of these two functions uses a Windows API function called GetVersion. This function returns both the Windows and the DOS version information in a number of type Long, which can easily contain all of the information. Versions numbers actually consist of two parts: a major and a minor number. For example, Windows 3.1 had a major number of 3 and a minor number of 10 (each part has two digits, so Windows 3.1 was actually version 3.10).

Each part of the version number can be any number between 00 and 99, which means each part of the version number fits into a single byte (a byte can contain numbers between 0 and 255). A number of type Long contains four bytes, which allows exactly enough room to contain two version numbers, each with a major and a minor number.

The exact equation Windows uses to encode both version numbers into a Long number is as follows:

```
GetVersion = ( (DOS major version) * 256 + (DOS minor
               version) ) _
* 65536 + (Windows minor version) * 256 + (Windows
           major version)
```

There's one interesting thing about this equation. You'll notice that Windows isn't consistent in how it reports the major and minor version numbers: For DOS, the major number is multiplied by 256, but for Windows the *minor* version number is multiplied by 256. Strange, huh?

The DOS Version() and Windows Version() functions pull out the major and minor version numbers, then put both parts back together in a single number, where the major part appears to the left of the decimal point and the minor part appears to the right. In other words, a version number like 3.31 will be returned as the number 3.31.

The DOSVersion() function begins by dividing the number from GetVersion() by 65536, which removes all the Windows version information, leaving only the DOS version information. Next, it gets the major part of the version number by dividing by 256. Finally, DOSVersion() adds the minor version divided by 100 to the major number. The Mod 256 extracts a single byte (the minor version number) from a larger number.

The WindowsVersion() function works in very much the same way as the DOSVersion function. The main difference is that WindowsVersion() uses Mod 65536 to extract the lower two bytes, which contain the Windows version information, from the Long number returned by GetVersion().

The Code

The following two functions return version information. Both of these functions use a Windows API call that must be defined in the (declarations) section of your module:

```
Private Declare Function GetVersion Lib "Kernel" () As Long
```

Here are the two functions:

```
Public Function DOSVersion () As Single
  '
  ' This function returns the DOS version number as a
  ' floating point number, such as 3.31 for DOS 3.31.
  '
  Dim ver As Long
  Dim DOSVer As Single

  ver = GetVersion()          ' Get DOS/Windows version
  ver = ver / 65536           ' Get just the DOS version
  DOSVer = ver / 256          ' Get major version number
  DOSVer = DOSVer + (ver Mod 256) / 100
  DOSVersion = DOSVer           ' Return version
End Function
```

```
Private Function WindowsVersion () As Single
'
  ' This function returns the Windows version number as
  ' a floating point number, such as 3.1 for Windows 3.1.
  '
  Dim ver As Long
  Dim WinVer As Single

  ver = GetVersion()            ' Get DOS/Windows version
  ver = ver Mod 65536           ' Get just the Win version
  WinVer = ver Mod 256          ' Get major version
  WinVer = WinVer + (ver / 256) / 100
  WindowsVersion = WinVer       ' Return version
End Function
```

Finding a Program's Directory

File: MISCTOOL.BAS

Purpose: Finding a program's full path name or the home directory of your program. This is very useful when you need to find your program's directory so your program can find its other files (to read and/or write).

If your program is a very simple program, you won't be interested in this section. But if you have other files you need to access, such as help files or INI files, you'll need to find the directory where your program resides. The functions in this section will do the trick.

Let's look at an example. Say you have a program called MyCalc located in the directory C:\PROG\MISC, and you need to display on-line help using a help file in this directory. As long as the current directory is C:\PROG\MISC, there's no problem. But a number of programs, allow you to set a default start-up directory different from the program's directory. In such cases, your program won't be able to find its help file unless you know which directory it's in.

Getting this information is easy. Visual Basic 2.0, 3.0 and now 4.0 provide a property that returns exactly this information. The following is what you'll see if you run your Address Book program and run the following lines in the Debug window:

```
Print App.Path
C:\SOURCE\ADDRESS
|
```

The path that you get is the directory that contains your .MAK file when you're running a program from within Visual Basic, and it's the directory that contains your .EXE program when you run a program as an EXE file.

The way this works is really simple. Visual Basic has an application object called *App*, which has a number of properties you can use to control your program or obtain information on it. Another such property is the EXEName property, which returns the name of your program as follows:

```
Print App.EXEName
ADDRESS
```

By the way, the App object was new to version 2.0 of Visual Basic. Getting this same information in Visual Basic 1.0 was much more difficult.

Building a Windows Screen Saver

File: SCRNSAVE.MAK, SCRNSAVE.BAS, BLANKFO.FRM, CONFIG.FRM

Purpose: A simple screen-saver module for Windows. You can easily write your own screen savers using the techniques outlined here.

Windows comes with several screen-saver modules, such as Flying Windows and a space-flight simulation. There are also a number of commercial screen-saver products. Have you ever wanted to write your own screen-saver module?

You may think that you'd have to write such a program in C or some other "real" language. Not so! It's much easier to write a screen saver in Visual Basic than in any other language. You can even make the screen-saver modules you write appear in the list of screen-saver modules in the Control Panel's Desktop dialog box, just like any screen-saver module you'd write in the C language.

In this section, we'll show you how to write Windows screen-saver modules entirely in Visual Basic, and we'll provide the full source code for a simple screen saver that displays random colored lines on a black screen. It unblanks the screen as soon as you move the mouse or press any key, including Shift.

How to Create a Windows Screen Saver

Screen-saver modules under Windows are ordinary programs, which is why they are so easy to write. Windows activates a screen saver by passing a special command line to your program. The command line your program will see is in the special Command$ variable. If Command$ contains the /c switch, your program should display its setup dialog box. The only other switch is the /s switch, which tells your program to blank the screen and start doing its job.

As soon as your program is finished with either task, your program needs to exit (with the End statement, for example). This is a rather subtle implication—after your program displays the setup dialog box, you'll quit, which means your screen-blanker code won't have a direct way to access the settings in the setup dialog. Later, we'll show you how to solve this problem the way Windows' own screen savers do.

Here is a summary of the steps you'll need to follow to build your own screen saver in Visual Basic (you'll find additional details following, where we'll walk you through the program John wrote):

1. **Sub Main.** Your program should start with a Sub Main that checks the command line to see which switch is present. Display a setup dialog box when the command line is /c, or blank the screen when Command$ is /s.
2. **SCR extension.** Your program needs to have the SCR extension, rather than the default EXE extension. John used the name SSVBLINE.SCR for

the name of the EXE file (see Figure 20.1). By convention, the names of all screen-saver modules start with SS.

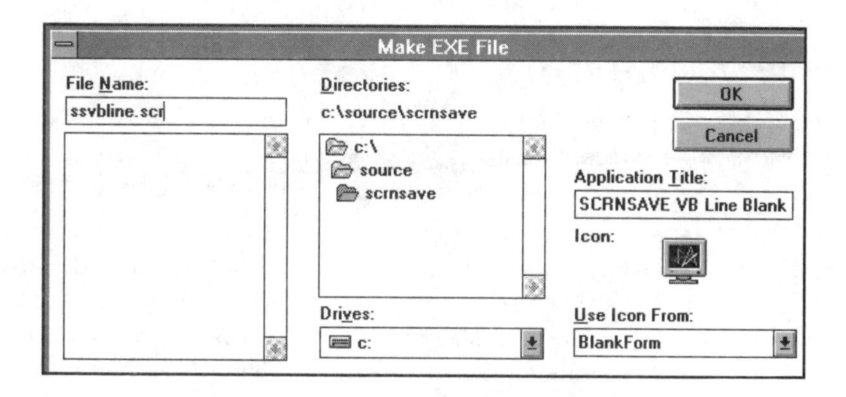

FIGURE 20.1 *This dialog box shows the File Name you'll want to use when you create a Visual Basic screen blanker.*

3. **Application title.** When you create an EXE program in Visual Basic, you need to set this field in the EXE Options dialog box from within the Make EXE File dialog box to a special name. As shown in Figure 20.2, the name must start with "SCRNSAVE " followed by the name that you want to appear in the list of screen-saver modules in the Control Panel. For example, John used the application title "SCRNSAVE VB Line Blanker" for the program you'll find on the disk; the name "VB Line Blanker" appears in the Control Panel.

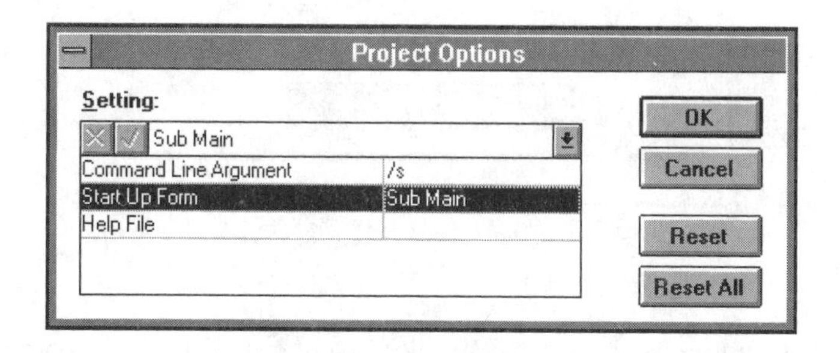

FIGURE 20.2 *This dialog box shows the Application Title and Icon Form you'll want to use when you create a Visual Basic screen blanker.*

4. **Copy to Windows directory.** The final thing you'll need to do is copy your new SCR file into your Windows directory so that Windows can find it.

How Sub Main Works

The example screen saver draws a number of random color lines on a black screen. It clears the screen after it has drawn 100 lines (you can change this to any number between 0 and 999). In this section we'll describe in detail how the program works.

Let's start by looking at the Main subroutine. The SCRNSAVE.MAK project includes a module called SCRNSAVE.BAS. This module contains a total of four subroutines, one of which is called Main. Whenever your program has a subroutine called Main, you have the option of making this the first piece of code that runs as soon as your program starts. In other words, you can have Main run without loading any forms, which is how this sample program is set up. You do this by first creating a subroutine called *Main*. Then you can use the Project Options dialog box (select the Project Options... option from the Tools menu) to set the Start Up Form to Sub Main (see Figure 20.3).

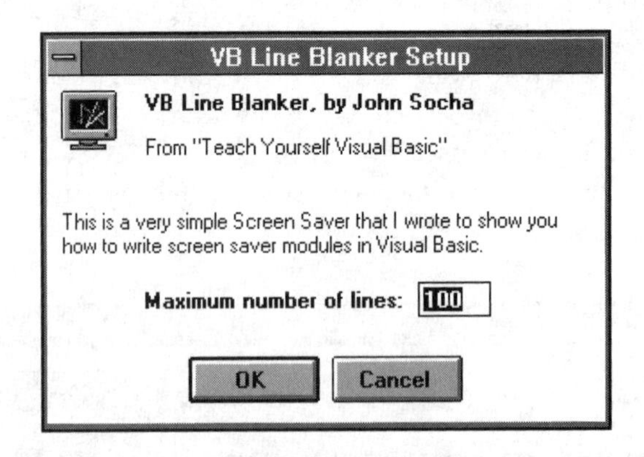

FIGURE 20.3 *You use this dialog box (select Project... from the Options menu) to set the Start Up Form to Sub Main.*

The job of subroutine Main is fairly simple, but there is one new command that requires explanation. You'll notice the first line uses a command called *GetPrivateProfileInt.* This is a Windows API command, which is defined in the (declarations) section of SCRNSAVE.BAS. This command reads a number (hence the Int, which is short for Integer) from an INI file. If you've ever looked into the bowels of Windows, you've discovered that there are a number of INI files that provide settings information to various Windows programs and to Windows itself.

One of these files, CONTROL.INI, provides information to various parts of the Control Panel. If you've used any of the screen savers in Windows, such as the Flying Windows module, you'll find a section in CONTROL.INI that looks something like the following:

```
[Screen Saver.Flying Windows]
Density=25
WarpSpeed=10
PWProtected=0
```

Each of the lines after the first line provides a number that the screen saver uses for its settings. WarpSpeed, for example, tells the Flying Windows module how fast to make the stars zoom by.

John's VB screen saver also has an entry it adds to CONTROL.INI to keep track of how many lines you want it to display before it blanks the screen, and the GetPrivateProfileInt command reads this number from the CONTROL.INI file. Let's take a look at the four parameters that this command takes.

First, the *secName* variable is a global variable that contains the name of the section in the CONTROL.INI file. The section name is the name that appears in square brackets, which is set to the following (the string doesn't include the brackets):

```
[Screen Saver.VB Line Blanker]
```

The next parameter, *keyName*, contains the name of the line you want to read in this section. VB Line Blanker only has a single line in its section, which looks something like the following:

```
MaxLines=100
```

The next parameter, 100, is the default number that GetPrivateProfileInt should return if it can't find the section you've asked for. This section won't exist until you select **Setup** for this screen saver and click on **OK**, which then writes an entry into CONTROL.INI.

Finally, the parameter *iniName* contains the name of the INI file from which you want to read. In this case, it's the CONTROL.INI file. When you provide a file name without a directory, Windows automatically looks in its own directory.

Now that you've learned about the GetPrivateProfileInt command, let's look at the other lines in the Main subroutine. The next section of code looks to see if the command-line switch is either /s or /c, and it displays the appropriate form for each case. The last two lines of code loop until no forms are visible. You need to do this because your program will quit as soon as the Main subroutine finishes running.

How the Blank Form Works

The screen-blanker form, BlankForm, is where all the nice animation takes place. As you can see from the source code, there isn't much code behind this function, but let's take a quick look at it since it has a few subtle points.

All of the drawing is done in the Timer event handler, set to trigger every 100 milliseconds, or 10 times a second. (You could set this to 50 milliseconds if you'd like the animation to be faster.) Tick_Timer() draws random lines and random colors using a function called Rnd. The Rnd function returns a floating-point number between 0 and 1. To draw random lines, to multiply Rnd by ScaleWidth and ScaleHeight (each time you use Rnd, you get a different value).

The same thing applies to colors. The numbers used for the red, green, and blue components of colors can range from 0 to 255, so the following expression provides a random color:

```
RGB(255 * Rnd, 255 * Rnd, 255 * Rnd)
```

There is one other detail about color. A standard form supports 16 colors by default, which means Blanker will be limited to a basic set of 16 colors unless you somehow define the additional colors it can use. To define additional colors, you can set the Picture property of the form to a bitmap that contains definitions for more colors. John used a file called rainbow.dib that contains a single black pixel, but it defines a full 256 colors. Once you set the Picture property to this bitmap, Blanker will use 256 of the different possible colors for the actual display.

The final detail you'll notice is that Tick_Timer() keeps track of how many lines it has drawn, and it erases the screen as soon as *numLines* exceeds *maxLines*.

The Form_Load event handler has a single call that's interesting: HideMouse. You'll find the HideMouse subroutine in SCRNSAVE.BAS, along with the

ShowMouse subroutine. These two subroutines allow you to hide the mouse pointer, and then show it again later. Both of these subroutines use a Windows API function called ShowCursor.

Now let's look at the other pieces of BlankForm. The code in the Form_KeyDown and Form_MouseMove event handlers takes care of unblanking the screen whenever you press any key (including Shift) or move the mouse. In the case of MouseMove, there's a bit of extra code that keeps the screen from unblanking when you knock your desk; you'll notice that you have to move the mouse at least three pixels from the last MouseMove before the screen unblanks. This means that if you very gently push the mouse, the screen won't unblank, but if you move the mouse at a normal rate, it will. Unblanking is accomplished by calling EndScrnsave, which makes the mouse pointer visible again, and then exits the program.

As to the form itself, you'll notice that it doesn't have a title bar or border. You can remove the title bar from a form by setting the form's caption to nothing (press **Space**, **Backspace**, then **Enter** in the settings box), and setting ControlBox to 0 – False. To remove the border, set BorderStyle to 0 – None.

How the Setup Form Works

The setup form is the easiest part of the program. Much of it should be familiar to you, but it does use a Windows API call: *WritePrivateProfileString*. This command is sort of the inverse of GetPrivateProfileInt, except that it writes a string to an INI file instead of an integer. For some reason, Windows doesn't provide a command for writing integers; it only allows you to write strings. No problem; Visual Basic makes this very easy. You'll notice that the third parameter is *txtMaxLines*, which is the string for the number that you need to write to the CONTROL.INI file. You don't actually have to write txtMaxLines.Text—it assumes that you need the text property when you use *txtMaxLines* as a string.

You'll also notice that code was added to the KeyPress event handler to make sure you can only type numbers into this text box.

Some Hints on Testing Screen Savers

There is one small trick we'd like to mention that you'll find very useful when you're writing your own screen-saver modules. To test your program, you need to be able to set the command line to either /c or /s, which you can do using the Project Options dialog box. You display this dialog box by selecting **Project...**

from the Options menu. When this dialog box appears, you can type **/c** or **/s**, and it will automatically be entered into the Command Line Argument field.

This field allows you to set the command line that your program will see whenever you run it from within Visual Basic, as opposed to a stand-alone EXE (or SCR) file. You can set this field to /c to test your Setup dialog box or to /s to test the screen-blanking part of your program.

The SCRNSAVE.BAS Module

Here is the file SCRNSAVE.BAS, which is a module that contains Main(), as well as several general-purpose subroutines.

```
Private Declare Function ShowCursor Lib "USER" _
(ByVal fShow As Integer) As Integer

Private Declare Function GetPrivateProfileInt Lib
"KERNEL" _ (ByVal lpszSectionName As String, ByVal
lpszKeyName As String, _ ByVal nDefault As Integer,
ByVal lpszFileName As String) As Integer

Public Declare Function WritePrivateProfileString Lib _
"KERNEL" (ByVal lpszSectionName As String, ByVal
lpszKeyName As String, _ ByVal nString As String, ByVal
lpszFileName As String) As Integer

'
' These variables support saving the maximum number of
' lines in the CONTROL.INI file, which is where the
' Windows 3.1 screen savers save setup information.
'
Public maxLines As Integer   ' Lines to show before CLS
PublicConst iniName = "CONTROL.INI"
PublicConst secName = "Screen Saver.VB Line Blanker"
PublicConst keyName = "MaxLines"
```

```
Public Sub EndScrnsave ()
  ShowMouse           ' Make mouse visible again
  End                 ' And exit
End Sub
```

```
Public Sub HideMouse ()
  '
  ' This subroutine makes the mouse pointer visible on
  ' the screen again.
  '
  While ShowCursor(False) >= 0
  Wend
End Sub
```

```
Public Sub Main ()
  '
  ' This next line of code gets a number from the
  ' CONTROL.INI file in your Windows directory. This
  ' number is the maximum number of lines to draw
  ' before clearing the screen.
  '
  maxLines = GetPrivateProfileInt(secName, keyName, 100, _

iniName)

  '
  ' Check to see if we should blank the screen, or dis
  ' play the Setup dialog box.
  '
  If InStr(Command$, "/c") Then
    SetupForm.Show 1
  ElseIf InStr(Command$, "/s") Then
    BlankForm.Show
  End If

  '
  ' Wait until there are no form visible, then quit.
  '
  While DoEvents() > 0      ' Loop until no forms visible
  Wend
End Sub
```

```
Public Sub ShowMouse ()
  '
```

```
  ' This subroutine hides the mouse pointer from the screen.
  '
  While ShowCursor(True) < 0
  Wend
End Sub
```

The BLANK.FRM Form

The BLANK.FRM file contains both a black form, which covers the entire screen when the screen saver is running, and the code that handles the screen blanking. The properties you'll need to set are in Table 20.1.

TABLE 20.1 *Properties You'll Need to Set for the Blank.frm Form*

Object	Property	Setting
Form	BackColor	&H00000000&
	BorderStyle	0 - None
	Caption	
	ControlBox	False
	Name	BlankForm
	ScaleMode	3 - Pixel
Timer	Interval	55
	Name	Tick

The following definitions should be in the (declarations) section of your form:

```
Private lastX, lastY     ' Last position of the mouse
Private numLines         ' Number of lines drawn so far
```

All of the following code is in the form:

```
Private Sub Form_KeyDown (KeyCode As Integer, Shift As Integer)
  EndScrnsave          ' End screen blanking
End Sub
```

```
Private Sub Form_Load ()
  Move 0, 0, Screen.Width, Screen.Height
  DrawWidth = 2
  HideMouse
End Sub
```

```
Private Sub Form_MouseMove (Button As Integer, Shift As _
Integer, X As Single, Y As Single)
  If IsEmpty(lastX) Or IsEmpty(lastY) Then
    lastX = X
    lastY = Y
  End If

  '
  ' Only unblank the screen if the mouse moves quickly
  ' enough (more than 2 pixels at one time).
  '
  If Abs(lastX - X) > 2 Or Abs(lastY - Y) > 2 Then
    EndScrnsave        ' End screen blanking
  End If
  lastX = X            ' Remember last position
  lastY = Y
End Sub
```

```
Private Sub Tick_Timer ()
  Dim X As Single
  Dim Y As Single

  numLines = numLines + 1    ' Count number of lines drawn
  If numLines > maxLines Then ' Time to clear screen yet?
    Cls            ' Yes, do so.
    numLines = 0       ' Reset the line counter.
    CurrentX = Rnd * ScaleWidth
    CurrentY = Rnd * ScaleHeight
  End If

  X = Rnd * ScaleWidth
  Y = Rnd * ScaleHeight

  Line -(X, Y), RGB(255 * Rnd, 255 * Rnd, 255 * Rnd)
End Sub
```

The SETUP.FRM Form

The Setup.frm file contains the form and code to handle the Setup dialog box, The properties you'll need to set are listed in Table 20.2.

TABLE 20.2 *Properties for Setup.frm*

Object	Property	Setting
Form	Auto3D	True
	BorderStyle	3 – Fixed Double
	Caption	VB Line Blanker Setup
	Height	3225
	Left	1035
	MaxButton	False
	MinButton	False
	Top	1140
	Width	4815
TextBox	Height	285
	Left	3120
	MaxLength	3
	Name	txtMaxLines
	TabIndex	0
	Text	100
	Top	1680
	Width	615

continued

Object	Property	Setting
CommandButton	Cancel	True
	Caption	Cancel
	Height	375
	Left	2400
	Name	cmdCancel
	TabIndex	1
	Top	2280
	Width	1095
CommandButton	Caption	OK
	Default	True
	Height	375
	Left	1200
	Name	cmdOK
	TabIndex	2
	Top	2280
	Width	1095
Label	Alignment	1 – Right Justify
	Caption	Maximum number of lines:
	Height	255
	Left	360
	Top	1725
	Width	2655

continued

Object	Property	Setting
Image	Height	480
	Left	120
	Name	Image1
	Picture	SCRNSAVE.ICO
	Top	120
	Width	480
Label	Caption	From "Teach Yourself Visual Basic "
	FontBold	0 – False
	Height	495
	Left	840
	Top	480
	Width	3735
Label	Caption	VB Line Blanker, by John Socha
	Height	255
	Left	840
	Top	120
	Width	3735
Label	Caption	This is a very simple Screen Saver that I wrote to show you how to write screen saver modules in Visual Basic.
	FontBold	0 – False
	Height	495
	Left	120
	Top	1080
	Width	4455

All of the following code is in the form:

```
Private Sub cmdCancel_Click ()
  Unload Me           ' Unload Setup form
End Sub
```

```
Private Sub cmdOK_Click ()
  i = WritePrivateProfileString(secName, keyName, _
txtMaxLines, iniName)
  Unload Me           ' Unload Setup form
End Sub
```

```
Private Sub Form_Load ()
  txtMaxLines = maxLines       ' Set to current max lines
  txtMaxLines.SelLength = 3   ' Select the current value
End Sub
```

```
Private Sub txtMaxLines_KeyPress (KeyAscii As Integer)
  If KeyAscii < 32 Then
    '            ' Let Ctrl keys pass through
  ElseIf KeyAscii < Asc("0") Or KeyAscii > Asc("9")
Then
    KeyAscii = 0       ' Discard chars other than digits
  End If
End Sub
```

Appendix A

Using the Commercial Software on the Companion Disk

The controls on the disk will only function in the 16-bit version of Visual Basic. Each Vendor makes a 32-bit OLE version of each control. Contact the vendor for ordering information about 32-bit OLE controls.

The disk at the back of this book includes the following custom-control files:

CDIALOG.VBX	Provided by Crescent Software, Inc. The documentation is in the file CRESCENT.WRI, which is a formatted Windows Write file you can print out.
MH??200.VBX	Four files provided by MicroHelp, Inc. The documentation is in VBT200.HLP, a hyperlinked Windows Help System file that also allows you to print out topics.

SHERDN01.VBX — Provided by Sheridan Software Systems, Inc. The documentation is in the file SHERIDAN.WRI, which is a formatted Windows Write file you can print out.

You'll also find three files with the same names as these files, except they have the extension VBR instead of VBX. These files are run-time versions of the VBX files. The license agreements from Crescent, MicroHelp, and Sheridan **permit you to redistribute ONLY the VBR files, royalty-free**. You're not allowed to redistribute the VBX files, except for MHFS200.VBX.

If you write a program using any of the custom controls, and you want to give it to someone else, you'll need to do the following:

1. Copy the EXE file that you made to another disk, and copy all other related files except for the VBX files.
2. Copy the VBR file with the same name as the VBX file you used.
3. Rename the VBR file you copied, changing its extension to VBX. You will now be able to run this program using the run-time version of the custom control.

Where to Put the VBX Files

For Windows to find the VBX files, it must be in the correct directory. Windows will search for your VBX files in the following directories (in this order):

1. The current directory.
2. The Windows directory (which contains the WIN.INI file).
3. The Windows system directory (which contains the system files, such as KERNEL.EXE).
4. *Windows 3.1 and later.* The directory containing your program.
5. Directories listed in the PATH statement.
6. The list of directories mapped in a network.

You should be aware of several things. First, you can place the VBX files in the same directory as your program, and Windows will always find them if you have Windows 3.1 or later. But if you have Windows 3.0, it may or may not, depending on what shell program you use to run your program. The Windows Program Manager will always set the current directory to the same directory as your program. However, Norton Desktop for Windows 2.0, for example, will not, which means your program may not run correctly if you use Norton Desktop 2.0 under Windows 3.0, unless you put the VBX files in the path or the Windows or System directory.

Microsoft recommends putting all VBX files into the Windows System directory. The Setup program on the companion disk will copy VBX files to your system directory if you check the last option: Install VBXs in SYSTEM directory.

Crescent Software Files

The custom controls and DLL functions provided by Crescent Software are a sample of their QuickPack Professional for Windows product. Their actual product contains far more custom controls and DLLs, and you'll find an advertisement with more details near the back of this book. Crescent Software has also agreed to offer QuickPack to readers at a special price. For more information contact

Crescent Software, Inc.

32 Seventy Acres

West Redding, CT 06896

(203) 438-5300

These are the functions described in this chapter that are provided by the Crescent Software custom-control file:

- ***Common Dialog Boxes.*** This is a set of custom controls that make it very easy to use Windows 3.1 common dialogs for Print, Print Setup, Open File, Save File As, Color, Font, Find, and Search and Replace. These controls are very useful.
- ***Play Command.*** This command allows you to play melodies on your computer. You'll hear songs come out of your speaker. If you're familiar with the DOS versions of Basic (such as QBasic), this command is almost exactly like DOS Basic's Play command.
- ***Financial Functions.*** There are a number of functions, provided as a Visual Basic module, for doing financial calculations.

There are a number of Crescent files included on the disk at the back of this book:

CDIALOG.VBX	The custom-control file that you can use for both run-time and design-time. Crescent allow you to freely distribute only this file, and you do *not* need to display a Crescent copyright notice or pay royalties to Crescent. You'll need the file QPRO.LIC in order to use these custom controls in Visual Basic's design mode.
QPRO.LIC	This file must be in your VB or Windows System directory in order for you to use CDIALOG.VBX in design mode. **DO NOT give this file to other people—you do not have a license to distribute it**.
SOUND.DRV	This is an updated sound driver for Windows 3.0 (don't use this with Windows 3.1). You are free to distribute this driver with any programs you create.
FNSPREAD.BAS	This file contains the financial functions described in this chapter. You're free to distribute programs you create using this module **as long as you do not distribute the source code**.
DEMOPLAY.*	This is a demo program, with source code, that shows how to use the Play command.
DEMOSCRL.*	This is a demo program, with source code, that shows how to use the instant-change scroll bars.

To use the common dialog boxes, you'll need to add the CDIALOG.VBX file to your project:

✷ Add CDIALOG.VBX to your program by selecting the Add File... item from the File menu in Visual Basic. Then double-click on the CDIALOG.VBX file.

MicroHelp Files

The custom controls and DLLs provided by MicroHelp as a sample of their VBTools product. Their actual product contains far more custom controls and DLLs, and you'll find an advertisement with more details near the back of this book. MicroHelp has also agreed to offer VBTools to readers at a special price. For more information contact

MicroHelp, Inc.
4359 Shallowford Industrial Parkway
Marietta, GA 30066
(404) 516-0899

There are four functions provided by the MicroHelp custom-control files:

- ***MhTag Custom List Box.*** This list box behaves exactly like Visual Basic's list box, but it has some very useful additions. Here are some of the improvements: you can select multiple items, it supports tab stops, and you can have multiple columns.
- ***Common Dialog Routines.*** MicroHelp has provided a number of subroutines and functions you can call to use the standard dialog boxes introduced in Windows 3.1 for such common tasks as Print, Print Setup, Open File, Save File As, etc. We've used these routines in the Address Book program that you'll find on the disk for the print and Print Setup dialog boxes. You're allowed to redistribute the COMMDLG.DLL file and the MHEN200.VBR file (which you'll need to rename MHEN200.VBX when you give copies to other people).
- ***MgGauge Analog Gauge.*** This is a special control that allows you to build special dash-board type gauges. For example, you could build a memory display that looks like a thermometer.
- ***MhFormScroll.*** This custom control allows you to add scroll bars to any form, which allows you to build forms that are larger than your screen. Anything inside the form (including controls) will scroll. This works at both run- and design-time, so you can build very large forms even on a small screen.

There are five MicroHelp files included on the disk at the back of this book:

MH??200.VBX	There are four custom-control files, with one for each of the custom controls listed above. The two question marks are any of the following letters: EN for common dialog boxes, FS for the Form Scroll control, GA for the

	Gauge control, and finally TG for the MhTag custom list box. These are the files you'll use when you're building your program. **DO NOT give this file to other people—you do not have a license to distribute them. You may, however, freely distribute MHFS200.VBX.**
MH??200.VBR	Run-time only versions of MH??200.VBX. When you want to give your program to other people, give them a copy of this files, and rename them so they have a VBX extension. MicroHelp allows you to freely distribute only these files, and you do *not* need to display a MicroHelp copyright notice or pay royalties to MicroHelp.
MHEN200.BAS	This file contains the definitions you'll need in order to use the common dialog routines. Simply include this file in your project.

To use any of these functions, you'll need to do the following:

1. Add one of the MH??200.VBX files to your project by selecting the Add File... item from the File menu in Visual Basic. Then double-click on the MH??200.VBX.
2. If you're going to use the common dialog routines, you'll also need to add MHEN200.BAS to your project.

Sheridan Files

The custom controls and DLL functions provided by Sheridan Software Systems as a sample of their 3-D Widgets product. Their actual product contains far more custom controls and DLLs, and you'll find an advertisement with more details near the back of this book. Sheridan Software Systems has also agreed to offer 3-D Widgets to readers at a special price. For more information contact

Sheridan Software Systems, Inc.
65 Maxess Road
Melvill, NY 11747
(516) 753-0985

These are the functions provided by the Sheridan Software custom-control file:

- ✱ *3-D Panel.* This custom control allows you to add 3-dimensional borders to your program. You can place these borders anywhere, including around other controls.
- ✱ *3-D Button.* A special version of the Command Button that allows you to put a picture inside a command button. The standard Visual Basic command button only allows text inside the button.

There are two Sheridan files included on the disk at the back of this book:

SHERDN01.VBX	The custom-control file that you can use for both run-time and design-time. This is the file you'll use when you're building your program. **DO NOT give this file to other people—you do not have a license to distribute it.**
SHERDN01.VBR	Run-time only version of SHERDN01.VBX. When you want to give your program to other people, give them a copy of this file, and rename it SHERDN01.VBX. Sheridan allows you to freely distribute only this file, and you do *not* need to display a Sheridan copyright notice or pay royalties to Sheridan.

To use the 3-D Panel and 3-D Button, you'll need to add the SHERDN01.VBX file to your project:

- ✱ Add SHERDN01.VBX to your program by selecting the Add File... item from the File menu in Visual Basic. Then you double-click on the SHERDN01.VBX file.

Appendix B

Glossary of Terms

ASCII. A standard that defines how numeric values are assigned to characters inside your computer. The ASCII standard defines which numbers will be assigned to all the characters on a U.S. keyboard, and assigns the numbers 32 through 127 to these characters. Other characters, such as ü are assigned numbers in the extended ASCII set (above 127 or below 32).

API. An acronym that stands for Application Programming Interface. Microsoft Windows has a number of subroutines and functions that you can call from within your Visual Basic programs, by using Declare to define the calls. These functions and subroutines are often called API calls. You can use calls to API functions and subroutines to extend you

Visual Basic programs. Part III of this book contains many examples of using APIs.

Argument. A value or special keyword used to supply information to a command or event handler. Arguments for event handlers can have three parts: the argument name, followed by the keyword AS, followed by a variable type.

Arrays. These can be control arrays, or variable arrays. In any case, an array is a collection of controls or variables that all share the same name. You refer to a specific control or variable within an array by providing an index in parentheses, such as lines(10). For control arrays, the index must match an index number you assigned to an element in the array. While for variable arrays, the index is "number" of the variable, starting with 1 for the first element (unless you use the To keyword to set a lower and upper limit for the index values). You use the Dim or Global keywords to define variable arrays.

Assignment operator. The equal sign is an assignment operator. It is used to assign a value to a variable.

Boolean. A number that has only two values: True and False, where False is 0, and True is -1, or any other number other than 0. Boolean expressions always return a 0 or -1, but commands like If..Then..Else that use Boolean expressions treat all numbers except 0 as True, and treats 0 as False. Boolean expressions always return an Integer value.

Boolean operators. Boolean expressions use Boolean operators: equal to, not equal, less than, greater than, less than or equal to, greater than or equal to, not, or, Xor, equivalent, implication.

Boundary conditions. Special cases that may require you to handle a programming situation differently. For example, you may have code that erases some previous object from a form, but you won't want to call that code the first time you open the form because there will be nothing there to erase.

[break]. One of three modes in Visual Basic. The other modes are [run] and [design]. Break mode is the mode when you've temporarily halted a program you're running inside Visual Basic, by pressing Ctrl+Break or selecting the Break from the Run menu. Whenever you're in break mode, you can use the Debug window, either to run commands, or to see the values assigned to variables.

Breakpoint. A line of code that you mark to tell Visual Basic you want it to stop running your program (and enter break mode) whenever it tries to run the specified line, i.e. reaches the breakpoint. You may designate multiple breakpoints. Useful for debugging.

Bug. Some type of failure in a computer program. If your program is not doing what it's supposed to do, your program has a bug. Debugging is the process of locating the problem and solving it.

Code window. This is where you place your Basic code. Double-click on a form or object to bring up the corresponding code window.

Combo Box. This is a standard Windows control. Normally you'll see a text box, with a down-pointing arrow on the right side. When you click on this arrow, you can select from the list of choices that appear.

Command. Visual Basic has a number of built-in commands, such as Beep, that you can use in your programs to tell Visual Basic what function you want it to perform for you. See also: Statement. The words command, statement, instruction, and code are sometimes used interchangeably by programmers.

Condition. Another word for a Boolean expression, which returns a True (-1) or False (0) as an number. The name condition is generally used when you have a Boolean expression in an If..Then statement. Conditions always return an Integer value.

Control. A control is a special type of object that appears inside a form (even if the control is not visible at run-time). The toolbox window contains icons representing the available control types.

Control array. Multiple controls with the same name, distinguished by an index number that follows the control name in parentheses.

Currency. A type of number that is useful for currency values. Visual Basic defines a total of five different types of numbers: Integer, Long, Single, Double, and Currency. The Currency type provides very accurate calculations for larger currency numbers, and has a range of -922,337,203,685,447.5808 to 922,337,203,685,447.5807 (almost 1000 trillion). Each Currency value uses eight bytes of memory.

Debug window. One of Visual Basic's windows that allows you to run individual commands immediately, by typing in the command and pressing the Enter key. You get to the Immediate Window by pressing F5 to run your program, then

Ctrl+Break. This is useful for checking you code, determining values of a variable, and other debugging activities.

[design]. One of three modes in Visual Basic. The other modes are [run] and [break]. You'll use design mode to create programs. The other two modes appear when you run a program you created in design mode.

Design-Time. Some properties are only available when you're in design mode, writing your program. For example, the Name property is only available in design mode. In other words, you can't obtain the Name of a control while your program is running. There are also properties that are only available at run-time.

DLL. An acronym standing for Dynamic Link Library. Microsoft Windows allows you to write subroutines and functions in many programming languages that you can use directly from Visual Basic or other programming languages. These code modules are loaded into memory whenever they're needed. As it turns out, most of Windows itself is built out of DLLs. You can use calls to DLL functions and subroutines to extend you Visual Basic programs. Part III of this book contains many examples of using DLLs.

Double. A type of number that can represent numbers with decimal points. Visual Basic defines a total of five different types of numbers: Integer, Long, Single, Double, and Currency. The Double type uses what's known as floating-point calculations, which are slower than Integer or Long calculations. But Double values can be any numbers between -1.8x10308 and 1.8x10308. They can also represent very small fractions, as small as 4.9x10-324. Each Double value uses eight bytes of memory.

dpi. An acronym that stands for Dots Per Inch, and refers to the density of dots on your screen or printer. Many laser printers print images at 300 dpi (although some newer laser printers use 600 dpi), while a VGA screen is defined to have 96 dpi. The lower the dot density, the courser the image will be. This is why printed output tends to look much better than what you see on your screen.

Dynamic array. A dynamic array is one that can change size while your program is running. Instead of declaring the array size with the DIM statement, the size is left out. Then later you set the size using a REDIM statement.

Element. A single item or instance in an array.

Event. Windows defines a number of events that Visual Basic supports, including Click, DblClick, MouseMove, and KeyPress. You can write code to handle any of these events using Event Handlers.

Event Handler. A subroutine that handles a type of Windows event. Controls and forms can handle a number of events, such as mouse clicks and moves, and key presses. See also: Subroutine, Function.

Extended ASCII characters. Special characters such as the paragraph mark (¶) and foreign-language characters such as ü are defined as extended ASCII characters. They are represented by by numbers outside the standard range of 32 and 127. See also: ASCII.

False. A number, 0, returned by a Boolean expression (condition). Any condition expression you write, such as 1=0, returns either True (-1) or False (0).

Flag. A variable that is used as a boolean value (either true or false) is often called a flag. In other words, since the flag can be either True or False, you can thing of this flag as being either raised (True) or lowered (False).

Floating-point numbers. Any number with something after the decimal point. For example 1.1 and 3.14159 are both floating-point numbers.

Focus. Focus refers to which control has the keyboard's focus of attention. The control object that is current or active is the one that has the focus. In a window full of text boxes, it would be the box where the cursor was. Moving the focus can be done with the Tab key (in most Windows programs) as well as with the mouse.

Form. According to Microsoft, a form is "a window or dialog box that you create with Visual Basic."

Form variables. Any variable defined in the (general) area of a form; and as such is available throughout the form.

Function. A piece of code, like a subroutine, that returns a value, like a number or a string. Functions start with Function Name As Type, and end with End Function. You can create a new function using the New Procedure... menu item in the Code menu when you have a code window active. See also: Event Handler, Subroutine.

Handler. See: Event Handler

Instruction. A command or statement that you write in Basic. The words instruction, statement, and command, and code are sometimes used interchangeably by programmers.

Integer. A type of number that can hold only whole numbers. Visual Basic defines a total of five different types of numbers: Integer, Long, Single, Double, and Currency. The Integer type is the smallest and fastest type of number to work with, and has a range of -32,768 to 32,767. Each Integer value uses two bytes of memory.

Long. A type of number that can hold only whole numbers. Visual Basic defines a total of five different types of numbers: Integer, Long, Single, Double, and Currency. The Long type is a little larger than an Integer, and calculations using Longs are slower than using Integers. But Longs allow you to work with whole numbers larger than Integers, with a range of -2,147,483,648 to 2,147,483,647. Each Long value use four bytes of memory.

Method. An action that can be performed on an object. For example the code myCombo.AddItem "Red" uses the AddItem method to add an item called "Red" to the myCombo object.

Modal form. A modal form is a form that always stays in front of the main window until you click on one of it's buttons to indicate an action. Any attempt to perform an action outside of a modal form (such as click on a different window) will be refused. Modal forms do not have resizeable borders, minimize or maximize buttons, or control menus.

Modular design. The modular approach to designing programs involves dividing the code into logical self-contained modules, with connections to other modules that are as simple as possible.

Module. A Visual Basic module is a file that contains nothing but code. You can include one or more modules in a project.

Modulo. A mathematical operation that calculates the remainder of a division.

Passing by reference. Refers to passing a reference to a variable rather than a copy of the variable's data. If a subroutine alters a variable that was passed by reference, the actual variable's value will be changed.

Passing by value. Refers to sending a copy of a variable to a subroutine, so that when the subroutine alters that variable, the original variable is not changed, only the copy contains the change. Requires use of the ByVal keyword.

Project. A project file is a special file (with the .MAK extension) that tells Visual Basic which forms (.FRM files), modules (.BAS files), and custom controls (.VBX files) belong to a program you're working on. You work with projects using the project window in Visual Basic.

Project Window. The window providing access to the forms, modules, and custom control files that are associated with the project.

Property. A special type of Visual Basic variable that describes an appearance or behavioral characteristic of an object . When you click on an object in design mode, that objects properties are shown in the properties window.

Properties Window. A window containing the properties of a form or control object. The select the form or control, then press F4 to bring the properties window to the front. With the exception of those properties that can only be set at Run-time, you can use this window to set the values for all other properties.

Pseudo-code. Code-like wording to indicate programming logic that will be used. Pseudo-code is not meant to be syntactically correct and often omits the actual keywords, opting instead for standard verbs.

Random access. A technique for reading and writing disk files that allows you to treat the file as if it contained an array of records.

Record. Each item in a random-access data file is called a record, which is similar in idea to the elements of an array. One record, for example, could be a single name and address (along with phone numbers).

[run]. One of three modes in Visual Basic. The other modes are [design] and [break]. Visual Basic displays [run] in it's caption whenever your Visual Basic program is running. You can enter design mode by pressing Ctrl+Break, which allows you to display the values currently assigned to variables. Pressing F5 while in break mode will take you back to run mode.

Run-Time. Some properties are only available when you're running your program (in run mode). For example, the CurrentX and CurrentY properties are only available in while you program is running. In other words, you can't set the CurrentX and CurrentY properties when you're designing your programs. There are also properties that are only available at design-time.

Single. A type of number that can represent numbers with decimal points. Visual Basic defines a total of five different types of numbers: Integer, Long, Single, Double, and Currency. The Single type uses what's known as floating-point calculations, which are slower than Integer or Long calculations. But Single values can be any numbers between -3.4x1038 and 3.4x1038. They can also represent very small fractions, such as 1.4x10-45. Each Single value uses four bytes of memory.

Statement. A statement is a single line in a Visual Basic program. Statements may include commands, like Beep, or they may be lines that provide information to Visual Basic, such as the End Sub statement in a subroutine. The words statement, instruction, command, and code are sometimes used interchangeably by programmers.

Step. Stepping through. Running your program one line at a time. Useful for debugging.

Strings. Characters that you work with in Basic. You can use any character inside a string, but the string must be enclosed between quotation marks. If you wish to use a quotation mark as part of a string, type the quotation character twice.

Subroutine. A piece of code that has a name, and can be run from other parts of a program. All subroutines start with Sub Name and end with End Sub. Visual Basic provides event handlers, which are pre-defined subroutines, and you can also create your own, using the New Procedure... menu item in the Code menu when you have a code window active. See also: Function, Event Handler.

Toolbox. Toolbox is the name of a window that contains the available controls. There are 23 controls in the standard edition of Visual Basic 3.0. When you incorporate controls from third-party vendors, they too will appear in your Toolbox window.

True. A number, -1, returned by a Boolean expression (condition). Any condition expression you write, such as 1=0, returns either True (-1) or False (0).

Twip. A twip is a unit of measurement created by Microsoft. It means "twentieth of a point" and is since a point measures 1/72 of an inch, a twip is equal to 1/1440 inch.

User-defined type. A compound variable that you define using the Type command. Compound refers to the combination of multiple variables of different types into a single variable.

Values. The actual numbers or strings in a variable.

Variables. Places where you can store numbers or strings of characters. Variables are stored in memory. Variable names must begin with a letter and can be up to 40 characters long

Variable array. A group of variables with the same name, distinguished from one another by an index number that follows the variable name in parentheses. Each individual variable in the array is called an element.

INDEX

A

B

E

K

L

M

Q

R

S

MicroHelp

Scrollable forms

If you've ever wanted to build forms larger than a screen or a window, now you can. MicroHelp's MhFormScroll custom control allows you to add scroll bars to any form or picture box. All you have to do is to add an MhFormScroll control to your form or Picture box, then set a few properties.

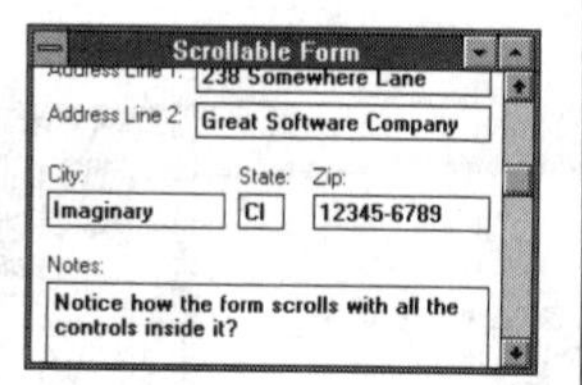

Custom List Box

A list box with some functions that aren't included in Visual Basic's list box:

- ❖ Searching
- ❖ Tab Stops
- ❖ Multiple Columns
- ❖ Horizontal Scroll Bar

Custom Gauge Control

The Gauge custom control makes it very easy to build progress bars and dials. You can also include pictures, allowing you to build thermometers, speedometers, and other graphical gauges. You can choose either a bar or a needle gauge.

Common Dialog Boxes

MicroHelp provides calls you can make to dialogs boxes for opening and saving files, selecting printers, printing, choosing fonts, and choosing colors.

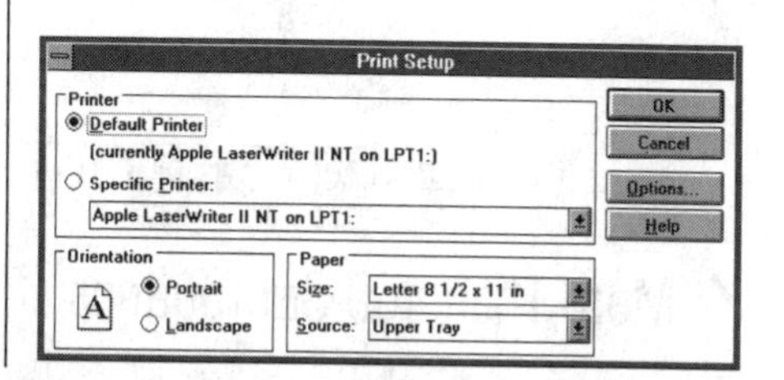

Sheridan Software

Sheridan Software provides two custom controls that let you add a 3-dimensional look to your program, as well as icons to the buttons in your programs.

3-D Panels

This custom control allows you to add various 3-dimensional borders to your programs.

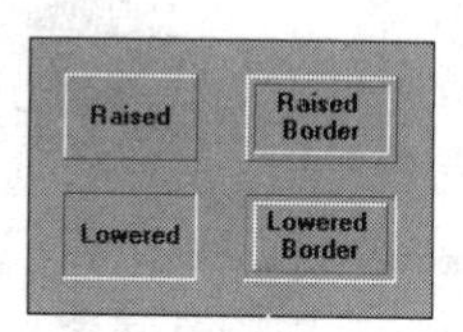

- ❖ Add 3-D borders around other controls
- ❖ Use as a 3-D progress indicator
- ❖ Display 3-D text

3-D Command Buttons

If you need to put an icon inside a button, this is the custom control for you. Visual Basic's own control only supports text.

- ❖ Add icons to your buttons
- ❖ Change the width of the bevel
- ❖ Add a 3-D effect to the caption

For more information about MicroHelp and Sheridan Software, please see Appendix B.

INSTALLING THE SOFTWARE ON THE DISK

Included on the disk is a Setup program designed to make installing the included files as simple as possible. To run the setup program, choose the Run... item from the Start menu and type **a:\setup** in the Run dialog box (or **b:setup** if your floppy disk is in drive B). Press return, and you should see a dialog box asking you to specify the drive and directory where you want the files installed.

For more information on how to install the various programs and files on the companion disk, please see *Installing the Companion-Disk Files* in Appendix A on page 487. For more information about the commercial software included with the book, please read Appendix B. Appendix B also contains information about the companies providing the commercial software and about your rights in using the files provided.